Russia's Age of Serfdom 1

The Blackwell History of Russia

General Editor: Simon M. Dixon

This series provides a provocative reinterpretation of fundamental questions in Russian history. Integrating the wave of new scholarship that followed the collapse of the Soviet Union, it focuses on Russia's development from the mid-seventeenth century to the present day, exploring the interplay of continuity and change. Volumes in the series demonstrate how new sources of information have reshaped traditional debates and present clear, stimulating overviews for students, scholars and general readers.

Published

Russia's Age of Serfdom: Russia and the USSR, 1649–1861
Elise Kimerling Wirtschafter

Forthcoming

Across the Revolutionary Divide: Russia and the USSR 1861–1945
Theodore R. Weeks

The Shadow of War: Russia and the USSR, 1941 to the present
Stephen Lovell

Russia's Age of Serfdom 1649–1861

Elise Kimerling Wirtschafter

Blackwell
Publishing

BLACKWELL PUBLISHING
350 Main Street, Malden, MA 02148-5020, USA
9600 Garsington Road, Oxford OX4 2DQ, UK
550 Swanston Street, Carlton, Victoria 3053, Australia

The right of Elise Kimerling Wirtschafter to be identified as the Author of this
Work has been asserted in accordance with the UK Copyright, Designs, and
Patents Act 1988.

Designations used by companies to distinguish their products are often claimed as
trademarks. All brand names and product names used in this book are trade names,
service marks, trademarks or registered trademarks of their respective owners. The
Publisher is not associated with any product or vendor mentioned in this book.

This publication is designed to provide accurate and authoritative information
in regard to the subject matter covered. It is sold on the understanding that the
Publisher is not engaged in rendering professional services. If professional advice
or other expert assistance is required, the services of a competent professional
should be sought.

First published 2008 by Blackwell Publishing Ltd

1   2008

Library of Congress Cataloging-in-Publication Data

Wirtschafter, Elise Kimerling.
    Russia's age of serfdom 1649–1861 / Elise Kimerling Wirtschafter.
        p. cm.
    Includes bibliographical references and index.
    ISBN 978-1-4051-3457-6 (hardcover : alk. paper) — ISBN 978-1-4051-3458-3
(pbk. : alk. paper)   1. Serfdom—Russia—History.   2. Russia—Social conditions.
3. Russia—Politics and government.   4. Russia—Civilization.   I. Title.

    HT807.W57 2008
    306.3'650947—dc22

                                                                    2007017674

A catalogue record for this title is available from the British Library.

Set in 10/12.5pt Minion
by Graphicraft Limited, Hong Kong
Printed and bound in Singapore
by C.O.S. Printers Pte Ltd

The publisher's policy is to use permanent paper from mills that operate a
sustainable forestry policy, and which has been manufactured from pulp
processed using acid-free and elementary chlorine-free practices. Furthermore,
the publisher ensures that the text paper and cover board used have met
acceptable environmental accreditation standards.

For further information on
Blackwell Publishing, visit our website:
www.blackwellpublishing.com

To my brother and sisters,
Judith, Michael and Anne, and Leslie,
with love.

To our Kimerling, Mazer, and Feigelson cousins,
with love.

To the memory of the Mazer and Feigelson cousins we have lost,
Robyn, Marissa, Ethel, Jill, and Sheri,
with love and sorrow.

Contents

Illustrations

Series Editor's Preface

Sweeping historiographical generalizations rarely inspire confidence. Although scholars on both sides of the Iron Curtain were bound to be influenced by the assumptions of the world that emerged from the ashes in 1945, we should resist the temptation to squeeze all of their efforts under the heading of 'Cold War historiography'. It is of course true that, in an attempt to understand a perceived enemy, both the USA and the states of Western Europe invested heavily in historical research in the second half of the twentieth century. In an attempt to justify a regime resting on a determinist historical doctrine, the Soviet Union did the same. Whatever their inspiration, however, the results were far from monochrome, and scholars on both sides of the ideological divide managed to preserve a sense of shared academic enterprise in the least promising of circumstances. We neglect their efforts at our peril. The same could be said of the work of historians writing in the tumultuous early years of the Bolshevik regime, to say nothing of the great names of nineteenth-century scholarship. If you think you have made a discovery about Imperial Russia, it is always worth checking to make sure that you were not trumped more than a hundred years ago by Vasilii Kliuchevskii or Sergei Solov'ev.

Yet there is no doubt that the opening of the archives under Gorbachev's *perestroika* and the collapse of the Soviet Union in 1991 have had a significant effect on thinking about the Russian past. At the most basic level, they have opened up so many new sources of information that historians have struggled to cope with the flow. Most have concentrated their attentions on the twentieth century. A small army of scholars is now advancing into the post-war world after combing the documents of the 1920s and 1930s. While the fiftieth anniversary of Stalin's death in 2003 offered them further encouragement, historians of Imperial Russia have grasped their own opportunities for commemoration, the tri-centenary of St Petersburg in 2003 being an obvious case in point. Whatever the period under review, new discoveries have thrown serious doubt on some persistent assumptions about the nature of Russian government and society. Censorship and surveillance remain important subjects for research. But now that social activity in Russia is no longer instinctively conceived in terms of resistance to a repressive, centralized state, there is room not only to investigate the more normal contours of everyday life, but also to consider its kaleidoscopic variety in the thousands of provincial villages and towns that make up the multi-national Russian polity. Although local history has never flourished in Russia in the way it has in, say, France or Germany, nineteenth-century antiquarians have bequeathed a promising enough legacy on which to build. One of their greatest preoccupations – religion – is at last gaining the recognition it deserves. Gender and culture in its widest sense are similarly prominent in recent writing. Scholars once preoccupied with pig-iron production are now inclined to focus on pilgrimages, icon veneration and incest. Once over-whelmingly materialist, they are now more likely to take 'the linguistic turn'. Imagery, ritual and ceremonial are all being reinterpreted. New sources have likewise prompted us to reshape questions about what we already know. In particular, a renewed awareness of Russia's Eurasian geopolitics in the present has opened up fruitful ways of thinking about imperial expansion in the past.

How can we take account of these 'extra' dimensions of Russian history without risking a descent into modishness? One way of squaring the circle is to adopt an unconventional chronological framework in which familiar (and still crucial) information can be presented in fresh and stimulating ways, interesting to both the student and the scholar. That is the aim of this series.

Each of its three volumes will cross a significant caesura in Russian history. The first is the physical and cultural move from Moscow to St Petersburg under Peter the Great at the beginning of the eighteenth century; the second the revolutions of 1917; the third the collapse of the USSR in 1991. It is tempting to represent each of these transitions as a stage in Russia's inexorable progress from darkness into light: from obscurantist Muscovite xenophobia to Enlightened Western cosmopolitanism in the eighteenth century; from repressive Imperial backwardness to modern Soviet Utopia in 1917; and from moribund Soviet Socialism to a fledgling capitalist democracy in 1991. Such Whiggishness is unconvincing. While there is no need to underestimate the impact of change, it is important not to explain continuity merely in terms of inertia. As Peter the Great himself put it: 'It is good to build anew, but the old that is good should not be thrown away.' Russia has always derived much of its stability and flexibility from time-honoured ways of doing things. It will be an important function of this series to explain why that was so.

Since it is natural enough now to look back on the Soviet period as a unity, many university history departments offer courses charting 'The Rise and Fall of the Soviet Union, 1917–1991'. Until recently, the story of the emergent Russian Federation in the 1990s has largely been told by and to students of politics. So there is not only a chronological divide to be crossed here, but also a disciplinary one. One reason why historians have yet to make the leap lies in their excessive attention (shared by most students of 'twentieth-century' Europe) to the inter-war years. This imbalance may partly derive from the fact that the history of European integration can seem insipid by comparison with that of the Europe of the dictators. But in Russia there is no reason to think the latter part of the twentieth century uneventful. And the 1990s are scarcely comprehensible if one knows nothing of either Khrushchev or Brezhnev. Demonstrating that contemporary history is no less significant a subject than politics in historical perspective, the final volume of this series will set Russian developments in the context of the wider international order. And since that order was in many ways shaped by the outcome of the Second World War, it is with the war that the book will begin. This was not only the Great Patriotic War that reinvigorated Russian nationalism, but also the war that cast a shadow over almost every aspect of the USSR for the remainder of its existence, from its command siege-economy to its literature, music and art.

It was also the war that provided the greatest single test for the Bolshevik regime born out of the revolutions of 1917 which will form the chronological pivot of the second volume in the series. With some distinguished exceptions, the Soviet and tsarist periods have tended to attract historians of different temperaments who have been reluctant to cross the boundary between the two. Yet the lived experience of Stalin's generation was quite different. Most aspects of the distinctive form of consumer society that emerged in the early Soviet period – tourism, the cinema and so on – had their origins in the commercial developments of late-Imperial Russia. Now that scholars are turning from the history of institutions and commodities to explore delicate inter-personal dynamics, the subject has become richer still. There is no need to stress the virtues of writing cultural history 'across the revolutionary divide': it is the *only* way to write about Russian modernism. The same applies just as importantly to music, and also to literature. And these are not the only continuities to explore. Though no attempt will be made to disguise the fact that the tsarist and Soviet regimes were ideological poles apart, both faced the same fundamental structural problem of governing a multi-national state. It is a similar story when one turns to the economy: the last three tsars and the early Soviet leaders were all trying to manage the politics of industrialization in an overwhelmingly agrarian empire. And the co-ordination of their efforts was made all the harder by the fact that they had to work across vast distances, linked by poor communications.

A sense of primitiveness has traditionally been associated in Western minds above all with 'Russia's Age of Serfdom', the subject of this first volume in the series. Questioned on humanitarian grounds since the later decades of the eighteenth century, serfdom seemed, by the time of its abolition in 1861, to meet few of the tsarist regime's most pressing needs. Once technological development had revolutionized both economic demand and military requirements, illiterate Russian peasants could neither supply nor operate the iron-clad navies that had replaced the old wooden fleets. The army's pitiful performance in the Crimean War seemed to exemplify serfdom's baleful influence on a modern army. Russia's principal continental rivals – Prussia and Austria – had abandoned serfdom in the aftermath of their defeat by Napoleon. Only the complacency of victory seemed to have ensured its survival under the tsars.

However, there is another side to the coin. If we look back over the period to 1649, when serfdom was incorporated into the Russian Law Code issued by Tsar Aleksei Mikhailovich, then serfdom appears as the most important of those features of early-modern Russia that used to be regarded as liabilities, but increasingly look like assets. Serfdom provided a cheap, unskilled workforce well suited to producing the low-grade finished goods, grain and forest products that were so heavily in demand in pre-industrial Europe. Serfdom gave the nobles a guaranteed workforce during a period when low population densities raised the cost of free labour. It gave the state a pool of military recruits and a more reliable basis for taxation than a geographically mobile peasantry could offer. And, cruel and degrading though it undoubtedly was, it protected the serfs themselves against the worst ravages of the market: unemployment and starvation. So long as Russia's nobles remained directly in control over their serfs, there was no need for an elaborate system of local administration. Once criticized for being slow to develop into a modern bureaucracy, the government of early-modern Russia depended instead on a fluid network of patronage relationships – rarely sufficiently rigid to deserve the name of factions – in which the power of individuals overlapped with and sometimes outweighed the power of institutions. Taken together, this far from modern political and social structure underpinned the most successful period of territorial expansion in Russian history. Though Russia's great power status has always depended heavily on the relative strengths of its international rivals, it was thanks to serfdom that Russia could first afford to play a part on the wider European stage. When Alexander II emancipated the serfs in 1861 in an attempt to shore up his failing dynasty, he inadvertently dismantled much of the scaffolding that supported the Russian old regime.

'Russia's Age of Serfdom' therefore provides a challenging but rewarding 'unity', ripe for a critical, investigative synthesis. That is precisely what Elise Kimerling Wirtschafter has given us in her striking new book. There could be no better start to the series.

Simon Dixon
University of Leeds

Preface

Russia's Age of Serfdom 1649–1861 offers a broad interpretive history of the Russian Empire from the time of serfdom's codification until its abolition following the Crimean War. As the book's title suggests, coverage focuses on those of the empire's European territories populated predominantly by ethnic Russian peasants. Although by 1650 the Muscovite state had become a multiethnic, multiconfessional Eurasian empire stretching from Europe across Siberia to the Pacific Ocean, the Romanov dynasty originated in Moscow, at the political and territorial center of European Russia, and the empire's governing classes viewed their history through a European prism. From the time of Prince Vladimir's conversion in 988, educated Russians identified with Christian civilization in its Eastern Orthodox or Byzantine form and by association with the cultural heritage of ancient Greece and Rome. Because of these ties to Western antiquity and because from the late seventeenth century Russia's educated service classes self-consciously embraced European culture, this book highlights Russian historical development within a European framework. If one thinks about European history in terms of a spectrum running from Britain in the west to Russia in the east, it is possible to recognize the European roots of Russian culture without downplaying the significant political divergences that separated Russia from other European powers of the day.

The narrative that follows is divided into three chronological periods, each containing chapters on society, politics, and culture. The chapters on society highlight the institution of serfdom, official social categories, and Russia's development as a country of peasants ruled by nobles, military commanders, and civil servants. These chapters also focus attention on the shift from a social order centered on the patriarchal household and immediate community to one in which individuals and groups also identified with a larger social collective or society. The political chapters illuminate both the idea and the reality of absolute monarchy in Russia, with special emphasis on the mobilization of human and material resources, the search for regular government, and the persistence of personal-moral, as opposed to legal-administrative, forms of authority. Finally, the cultural chapters trace the emergence of modern Russian culture out of and alongside Orthodox religious culture, a process embodied in the Europeanization and growing independence of Russian elite society and in the emergence of political and cultural dissent. Rather than provide encyclopedic empirical coverage, the book highlights key analytical themes, so that the reader can assimilate problems of interpretation with reference to a traditional historical framework.

Throughout *Russia's Age of Serfdom*, dates are give in the Old Style, based on the Julian calendar used in Russia from the reign of Peter I until January 1918. When the New Style (NS) dates of Europe's Gregorian calendar are used, this is indicated in the text or notes. During the eighteenth century, the Russian calendar lagged 11 days behind the European calendar and during the nineteenth century 12 days.

Finally, I would like to acknowledge the personal and professional debts incurred in the process of writing this book. I am grateful as always to Marc Raeff and Gregory L. Freeze, teachers, mentors, and friends, for inspiring my interest in Russia's age of serfdom and for guiding my education in Russian history. Simon Dixon invited me to write the volume and read the entire manuscript with care, sensitivity, and depth. Tessa Harvey of Blackwell Publishing brought professional grace and enthusiasm to the project and commented on the narrative from the perspective of an intelligent non-specialist reader. Marc Raeff, James Melton, and David Moon shared their knowledge and offered crucial comments on specific chapters. Linda Hart brought her artistic eye and technical wizardry to the rendering of charts and maps. My mother, Rita Kimerling, read the entire manuscript with classic concern for commas and word choice. California State Polytechnic University at Pomona supported completion of the book with sabbatical leave, mini-grants from the Faculty Center for Professional Development, and released time through the Research, Scholarship, and Creative Activity Program. Last but not least, my husband Gary and our children, Eric, Carla, and Valerie, nourished the book, and its author, with unfailing love and energy. My daughter Carla also deserves special mention for typing the bibliography in the midst of her own rigorous academic and athletic (Go 'Cats!) schedule.

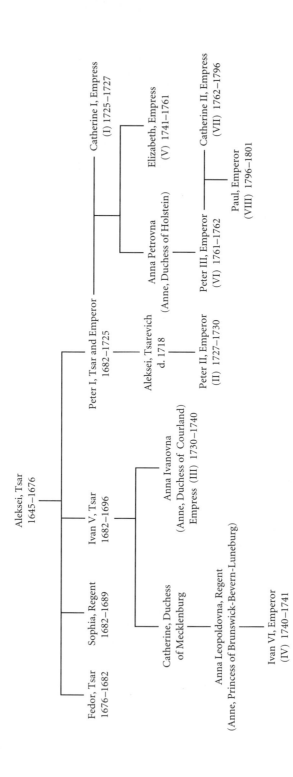

FIGURE 1 Succession to the throne, 1645–1796*

* Roman numerals indicate the order of succession after Peter I.

FIGURE 2　Wedding feast of Peter I and Catherine, 1712. Etching by Aleksei Zubov.
Source: Slavic and Baltic Division, The New York Public Library, Astor, Lenox and Tilden Foundations.

MAP 1   Russian imperial expansion, ca. 1700–1800.
Source: Adapted from Geoffrey Hosking, *Russia and the Russians: A History* (Cambridge, MA, 2001), pp. 188–9.

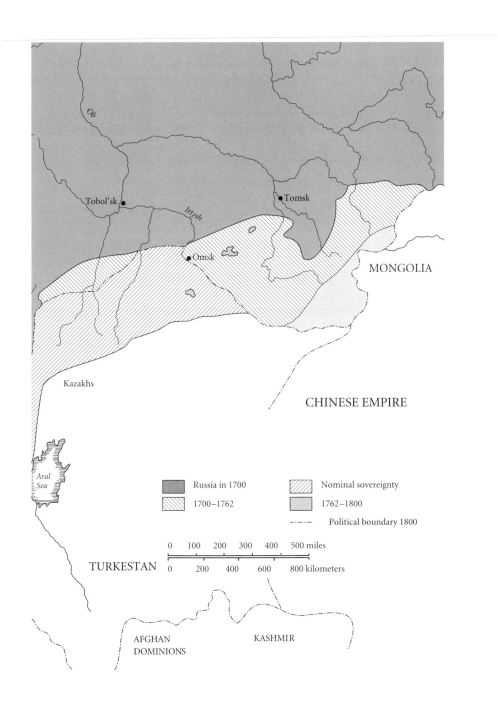

Ob

Tobol'sk

Irtysh

Tomsk

Omsk

MONGOLIA

Kazakhs

CHINESE EMPIRE

Aral
Sea

Russia in 1700

1700–1762

Nominal sovereignty

1762–1800

Political boundary 1800

| 0 | 100 | 200 | 300 | 400 | 500 miles |

TURKESTAN

| 0 | 200 | 400 | 600 | 800 kilometers |

AFGHAN
DOMINIONS

KASHMIR

Regions

I	Central Non-Black Earth	VI	Mid-Volga	XI	Belarus
II	Northwest	VII	Lower Volga and Don	XII	Left-Bank Ukraine
III	Northern	VIII	Southern Urals	XIII	Right-Bank Ukraine
IV	Northern Urals	IX	Baltic	XIV	Southern Ukraine (New Russia)
V	Central Black Earth	X	Lithuania		

MAP 2   Regions and provinces of European Russia, mid-nineteenth century.
Source: Adapted from David Moon, *The Abolition of Serfdom in Russia* (Harlow and London, 2001), pp. xviii–xix.

Part I

Russian Absolute Monarchy
1649–1725

In the late eleventh and twelfth centuries, a "papal revolution" in Catholic Europe effectively separated a civil sphere of monarchy and lordship from a religious sphere of canon law and church governance. This separation into spheres of civil and religious authority then paved the way for the development of "national" states with centralized systems of law and administration. Modern political thought followed, appearing in the "city republics" of Renaissance Italy, though only in the sixteenth and seventeenth centuries did the Protestant Reformation and subsequent wars of religion convince Europe's governing classes of the need for a strong state power. Following decades of bloody and destructive religious strife, national political claims began to take precedence over Catholic universalism, and the theory of absolute monarchy acquired unprecedented legitimacy. In powerful states such as Britain, France, Austria, and Prussia, recognition of the need for good order accorded well with the ambitions of "modern" state building.[1]

In recent decades, a growing number of historians have expressed dissatisfaction with the concept of absolute monarchy that long has dominated depictions of early modern states. These historians correctly note that the terminology of absolutism implies a degree of control and coherence unthinkable before the advent of mechanized systems of production, transportation, and communications. This is all well and good, except that when previous generations of historians used the phrase "absolute monarchy," they by no means intended to imply that absolute monarchs wielded absolute control. In their vocabulary "absolutism" referred not to the "absolute" power of a modern centralized state, but to a set of political institutions and relationships presided over by a monarch whose authority was assumed to be God-given and hence "absolute."[2] That said, it is important to remember that despite the absence of constitutions, civil liberties, and democratic representative government, early modern monarchies exercised much less *effective* control over the lives of their subjects than do today's liberal democracies over their free citizens. The political principles of old regime monarchies may have been undemocratic, hierarchical, and absolutist, but their administrative reach and ability to know what their subjects were doing remained exceedingly limited. For that reason, it is useful to think of "absolute monarchy" as a concept that conveys the modern aspiration to control rather than the reality of actual control.

Already in the middle ages, the monarchs of Western and Central Europe began to accumulate judicial and legislative powers that eventually allowed them to assert authority over the great lords and bishops of their realms. By the seventeenth century, the concentration of political power could be seen in central offices of government, and in the appearance of rulers whose authority exceeded the traditional functions of judge, lawgiver, and military commander. Early modern monarchs sought to mold socioeconomic development, and they viewed legal prescriptions as administrative tools designed to impose change, mobilize resources, and encourage productivity. In order to subordinate noble elites and keep external enemies at bay, monarchs needed armies and revenues, and in order to maintain armies and collect revenues, they needed regularized bureaucracies and cadres of trained officials able to track resources and regulate subject populations. Even more important, monarchs needed large numbers of subjects whose labor power could be exploited and wealth extracted for the "common good" of the country or national state. What distinguished absolute (or administrative) monarchies from their immediate predecessors was that "they made the state a part of everyone's daily existence."[3] Social relationships remained rooted in hierarchies of birth that people continued to accept as part of the divine order. Economic relationships, while increasingly commercialized, remained untouched by industrial transformation. Administrative authority remained *de facto* dispersed and rural lands undergoverned, but the aspiration of monarchy to regulate behavior and impose control appeared thoroughly "modern."

The development of a Russian "national" state did not follow the historical pattern of a single monarch bringing great lords and bishops under his authority and control. In Russia, centralized monarchy arose toward the end of the fifteenth century, as the grand prince of Moscow liberated his lands from Mongol rule (established in Russia since 1240) and subjugated the independent principalities of other princes whose lineage he shared. The process of uniting the "Russian" lands ended around 1521 with the annexation of Riazan, and in the reign of Ivan IV (ruled 1533–84), serious institution building began with the creation of central administrative offices and standing military units. The first Russian ruler to be crowned tsar, Ivan IV also transformed Russia into an expansive imperial power when he conquered the khanates of Kazan (1552) and Astrakhan (1556). But Ivan left a problematic legacy. Acts of mass murder and terror, unleashed against individual subjects and entire territories, marred his successes, leading in turn to depopulation and economic devastation. Recovery began under Ivan's son, Fedor (ruled 1584–98), a man with serious disabilities, whose brother-in-law, Boris Godunov, actually governed the tsardom. When Fedor died childless in 1598, the ruling dynasty came to an end and instability again erupted. Russia entered a period of unprecedented social rebellion, civil war, and foreign occupation aptly called the Time of Troubles. Only after the election of Mikhail Romanov as tsar in 1613 did order finally return, and by the 1630s a process of "modern" state building got under way. The emergence of a Russian absolute monarchy designed to mobilize the resources of society for military and political purposes could be glimpsed in central administrative offices, the core of a standing army, liturgical reforms, subordination of the church to the monarch, and codification of serfdom. Like the Wars of Religion in Western and Central Europe, the Time of Troubles in Russia had shown the need for a strong state power, which powerful subjects, institutions, and territories at last seemed prepared to accept.

Chapter 1

Face to Face in Russian Society

Throughout Russia's age of serfdom, the basic unit of social organization remained the patriarchal household, composed of a nuclear, co-resident, or multigenerational family and its dependents. Until relatively recent times, patriarchy also represented a global institution – an institution that in practically every society gave to a family's senior adult male absolute authority over his wife, children, wards, and servants. Current scholarship tends to situate patriarchy within the history of the family and gender relations. From this perspective, patriarchy appears to be an authoritarian institution designed to ensure male dominance and the subjugation of women and children.[1] Our present-day sensibilities, influenced as they are by the civil rights and feminist movements of the late twentieth century, affirm the authoritarian image. But what did Russians of the seventeenth and eighteenth centuries think of the patriarchal relationships that defined their lives? And why did generations of women accept as natural and God-given the hierarchies of age and gender embodied in patriarchy?

Some historians respond to these questions by rejecting stereotypes of female passivity, highlighting instead the social spaces in which women carved out an autonomous existence and played meaningful public roles. In both Muscovy and Imperial Russia, noblewomen achieved autonomy through the administration of dowry estates, which remained their personal property even after marriage. A second autonomous space, limited to the Muscovite era, arose in the special women's quarters or *terem*, where elite women lived in semi-seclusion from male society. Despite the apparent isolation of these women, the *terem* became a forum from which they negotiated marriage arrangements, dispensed charity and patronage, and helped relatives forge political alliances.[2] To a significant degree, segregation in the *terem* brought not marginalization, but power and influence.

Clearly, to the men and women of early modern Russia, the hierarchies of age and gender associated with patriarchy did not seem as oppressive as they do today. Injustice and inequity did not go unrecognized, but basic problems of physical survival tended to override any budding concern for egalitarian principles. Among laboring people, women had no choice but to work, both in the home (cooking, cleaning, and clothing) and alongside men in fields or workshops. If women did not die young from childbirth or disease, they might nonetheless die relatively young from the cumulative exhaustion and physical weakness brought on by childbearing, years of heavy physical labor, and the chronic infections that plagued rich and poor alike. With the exception of childbearing, God's unique gift to women, men worked equally hard and suffered equally from disease. Men, women, and children labored together, according to a customary division of tasks, not because patriarchy required them to do so, but because they needed to do so in order to survive. What patriarchy did do, in the eyes of those who accepted its strictures, was to impose control on potentially explosive social relationships. By articulating a moral ideal of obedience, duty, and obligation, patriarchy created the basis for good order in the family and by extension in society at large.

That so many people could remain obedient in the face of patriarchal inequities seems mind-boggling in a world of mass mobility and political contestation. But not unlike our own ancestors of no more than a couple of generations past, Russians of the Muscovite and Imperial periods imbibed a culture of duty – duty to family, country, church, tsar, and God. Duty meant obligation, and to fulfill one's obligations – whether as husband, wife, parent, child, servant, or superior – brought peace of mind, which in turn represented freedom and happiness. Whatever suffering the individual might be called upon to endure, he or she also believed that the fulfillment of duty ultimately brought happiness, if not in this life, then in the life to come. Similarly, whatever the individual might strive to achieve, he or she also knew that the fulfillment of duty always took precedence over the satisfaction of personal desire. Self-mastery, both in exercising authority and in submitting to it, ensured social order.

Indeed, the call to duty was a two-way street. Alongside deference to authority, patriarchy also taught that the household head fulfilled duties to family members and other subordinates. The duty to protect and provide for dependents; the duty to love a wife, honor parents, and educate children; the duty to treat servants kindly and to discipline them justly; the duty to show generosity toward the unfortunate – these were just some of the obligations imposed by God on persons in positions of power. Literature, legal prescription, and religious teachings all assumed that if the individuals joined together in a household carried out their duties, human passions would be mastered and good order prevail. Patriarchy did not then represent a mechanism for imposing male dominance and female subjugation, though this might be one of its results. Patriarchy developed as an institution designed to reconcile individual desire with social order. By organizing household relationships around the principles of obedience, duty, and obligation, patriarchy effectively harnessed human passions in the interest of a shared good. The wellbeing of the individual person simply could not be disentangled from the wellbeing of the entire family.

Of course, it is impossible to know the extent to which individual Russians lived up to the principles of obedience, duty, and obligation that defined the patriarchal ideal. Hagiography, biography, memoirs, literature, and judicial testimony are filled with stories about the abuse and humiliation suffered by dutiful wives, children, and servants. Much cruelty no doubt remained hidden, and officials proved reluctant to intervene in private household relations. Both the church and government recognized a need to condemn offenses such as forced marriage (even of serfs) and unjustified physical violence. Consistent with the religious and official admonitions, more formal mechanisms of social and economic self-defense also developed, as Russians of all statuses, including serfs, employed legal prescriptions and judicial proceedings to defend family honor, challenge abuse, or petition for redress of grievances. Muscovite and Imperial authorities dealt gingerly with the "right" to complain and tried repeatedly to limit petitioning, but the government never completely blocked the channels leading to justice through the intervention of higher authority. Appeals to the tsar, primarily for nobles and only occasionally for ordinary Russians, remained a basic feature of legal-administrative practice until the final demise of the Romanov monarchy.

The concrete results that Russian subjects achieved through petitioning cannot be calculated with any certainty, but in the realm of social relationships, the promise of redress seemed more important than the reality. Courtiers and nobles enjoyed decisive advantages in the art of supplication, because of their personal access to powerful patrons and even to the monarch. Elite individuals repeatedly appealed for help when they fell into debt, faced the possibility of an unfavorable judicial decision, or sought to advance or rescue a career. Landowners also sometimes responded when peasants complained of excessive obligations or cruel treatment at the hands of stewards or village officials. Such responses followed closely the dictates of patriarchy. When transposed into the public realms of society and polity, patriarchy encouraged reliance on personal relationships and interventions. Our modern ideal of a private life protected from the sphere of public action simply did not apply. Most Russians lived within the confines of the family and locality, separated from the monarchy by geographic distance and primitive communications. In these circumstances, personal relationships and appeals to private interventions constituted an effective social glue that integrated people into the Muscovite and Imperial systems of government. Precisely because legal-administrative power barely touched the patriarchal household, personal relationships dominated political life.

───────   Serfdom and Muscovite Social Organization   ───────

In 1648–9 an Assembly of the Land (*zemskii sobor*) gathered in Moscow to approve the project for a Law Code (*Ulozhenie*) that defined the organization of Russian society and government.[3] Although the patriarchal household remained Russia's primary social institution, legal prescriptions made clear that the monarchy intended to harness the human and material resources of the Russian people. The Law Code of 1649 codified serfdom and identified a variety of social groups and ranks distinguished by their service obligations, legal privileges, and occupational or economic functions. With respect to peasants living on noble lands, the Law Code envisioned a class of agriculturalists who provided revenues and recruits for the monarchy, together with a reliable livelihood for the tsar's noble servicemen. Not only nobles, who since the mid-sixteenth century had been required to serve, but all groups in society would fulfill obligations to the tsar and his government. To that end, officials began to ascribe peasants and townspeople to the communities in which they lived and into which future generations would be born. With the exception of clergy, whose special calling fell under church authority, all the tsar's subjects became members of legally defined social categories. Numerous, changeable, and imprecise, the categories or ranks (*chiny*) of Muscovite society embodied the amorphousness of a social structure that to this day confounds historians. The categories cannot be ignored, however, because of their critical role in Russia's long-term social development. In Muscovite times, and continuing throughout the age of serfdom, birth into one or another official category remained at the heart of Russian social organization.

By the mid-seventeenth century, serfdom stood at the center of Russian society, and the enserfment of the Russian peasantry had set the stage for defining and binding other social groups. The actual process of enserfment dated from the late fifteenth century, when the Moscow grand prince emerged to become the ruler of a centralized Russian monarchy. At that time, provincial nobles began to receive land grants in return for military service, and in order to supply a labor force for noble lands, the monarchy took steps to restrict peasant movement and enforce peasant obligations to the landowner.[4] Law Codes of 1497 and 1550 continued to guarantee peasants a right to move, but only for a two-week period around St George's day (November 26), which marked the end of the harvest season. During the 1580s decrees on "forbidden years" temporarily banned peasant movement in specified areas, and in 1592/93, historians infer from court cases, all peasant movement became permanently illegal. Still, peasants continued, with relative ease, to flee the clutches of increasingly vigilant landowners. The monarchy could do little to prevent peasant flight and even imposed a statute of limitations (five to fifteen years) on the right of landowners to reclaim fugitives. Only with the promulgation of the Law Code of 1649 did the government eliminate the statute of limitations and commit itself to enforcing prohibitions on peasant movement. Seigniorial peasants belonging to noble landowners became serfs in the full legal sense, and peasants living on state, church, and crown lands also became bound to their communities. To the extent that no peasant enjoyed an unequivocal right to move, and all owed labor or monetary dues to a legally recognized authority, it can be said that the entire peasantry had become "enserfed" or bound to the state, church, crown, or nobility.[5]

Based on the household census of 1678, historian Ia. E. Vodarskii estimates that the population of male serfs and state peasants in Russia, including Ukraine, numbered 3.4 million and .9 million respectively.[6] In 1678 peasants accounted for 89.58 percent of the male population, and in 1719, the year of the first poll tax census, the figure reached 90.18 percent. In 1857, the year of the last census prior to the emancipation of the serfs, the proportion fell to 83.67 percent. But in 1914–17, by which time military recruits no longer left their original social status, the proportion again rose to 86 percent.[7] However historians calculate population data from the late seventeenth to the early twentieth century, the proportion of peasants reaches a consistent 80 to 90 percent. Until the era of Soviet industrialization in the 1930s, Russian society remained overwhelmingly peasant, diversified by a smattering of dynamic urban classes (educated and uneducated) and ruled (or ostensibly guided) by relatively small noble, bureaucratic, and professional elites.

The status of Muscovite peasants changed over time, and their obligations varied according to region and category of peasant (state, church/monastery, crown, or seigniorial). Even so, the basic forms of Muscovite exploitation survived until the abolition of serfdom in 1861.[8] Seigniorial peasants, or serfs, performed labor services for the noble landowner, an obligation referred to as *barshchina*, or paid dues in money or kind, referred to as *obrok*. On some estates they did both. In addition, seigniorial peasants delivered a range of agricultural products and supplies to the landowner and might be required to perform construction or repair work on his (or her) property. Levels of exploitation also varied. The government did little to regulate the master–serf relationship, so that despite customary and legal restrictions, the landowner usually could impose any obligation he wished. But peasants of all categories also played a role in defining their obligations. They appealed to landowners, to government and church officials, and even to the tsar when the demands placed upon them became too onerous.[9] They also might show up late for obligatory labor and take long or frequent breaks during the workday. Landowners, moreover, had an interest in nurturing rather than draining the economic strength of their peasants. Prosperous peasants increased the wealth of the landowner, whereas poor peasants dragged him down.

It is impossible to measure the levels of exploitation imposed on Muscovite peasants, but historians generally believe that serfs who paid dues in money or kind (*obrok*) enjoyed greater freedom and lighter obligations than those who performed labor services (*barshchina*) under the direct control of the landowner or, more likely, his representative. Church peasants belonged in effect to a private landowner and, like serfs, performed additional labor obligations for the monarchy. State and crown peasants did not have churchmen or private landowners feeding at the community trough, but in addition to paying dues, they also performed labor services. All peasants, moreover, paid taxes to the government. Until the mid-seventeenth century, the government levied a direct tax based on the quantity and quality of land cultivated by each household. Beginning in 1645–7, the household assessment combined the value of land holdings with an additional flat tax. Finally, in 1679, following completion of the household census of 1678, the government began to collect a fixed payment from individual households. Land no longer figured into the equation, and peasants could lighten their tax burden by living together in households composed of multiple generations (grandparents, parents, children, and grandchildren) or co-resident brothers and their families.[10] The levy on households remained in place until the 1720s, when Peter I significantly increased government revenues by imposing a poll tax or capitation on the "head" of every male peasant.

In addition to the fulfillment of labor and tax obligations, some peasants also performed military service for the monarchy. During the sixteenth century, the government drafted auxiliaries (*pososhnye*), who lacked military training but could be employed in construction, digging, and carting. Other (not necessarily peasant) dependents of nobles – for example, the "boyars' men" (*boiarskie liudi*) and "donated men" (*datochnye*) – accompanied their masters who served in the cavalry militia, and sometimes they too ended up performing combat functions. Beginning in 1630, the Muscovite government established "new-model infantry and cavalry regiments," conscripted from landless noble servicemen, Tatar converts, peasants, and Cossacks. The appearance of these regiments signaled the development of a regular army on the European model and greatly increased the service burden imposed on peasants and other groups in the laboring population. Conscription levies, based on the number of peasant households held by a landowner, became an established feature of Russian life. In 1630/31 the burden stood at one recruit per ten households, and in 1646 at one per twenty. By the 1660s, the government conducted general levies throughout Russia. Historians estimate that during the Thirteen Years' War (1654–67) with Poland military drafts swept up about 100,000 men, many of whom served for life. The introduction of lifelong service stood in sharp contrast to the traditional practice of calling noble servicemen and their dependents to arms for the duration of seasonal military campaigns. This and the recruitment of laboring men into new-model forces constituted important steps toward the establishment of regular conscription. Indeed, in the early eighteenth century, the tentative drafts of the

Muscovite government became massive annual levies borne overwhelmingly by Russian peasants.[11]

Historians long have recognized the connection between the Russian monarchy's military needs and the development of serfdom. From the outset, serfdom developed as a mechanism to support noble and church landowners and to mobilize resources for the government. To ensure compliance, officials bolstered the authority of the peasant commune by introducing the principle of collective responsibility (*krugovaia poruka*) for the fulfillment of labor, monetary, and service obligations. Collective responsibility meant that the entire village community became liable for meeting the obligations of all its members. The commune, which served as the intermediary between the community and the landowner or government, distributed and administered these obligations. Controlled by the heads of member households and elected peasant officials, the commune supervised agricultural production in open fields and regulated the use of pasture, forest, and water resources held in common. Although communal regulation of production and common resources reached back into earlier times, before peasants became subject to government and landowner demands, with the introduction of collective responsibility the commune's authority and functions increased substantially.[12] For officials and landowners, the commune represented a highly effective instrument of administrative control.

For peasants, the commune remained a time-honored institution that served the social and economic requirements of the entire village community. As members of the commune, peasants collectively devised strategies of production and community organization both in response to higher levels of exploitation and in keeping with the primary need to provide subsistence for member households. The commune helped peasants adapt to changed conditions by altering established practices and introducing innovations that did not threaten security. Leveling mechanisms such as communal land tenure and periodic repartition of land aimed to ensure that every household possessed sufficient resources to meet its obligations. Although as late as the fifteenth and sixteenth centuries Russian peasants held their arable land in hereditary household tenure, in the seventeenth and eighteenth centuries, beginning in areas of especially harsh exploitation such as the seigniorial *barshchina* estates of the Central Non-Black Earth region, a shift to communal land tenure occurred. From the Central Non-Black Earth region the practice quickly spread to the Central Black Earth region, and from the mid-eighteenth century communal land tenure and periodic repartition of land became widespread throughout central European Russia. In the Northern and Urals regions, in Siberia, and along the old steppe frontier of the southeast, communal tenure and periodic repartition did not make significant inroads before the early nineteenth century. Nor did these practices ever become established in Ukraine, Belarus, Lithuania, or the Baltic provinces. As the regional variations show, the pressures producing the shift resulted from conditions in peasant society and from the demands of landowners and officials. In contrast to the idealized images propagated by later generations of Russian radicals, the egalitarian collectivism of Russian peasants had nothing to do with any innate "peasant socialism."

Like peasants across the globe, Russian peasants lived off the land. They farmed primarily to meet subsistence needs and engaged in production for profit on the open market only as a secondary consideration. Peasants planted much of their arable land with grains, mainly rye or oats, but also barley or wheat in some regions. Methods of cultivation varied, and simple systems survived into the nineteenth and twentieth centuries: slash-burn, field grass-husbandry, long and short fallow, two-field, and three-field. The most advanced of these systems, the three-field, tended to become dominant over time. But again, the shift came quite late and did not reach all areas. Beginning in the fifteenth century, population pressure and the demands of large noble and church landowners led some peasants to move from the two-field to the three-field system of production. In the two-field system, dating back to the late middle ages, peasants divided arable land into two fields which they cultivated in alternate years. In the three-field system, a more intensive form of cultivation, arable land was divided into three open fields, which were further divided into strips farmed by individual households. Peasants planted one field with a winter crop and a second field with a spring crop, leaving the third field fallow to allow the soil to replenish. As in the two-field system, peasants alternated the fields under cultivation from year to year. In the sixteenth and seventeenth centuries, the three-field system first became dominant in the Central Non-Black Earth and Northwestern regions and then spread out, along with peasant settlement and population growth, into the Central Black Earth and Mid-Volga regions. During the eighteenth and nineteenth centuries, the system reached further south and east into the open steppe and Siberia.[13]

Whether one looks at communal land tenure, periodic repartition of land, or development of the three-field system, the peasant's relationship to the land appears at once moral and practical. No matter how oppressive serfdom became, peasants enjoyed a near universal right to arable land. The irony is that access to land became stronger as serfdom became more entrenched. The peasant's right to arable land served the interests of all parties to serfdom – the government, landowner, peasant commune, and individual household – by guaranteeing that each family possessed enough land to meet not only subsistence needs but also monetary and labor obligations. In addition, because arable fields varied in quality and accessibility, the commune allotted land in strips, so that each household possessed equal access to the most fertile, least productive, most convenient, and least accessible fields. As long as the peasant commune possessed or "owned" the land (which legally also could be said to belong to the state, church, crown, or noble landowner), member households cooperated to ensure that each family used its land effectively and in a manner consistent with the needs of the entire community. Planting and harvesting, the use of fallow land to graze livestock, the choice of crops, and changes in methods of cultivation – all these practices needed to be managed collectively within the framework of the peasant commune.

As individual peasant households grew or declined, in accordance with the coming and going of the generations, the number of able-bodied adults and dependents also changed. Consequently, land distribution and the allocation of obligations depended on the size of the household and especially on the number of husband–wife labor teams (*tiaglo*) within a household. Because a large household was more likely to occupy a prosperous, secure, and powerful position within the community, near universal and early marriage remained characteristic of Russian peasant society into the twentieth century. Peasant families often lived together in multigenerational households that included a father and mother, their married or unmarried children, and grandchildren. As families grew, they became entitled to larger shares of land, which then could be inherited by the adult sons of the household head. When the senior adult male died, married sons tended to part ways and establish their own separate households. These separations led in turn to further adjustments in the distribution of communal resources, especially arable land, and to reallocations of the tax and other obligations owed by individual households. The principle of collective responsibility made wealthier households responsible for the obligations of the poor, which meant that all peasants had a stake in preserving the economic viability of each and every household.

Shared interests notwithstanding, Russia's harsh natural environment guaranteed that not every crisis could be averted. Depending on the region, growing seasons could be short (less than six months in the forest heartland) and rainfall unreliable (in the steppe zone). Crop failure, epidemic, and even starvation represented very real possibilities. Although peasant society displayed a remarkable durability, individual families remained painfully vulnerable to economic crisis. Some died out or became absorbed into larger households, and others, judged unworthy of communal support, suffered exclusion from the community. The organization of the Russian village aimed to prevent such drastic outcomes, and on average the agricultural economy met the everyday needs of peasants while also providing adequate support for landowners and the monarchy. The deep structures of production and community relationships helped peasants adapt to environmental fluctuations caused by weather, war, and patterns of exploitation. For this reason, peasants did not look to innovate, but rather approached life and work so as to avoid risk. Their risk-averse strategies stood well the test of time. The basic organization of peasant society, developed already in the Muscovite period, survived until its forced destruction in the Stalinist collectivization drive of 1930.[14]

Serfdom defined the relationship of peasants to the land and the degree of exploitation they endured, but serfdom also represented a moral order. As social subordinates, all peasants were expected to be obedient and hard-working. Within the household, the senior adult male reigned supreme. Within the village, household heads, elected peasant officials, appointed stewards, and on occasion the landowner himself governed with few constraints. But the various authorities and social superiors who lorded it over peasants, including government officials and the tsar, also were responsible for the wellbeing of the people under their command. Paternalistic solicitude, moral guidance, fairness in the meting out of punishments, assistance in times of hardship – these were just a few of the responsibilities that accompanied power and the right of economic exploitation. Across Russian society, hierarchy and obedience to hierarchy were regarded as divinely ordained, but so too was fulfillment of God's commandments. No person or power, not even the tsar, stood above or outside God's law.

Of course, here on earth God's law was not sufficient to ensure justice, equity, or good will. Landowners and officials abused their subordinates, and peasants defied the divine order by openly rebelling. The Stepan Razin revolt of 1670–1 erupted under the leadership of a Don Cossack whose Cossack followers had for decades been experiencing losses of autonomy and privilege as the Russian government extended its reach into the steppe frontier. Among Razin's supporters, fugitive peasants, townspeople, and non-Russian Finnic and Turkic minorities in the Volga basin likewise had been feeling the heavy hand of increased government or landowner control. Razin's revolt also sparked significant peasant unrest in the Mid-Volga region and in limited areas of the Non-Black Earth and Central Black Earth regions.[15] But open rebellion was a dangerous game, and most peasants contented themselves with less dramatic forms of protest: work slowdowns and stoppages, non-payment of taxes and dues (which might not at all represent protest but rather result from genuine hardship), petitions for redress of grievances (which also implied recognition of established authority), and flight (which officials and landowners sometimes tolerated in order to attract labor to underpopulated regions and borderlands). Although any and all forms of protest were illegal, and if necessary repressed by military force, peasants sometimes managed to reduce obligations, achieve intervention by a higher authority, or create a new social identity. There is no reliable way to measure the levels of abuse inflicted on Russian peasants; much depended on the character and moral qualities of their superiors. Like the forces of nature, which threatened physical survival, the forces of authority could be arbitrary, unpredictable, and overwhelming. But such was the natural order of things, accepted or at least expected by peasants and other groups in Russian society.

Living only slightly above peasants in terms of social status and the burden of obligations were the ordinary townspeople or *posad* people (*posadskie*), defined as registered members of the urban community (*posad*).[16] According to the household census of 1678, the urban population of Russia, without Ukraine, numbered

about 185,000 males; of these, 134,000 belonged to the official townspeople.[17]
Legislation from 1600–2 identified two markers of townsman status: 1) social
origin or birth into the urban community, and 2) participation in trade or craft
production within the urban community. Townspeople were supposed to be registered to their communities of origin and/or employment, and like peasants, they
paid taxes and performed service for the monarchy. Unlike peasants, however,
their livelihood could not be secured with access to a plot of land. In trade and
craft production, townspeople always faced competition from non-members
of the urban community, who did not share in the tax and service obligations of
registered townspeople. Numerous peasants and dependents of church and noble
landowners lived in "white" or tax-exempt settlements (*slobody*) that formed around
official urban communities. Data from the first half of the seventeenth century
(excluding Siberia and Ukraine) reveal that out of 107,413 households in 226 towns,
only 29 percent, located in 73 towns, belonged to the official (and therefore taxed)
townspeople.[18] No matter how the government defined membership in the urban
community, townspeople shared their social and economic space with a host of
permanent "outsiders."

To meet their tax and service obligations, urban communities sought to preserve, and hopefully also to augment, the number of their members. Individual
townspeople, by contrast, sought to escape taxation by fleeing to the white settlements or mortgaging themselves to wealthy individuals. Because, as with peasants, the government made the entire urban community responsible for paying
communal taxes (additional taxes were assessed individually), a larger number
of townspeople meant a lighter individual tax burden. Beginning in 1619, the
government responded to complaints about lost townspeople by conducting
investigations to recover runaways and dependents. Three decades later, the
Law Code of 1649 abolished tax-exempt settlements and granted townspeople a
monopoly on trade and manufacturing within the urban community. In addition, privately held settlements and estates located within or adjacent to towns
became state property, incorporated into the urban community together with their
commercial and manufacturing population. These settlements might contain
dependents (*zakladshchiki*) who had mortgaged themselves to wealthy masters,
peasants and slaves (*kholopy*), limited service contract slaves (*kabal'nye liudi*), and
various "men recruited for service" (*sluzhilye liudi po priboru*), including musketeers
(*strel'tsy*), artillerymen or gunners (*pushkari*), artillerymen responsible for light
cannon (*zatinshchiki*), fortress gate-guards (*vorotniki*), new Cossacks (enrolled
in service after the Smolensk War of 1632–4), infantrymen (*soldaty*), coachmen
(*iamshchiki*), and keepers of hunting dogs (*psari*).[19] Free persons who resided on
church lands located within towns and who made a living from trade or handicrafts
also became members of the urban community, as did ecclesiastical groups such
as priests' children, church readers (*tserkovnye d'iachki*), and sacristans (*ponomari*).

Others, such as permanent contract slaves (*vechnye kabal'nye liudi*) and peasant farmers (*pashennye krest'iane*), had to sell their shops and enterprises to official townspeople and return to the homes and estates of their masters. Peasants continued to be allowed to trade and produce handicrafts in towns, but only on a temporary basis. No longer were they permitted to operate permanent shops or businesses.

Among the "men recruited for service," those who lived outside the private settlements represented yet another category of urban resident engaged in trade and handicraft production. Toward the mid-seventeenth century, these men numbered over 60,000 in 150 cities and included musketeers, Cossacks, artillerymen, dragoons, fortress guards, state carpenters, and state farriers.[20] All enjoyed the right, according to the Law Code of 1649, to sell their shops and leave the taxpaying population. But among those who continued to ply an urban trade, artillerymen, fortress guards, and state artisans were required to fulfill tax and service obligations together with the townspeople. By contrast, musketeers, Cossacks, and dragoons – groups that theoretically received government salaries for military service – paid customs duties and taxes on their shops but were not included in the urban tax assessment (*tiaglo*) and did not perform the service obligations of townspeople. The Law Code went a long way toward delineating the economic privileges and occupational functions of official townspeople; however, as the persistent presence of the "men recruited for service" suggests, towns were dynamic and diverse places. Urban populations remained far too adept at evading authority to make towns the preserve of a relatively small group of legally recognized residents.

The most privileged groups in the urban population included elite merchants (*gosti*), the "merchants' hundred" (*gostinaia sotnia*), and the "cloth hundred" (*sukonnaia sotnia*). The members of merchant categories usually came from townspeople who had risen to become commercial agents for the state treasury and financial advisors to the ruler. The elite merchants, numbering thirteen in 1649, each held a special charter granted by the tsar. Elite merchants paid taxes in connection with some privileges, but were free from quartering obligations and enjoyed a variety of special rights: the right to be judged in the tsar's court, the right not to kiss the cross (a form of judicial test used to determine guilt or innocence), and the right to travel abroad for trade, heat homes and baths, brew drink, and even possess patrimonial estates (*votchiny*).[21] The trading people of the merchants' hundred, numbering 158 in 1649, ranked just below the elite merchants. In 1613 the hundred received a collective charter granting its members most of the privileges enjoyed by elite merchants. Members of the merchants' hundred did not, however, possess the right to travel abroad or possess patrimonial estates. The trading people of the cloth hundred, numbering 116 in 1649, came from wealthy provincial merchants and enjoyed privileges comparable to those of the merchants' hundred. Both groups served in Moscow customs houses and the mint, though in positions below those held by elite merchants. On the Muscovite social scale the elite merchants ranked just below hereditary noble servicemen (discussed below), whereas the trading people of the merchants' hundred and cloth hundred were close in social status to the "men recruited for service."

The "men recruited for service" (*sluzhilye liudi po priboru*) occupied the lowest rungs of the Muscovite service hierarchy. Encompassing a variety of military ranks associated with different forms of weaponry and organization, they also frequently overlapped with the urban and peasant classes.[22] The "old formation" servicemen consisted of musketeers (*strel'tsy*), town Cossacks (*gorodovye kazaki*), artillerymen or gunners (*pushkari* and *zatinshchiki*), and fortress gate-guards (*vorotniki*). The "new formation" servicemen counted among their numbers infantrymen (*soldaty*), cavalrymen (*reitary*), and dragoons (*draguny*). The old formation servicemen can be described as functional or proto-professional ranks in which membership was hereditary and all males served for life. But in addition to their military obligations, the old formation servicemen also engaged in petty trade and agriculture in order to support their families. An important group among the urban classes of Moscow and provincial towns, they became prominent participants in urban riots and disorders of the seventeenth and early eighteenth centuries.

In contrast to the old formation servicemen, whose service ended up being part-time and whose military skills were becoming obsolete in the seventeenth century, the men of the new formation forces represented the core of the future standing army. Trained in linear tactics and the use of flintlock muskets, these servicemen were supposed to form "regular troops paid and supplied by the central government." But because government resources always fell short, the new model forces sometimes quartered in military settlements, where they "were required to provide for themselves much as the traditional forces did."[23] The new model regiments became established from the 1630s to the 1650s, and in the second half of the seventeenth century the peasant recruits who manned these forces began to serve for life. In addition to peasants, the government also conscripted landless provincial nobles, especially after 1678, when nobles possessing fewer than 24 peasant households were excluded from service in the noble cavalry militia. These nobles were required instead to serve as infantrymen or cavalrymen in the new model forces, a status that despite offering some limited opportunities for promotion to officer rank, generally meant downward social mobility.[24] Still, at a time when the traditional militia was becoming militarily obsolete, conscription into the new model forces provided poor provincial nobles with a livelihood and a way to transition into the future standing army.

Prior to the creation of new model regiments, all noble servicemen, both high and low, belonged to the elite category of "hereditary servicemen" (*sluzhilye liudi po otechestvu*).[25] Distinguished by their right to exploit peasant labor, a right explicitly denied the "men recruited for service," these ranks eventually agglomerated into the landowning nobility of Imperial Russia.[26] Like the "men recruited for service," hereditary servicemen also belonged to a variety of ranks, ranging in their case from privileged members of the tsar's council or duma (*dumnye chiny*) to men serving from the metropolitan Moscow list (*chiny moskovskie* or *sluzhilye liudi po moskovskomu spisku*) to men serving from provincial towns. The nobles serving from provincial town lists began to comprise a social group in the reign of Ivan III (ruled 1462–1505), when in return for grants of populated land, they agreed to serve the tsar in the noble cavalry militia. Also called *pomeshchiki* or holders of "conditional land grants" (*pomest'ia*), their ranks included, in ascending order, boyars' sons from the town lists (*gorodovye boiarskie deti*), boyars' sons from the court lists (*dvorovye boiarskie deti*), and selected nobles (*vybornye dvoriane*).[27] In the seventeenth century, another category of servicemen called *zhil'tsy* (sing., *zhilets*), literally "residents," stood at the head of the town lists and served in lower-level military and administrative positions. Some historians also describe *zhilets* as the lowest metropolitan Moscow rank, noting that servicemen of this rank performed ceremonial duties and served in the tsar's personal bodyguard.[28] Clearly, a man who began his service career as a *zhilets* might be able to advance into the Moscow ranks, which included, in ascending order, Moscow nobles (*dvoriane moskovskie*), *striapchie*, and *stol'niki*. The Moscow nobles held offices such as governor, ambassador, chancellery official, and regimental commander, whereas the higher Moscow ranks, the *striapchie* and *stol'niki*, held more prestigious positions such as town governor and military commander.

At the very top of the Muscovite service hierarchy stood the members of the tsar's council, the "duma ranks," which included, in ascending order, duma nobles (*dumnye dvoriane*) and duma secretaries (*dumnye d'iaki*), *okol'nichie*, and boyars (*boiare*). Appointment to the council, called the Boyar Duma by historians, occurred in recognition of distinguished service and represented the peak of social privilege and political power. Council members advised the tsar and helped to make decisions about domestic and foreign policy. Constantly on the go in service to the sovereign, they commanded armies, governed provinces, supervised the government's central administrative offices (*prikazy*), and heard judicial appeals. Men of duma rank usually held this appointment for life, though only after years of military or civil service and only so long as they did not suffer disgrace or exile.

During the course of the seventeenth century, the composition and size of the tsar's council fluctuated. Overall, however, its membership increased and thus became less distinguished. In 1613, the year of Mikhail Romanov's election to the throne, only 20 men sat in the council; by 1649 the number had risen to 52. After 1676 appointees to duma rank also included growing numbers of younger men with no service experience outside the court. In 1682 Tsars Peter I and Ivan V ascended the throne, and 107 individuals held duma rank; by 1690 the number reached 153. At century's end, the men of duma rank had become far too numerous to act as an effective decision-making body. The "inflation of honors" rendered duma rank less exclusive and encouraged rulers to bypass the council and rely instead on a select circle of chosen advisors. When in 1711 Peter I established the Senate, thereby abolishing the traditional council, his action caused neither administrative disruption nor even elite protest.[29]

The precise relationship between lineage, service, and political power in Muscovy is not always easy to define. To a significant degree, the most powerful men in Muscovy held rank and office at the ruler's pleasure. The tsar appointed individuals to duma rank, and his disfavor could bring removal from the council. But the ruler also needed the consent and assistance of powerful nobles in order to govern his vast and diverse territories. Nor did he enjoy complete freedom in making appointments. Although the tsar appointed personal favorites and relatives to his council, the men of duma rank nonetheless tended to come from a relatively small group of princely and Moscow boyar families. Not all men of power and wealth attained duma rank, yet the men of duma rank included Russia's richest landowners and most important generals and officials. No one sat in the tsar's council by hereditary right, yet the ruler remained morally, politically, and even legally obliged to select his advisors based in part on genealogy.

Beginning in the late fifteenth century, as the Moscow grand princes consolidated their rule over the appanage territories and brought local princes and service elites into the Muscovite polity, a place system developed to regulate relations within the newly constituted governing class. Called *mestnichestvo*, the place system combined lineage and service to establish a rank ordering of elite families that determined precedence in service appointments and at court. No individual was supposed to occupy a position or receive an appointment above another whose family held a higher place in the genealogical hierarchy. *Mestnichestvo* disputes undermined the corporate power of the nobility and kept many a family and official busy with time-consuming litigation. But *mestnichestvo* also represented a source of social cohesion, based on shared notions of family honor, and a real limit on the power of the tsar. Before the abolition of *mestnichestvo* in 1682, the ruler may have been free to appoint favorites and men of undistinguished lineage or service to high office and duma rank, but not with complete disregard for the genealogical hierarchy institutionalized in *mestnichestvo*.[30]

Data from the seventeenth century show that successive rulers often appointed council members from a small group of prominent families. About 43 percent of appointees had a relative already sitting in the tsar's council. During "the entire seventeenth century 36 percent of all boyars and *okol'nichie* were direct descendants of men who held the same ranks at least thirty years earlier." Heredity and lineage clearly mattered, but they were not sacrosanct or inviolable. The tsar could at any time bring representatives of new families into his council, a practice that increased as the seventeenth century progressed. During the reign of Aleksei

Mikhailovich (ruled 1645–76), appointments to the council included "unprecedented numbers of social upstarts." From 1659 to 1676, a mere 16 percent of "appointees to the Duma's top ranks had direct ancestors who had served in the same capacity."[31] These changes in the composition of the tsar's council illustrate the fact that while Muscovy boasted a rich and powerful noble elite – one that supplied the monarchy with generations of officials, generals, and courtiers – no individual except the tsar possessed an hereditary right to any office or rank. In order to govern, tsars relied on the entrenched Muscovite elite, but also regularly added to it. Throughout the period of Romanov rule, lasting from 1613 to 1917, the Russian nobility remained relatively open to newcomers, and the only way for a commoner to achieve nobility was through service to the sovereign.

Service also provided access to land ownership and hence to noble wealth. From provincial servicemen to men of duma rank, Russian nobles enjoyed the right to possess populated estates. Some held land on condition of service, the *pomest'e* estates described above, and others owned land outright as patrimony or *votchina*. Nobles of all ranks could hold both kinds of property, though men of higher rank depended less on conditional grants of land. Ownership of *votchina* also carried greater prestige and allowed nobles to move serfs between estates. Even more striking in effect than the form of land tenure were the differences in wealth that divided Russian nobles. Among the duma men of 1678, for example, boyars owned an average of 862 peasant households, while *okol'nichie* owned 226.[32] Significant economic differentiation remained characteristic of the Russian nobility until the end of the monarchy in 1917.

The sources of inequality changed over time; however, the practice of partible inheritance, on the basis of which all sons (and some daughters) became heirs, stands out because of its social and political implications. Sons usually received equal portions of their father's estate, so that over the generations, land holdings tended to fragment and family wealth easily dissipated. In order to preserve a family's wealth (and attendant status), it became necessary to purchase land, marry one's sons to women with dowries in land, or seek additional grants of land through service to the tsar. For generations a core group of noble families managed to maintain their property and social position independent of service. Yet still their senior males served. Many other families, moreover, depended almost entirely on service to ensure the prosperity needed to support a noble way of life. In Muscovy, and later in Imperial Russia, service to the tsar brought access to power, status, and wealth just as often as wealth brought access to power, status, and the tsar.[33]

Indeed, if one focuses on the connection between land ownership and political power, the legal and economic distinctions dividing nobles appear less striking. From the mid-sixteenth century, all nobles were required to serve; consequently, the distinction between lands held on condition of service and those held as patrimony became less significant in defining noble status. (In the early eighteenth century, Tsar Peter I abolished the distinction outright.) Wealth, status, and power always would be linked in Russia; however, by the late seventeenth century, it also became clear that while wealth facilitated access to rank and office, land ownership did not automatically confer rank or office. The boyars and other duma ranks can be described as a class of aristocratic magnates whose power rested on inherited wealth and closeness to the tsar. These men advised the tsar directly; served as policymakers, generals, and high-level officials; and during times of disputed succession, decided who would rule. But the duma ranks were not inherited, and although the tsar frequently appointed great nobles to such rank, he also could elevate men of lesser status or undistinguished service. Muscovy's hereditary servicemen (*sluzhilye liudi po otechestvu*) thus constituted both a service class and a landowning nobility with no clear distinction between the two.

Beyond Moscow, among townspeople and provincial nobles, appointment to office and rank likewise depended on the tsar's favor. During the seventeenth century, the elective offices found in provincial towns tended to be replaced by appointed officials representing the central bureaucracy in Moscow.[34] Nor did Muscovy develop corporate bodies – bodies such as diets, *parlements*, provincial estates, Estates General, or the English Parliament – in which nobles sat based on property ownership or inherited title.[35] Historians incessantly debate whether or not Muscovy's nobles constituted an autonomous landed gentry with local roots and a meaningful corporate identity or a service class beholden to the tsar. Nobles up and down the social hierarchy looked after their estates and families, served in local or central offices, and developed relationships with neighbors and relatives. But lacking the independent power embodied in inherited offices and corporate bodies, they belonged to a service class, composed of individuals in direct and personal relationship to peers, superiors, and the tsar.

The profusion of social ranks and categories that made up Muscovite society can seem painfully complicated and arcane to a modern-day brain. The lists of categories and sub-categories, each defined by specific service or socioeconomic functions, overwhelm and confuse those of us accustomed to a system in which precise legal rights are accorded to individuals rather than social collectivities. But it is impossible to describe seventeenth- and even eighteenth-century Russian society without noting the multiplicity of categories. The Muscovite ranks revealed a legalistic understanding of society, though not one grounded in the rule of law or the principle of inalienable natural rights. The Muscovite ranks represented medieval grants of privilege that the tsar could rescind at any time. Although such privileges could be inherited, they did not automatically confer membership in any particular social or political institution. Individuals or collectivities received privileges, and through the granting of privileges the monarchy could move people between established, or not so established, categories and statuses.

The Muscovite ranks are best understood as tools of administration imposed by the government on subjects and servitors of the tsar. Designed to mobilize resources for the monarchy and bring order to fluid, diverse, and dynamic social relationships, the ranks did not always correspond to actual conditions on the ground. Especially in the towns, people of various origins and legal statuses could be found engaging in trades meant to be the preserve of official townspeople. The gap between official definitions and concrete realities suggests that the government remained legally free but practically limited in its ability to mold social relationships and institutions. For this reason, the Muscovite vocabulary of social ranks often appears inadequate to encompass the substance of actual relationships. Yet in a culture dominated by Orthodox Christian universalism, this vocabulary, however cumbersome and confused, gave broad secular meaning to the activities and obligations of everyday life. From the monarchy's point of view, the definition of ranks represented a giant step toward realization of the effective population controls needed to support modern state building. From the historian's point of view, it marked the onset of a long process whereby Russians, both individually and collectively, ventured beyond familism, localism, and parochialism into "society."

—— Social Organization in the Reign of Peter the Great ——

During the reign of Tsar Peter I (ruled 1682/89–1725), the need to mobilize Russia's human and material resources took center stage in the development of social policy and political institutions.[36] In the seventeenth century, the Muscovite government bound peasants and townspeople to their communities of origin or residence for purposes of taxation and conscription. Muscovite law also established a clear connection between social rank or status on the one hand and service or economic function on the other. Family relations and local ties continued to define the realities of everyday life, but in "society" writ large functional attributes mattered most. Although the Petrine reforms did little to change these basic patterns, they did much to enforce legal distinctions and obligations to the state more effectively. Social and political relationships that the Muscovite government left vague and amorphous, Peter's government set out to define and regulate.

Emblematic of the Petrine government's drive to control population and resources was the introduction of the poll tax or capitation. Decreed in 1718 and implemented from 1719 through 1728, the poll tax reform identified the social groups liable for taxation and imposed an annual monetary payment on every male soul ascribed to one of these groups. The vast majority of Russian subjects, primarily peasants and townspeople, fell into the taxpaying population, while a range of smaller groups – nobles, ordained clergy, and various nonnobles in military or civil service – remained exempt. The reform began with a population count of taxable males, a process repeated in subsequent censuses of 1743–7, 1761–7, 1781–2, 1794–5, 1811, 1815–17, 1833–6, 1850–3, and 1857–8.[37] In each instance, officials compiled lists, which then served as the basis for collecting the capitation and conscripting recruits. As in Muscovite times, the fulfillment of obligations, in this case payment of the capitation and delivery of recruits, was the responsibility of the entire peasant or urban community, with landlords or local officials determining precisely how the burden would be distributed.

Historians no longer follow the lead of prerevolutionary historian Pavel N. Miliukov (1859–1943), who claimed that the fiscal and military policies of Peter I ruined the Russian population and devastated the economy. But they do recognize that the burden of taxation and service imposed by Peter was unprecedented in the history of Russia. Instead of taxing every household or the amount of the land or capital held by a household, the government now taxed every male living in every household (74 kopecks a year, reduced to 70 soon after Peter's death). And instead of haphazard calls to arms, in 1705 the government instituted regular conscription levies which transformed recruits into lifelong soldiers, known collectively as the "lower military ranks." Back home in the peasant village or provincial town, as the monarchy's standing army grew, so too did the quartering, carting, and provisioning obligations imposed on local (primarily peasant) populations. Introduction of the capitation, like census-taking across Europe, gave to the government an effective tool for tracking a dynamic and, in the Russian case, residentially bound population. As a result, taxes could be collected, recruits mustered, and labor services imposed.

Although conceived as a tool of administration, the capitation also had significant social consequences. Above all, it created in Russian society a fundamental divide between the privileged few who enjoyed exemption from the tax and the unprivileged many who filled the ranks of the army and labored to support social elites and government institutions. The taxpaying population encompassed Russia's commercial and laboring classes, the "common people" and backbone of the economy. Groups exempted from the capitation included nobles, ordained clergy, technical and cultural specialists, and upwardly mobile groups that might some day achieve noble status by rising in the service hierarchy. The poll tax divide did less to highlight differences between untaxed nobles and taxed nonnobles (high versus low) than between untaxed service classes (high and low) and taxed commercial and laboring classes (also high and low in terms of socioeconomic standing).

The poll tax reform also can be seen as part of a larger process of agglomeration from the multiple Muscovite ranks into the larger social categories of the Imperial period – the *sostoianiia* (sing., *sostoianie*) or *sosloviia* (sing., *soslovie*).[38] Like the Muscovite ranks, the Imperial "estates" (an inadequate translation but the best available) were hereditary legal categories defined by privileges, obligations, and service or socioeconomic functions. The main categories included the nobility, clergy, merchants and townspeople, and various subcategories of peasants (state, church/monastery, crown, and seigniorial). Although legal distinctions further subdivided the clergy, urban classes, and peasants, the members of each of the main categories shared a common set of obligations to the monarchy. In addition, around the edges of the main categories, Petrine legislation delineated a host of smaller groups, the "people of various ranks" (*raznochintsy*), defined by service, socioeconomic, and cultural functions.[39] Agglomeration from ranks into estates strengthened the government's ability to manage the Russian population, especially servicemen and taxpayers, but as the phenomenon of the *raznochintsy* attests, social boundaries remained porous and indeterminate. At the same time that policymakers sought to regulate society by assigning every subject to an appropriate legal status, they also contributed to social mobility by freeing from the capitation a variety of specialists and servicemen recruited from the taxpaying population: common soldiers, petty clerks in the bureaucracy, and technical specialists and craftsmen in government service. Changeable social definitions and an amorphous social structure thus accompanied the process of social agglomeration, a process conceived and engineered by the central government.

The combination of stricter regulation and social amorphousness that resulted from the poll tax reform is strikingly evident in the relationship of Peter I's government to the Russian peasantry. As noted above, the basic organization of peasant society barely changed before the onset of Soviet modernization in the second quarter of the twentieth century. By contrast, the main innovations of the Petrine period, imposition of the capitation and regular conscription, altered forever the role of the government in peasant life. The first step in imposing the capitation was the population count of 1719–28, elaborated in a table of 1738. The table identified a total peasant population of 5,331,673 male souls (93.5 percent of the taxpaying population), including 1,022,081 state peasants (18.2 percent of taxpayers) and 4,279,492 church, crown, and seigniorial peasants (75.3 percent of taxpayers).[40] Regular conscription began years before the poll tax reform, but once the population count was completed, it also became the basis for determining who was liable for military service. While estimates of the number of inductees into Peter's army vary, one recent account gives a figure of at least 205,000 in the period 1700–11 and "a bare minimum" of 140,000 in 1713–24.[41] Peter's conscription levies took in townspeople (a category numbering 188,665 male souls, according to the 1738 table) and in 1721 even clergy, though the vast majority of recruits came from the peasantry.[42]

For Russian peasants, regular intrusions by the government, primarily in the form of conscription levies, constituted the most significant effect of Peter I's policies. Within each peasant (and urban) community, conscription created a painful source of conflict, as landowners and village (or town) officials set about deciding whose son, husband, father, or brother would be sent to the army. Peasant (and urban) communities could use conscription levies to rid themselves of troublesome or economically weak members, but all too often it proved necessary to take a healthy adult male from an upstanding family. However implemented, the loss of an able-bodied adult male represented a blow not only to his loved ones, but also to the community as a whole, concerned as it was to ensure the viability of member households. Landowners and village officials tried to limit the impact of conscription by selecting single men from larger households and sparing households with fewer grown males. But corruption and abuse, the ability of the wealthy to pay a bribe or purchase a substitute, and the vagaries of village politics did not always make for an equitable selection process.[43] Prior to 1793, conscription brought permanent year-round service, which continued until disability or death ended a soldier's active military career. Not surprisingly, peasants viewed conscription as an unmitigated disaster and mourned each recruit as dead. Hence the peasant proverb: "One son is not a son. Two sons are half a son. Three sons are a son."[44]

Once a recruit was carried off, sometimes in chains, his family and community still faced the problem of what to do with his wife, assuming he had one, their offspring, and any children that she might produce in the future. Soldiers conscripted from the taxpaying population, including serfs, became legally free – free from the capitation and from any obligations previously owed to the landowner or community. Soldiers' wives and any children born to soldiers after the start of active service also enjoyed legal freedom. If a couple had children prior to the husband's conscription, these children remained in their father's former status and would have been entitled to full membership in the peasant (or urban) community. But a wife left behind with no children, in light of her legal freedom, had no place in village society. Unable to remarry without proof of her husband's death, she lived at the mercy of in-laws, relatives (perhaps her own natal family), and neighbors. If a soldier's wife eventually gave birth to illegitimate children, they too shared her precarious status. To cope with the uncertainty, soldiers' wives sometimes left the village voluntarily, if they were not already driven out by force, and went to live in towns or alongside the troops. The government also eventually responded to the welfare problem posed by abandoned wives and illegitimate children. A decree of 1721 created the category "soldiers' children" (*soldatskie deti*), defined as children born to fathers in active service, and legislation from the early nineteenth century added to the category illegitimate children of soldiers' wives and daughters. Soldiers' children belonged to the military domain (*voennoe vedomstvo*), and the males among them were obliged to attend garrison schools and enter military service. The category "soldiers' children" thus embodied the possibility of upward social mobility that was built into the Petrine service state. Soldiers' wives, by contrast, continued to lack secure social moorings. While they might find an informal or even illicit place in society, especially among the laboring classes of the towns, their plight illustrated all too starkly the social disruptions caused by Peter's poll tax and military reforms.

Townspeople likewise suffered from the consequences of conscription, but because Russia's official urban population remained small (3.3 percent of the taxpaying population, according to the 1738 table), the actual number of urban residents affected was never very large. Of greater concern to urban communities and government officials was the continuing presence of unregistered town residents, some of whom encroached on urban trades and none of whom fulfilled the tax and service obligations of official townspeople. Data from 1701 show that out of 16,500 households counted in Moscow, only 6,800 belonged to registered urban residents.[45] Of course, Moscow was the administrative and cultural center of the country, and many householders belonged to social categories that carried their own service obligations – nobles, clergy, civil servants, and military servicemen. Still, throughout the eighteenth century, peasants, *raznochintsy*, and even local officials continued to practice urban trades that were supposed to be the preserve of registered townspeople.

In its treatment of townspeople, the government of Peter I followed precedents enshrined in the Law Code of 1649, which had attempted to restrict urban trades to specific social categories by defining who could trade what and where they could operate. In an effort to enforce privileges and obligations, Petrine legislation also divided urban residents into regular and irregular "citizens." Irregular citizens, sometimes called the "base people" (*podlye liudi*), tended to be wage laborers who lacked capital, a profession, or membership in a craft organization. Regular citizens belonged to one of three guilds, depending on occupation and the amount of capital a person possessed, or to craft organizations (*tsekhi*), designed to supervise craftsmen and ensure their inclusion in the taxpaying community. Like the peasant commune, the guilds and craft organizations administered their own affairs. In addition, regular citizens came under the authority of a special legal-administrative body or court, the magistracy, to which they sent elected representatives.[46]

Probably the most dramatic social changes associated with the reign of Peter I affected the nobility and educated service classes. In Muscovy, there had existed an array of noble ranks, with men of duma rank occupying an exalted status that clearly distinguished them from poor provincial nobles. Petrine legislation made these distinctions less transparent by agglomerating the multiple noble ranks into a single noble status and linking that status directly to service. The nobility remained internally differentiated with respect to wealth and social prestige, and the tsar continued to appoint individuals from elite noble families to the highest positions in military and civil service. But in strictly legal terms, Peter equalized or leveled the various noble ranks, so that in principle all nobles enjoyed the same rights, privileges, and obligations. Ranks did not disappear; however, from the time of Peter onward, they referred solely to a man's position in the service hierarchy.

In 1722 Peter I, called Emperor since October 1721, bureaucratized military, civil, and court ranks (and radically altered terminology) when he introduced the Table of Ranks. One of the most significant and enduring of Peter's innovations, the Table of Ranks consisted of fourteen classes or grades, each of which corresponded to specified titles (*chiny*) and offices (*dolzhnosti*) in the service hierarchy. A "place system" of a different sort, the Table of Ranks tied noble status and the attainment of noble status to service rank. In military service, promotion to rank 14, the lowest commissioned officer rank, brought automatic ennoblement. In civil service, any official who reached rank 8 became a noble, whereas those serving in ranks 14 to 9 or in administrative positions that fell below the Table of Ranks could be noble or nonnoble.[47] Somewhere around the age of fifteen, a young nobleman began his career in the military or bureaucracy, supposedly on the lower rungs of the service ladder. Promotions occurred more rapidly in military service, which nobles preferred anyway, and members of prominent families also benefited from connections to powerful patrons. As in Muscovy, the attainment of high position hinged on lineage, the tsar's favor, and a measure of merit.

The Table of Ranks did not transform the Petrine service state into a meritocracy, but it did regularize and institutionalize promotions based on talent and zeal. The dramatic growth of the military and bureaucracy, combined with the pressing need for educated servicemen and technical specialists, increased the opportunities for men of humble origins to rise. Promotion in service became more closely linked to education, and clear criteria of merit joined birth and patronage in the calculus of advancement. At the same time, even though social origin became less important in defining service position, elite status and high position tended to go hand in hand. Nobles, and to a lesser degree the sons of nonnoble officials, enjoyed greater access to education and thus could more readily be identified as men of talent. Petrine policy sought not to dislodge Russia's great nobles from their position of social and political dominance, but rather to ensure that all nobles acquired the education and skills needed to compete in a modern European world. On a scale unimaginable to Peter's predecessors, service defined the lives of nobles and the meaning of noble status. For nobles, as for peasants and townspeople, the burden of service increased enormously. In the case of nobles, the government also began to intervene in everyday life. Ordered to shave their beards, adopt contemporary European dress, congregate in mixed social company, and educate their children to meet the military and administrative needs of the monarchy, nobles no longer enjoyed the possibility of leading quiet provincial lives. Although in Muscovy noble service already had become obligatory, in Peter's Russia this service became lifelong, year-round, and much more strictly enforced. Nobles became part of a single noble class (*dvorianstvo*), which in turn represented the core of the educated service classes.

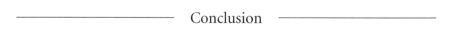

Conclusion

Historians long have noted the absence of a clear distinction between civil administration and social institutions in eighteenth-century Russia.[48] Already implicit in the organization of Muscovite society, the pattern became particularly noticeable in the hands of Peter I's activist and self-consciously reformist government. The reason for the blending of government and society was not the autocratic nature of the monarchy or the servility of the Russian people; it was the institutional weakness of both the state and society. During the seventeenth and eighteenth centuries, the absolute monarchies of Central and Western Europe expended great effort to plug new government institutions into corporate bodies that had functioned in society since the middle ages. The Russian monarchy, by contrast, itself initiated the building of both local and central (translocal) institutions, which it then called upon different groups in "society" to fill. One result of the Russian reliance on government initiative was a relatively peaceful process of state building in the seventeenth (after 1613) and eighteenth centuries. Although between 1682 and 1801 court coups occurred with frightful regularity, Russia's social elites did not mount any organized opposition to established political institutions before 1825. Other consequences of the government's role as initiator included a lack of formal institution-based social integration and a reliance on personal authority and relationships to negotiate public life. Before the mid to late nineteenth century, Russians outside of government did little to build institutions that connected individuals, families, and communities to their cohorts in other localities.

For most Russians, links to the monarchy remained tenuous and transient throughout the age of serfdom. Because nobles served the tsar directly, they always were tied to the monarchy and its administrative center through personal relationships and vertical institutional structures. The very limited links to the political center maintained by peasants and townspeople also tended to be personal and vertical. Laboring people generally handled their own daily affairs within the confines of self-governing and largely self-sufficient communities that had little need for a larger "society" or government. When relations of trade, marriage, or service required formal legal sanction or mediation across the boundaries of community, then peasants and townspeople, like nobles, turned to government officials for assistance. This brought them into direct contact with the monarchy, but only because outside the immediate village or urban community locally constituted bodies designed to mediate civic relations did not exist. Appeals beyond one's immediate neighbors had nowhere to go other than to the noble landowner (sometimes mediated through his steward) or town official. Appeals beyond the landowner or town official, or against them, had nowhere to go other than to a higher government authority. Finally, appeals beyond high-level government officials, or against them, had nowhere to go other than to the tsar. The same can be said of church peasants and servicemen, who could appeal to the monastery head, then to the bishop, and eventually to the patriarch (later the Synod) or tsar. Beyond the tsar, there was no one and nothing, except for God and conscience.

Chapter 2

Building a Service State

The present defines understanding of the past, and for today's historians the memory of communist dictatorship in Soviet Russia raises the question of how best to characterize the centralized monarchy of Muscovy. The question seems straightforward enough, but it is colored by assumptions concerning the "inevitability" of authoritarian government in Russia and the country's "fitness" for democracy. Equally problematic, current knowledge and available sources produce a decidedly ambiguous picture that can be interpreted in different ways. In contrast to documents from the Petrine era, which offer bold statements of absolutist political theory, Muscovite sources provide only the most tentative articulation of political principles. The contrast between Muscovite silence and Petrine eloquence is striking, but the meaning of the contrast continues to baffle historians. Is it substance or merely style? Did Tsar Peter I's concrete declarations of absolutist political theory represent a departure from a Muscovite politics built upon consensus and collective governance? Or did Peter merely impart a more modern or European form to a traditional patrimonial state in which the monarch viewed the territories under his authority as personal property to be exploited as he saw fit?[1] What, historians continue to ask, was the basic quality of Russian monarchy prior to the Petrine declaration that the Russian ruler is 'an absolute monarch [*samovlastnyi Monarkh*] who need answer to no one on earth about his affairs, but has the power and authority as a Christian Sovereign to rule his dominions and lands by his own will and good judgment'?[2]

In recent decades, anthropological conceptions of political culture have encouraged historians to downplay the images of autocratic government found in sources from the Muscovite era. Sensitive to dynamics and nuance, these scholars focus on how the monarchy functioned in concrete situations and relationships. From a variety of perspectives, the effective power of the Russian monarch does indeed appear limited. Because Muscovite tsars often took wives from the elite nobility, they remained tied by relations of kinship to the social class whose cooperation they needed in order to govern. In addition, given the territorial expanse and primitive communications of the Russian lands, even the most awe-inspiring tsar could hardly command absolute obedience from his people. The tsar might decree, but his subjects, including officials, did not (or could not) always obey. To mobilize resources and protect his territories, the ruler not only needed the help of honest officials committed to implementing the law; he also needed to communicate with his people. This he did by consulting representatives from the clergy, elite nobility, noble and nonnoble service classes, and townspeople. Both the tsar's council and the Assembly of the Land provided effective channels of communication that allowed the tsar to admonish and hear out his subjects. Judicial proceedings provided yet another means of communication. Russians of all classes, including peasants, used government offices and legal prescriptions to pursue litigation that protected their privileges and honor, while at the same time integrating them into social networks and political institutions. Finally, historians of an anthropological bent suggest, the Russian language of servility and supplication, so often cited by foreign observers as evidence of the tsar's omnipotence, should be interpreted as baroque play or a façade of symbolic subjugation that enabled powerful grandees at once to oppose rivals, negotiate political power, and preserve social peace.[3]

Yet at moments of crisis and confusion over the succession to the throne, peace was not preserved. Although Muscovite tsars (and officials) ruled through laws, Russia developed no formally constituted bodies to limit their power. For this reason, historians who emphasize legal prescriptions and institutions, those who adopt a more formalistic approach to the problem of political culture, tend to conclude that the Muscovite tsar became a theoretically all-powerful sovereign, capable of suppressing any dissent and removing any challenger, long before Peter I's explicit articulation of absolutist political principles. To legal-minded historians, whether of prerevolutionary Russia or Cold War Europe and America, it makes no difference that the ruler's effective power remained weak or that "autocracy" constituted a theory more than a description of concrete practice. To this day, what matters most to such historians is long-term development toward constitutional government and the rule of law. If the formalistic approach represents an anachronistic imposition of Western experience onto Russian history, so be it, say the legal-minded historians. Before the communist revolution, significant numbers of Russians struggled, and in the post-communist era continue to struggle, for the realization of civil liberties and political democracy in Russia.

Historians who prefer a legal-institutional analysis repeatedly draw attention to modern Russia's political divergence from the other great powers of Europe. At the core of their analysis lies the absolutist power of the Russian monarch. In Britain, France, Austria, and even the German states, limited monarchy (and eventually parliamentary government and the rule of law) arose from medieval territorial privileges and from the cumulative effects of institutional competition and juristic posturing among recognized corporate bodies. Monarchs who asserted a divine right to absolute sovereignty had to contend with the authority and pre-rogatives of corporate bodies. In need of resources but short of effective power, monarchs pursued dynastic or state interests through cooperation with, or opposition from, these bodies. Negotiation and struggle thus occurred within a formally constituted and legally explicit framework. In Russia, by contrast, the monarch may have been vulnerable to overthrow, weak in administrative reach, and obliged to rule through noble elites. But he nonetheless remained the sole source of formal legislative authority and the final source of earthly justice. At no time before the creation of an elected Duma in 1906 did any representative institution exercise legislative, administrative, or judicial authority independent of the ruler. The right of the people to resist a tyrant and the obligation of the monarch to consult society and seek advice represented moral but not legal or institutional limits on his power.[4] That the Muscovite tsar felt morally or polit-ically compelled to take account of opinions and proposals put forth by bishops, elite nobles, and other representatives of his people – that he sometimes chose or was forced to consult with and rule through assemblies or men of duma rank – did not change the fact that once the monarch decided and decreed, his decision could not be challenged. Tsars were themselves expected to obey the law, but they also could change the law, or overturn any judicial or administrative decision based on the law, at will.

――――   ## Political Institutions in the Seventeenth Century   ――――

In 1598 the dynasty that had ruled the Russian lands since the legendary founding of the Kievan polity in 862 died out, unleashing a succession crisis that soon led to full-scale civil war and foreign occupation. The Time of Troubles came to an end in 1613, after Russian troops expelled Polish occupiers from the Kremlin and an Assembly of the Land, composed of elite nobles and several hundred repres-entatives of the free population (provincial nobles, musketeers and other low-ranking military servicemen, townspeople, clergy, Cossacks, state peasants, and crown peasants), elected Mikhail Fedorovich Romanov (ruled 1613–45) to be tsar.[5] Any ruler chosen in 1613 would have lacked immediate authority and legitimacy, but Muscovites of the time also were eager to restore peace and reclaim their country. For this reason, they accepted Mikhail, clearly a compromise candidate, "as the God-chosen successor of the defunct sacred dynasty."[6] For his part, Mikhail suc-cessfully associated himself with the old dynasty (Anastasia, the most beloved wife of Ivan IV, had been a Romanov) and moved to restore the political arrangements in place before the onset of the troubles. The young tsar did not hesitate to punish challengers and suspected traitors; however, in his role as God's vicar on earth, he combined repression with traditional expressions of piety and divinely sanctioned autocratic power. To govern his realm, Mikhail relied on elite noble families that had survived the Time of Troubles and on the Assembly of the Land which had brought him to power. Equally important, he relied on his father, Metropolitan Filaret, who in 1619 returned from Polish captivity to become, until his death in 1633, patriarch of the Russian Orthodox Church and the actual ruler of Russia. Together, father and son presided over the restoration of institutions and practices that had defined the monarchy of the late fifteenth and sixteenth centuries, while also strengthening the power of the church and government bureaucracy.

Alongside the hereditary monarchy embodied in the divinely elected Romanov dynasty, the basic institutions to emerge from the period of political centralization prior to 1598 and again from the Time of Troubles included the tsar's council, the Assembly of the Land, and a collection of administrative offices or chancelleries called *prikazy*. Dating from the later fifteenth century, the tsar's council consisted of appointed members, the men of duma rank, usually chosen from a core of several hundred noble families living around the court. The men of duma rank advised the tsar, conducted his foreign policy, commanded his armies, decided judicial cases, and oversaw central and local administrative offices. Limited to between 28 and 39 members in the reign of Mikhail Fedorovich and reaching as many as 74 members under Aleksei Mikhailovich (ruled 1645–76), membership in the tsar's council further increased to between 66 and 107 during the brief reign of Fedor Alekseevich (ruled 1676–82).[7] The tsar's council possessed no formal legal status, and as its membership grew, its political weight declined. In the period 1650 to 1676, the government of Aleksei Mikhailovich issued 618 legislative decrees, 588 of which were "privy" or tsarist decrees (*imennye ukazy*) issued in the tsar's name only.[8] Increasingly, the tsar bypassed traditional channels of communication and instead solicited advice in "private" meetings with individual commanders and officials. These individuals might also be men of duma rank, but the locus of their power had changed and their relationship to the tsar had ceased to be mediated through membership in his council. As Muscovy's military forces and government bureaucracy developed apace, and as the men of duma rank became more absorbed in routine administrative or court affairs, policy discussions tended to become the preserve of the tsar and a handful of close associates. The shift may not have been all that perceptible to the people involved, for even in the old days the men of duma rank had served at the ruler's pleasure. Neither the council members of past generations nor the new favorites of seventeenth-century Muscovy ever shared formal power with the monarch.

The same can be said about the Assembly of the Land, an institution that first appeared in the reign of Ivan (IV) the Terrible (ruled 1533–84). According to Soviet historian L. V. Cherepnin, in the period 1549 to 1683 a minimum of 57 assemblies convened, including three church councils from the second half of the sixteenth century and three councils from the second decade of the seventeenth century that cannot be fully verified. Most of these gatherings were called by the tsar, others in response to demands emanating from society or "the land," and still others to elect a new tsar, including two in 1682 (the first to elect Peter I and the second to rescind that decision by crowning Ivan V and Peter I as co-tsars).[9] Few historians accept Cherepnin's list in full, and few would claim that a precise count even is possible. As noted above, a broadly representative assembly convened in 1613 to end the succession crisis and civil war by crowning Mikhail Romanov. That body remained in place until 1615, when new delegates gathered in an assembly that met until 1622. Thus between 1613 and 1622, the Assembly of the Land appeared to function as a regular body with significant powers of government. Subsequent assemblies met in 1632 to discuss impending war with Poland; in 1637, 1639, and 1642 to consider relations with the Crimean Khanate and the Ottoman Empire; in 1645 to confirm the accession to the throne of Aleksei Mikhailovich; in 1648–9 to approve the new Law Code (*Ulozhenie*); in 1650 to deal with rebellion in Pskov; and finally in 1651 and 1653 in connection with Muscovy's incorporation of eastern Ukraine and another war with Poland.[10] Accounts of assemblies called after 1653 are questionable.

Given the available documentation, it also is impossible to know exactly how often the Assembly of the Land met or for how long. Clearly, the assembly did not evolve into a formally constituted body possessing institutionalized authority defined by law. No record of assembly deliberations and procedures has ever been found, and historians lack even the most fragmentary information about procedures for the "election" of delegates. The assembly's composition also varied; peasants participated only in 1613, and there is no evidence of an assembly seeking to regularize its status or limit the powers of the tsar. Even at the height of its power in the reign of Mikhail Fedorovich, the Assembly of the Land is best described as a consultative body with no formal legislative authority. Although the assembly appears to have played a significant political role, this role never became constitutional. Rather, assemblies encouraged recognition of the tsar's authority and demands by communicating with the countryside and provincial towns during periods of political or military uncertainty.[11]

By 1650 or so, political and social order returned to the Russian lands, and significant progress in constructing an apparatus of central administration and national defense became evident. The practice of consultation did not entirely disappear; however, the bureaucratic classes that manned government offices in Moscow and the provinces allowed the monarchy to govern its territories directly, instead of relying on consultations with representatives from various localities and social groups. In subsequent reigns, during periods of reform and statutory innovation, Russia's rulers continued to call together *ad hoc* assemblies or commissions to discuss policy and sound out public opinion. The Muscovite tradition of consultation never became a formal mechanism of government, but it did remain part of Russian political life until the end of the monarchy in 1917.

By far the most sustained institutional development of the seventeenth century occurred in the central administrative offices or chancelleries, which in contrast to the tsar's council and the Assembly of the Land, carried over into the age of reform initiated by Tsar Peter I. Established by the mid-1550s, Russia's central chancelleries represented the core of a "modern" bureaucracy staffed by secretaries (*d'iaki*) and clerks (*pod'iachie*) who received their training on the job and whose status tended to become hereditary. During the sixteenth century, the main function of the bureaucracy had been to raise, finance, and supply the army.[12] In the seventeenth century, its structure and composition became significantly more complicated, with the result that historians' estimates of the actual number of chancelleries show considerable variation. N. F. Demidova, who counts the number of chancelleries functioning in a given year, provides figures that range from 44 in 1626 to 58 in 1698, 44 being the lowest number with peaks of 57 and 59 reached in 1664 and 1677 respectively. Somewhat higher than Demidova's figures are those of Peter B. Brown, who estimates the number of chancelleries existing for each decade of the seventeenth century (68 in the 1620s, 66 in the 1660s, 65 in the 1670s, 61 in the 1690s) and arrives at a total of 136 chancelleries for the period 1613 to 1700. Other estimates include a total of 77 chancelleries in the seventeenth century, to which Borivoj Plavsic adds another 10 to 20. Finally, N. V. Ustiugov identifies 40 "permanent central institutions" or chancelleries in seventeenth-century Russia and settles on a figure of 80 after adding together permanent and temporary chancelleries.[13]

That some chancelleries were temporary in nature – established to carry out a specified task on a limited basis – partly accounts for the fluctuation in numbers. The Foreign Affairs Chancellery (*Posol'skii prikaz*), by contrast, performed specialized duties that required a sizeable permanent staff trained in diplomatic protocol and foreign languages. Offices such as the Siberian Chancellery, formed in 1637 from the Chancellery of the Kazan Palace, managed the affairs of a particular geographic region and also might contain smaller chancelleries responsible for concrete jobs. Within the Siberian Chancellery, for example, a special Chancellery for Merchant Affairs developed to handle matters relating to the fur trade. Among the largest and most important chancelleries, historians also usually mention the Military (*Razriadnyi*) and Service Land (*Pomestnyi*) Chancelleries, and alongside these provide additional listings that include a variety of fiscal, economic, and judicial or policing offices (the Secret, Felony, and Petitions Chancelleries).

Descriptions of the chancellery system generally portray not a system, but a hodgepodge of offices with overlapping functions and no clear hierarchy, structure, or procedures. A handful of recent histories question this appraisal based on: 1) the presence of "staff budgets," which indicate permanent cadres of "professional administrators" or chancellery men (*prikaznye liudi*); and 2) the presence of "administrative manuals," which indicate defined lines of authority and rules of procedure.[14] Whether or not chancellery officials understood or consistently followed rules of procedure remains an open question. Certainly, there is evidence that they attempted to decide cases in accordance with legal prescriptions. But lawsuits dragged on for years, even decades, and officials regularly supplemented their salaries, income from estates, and legitimate fees with informal payments and gifts – tokens of supplication and gratitude – that easily crossed the line into outright and, according to state law, illegal bribes. Such practices remained commonplace throughout the age of serfdom, and not surprisingly, Russian opinion regarding the effectiveness of both the Muscovite and Imperial bureaucracies has been overwhelmingly negative.[15] Historians regularly acknowledge the presence of conscientious enlightened officials in the upper reaches of the bureaucracy, and there is no reason to doubt that at least some of their subordinates were similarly high-minded. But the literary images of corruption and abuse are difficult to set aside, and the gathering of documentation is far from complete.

Whatever the professional quality of Muscovite government, bureaucratic development in the seventeenth century marked the founding of modern administrative monarchy in Russia. The presence of high-ranking secretaries in the tsar's council, the duma secretaries (*dumnye d'iaki*), revealed that service in the bureaucracy sometimes carried great prestige. Sustained growth in the number of officials likewise suggested that a stable process of change had begun: the total number of "chancellery people" (*prikaznye liudi*) employed in Moscow institutions rose from 656 in 1626 to 2,762 in 1698. These figures included 33 and 23 judges (*sud'i*), 46 and 86 chancellery secretaries (*d'iaki*), and 575 and 2,648 clerks (*pod'iachie*).[16] Two or more "judges" appointed from the boyars, *okol'nichie*, duma secretaries, and chancellery secretaries usually headed each chancellery, and within the chancelleries, department or "desk" heads and staff came from the secretaries and clerks.[17] In addition, the Moscow chancelleries extended their authority into provincial towns through administrative offices (*izby*) that came under the authority of appointed governors (*voevody*). Appointed officials serving in government offices began to replace or co-opt locally elected officials serving in provincial offices (*gubnye* and *zemskie izby*), which, not unlike peasant communes, administered community affairs and justice. While the office of governor tended to become permanent in towns where it existed, government offices and officials also might be assigned to carry out specific tasks on a temporary basis. In 1626 the number of local government offices stood at 185, reaching 212 in 1645 and 302 in 1698. More indicative of dramatic growth was the number of officials: in the 1640s, 26 secretaries and 1,522 clerks served in local government offices, whereas by the 1690s these numbers rose to 45 secretaries and 3,791 clerks.[18] Over time, the bureaucracy came to comprise distinct classes of officials, at least some of whom identified the good of Russia with strong state power.

The degree of bureaucratic growth does indeed seem impressive, as does the development of identifiable "civil servants." But given the great expanse of Muscovy's Russian and non-Russian lands, the presence of government officials can only be called a drop in the ocean. Throughout the seventeenth and eighteenth centuries, the transition from local self-government to central bureaucratic government progressed unevenly and remained incomplete. Even in the nineteenth century, administration in general and local administration in particular represented the Achilles heel of the Russian state system. At the same time, however, the organization of Russian society, especially peasant society, suited the limited government presence. In Muscovy, as in other parts of early modern Europe, the central government provided only minimal, mainly military, protection to the population under its authority. One can argue quite convincingly, moreover, that the vast majority of Russian subjects preferred to remain in a condition of freedom *from* the structures and demands of government. Judging by the sources of popular rebellion from the seventeenth to the twentieth century, it seems that the spread of government power into the countryside and borderlands, the latter continuing to fluctuate throughout the age of serfdom, tended to foster discontent and instability rather than national identity and social control. Except for taxation and conscription, which the government did manage to impose with relative consistency, the natural freedom of everyday life allowed people to elude administrative authority.

Muscovite institutional development succeeded in placing political relationships on a relatively firm foundation, but the bureaucracy did not reach deeply or effectively into society. The only broadly based social institution of the period remained the Russian Orthodox Church. Russia joined the Christian world in 988, when Prince Vladimir of Kiev accepted baptism from the bishop of Korsun in order to marry Anna, sister of the Byzantine co-emperors. More than half a century later, in 1054, Christianity became formally divided between Roman Catholicism and Eastern Orthodoxy. In the west, the Roman Catholic Church continued to develop a Latin religious culture and liturgy under the centralized authority of the pope. In the east, the more loosely administered Orthodox churches sanctioned a variety of liturgical languages and practices under the authority of four patriarchs (Constantinople, Alexandria, Antioch, and Jerusalem) who presided over autocephalous "national" or territorial metropolitans. The Russian Church adopted the Byzantine form of Eastern Orthodoxy and thus came under the authority of the patriarch of Constantinople.

The Russian church also enjoyed access to a Slavonic liturgy and translations from the Bible dating back to the late ninth century. In the tenth and eleventh centuries, the available Slavonic translations included the New Testament, parts of the Old Testament (especially *Psalms*), the texts of the Eucharist and the sacraments, and the corpus of Byzantine hymnography. The Russian church accorded enormous deference to the Byzantine church – virtually all the metropolitans of Russia were Byzantine appointees – but the Russian church also developed distinctive liturgical practices and over time acquired a measure of institutional autonomy. *De facto* independence came after the 1439 Union of Florence, which briefly reunited the Catholic and Orthodox Churches: Russia refused to accept the union, and in 1448 a council of Russian bishops bypassed the patriarch of Constantinople in consecrating Metropolitan Ion. Soon thereafter, in 1453, the Byzantine Empire fell to the Ottoman Turks, a Muslim people, and in 1459 a council of Russian bishops declared that henceforth the Russian metropolitan would be chosen in Moscow by order of the grand prince, rather than through dealings with the Greeks. The fall of the Byzantine Empire also left the Russian grand prince as the world's only fully independent Orthodox ruler, a harsh reality that allowed subsequent tsars to assume the mantle of the Orthodox emperor responsible for protecting the universal Orthodox Church and all Orthodox Christians. The end of Mongol rule in 1480 brought still greater independence, and in 1562 the patriarch of Constantinople recognized the 1547 crowning of Ivan IV as tsar. By 1589 the Russian Church obtained its own patriarchate centered in Moscow. Russia had become the New Israel, Moscow the New Jerusalem, and "defense of the [Orthodox] faith" synonymous with "loyalty to the [Russian] tsar."[19]

Even before the establishment of a patriarchate in Moscow, the Russian church had become a powerful and influential institution.[20] Although formally subordinate to the Byzantine church until 1459, and long vulnerable to interference by Russian princes, the church dominated the literary culture of Muscovy and controlled huge tracts of populated land. In the mid-seventeenth century, Patriarch Nikon possessed about 35,000 serfs, and according to data from the first poll tax census, conducted in 1719–28, church peasants comprised close to 14 percent of the entire peasant population. (Crown peasants, those considered the private property of the royal family, comprised only about 9 percent.[21]) Following the Time of Troubles, under the leadership of Patriarch Filaret, the church became a veritable state parallel to the monarchy and its bureaucracy. The "patriarchal court" mirrored the tsarist court, and based on a charter granted by Tsar Mikhail Fedorovich in 1625, all clergy in Filaret's eparchy, together with servicemen and peasants subject to monasteries and churches, came under the judicial authority of the patriarch.

The Russian church always enjoyed a measure of independent judicial authority, though even after 1625 this authority remained divided between the patriarch, abbots, and bishops. No uniform code of laws or integrated system of courts defined the judicial authority of either the church or the monarchy. People had recourse to multiple courts and sets of regulations depending on location and circumstances.

Questions of marriage, family relations, and religious belief tended to come under canon law and be decided by church courts, which also exercised judicial authority over ordained clergy, non-ordained churchmen of all ranks, and the servicemen, traders, craftsmen, and peasants living on church lands. Serious criminal offenses usually came under government courts, and lawsuits pitting laypersons against persons under ecclesiastical authority also might be subject to secular justice. Although from the earliest days of Russian Christianity a division of judicial authority existed, the competence of church and government courts, and the laws governing their decisions, overlapped to a considerable degree.

The delineation of legal-administrative authority improved somewhat by the mid-seventeenth century, when both the church and monarchy took steps to promote centralization and standardization. The Law Code of 1649 established a Monastery Chancellery that became responsible for all civil suits involving church personnel, servicemen, and peasants, whether or not their judicial opponents also lived under church administration. Once again, however, the effort to delimit judicial authority by broadening the jurisdiction of government courts fell short. Tsarist charters (*gramoty*) recognized the independent judicial powers of the patriarch and bishops, and in 1677 the Monastery Chancellery was abolished. Church councils of 1666–7 and 1675 also ensured that in civil suits bishops would exercise judicial authority over all persons living on church lands or under church administration. In criminal cases, persons of ecclesiastical rank did become subject to government courts, though only after being defrocked. In religious and marital cases, even laypersons came under church courts.

Muscovy's complicated judicial jurisdictions represented just one aspect of an ambiguous political reality. Although the Law Code of 1649 forbade further expansion of ecclesiastical landholding and allowed the monarchy to achieve some success in containing the power of the church, the precise relationship between tsarist and patriarchal authority remained negotiable and in legal terms undefined. The church retained absolute authority in matters of dogma, and both custom and law required that the tsar obey the canons of the church, an arrangement regularly reinforced by religious observances. Beginning in 1548 and continuing until Peter I took charge of the government in 1694, Russian tsars publicly displayed their obedience to the church by participating in the Palm Sunday ceremony. A dramatic moment in the liturgical calendar, the ceremony re-enacted Christ's entry into Jerusalem. The patriarch, and before 1589 the metropolitan, played the role of Christ, with the tsar leading his horse through the center of Moscow.[22] The ruler's symbolic humility before the patriarch must have carried a powerful political message. But sacred rituals do not a functional government make, and in concrete practice, Muscovite tsars, like Byzantine emperors, repeatedly interfered in church appointments and even in religious controversies. In both Moscow and Constantinople, the Byzantine tradition of emperor and patriarch working in harmony for the good of the church and the salvation of the people almost always assigned primacy to the emperor.

Open confrontation between the secular and spiritual heads of the Orthodox community rarely occurred, but if a conflict did erupt, the Byzantine emperor and later the Muscovite tsar tended to predominate. After Metropolitan Filipp repeatedly used church services to denounce Ivan IV's violent repressions, the tsar had the metropolitan removed from office, defrocked, imprisoned, and eventually murdered. In the reign of Aleksei Mikhailovich, tsarist and patriarchal power once again clashed, though without such bloody consequences. The main source of conflict was Patriarch Nikon's desire to restore to his office the political ascendancy enjoyed by Filaret between 1619 and 1633. Aleksei did indeed look to Nikon for moral guidance and religious instruction, but he in no way viewed the patriarch as a co-ruler or political equal.

Nikon accepted the patriarchate in 1652, after a public entreaty by the tsar in Moscow's Dormition Cathedral (*Uspenskii sobor*). The following year, with the tsar's unequivocal support, Nikon began to preside over a reform of the Russian church that already had begun under the influence of high-ranking churchmen from Constantinople and the Greek diaspora. Based on a comparison of contemporary Greek and Russian Church Slavonic liturgical manuscripts, carried out by Jesuit-trained scholars from Ukraine and Belarus, the reform aimed to identify Russian divergences from Greek practice and to purify the Russian church by bringing Russian practice into conformity with the liturgies and rituals of the Greek church. Prior to becoming patriarch, Nikon belonged to a group of reformers concerned with the personal behavior and piety of Orthodox clergy. As bishop, metropolitan, and patriarch, he acquired a reputation for imposing strict discipline and harsh punishments on subordinates. Nikon's interest in correcting the service books thus began as part of a broader moral reform of the Russian church. But then Nikon used the reform process to introduce by decree additional changes in the forms of Russian worship – changes that he enforced in a ruthless and tyrannical manner. Backed by the full coercive powers of the monarchy, Nikon insisted that the sign of the cross be made with three fingers rather than two, in clear violation of the practice established by the Stoglav (Hundred Chapters) Council of 1551. In addition, the patriarch ordered alterations in the design of liturgical vestments and the wording of prayers. Opposition to the substance of Nikon's reforms, particularly to the new service books, and to his increasingly violent methods of church administration quickly produced religious dissent and schism (*raskol*). To this day, Russian Orthodox believers remain divided between the official church and various forms of "Old Belief" which reject the liturgical changes imposed under Nikon.[23]

For the most part, tsar and patriarch cooperated in implementing Nikon's reforms, which received formal church sanction at councils held in 1654, 1655,

1666, and 1667. But while Nikon's reforms proved lasting, his political power did not. The patriarch's severity and ambition generated enmity among elite nobles and churchmen. When Aleksei Mikhailovich returned from the second Livonian campaign in 1657, he too began to see Nikon as a political threat and liability. Shunned by the tsar, Nikon retired to the Resurrection (*Voskresenskii*) Monastery in 1658, all the while insisting that his patriarchal authority be respected. Uncertainty about the status of Nikon and his relationship to the tsar continued until 1666, when Aleksei presided over a council of Russian and Greek hierarchs, including the patriarchs of Jerusalem and Antioch, who condemned and deposed Nikon. Stripped of the patriarchate and priesthood, and reduced to the status of a lay monk, Nikon became a prisoner in the Ferapontov Monastery. In 1676 the government moved him to the Kirillov Monastery, and in 1681, while en route back to the Resurrection Monastery, the defrocked patriarch died. Beginning in 1682, the Russian church once again commemorated Nikon as patriarch, but his legacy, schism and pretensions to political power, remained a source of social and political instability.

Seventeenth-century Muscovites achieved much in developing the institutions of the church and monarchy, especially in light of the instability wrought by decades of devastation from the reign of Ivan IV through the Time of Troubles. The years after 1613 began a period of recovery, which by 1649 had produced dynamic patterns of institutional centralization and standardization. The Russian Orthodox Church had never possessed greater power or wealth, and the Russian monarchy had never mobilized the human and material resources at its disposal more effectively. The government that served the monarchy had never been better educated or professionally organized, and the Muscovite military, while still beset with manpower and logistical problems, had never been better poised to secure the empire's borders or bolster Russian diplomacy. In the realm of state building, defined as the construction and maintenance of instrumentalities of governance and national defense, Russia by the late seventeenth century was on the way to achieving greatpower status in Europe.

For the Russian people, the institutional successes of bishops and bureaucrats came at a cost. The imposition of serfdom and the binding of all Russian subjects to local communities and social ranks brought unprecedented levels of economic exploitation, taxation, and conscription into military service. Across society, people experienced tighter regulations and harsher discipline at the hands of church and government officials. The drive to centralize religious authority and standardize ritual practice was so great that it produced schism among Orthodox believers and a showdown between Patriarch Nikon and Tsar Aleksei Mikhailovich. Russian tsars, like their Byzantine predecessors, always had asserted authority over the church and clergy. The pretensions to political power displayed by Patriarchs Filaret and Nikon surely represented exceptions. But these pretensions arose at a time when both church and monarchy strove to establish more effective control over the

Russian populace. In the conflict with Patriarch Nikon, the monarch's power clearly emerged victorious. But the *de facto* achievement of superior government power did not change the institutional ambiguity embodied in the relationship between an autocephalous patriarch and a most holy and pious Orthodox tsar. By custom and canon, both patriarch and tsar were essential to the integrity of the church and the salvation of the people. Regardless of how often the tsar predominated over the patriarch in practice, the "symphony" of church and state did not allow for a precise legal or institutional definition of the relationship between ecclesiastical and secular power.

Nor did the political and institutional developments of the seventeenth century make clear the relationship between the monarchy, bureaucracy, and nobility. In practice, the tsar seemed once again to reign supreme. All nobles were required to serve the monarch, and the vast majority also depended economically on the land grants and appointments to rank that he dispensed. But with the codification of serfdom, nobles also became masters and judges in their own right, and increasingly the monarch relied on their authority to govern the peasants. The most elite nobles, those of great wealth and ancient lineage, also felt entitled to approach and advise the tsar. The tsar controlled appointments to high office, and for serious crimes such as disloyalty, he could deprive nobles of rank, property, and even life. Once again, however, the *de facto* power of the tsar left the precise nature of his relationship to the nobility undefined. In times of uncertainty about the succession, the actions of noble factions at court tended to become decisive. In all areas of institutional development, the tsar's power appeared secure and unassailable, yet it remained legally and institutionally ambiguous. It seems, then, that the question of whether or not Tsar Peter I changed the quality of Russian government and set Russia on a new historical path may be the wrong question to ask. In light of the social and political arrangements prevailing in the seventeenth century, the Petrine reforms can also be understood as responses to a series of pressing and unresolved problems – problems related to national security, the relative authority of church and state, and the relationship of the monarch to the patriarch and elite nobility.

Tsar Peter I

A towering historical persona, both literally and figuratively, Tsar Peter I stood 6 feet 7 inches in height and remains to this day a symbol of modern Russia's complicated relationship to "the West" (defined as Western, Central, and even East Central Europe). Throughout the Imperial period, generations of Russian intellectuals debated the significance and consequences of Peter's reign in order both to understand Russia's place in world history and to address the burning questions of their own times. Some described Peter as emblematic of the "good tsar." Others saw in him a reformer, revolutionary, visionary, or tyrant. Still others associated his indomitable personality with the reign of the Antichrist. Regardless of any specific characterization, all observers spoke to the enormity of Peter's physical and moral presence. Well-nigh mythologized as the creator of modern Russia, Peter introduced reforms and innovations that reached into every dimension of Russian life. Ever since his death, moreover, scholars and other commentators have found it impossible to discuss Russia's history or contemporary condition without reference to the institutions Peter established, the empire he forged, the society he harnessed, and the European culture he embraced. Peter's path to power was fraught with danger, and his reign was plagued by opposition, including that of his son and heir Aleksei, but ultimately his vision prevailed. From the time of Peter onward, the Russian monarchy self-consciously followed a European road to modernity.[24]

On May 26, 1682, Tsar Peter I became co-ruler with his sickly half-brother Ivan V. Ivan's sister and Peter's half-sister, Sophia, served as *de facto* regent in an arrangement designed to prevent open conflict between court factions grouped around the Miloslavskii family of Ivan's mother and the Naryshkin family of Peter's. Peter and his supporters broke with Sophia in July 1689, and in early September the regent found herself confined to a convent. Although the reign of Peter usually is dated from 1689, he remained under his mother's influence until her death in 1694, and he did not formally become sole ruler of Russia until Ivan's death in 1696. Even then, however, Peter's hold on the throne appeared open to challenge. The Moscow musketeers (*strel'tsy*), who had supported Sophia in 1682 and 1689, continued to pose a danger. In 1698 the third musketeer rebellion of Peter's reign erupted, forcing him to cut short the Grand Embassy to Europe. Upon receiving news of the rebellion, the tsar hurried back to Moscow, where between October 1698 and February 1700 close to 1,200 rebels were publicly tortured and executed.[25] The suppression of the mutinous musketeers and the subsequent disbanding of their regiments at last lifted the cloud of uncertainty that for years had hung over Peter's claim to the throne. But opposition to Peter and his policies did not end in Moscow. Another group of musketeers rebelled in Astrakhan in the summer of 1705, and Don Cossacks led by Kondratii Bulavin spearheaded a mass rebellion in the Lower Volga and Don region in 1707–8. The last popular movement to threaten Peter began in 1708, when Ukrainian hetman Ivan S. Mazepa and several thousand followers joined the Swedish king Charles XII in military action against Russia. Peter's army vanquished the Swedes at Poltava in 1709, and from that time onward the tsar faced no further "internal resistance of a mass or organized military nature."[26]

By the time Peter defeated the last organized opposition to his accession, his priorities as a ruler had been formed. Indeed, already before the 1689 break with Sophia, Peter pursued interests that foreshadowed the ruler he would become.

Kept away from the Moscow court during his youth, Peter spent much of his time in the village of Preobrazhenskoe, where he studied shipbuilding and navigation, commanded new model "play regiments" (the future Preobrazhenskii and Semenovskii Guard Regiments), conducted war and naval games, and kept raucous company with the usual array of courtiers and relatives, but also with commoners such as Aleksandr D. Menshikov and foreigners such as the Scottish general Patrick Gordon and the Swiss mercenary Franz Lefort. Peter's contacts with Europeans, including visits to the Foreign Quarter of Moscow, opened his eyes to the wonders of European technology and the pleasures of European sociability. Modestly educated, primarily in Muscovite traditions with a smattering of arithmetic and geometry, Peter possessed abundant intelligence and became a lifelong learner, determined to bring to his country the social mores and operational sciences of contemporary Europe.

After securing his first military victory against the Turkish fortress of Azov in 1696, Tsar Peter I set off on the Grand Embassy to Europe, where between April 1697 and August 1698 he visited Courland, Brandenburg, the Dutch Republic, England, Austria, and Galicia. The tsar spent most of his time in the Dutch Republic and in England, observing firsthand the achievements of modern navigation, shipbuilding, carpentry, architecture, engineering, and medicine. While abroad, he himself studied shipbuilding and, more importantly for Russia's future development, enlisted the services of foreign experts capable of transmitting up-to-date technical knowledge to a new generation of educated Russians. In the decades to come, young Russians also regularly went abroad to study the mechanical trades and to acquire scholarly learning. Endowed with limitless curiosity and energy, Tsar Peter returned from his European travels "not just a changed man but also a man more convinced than ever that Russia must change."[27]

Although periodically subject to the influence of favorites and factions at court, and almost always dependent on others to carry out his concrete orders, Tsar Peter I suffered neither fools nor foes in pursuing his vision of change for Russia. Crude, cruel, and violent, the monarch stopped at nothing to secure Russia's status as a great power in Europe and Asia. Peter's ambition did not blind him to concrete reality: he correctly suspected disaffected or incompetent subordinates of thwarting his aims and in response appointed personal spies to report on disobedience to his orders. Peter also experienced the feelings of awe before God and His Creation that were appropriate to a Christian believer. In official pronouncements, the tsar repeatedly attributed his country's successes and failures to divine providence. Peter likewise understood that his personal wellbeing depended on the divine will. Of the eight children Peter's second wife Catherine bore for him, only two survived childhood: the future Empress Elizabeth and Anna, mother of the future Emperor Peter III. Tsar Peter knew only too well that immediate life and the historical fate of his beloved Russia lay in the hands of the Almighty. But like absolutist rulers across the globe, Peter possessed little sense of the practical limits to his own earthly power. He readily assumed that his policies and his understanding of Russia's greater destiny corresponded to the will of God. Peter had survived a violent and turbulent childhood, and as an adolescent tsar he had faced the uncertainty represented by enemies and opportunists conniving in the shadows. But Peter's was a restless and energetic soul that pushed him to confront danger with action. Act he did time and again. Still, there remained a problem that Peter's actions seemed unable to resolve and that haunted him throughout his reign. This was the problem of the succession, a problem that might not have arisen if Peter had been less the revolutionary and more the traditionalist bound to custom.

That Tsar Peter I was a man capable of deep and abiding affection is evident from his friendship with the ambitious and corrupt Aleksandr Menshikov and from his love for his second wife and wartime companion, Catherine Alekseevna, the future Empress Catherine I. But in general, Peter employed tyrannical methods of government and treated with utter ruthlessness anyone who thwarted or was perceived to thwart his aims. For persons within sight of Peter or one of his spies, disobedience in matters small or large invariably led to punishment. Present-day historians note with bemusement and a touch of sympathy Peter's use of coercion to Europeanize the social habits of his countrymen. On August 26, 1698, for example, just one day after Peter returned to Moscow to deal with the musketeer rebellion, he began a campaign against traditional Russian beards and dress. Peter personally cut off the beards of courtiers close at hand and ordered that all servicemen should be clean-shaven. On September 1, at a New Year's banquet, he employed a court jester to shave the face of any guest who had not yet complied with the new sartorial order. No matter that the shaving of beards represented an affront to established religious belief. Peter had decided that a clean-shaven face in no way offended God.

At play and in work, Tsar Peter I insisted that his will be done. The monarch's social assemblies and court celebrations were not for the temperate or the timid. Peter regularly entertained and shamed his subjects by forcing them to participate in mock rituals and bizarre jokes. At banquets, he insisted that guests drink huge amounts of alcohol, and even foreign diplomats found it difficult to escape the obligatory drunkenness. Peter enforced sociability the way he enforced military service, by punishing noncompliance. Courtiers who neglected to attend boat parties and other festivities were required to pay fines or consume excess drink. Peter even decided what his guests would be allowed to drink. In August 1721, at a party to celebrate a ship launching, the tsar ordered that only Hungarian wine be served. Aleksandr Menshikov was caught consuming Rhine wine, however, and as punishment he was compelled "to drink a penalty of two bottles of strong wine, after which he collapsed in a drunken stupor."[28] Being a close companion of Peter, and a man of similar taste, Menshikov may have welcomed his punishment. But the fact that sociability had to be imposed suggests that not all Peter's associates shared his capacity for raucous behavior. Across Europe, the entertainments of the day embraced the freakish and carnivalesque, but Petrine sociability also represented an assertion of absolutist political principles. Together with the prosecution of political crimes and the imposition of lifelong service, the enforcement of sociability made clear that the personal power of the monarch reached into the life of every Russian subject.[29]

Tsar Peter I never hesitated to use violence and humiliation to command obedience from his subjects or to transform the elite among them, he hoped, into educated Europeans. Yet despite the fear that Peter inspired in those around him, he proved unable to overcome the recalcitrance of his son Aleksei (1690–1718), whose indifference to military affairs and European learning challenged the monarch's understanding of Russian greatness.[30] Aleksei was Peter's son by his first wife, Evdokiia Lopukhina, who in 1698 had been banished to a convent by her husband. The very facts of Aleksei's birth no doubt encouraged Peter's suspicions about his son's character and intentions. From Peter's point of view, it was essential to provide the tsarevich with a European education, the education Peter had never received, so that Aleksei could become an imposing and effective ruler. In addition, like all reigning monarchs (and fathers), Peter assumed responsibility for finding his son a suitable bride. Aleksei was married to Princess Charlotte-Christina-Sophia of Wolfenbüttel in 1711, and while Peter developed a sincere fondness for his daughter-in-law, Aleksei grew ever more discontented. Unhappy in his marriage and unreceptive to his father's vision of the person he should be, Aleksei took up with a mistress in 1714 and began to keep company with his maternal relatives, disaffected clergy, and other potential opponents of Peter.

Already by 1715, Peter became convinced that, if Aleksei succeeded him, all the progress Russia had achieved would be lost. In October 1715, Charlotte gave birth to a healthy baby boy, the future Emperor Peter II, and then died of postnatal complications. Later in the month, Catherine too gave birth to a son, also named Peter. Aware of Tsar Peter's displeasure and eager to be free of his heavy hand, Aleksei used the occasion of his wife's death and the birth of two potential heirs to express his willingness to give up the throne and enter a monastery. This could have ended the matter; however, the question of Aleksei's future remained undecided, and Peter continued to badger his son. In August 1716, while in Copenhagen preparing for an abortive naval operation against Sweden, Peter sent a summons to Aleksei to join him on campaign. The summons made clear that if Aleksei did not intend to fight alongside his father in Europe, then it was time for him to choose the monastery to which he would retire. Instead of obeying Peter and deciding to share in the tsar's military labors, Aleksei fled to Vienna, where he found refuge at the court of his late wife's brother-in-law, Emperor Charles VI. If previously Peter had been reluctant to see in his son an overt oppositionist and had preserved some hope for his eventual rehabilitation, Aleksei's flight to Vienna convinced the tsar that treachery was afoot.

Historians disagree as to whether or not Aleksei and his circle, or others sympathetic to his plight, actually aimed to oppose Peter. Surely, there were individuals among the clergy and elite nobility who hoped that the Petrine revolution would be reversed once its architect passed on. Yet the evidence for any concrete conspiracy seems vague and inconclusive.[31] After learning of Aleksei's flight, Peter sent two trusted agents to locate the tsarevich and bring him back to Russia. Aleksei agreed to return after receiving assurances that he would be allowed to marry his mistress and live in peace. But when Aleksei arrived in Moscow in January 1718, Peter also insisted that he renounce his claim to the throne and identify the persons who had helped him to flee abroad. Peter's decision to remove Aleksei from the succession did not pose an immediate problem; already in 1715, the tsarevich had declared his willingness to give up the throne. An imperial manifesto of February 3, 1718 turned this willingness into law. The manifesto formally removed Aleksei from the succession and proclaimed Peter Petrovich, age two, the new heir.

Once again, Peter's relationship with Aleksei seemed to have reached a resolution, however unhappy. But the apparent resolution still was not enough for Peter, who began a hunt for Aleksei's accomplices. During 1718 associates of Aleksei and his mother Evdokiia suffered torture, execution, corporal punishment, exile, and imprisonment. The abbess and another nun from the convent where Evdokiia lived were punished with the knout and banished. Outright execution befell Avraamii Lopukhin, Evdokiia's brother. Even Peter's half-sister, Mariia Alekseevna, was temporarily imprisoned in the Schlüsselburg Fortress for acting as a liaison between Aleksei and his mother. Finally, Aleksei himself faced charges of treason. Specifically, he was accused of soliciting Austrian aid to overthrow and assassinate Peter. In June 1718, the Secret Chancellery opened in St Petersburg to investigate the case against Aleksei, who by that time had been imprisoned in the Peter and Paul Fortress. On June 19 and again on June 24, Aleksei suffered interrogation under torture. The interrogation continued in the afternoon of June 24, after a court had pronounced Aleksei guilty and condemned him to death. On June 26, one last interrogation occurred, and that evening Aleksei died from the combined effects of torture and tuberculosis.[32]

Tsar Peter I showed no mercy toward Aleksei, and for a brief period at least, he could believe that he had rescued Russia from the danger posed by a hostile heir. But then, less than a year after Aleksei's death, on April 25, 1719, Peter Petrovich died, leaving the monarch without a male successor. From Peter's perspective, the preservation of Russia's great-power status once again seemed in question. A solution was found in the 1722 Law on the Succession, which gave to the reigning sovereign the authority to choose his successor. The law compared Aleksei to the evil Absalom and then invoked Biblical and Russian historical precedents to justify ignoring the time-honored principle of seniority. Citing the examples of the biblical patriarch Isaac and the Muscovite tsar Ivan III, the law declared that in cases of unworthy heirs, God Himself blessed violations of seniority. But if to dispense with seniority carried divine sanction, Peter's decree went beyond the question of passing over one son or grandson for another. The Law on the Succession did more than dismiss adherence to seniority as "not a good custom"; it stated outright that the monarch may appoint as his successor "whom he wants." Try as Peter might to present his actions as a response to Aleksei's betrayal, the Law on the Succession was a radical move and a bold statement of absolutist monarchical pretensions: anyone who opposed the new order of succession would be considered a traitor subject to capital punishment and church oath.[33]

Peter had good reasons for doing the things he did, yet in doing what he did, the tsar never hesitated to use violence. In pursuing his vision of change for Russia, Peter brutalized associates and ignored centuries of custom and historical precedent. Not surprisingly, ever since Peter's death Russian intellectuals have debated the appropriateness of his policies and methods. Historians too continue to discuss whether or not his tyrannical actions represented a necessary tool of progress. Without coercion, many conclude, Russia would not have joined the ranks of the modern European powers. Yet when measured in terms of human suffering, the price of Petrine progress appears problematic and the results more ambiguous.[34] Clearly, the removal of Aleksei from the succession aimed to preserve the Petrine revolution. Whether or not this goal required such action is unclear. For the rest of the eighteenth century, the Law on the Succession caused chronic political instability, which did not, however, undo the Petrine reforms. Peter's most important innovations struck deep roots, though historians continue to disagree as to whether or not his policies were truly revolutionary. Peter's reforms appear least radical in their socioeconomic dimension, most immediately revolutionary and ultimately most enduring in their cultural dimension, and most immediately effective in their institutional (especially military) dimension. Scholars evaluate the success and impact of Peter's reforms in a variety of ways, and their often ambivalent conclusions differ depending on the areas of Russian life being examined.[35] Most agree, however, that military necessity drove Peter's early reforms.

When Peter I acceded to the throne, he inherited Muscovy's main enemies to the north, west, and south. In the seventeenth century, these included Sweden, the Polish-Lithuanian Commonwealth, the Crimean Khanate, and the Ottoman Empire. Following the Time of Troubles, the Muscovites had paid a heavy price to attain peace with their opportunistic neighbors. The Treaty of Stolbovo (1617) gave to Sweden a large territory along the shores of Lake Ladoga and left Russia completely cut off from the Gulf of Finland. In the Deulino armistice (1618), Muscovy ceded to Poland significant lands along the country's western border, including the strategically important city of Smolensk. Throughout the seventeenth century, Russian leaders set their sights on recovering the territories lost to Sweden and Poland. In 1656–8 Aleksei Mikhailovich used military action to challenge Swedish domination of the Baltic trade. Muscovy also butted heads with Poland over Ukraine, where in the 1620s the Orthodox population began to seek Russian protection against Polish Catholic rule. In 1648 Ukrainian Cossacks rebelled against Poland, and in 1654 they took the oath of allegiance to the Russian tsar. That same year, Muscovy conquered Smolensk. Thus began the Thirteen Years' War between Russia and Poland, which, according to the truce of Andrusovo (1667), left Moscow in control of Left-Bank (eastern) Ukraine, Kiev, and Smolensk.[36]

Russian gains in Ukraine meant that Muscovy also began to share a border with the Ottoman Empire. In 1676 Poland surrendered a large part of Right-Bank (western) Ukraine to the Ottomans. This led to the first Russo-Turkish War (1677–81), which did not, however, result in any territorial changes for Russia. At the time, Ottoman policy focused more on making gains in southeastern Europe than on stopping Russian advances in Ukraine. Besides, the Crimean Tatars, vassals of the Ottomans, could be counted on to raid Russian settlements in the southern borderland. The Girei dynasty which ruled the Crimean Khanate traced it origins back to Chinggis Khan. For this reason, from the Russian perspective, Tatar raids meant more than immediate devastation; they also recalled past subjugation to Mongol rule. So in order to deal with the Tatar threat, secure Russian possessions in Ukraine, and avenge the humiliation of Russian ambassadors, Muscovy declared its intention to free Crimea of the Tatars. The Crimean campaigns of 1687 and 1689, led by Sophia's favorite Vasilii V. Golitsyn (1643–1714), involved little direct combat and did nothing to enhance Russian security. To the contrary, the campaigns laid bare Muscovy's limited military capability, particularly the inability to sustain combat operations in distant theaters. Seventeenth-century advances in military technology, tactics, and operations, however impressive on the surface, had failed to solve the deeper structural problem of "endurance" – the combined effect of logistics, transport, training, reinforcement, and finance.[37] Simply put, Muscovite military capability proved inadequate to support Muscovite military ambitions.

At the turn of the eighteenth century, Tsar Peter I took steps to overcome the manpower, financial, and logistical limitations imposed by Muscovite institutions. To meet the demands of national defense, but also to make clear that Russia was a serious player in world politics, Peter established a standing (really a semi-standing) army based on regular conscription levies and a navy built with foreign and newly acquired Russian expertise. The Muscovite government had created the core of a regular army with the introduction of new model regiments in the second quarter of the seventeenth century. Peter's own father, Tsar Aleksei Mikhailovich, also had taken steps to secure Russian sea power, when he tried, and failed, in a military campaign of 1656 to recover the port of Narva and additional Baltic coastland lost to Sweden in 1581. A more direct precedent for Peter's navy could be found in Aleksei's effort to build a flotilla of warships to service the Volga–Caspian trade route. A three-masted ship, the *Eagle*, was in fact built in 1667–8, only to be destroyed in 1670, when Stepan Razin's rebels attacked Astrakhan. In his Military Statute of 1716 and Naval Statute of 1720, Peter readily acknowledged Aleksei's military reforms as a model for his own.[38] But no matter how deeply rooted in Muscovite precedent, Peter's policies achieved a scope and intensity that went well beyond anything his predecessors had attempted or even imagined.

In contrast to previous rulers, who focused on protecting borderlands, recovering lost lands, and promoting foreign trade, Peter's military ambitions were aggressive, strategic, and intent on asserting Russian power. As early as 1695, Russian troops tried and failed to take the Turkish fortress at Azov. A follow-up campaign in 1696 brought success, and Peter ordered the building of a naval fleet in the Sea of Azov. The purpose of the fleet was to challenge Ottoman control of the Black Sea and to disrupt communications between the Turks and Crimean Tatars. Such goals seemed attainable until Peter fought a third war against Turkey in 1711; this war almost ended in disaster for Russia. Following the battle on the Pruth River in Moldavia (July 9), in which the combined Turkish and Tatar forces greatly outnumbered those of Russia, Peter agreed to surrender Azov (regained by Russia in 1739), dismantle his southern fleet, and level fortresses at Taganrog and Kamennyi Zaton.[39] Not until the reign of Catherine II (ruled 1762–96) would Russia achieve significant gains against the Ottoman Empire. Advances in Central Asia – Russia and Persia fought a war in 1722–3 – likewise produced only modest results. In neither the Ottoman nor the Persian theater did Peter definitively establish a Russian military presence.

A very different story unfolded in Europe. The military enterprise that most fully embodied Peter's ambition and success – and that established Russia's status as a world power – was the Great Northern War against Sweden. Charles XII had acceded to the Swedish throne in 1697, at the age of fourteen, and assumptions about the weakness of the young king encouraged neighboring monarchs in Denmark and Poland, Frederick IV and Elector Augustus of Saxony, to join with Peter in a plot to destroy Sweden's Baltic empire. Denmark and Poland began military operations in the spring of 1700, and Russia declared war on August 9. In Peter's judgment, circumstances seemed propitious. But Charles proved to be a more than formidable foe. Even before the Russian declaration of war, the Swedes moved against Copenhagen by sea, and Denmark sued for peace. Peter's forces began their participation in the war by besieging the Swedish fortress of Narva; the siege lasted until November 20, when the Swedish infantry routed the Russian army. A mere 9,000 Swedish troops crushed Russian forces numbering 40,000. Charles then moved to relieve Riga, under siege by Augustus since June.

At Riga the Swedes again emerged victorious, defeating a force of Russian, Polish, and Saxon troops and opening the door to a Swedish invasion of Poland.

Swedish successes in this early phase of the war, particularly the victory at Narva, represented the wake-up call that compelled Peter to reorganize the Russian army. Peter's primary task, which he achieved by revamping the Russian military system, was "to translate . . . resources – human, material, and financial – into power."[40] The introduction of mass conscription, the sufficiently effective imposition of military discipline, the intensification of tax collection, the manufacture of armaments and military cloth, the development of a system of military transport and supply, the formation of an educated officer corps, and last but not least, the mastery of strategic planning and an emphasis in operational practices on fortification, troop mobility, and naval support – these were the components of Peter's military reforms that over the course of two decades eventually led to victory. Russian military successes against Sweden actually began as early as December 1701, before any improvements in military organization could have taken effect. But it was Peter's ability to sustain the military effort – to surmount, to a degree, the problem of endurance – that allowed Russia to defeat Sweden. Russian victories came and went, as did Swedish ones, and only after years of grueling combat did the reality of Russian power become clear.[41]

Following a summer campaign in 1704, Russia controlled Dorpat and Narva, Swedish Ingria, and the Neva River. Already in 1703, Peter had founded the city of St Petersburg, the new capital of the Russian Empire and the site of a permanent Russian foothold on the Baltic Sea. These successes proved lasting, yet the war barely had begun. Swedish gains in Poland and Saxony led to the abdication of Augustus in 1706, which freed Charles to move against Russia. This he did at the beginning of 1708, though instead of marching toward Moscow, Charles led his troops south into Ukraine. There he joined forces with the Cossack hetman Mazepa, previously an ally of Russia. Not until June 28, 1709, did Charles face a day of reckoning: at the fortress of Poltava the Swedes suffered a decisive defeat, and their king fled to the Ottoman Empire. Russia's combat fortunes surely had improved, yet Peter's trials were far from over. The Ottomans declared war in 1710, and as noted above, the battle on the Pruth (1711) led to painful territorial losses and also forced Peter to grant Charles safe passage back to Sweden. Charles returned to Sweden in November 1714, by which time the Russians and Ottomans had concluded the Peace of Adrianople (1713). Russia also had made significant gains in Swedish Pomerania and Finland. Still, Charles refused to quit. In 1716 the Swedes attacked Danish possessions in Norway, and not until 1718, with Russia, Poland, Saxony, Prussia, Denmark, and Britain all ready to oppose Sweden, did peace negotiations begin. Military operations continued, however, even after Charles died in battle at the end of the year. To ensure an end to the war, Russian troops kept up the pressure by conducting destructive raids into Swedish territory in 1719,

1720, and 1721. Finally, on August 30 (September 10) 1721, Russia and Sweden signed the Treaty of Nystad.

Based on the terms of Nystad, Russia acquired Livonia, Estonia, Ingria, part of Karelia, and the Baltic islands of Oesel and Dagoe. Russia returned Finland, except for Vyborg, and also paid an indemnity to Sweden. More important than the specific territorial gains, Russia replaced Sweden as the dominant Baltic power and established its position, maintained to this day, as a great power in modern Europe.[42] Peter could not have hoped for a more glorious conclusion to the years of military struggle. Less than two months after the conclusion of the peace with Sweden, Peter's subjects acknowledged his achievements. On October 21, 1721, the members of the Senate (an appointed administrative body established in 1711) awarded to their victorious monarch the titles "Father of the fatherland, All-Russian Emperor, and Peter the Great."[43] For Russia, the Great Northern War had been long and costly, yet over the years Peter had done much to reform Russian institutions and to secure the empire's western and, to a lesser degree, southern borders.

Alongside the victory against Sweden the most striking success of Peter's reign was the organization of a modern military machine capable of sustaining Russia's great-power status. By the time of his death in 1725, Peter commanded an army of 130,000 regular troops, 75–80,000 garrison troops, and 20,000 Cossack irregulars. The empire's navy, created almost from scratch, consisted of two ships-of-the-line, sixteen frigates, and "scores of galleys, bomb boats, and other craft."[44] A system of mass conscription established in 1705 kept the Russian military supplied with manpower, and some 200 factories produced manufactured goods that included weapons, ammunition, cloth for uniforms, and sailcloth. Peter also had established central government offices responsible for delivery of provisions and supplies to the troops. The Commissariat Chancellery assumed responsibility for pay, clothing, ammunition, and equipment, while the Provisioning Chancellery provided food and forage, or the funds to procure them. Revenues to support the military came from the capitation, introduced in 1719–28, and from a host of direct and indirect taxes imposed on specific social groups, economic activities, and consumer necessities. Additional sources of revenue included licenses to sell liquor and government monopolies on products such as salt, potash, tar, and Siberian furs. Under Peter, government revenues increased from 3.6 million rubles in 1701 to 8.7 million in 1725. But still the government always seemed to be short of funds. Throughout Russia's age of serfdom, the army suffered from inadequate resources, which meant that soldiers and commanders on the ground often had to meet their own subsistence needs. Soldiers earned wages at outside labor, and commanders improvised with the resources at hand. Much also depended on what regiments could collect from local populations. Peter's regular standing army did not then always appear to be standing; however, its soldiers became steeled in lifelong service, and its officers increasingly possessed a modicum of education.[45]

The appearance in Russia of nonecclesiastical educated classes stemmed in large measure from the technical qualifications that became necessary for advancement in military and civil service. Peter encouraged the spread of education both by promoting individuals with specialized knowledge and by founding state schools. The Moscow School of Mathematics and Navigation, established in 1701, stands as one of the tsar's most successful educational endeavors. By 1715, when Peter transferred the higher classes of the Moscow School to the new St Petersburg Naval Academy, 1,200 students had passed through its doors, having received instruction in literacy, arithmetic, geometry, trigonometry, navigation, navigational astronomy, and geography. The St Petersburg Naval Academy operated until 1752, at which time it became amalgamated into the Naval Cadet Corps, together with the Moscow School and a naval artillery school also founded by Peter. The Naval Cadet Corps remained the premier institution for training Russian naval officers until the end of the monarchy in 1917.

The history of the Naval Academy illustrates the importance that Russian monarchs attached to advanced technical education. But Peter and his successors also understood that educational progress required the development of government-sponsored primary education. In both Moscow and St Petersburg, Peter established medical, engineering, and artillery schools, all of which offered general primary and more specialized technical education. Peter even tried to establish a network of primary schools that would feed into the technical institutions. As early as 1703, he ordered that cipher schools under the authority of the Admiralty be opened in provincial towns. The cipher schools served a socially mixed population that included the children of nobles (until 1716), townspeople (until 1720), clergy (until 1722), nonnoble officials, and military servicemen. The cipher schools did not long outlive Peter; the handful that remained in 1744 merged with the garrison schools for soldiers' sons, also dating from Peter's reign. But together the cipher schools and garrison schools set a precedent for government-sponsored primary education open to diverse social groups.[46]

Throughout his reign, Peter I's military and educational reforms proved their worth. Data from 1720–1 show that only 12.6 percent of 2,245 officers in the field infantry and cavalry were foreigners.[47] There also was more to Peter's vision of change than military power and the development of the institutions and educated personnel needed to sustain that power. Peter possessed a relatively modern conception of good government, which to him meant regularized administration placed on a firm financial footing and operating on the basis of formal rules and procedures. Such a government would function effectively (or mechanistically), much as a clock, whether or not the monarch could personally be present. Written rules of behavior and the procedures for conducting legal-administrative affairs would be so explicit and so comprehensive that individual officials could not possibly ignore their duties. To achieve regular government, Peter defined the order of service in military and civil administration by introducing legislation such as the Military Statute (1716), the Naval Statute (1720), and the General Regulation (1720). New institutions such as the Senate, established in 1711, and the colleges, established in 1717–18, organized administrative tasks based on Peter's decrees and instructions. Historian Marc Raeff traces Peter's understanding of government to the "well-ordered police state" (*Policeystaat*) of seventeenth- and eighteenth-century German cameralism. According to cameralist thought, the functions of government included not only the mobilization of human and material resources to serve the common good, but also the proper ordering of social and moral life. Through institution building and legal prescription, the cameralist government, a form of European administrative monarchy, initiated and directed social change so as to realize the material and spiritual potential of the state (understood as a particular territory) and its inhabitants.[48]

Peter was not the last great reformer among the monarchs of Imperial Russia, but prior to the emancipation of the serfs in 1861 his successors did not substantively depart from his understanding of good government. Indicative of the centrality of Peter's cameralist orientation, his most important institutional innovations remained operative until the end of the monarchy in 1917. His concept of directed progress achieved through regular government informed Russian policymakers and high-level officials during the entire Imperial period. The Senate, one of the most enduring of Peter's new institutions, embodied his approach to administration. At the time of its creation in 1711, the purpose of the Senate was to govern in Peter's absence, which was frequent because of his personal involvement in military campaigns. Over time, the Senate evolved into the empire's highest instance of judicial appeal, short of the ruler, and it continued to fulfill this function even after the liberal judicial reforms of 1864. Appointment to the Senate was a mark of honor and usually occurred after years of sacrifice in service. The members of the Senate represented the cream of Russian officialdom. Although the Senate still awaits its modern historian, scattered protocols of its proceedings suggest that throughout the life of the empire senators conscientiously carried out the Petrine mandate to oversee administration and ensure observance of the law.

In establishing the Senate and later the colleges, Peter sought to bring greater coherence and efficiency to Russian government. The collegial reform, based on Swedish and German models, reorganized the Muscovite chancelleries, which under Peter had ceased to function as a central government. Peter also hoped to enhance effectiveness and limit corruption by making administrative authority and responsibility collegial or collective. (In the early nineteenth century, Emperor Alexander I instituted a centralized ministerial system with a single minister at the head of each ministry.) Under Peter, decrees of 1717 and 1718 created nine colleges to deal with military, diplomatic, judicial, economic, and financial matters: War,

Admiralty, Foreign Affairs, Justice, Commerce, Mines and Manufactories, State Receipts (*Kamor*), State Revenues and Expenditures (*Revizion*), and State Office (also concerned with expenditures).[49] Together the colleges made up much of the government's central bureaucracy, and within their specialized areas of competence, they also linked local with central administration.

In 1721 Peter extended the collegial principle of central administration to the organization of the Russian Orthodox Church, abolishing the patriarchate and establishing in its place a Synod composed of appointed bishops. From 1722 the Synod, like the other colleges, was supervised by a lay procurator who functioned as the eyes and ears of the monarch. The abolition of the patriarchate clearly violated canon law, yet Peter requested and succeeded in gaining formal recognition of the Synod from the patriarchs of Constantinople, Alexandria, Antioch, and Jerusalem.[50] In addition, Peter compelled 87 senior Russian clergy from St Petersburg, Moscow, and the provinces to sign, along with himself, the final version of the Ecclesiastical Regulation.[51]

Peter's ecclesiastical reform eliminated the political ambiguity in church–state relations by transforming the church into a "government bureau" administered by the Synod in the name of the monarch. The reform reduced the church's judicial powers and increased the authority of secular courts over the clergy. The monarch also began to approve all consecrations of bishops. The clergy became in effect a category of state servicemen required to keep vital statistics, read out official decrees, and even violate confession by reporting intended crimes.[52] At the same time, the church and clergy continued to occupy a special and relatively independent status within the Petrine service state. This resulted from their role in salvation, which compelled the government to leave matters of religious observance and divine law – the sacrament of marriage, for example – in the hands of ecclesiastical authorities. Peter's insistence that steps be taken to improve the overall educational level of the clergy likewise helped to sustain the church's independence. Between 1721 and 1724, Russian bishops opened 45 ecclesiastical schools, and over time some of these schools developed into seminaries providing a Latin curriculum based on that of the Kiev and Moscow Academies (see chapter 3).[53] In the church, as in the army and bureaucracy, Peter needed educated servicemen to carry out their respective duties for the common good.

Peter's search for regular government also led him to reorder relations between the service classes, particularly the nobility, and the monarchy. This he did through the Table of Ranks, which defined the relationship between service and noble status. Like the Senate and the Synod, the Table of Ranks proved to be one of Peter's most successful institutional reforms. According to legislation of 1722, the Table of Ranks consisted of fourteen classes or grades that corresponded to specific ranks in military, civil, and court service. The military ranks were then further divided into infantry, guard, artillery, and naval ranks. Each office or position in the various branches of service carried a specific rank, and when a serviceman received promotion to a higher office, he also was supposed to be awarded the corresponding rank. Because promotion in rank sometimes occurred before an appropriate office actually became vacant, the desired correspondence between rank and office could be difficult to maintain. The principle was clear, however, and throughout the Imperial period the Table of Ranks effectively achieved its purpose: to regularize and institutionalize promotion in service and to tie the attainment of noble status to service. In civil service, nonnobles became ennobled at rank 8 in the Table of Ranks and in military service at rank 14. The Table of Ranks did not eliminate lineage as the foundation of social status or patronage as a necessity in career advancement. A successful service career always required good social connections. But by systematizing the relationship between rank, service, and ennoblement – only through service could a man achieve noble status – the Table of Ranks introduced merit as the primary justification for social mobility.[54]

An overview of Peter's most important institutional reforms shows that after responding to the exigencies of war and political instability at court, the monarch built upon the achievements of the seventeenth century and attempted to address the outstanding issues that Muscovite institutions and the policies of his predecessors had failed to resolve. In military affairs, Muscovite rulers did much to establish the core of a modern European army, including the introduction of "standing" regiments, and they took tentative steps toward implementing a system of mass conscription. In mobilizing the human and material resources of the empire, Muscovite rulers also went a long way toward defining service classes that performed specific duties, some of which required specialized training, for the monarchy. Finally, Peter's predecessors began the arduous and complicated process of developing a competent bureaucracy both by expanding government offices and recruiting personnel. Even after Peter added his contributions, much work remained to be done, but already in the seventeenth century the seeds of absolute monarchy had been sown.

In other areas of government, by contrast, Peter rightly felt the need to impose bold and forceful measures in order to overcome the barriers blocking further progress. Peter made mass conscription and obligatory service a daily reality for practically the entire Russian population, but especially for peasants and townspeople who provided recruits and for nobles who became military officers and civil servants. Under Peter service became year-round and lifelong. Peter's taxation and other economic policies likewise intensified the mobilization of Russia's material resources to an unprecedented degree. In the Table of Ranks, Peter institutionalized and bureaucratized the relationship between service and noble status both to encourage the promotion of worthy nonnobles and to compel nobles to educate their children. Finally, Peter eliminated the uncertainty surrounding the relationship between the monarch and the patriarch by abolishing the patriarchate and placing church administration clearly under his command. The church continued to function as a parallel "state"; only now it was headed by the Synod, just as civil administration was headed by the Senate. The monarch stood above both the Synod and the Senate, and above him there was no one but God.

Conclusion

The central quality of Petrine regular government was the combination of bureaucratic rationality with personal rulership. The result was regular government that was far from regular. Between 1649 and 1832, despite numerous attempts, no new code of Russian laws would be written. Nor did the 1832 codification actually deserve the name: the codification produced a "complete" collection of laws issued since 1649 and a digest of those still in effect. Any reading of Petrine and subsequent eighteenth-century legislation reveals much confusion and inconsistency. In practice, even when legal prescriptions seemed clear, the officials responsible for their implementation could be poorly educated, overwhelmed by their duties and physical ailments, or simply dishonest. Peter's reforms also did nothing to improve local administration, which continued to rely on seigniorial power and community self-government. Nor did Peter trust officials to carry out his orders. Instead of allowing official decisions to work their way through defined channels of authority, Peter relied on financial inspectors (*fiskaly*) from 1711 and on procurators from 1722 to report on irregularities in the government's local and central offices. Appointed directly by the monarch to serve as his eyes and ears, the inspectors and procurators brought imperial power into the routine functioning of the bureaucracy. The system of procurators even included the appointment of a procurator general to supervise the Senate.[55] Peter and the rulers who followed him may have embraced a vision of regular government, but they never understood regular government in terms that might limit their personal power. Good government for Peter, and throughout the Imperial period, required not "the rule of law," where the law reigned supreme, even if in a particular instance the law appeared to stand in the way of justice. To the contrary, good government in Imperial Russia relied on "the rule of laws," where in the name of justice, the monarch could at any time intervene in routine administration and change the law retroactively.

By the end of Peter's reign, Russian government had moved from a caretaker posture designed to protect the tsar's realm to a posture of active intervention in social, economic, institutional, and cultural development. Similarly, in military and diplomatic affairs, the empire had moved from a defensive posture aimed at protecting borders and recovering lost lands to a posture of aggressive imperialist expansion. The transformation had been achieved by building a service state designed to mobilize and expand the human and material resources of the empire. Equally important, political arrangements that previously had projected a measure of consensus and consultation between the monarch on the one hand, and the patriarch, men of duma rank, or representatives of the land on the other, now projected the absolute power of a secular ruler who answered to no earthly authority other than his own conscience. In practice, absolutist political power was far from absolute, but the principle could not have been clearer. No matter how much the monarch depended on landowners, military officers, and civil servants to govern the empire, he commanded their obedience because they served him personally. The tension between bureaucratic rationality and personal rulership remained characteristic of Russian government until the revolution of 1917. Good government hinged on observance of the law, but it was left to human beings, that is to persons in positions of authority (not to individual subjects or citizens exercising conscience), to determine if adherence to the law coincided with justice. Where law and justice seemed to clash, the course of action leading to justice always could be taken.

Chapter 3

Muscovite Tradition and Petrine Cultural Revolution

Russia's attainment of great-power status in the early eighteenth century resulted to a significant degree from the conscious adaptation of European learning. Throughout the reign of Peter I, the government worked feverishly to import Western ideas and to educate Russian specialists capable of mastering modern science and technology. Although the demands of state building and national defense required that initial efforts focus on training administrative and military personnel, the Petrine program of cultural change ran much deeper than the satisfaction of narrow utilitarian needs. When Peter took over the reins of government, Russia's only institutions of higher education were the ecclesiastical academies of Kiev and Moscow, the latter really a school established just a few years earlier. In 1725, the year of Peter's death, the St Petersburg Academy of Sciences, modeled after learned societies across Europe, began to hold regular meetings. For decades, the academy's development depended on the importation of scholars, primarily Germans, from abroad. But the academy also supported a gymnasium and university, both designed to prepare Russians for a life of scholarship, scientific discovery, and literary accomplishment. If at the start of the eighteenth century Russia lacked the educated people needed to participate in the progress of European letters, arts, and sciences, by mid-century it became possible to speak of Russian science, Russian scholarship, Russian literature, and Russian educated classes fully versed in modern learning and Enlightenment culture. The magnitude of the transformation, the depth and breadth of change, constituted nothing less than a cultural revolution – a revolution inaugurated by Peter's insistence that his subjects become educated Europeans.[1]

———— Muscovite Culture in the Seventeenth Century ————

Beginning with Prince Vladimir's conversion in the late tenth century, Russian culture developed within a framework defined by Eastern Orthodox Christianity. Pre-Christian Slavic traditions also contributed thematic content and artistic genres and motifs, but on the whole Russian high culture, both written and visual, became synonymous with the culture of the Russian Orthodox Church. In the eighteenth century, the culture of Russia's educated classes began also to develop in a European context, becoming further differentiated, though not entirely removed, from the culture of the common people. Blending popular traditions, Orthodox religious beliefs and practices, and European letters, arts, and sciences, a secular culture took shape, which in the nineteenth and early twentieth centuries achieved pan-European recognition. The stunning originality of Russian literature and arts in the Imperial period tends to overshadow the richness of the Muscovite cultural legacy. Yet Russia's rise to cultural prominence began in the seventeenth century, when church reform, territorial incorporation of Ukraine, and the importation of educated monks and servicemen versed in Latinist learning opened the door to the modern culture of post-Reformation Europe. At once devoted to tradition and receptive to innovation, Muscovite artists and intellectuals did not deliberately seek change. They did, however, create multidirectional development, potentiality, and confusion, out of which Peter I's directed cultural revolution emerged.

Seventeenth-century Muscovy handed to Peter a vibrant literary heritage, dynamic and multifaceted, that anticipated the cultural changes to come. Translations, compilations, and original Russian works made available, though not widely accessible, an array of religious, scholarly, and artistic material. Religious subject matter dominated literary output – devotional works comprised 95 percent of printed titles in the seventeenth century – and most authors came from the clergy, which well into the eighteenth century remained the most educated class in society.[2] The church's centrality endured. Yet the range of literary forms and content makes it impossible to identify seventeenth-century literature with any narrow social or institutional milieu. The people and places depicted could be historical or imaginary; local, Russian, or foreign; ancient, medieval, or contemporary. Slavic folklore, Russian and classical history, the Hebrew Bible, the Gospels, the teachings of Eastern Orthodoxy, and the literature and learning of foreign lands all provided Russians with models of cultural expression.

The largest body of seventeenth-century literature came from within the church and encompassed devotional and biblical readings; chronicles and works of history; sermons, homilies, and collections of aphorisms; selections from the writings of Russian churchmen and Eastern Church fathers; lives of saints, local, Russian, and foreign; and finally, biography and autobiography, including most famously the autobiography of Archpriest Avvakum, martyred leader of the Old Believers. Scholarly works, also often of church provenance, comprised another significant literary corpus. Translations and compilations devoted to cosmology, astrology, geography, anatomy, medicine, trigonometry, surveying, agriculture, and firearms provided technical knowledge and introduced Russians to classical writers, European philosophy, and the scientific discoveries of Nicolaus Copernicus, Johannes Kepler, and Galileo Galilei. Translated and original works of scholarship also taught the liberal arts, including grammar, rhetoric, and poetics. Together with histories and historical legends about Russia and foreign lands, manuscript newspapers, produced from 1621, and travel accounts brought awareness of worlds beyond Muscovy's frontiers and in remote regions such as Siberia and the Far East. Publicistic writings served political and ideological purposes, both secular and religious. The range of these writings is evident from descriptions of Muscovy's social and political order, projects of reform, Orthodox critiques of Catholicism and Protestantism, and polemical literature associated with struggles over education, religious doctrine, and church reform, including works by advocates and opponents of Old Belief. Educational literature – primers, moral instructions, testaments, practical manuals, and calendars – aimed to provide useful information and teach proper behavior. Finally, a bourgeoning artistic literature consisted of translations, adaptations, and Russian originals produced in Moscow and the provinces. Stories, tales, fables, parables, anecdotes, drama, and poetry portrayed heroes and heroines who could be purely imaginary or based on biblical or historical figures. Although artistic literature remained predominantly religious, moralistic, historical, or panegyric in content, it also highlighted conditions of everyday life and employed satire, chivalric romance, fantasy, adventure, the bawdy, and the risqué to both instruct and entertain.[3]

Throughout the seventeenth century, Russian literature circulated primarily in manuscript form, and among present-day historians the origins of key works continue to be contested.[4] Book publishing did not begin to fix Russia's literary heritage before the late 1550s. At that time, the government opened an official printing house (*pechatnyi dvor*) in Moscow. In 1564 the printing house issued its first publication, the *Book of the Apostles* (*Apostoly*, that is, *Acts* and *Epistles*), and over the course of the century printed around 24 titles. During the seventeenth century, the Moscow press, under the supervision of the patriarch from 1653, and three presses at provincial monasteries published about 500 titles. Toward the end of the century, the number of titles reached six or seven a year. Although the printing operations of the seventeenth century did not a "printing revolution" make, Russia's breakthrough in print culture appeared on the horizon. In the first quarter of the eighteenth century, roughly 45 titles came out each year, and by 1788, the number reached 500.[5] The eighteenth century represented the watershed, yet given the overall paucity of historical sources for the Muscovite period, the impact of the literature available to reading and listening Russians already by the mid-seventeenth century should not be underestimated.

Whether copied in manuscript form or printed at a press, whether produced in Muscovy or imported from abroad, and whether written in Greek, Latin, Polish, Church Slavonic, chancery Russian, or a hybrid vernacular, the literature of seventeenth-century Muscovy became a force for cultural change. An early chink in the armor of Russian tradition occurred when the service books of the Orthodox Church came under scrutiny. Already in the sixteenth century, religious author-ities, concerned about the moral condition of the church, began to question dif-ferences found in the Russian and Greek liturgies. Tradition held firm, however, when the Stoglav (Hundred Chapters) Council of 1551 upheld Russian practices, rejected Greek innovations, strengthened the authority of Muscovite bishops, and enacted measures to improve the moral behavior of the clergy and laity. Following the Time of Troubles in the early seventeenth century, concerns about moral behavior and liturgical practices revived, and by 1640 a group of religious reformers called the zealots of piety emerged as advocates for broad reformation of the Russian church. Before becoming patriarch in 1652, Nikon himself identi-fied with the zealots of piety, whose ranks included both future supporters and opponents of his reforms. Tsar Aleksei Mikhailovich also strongly encouraged the zealots of piety, especially their efforts to reform religious life by improving morals, elevating the spiritual and intellectual capacities of clergy and laity, and correct-ing liturgical abuses. The Nikonian liturgical reforms of the 1650s, the cause of deep schism in the Russian church, grew out of the program of religious reforma-tion conceived by the zealots of piety.[6]

In the mid-seventeenth century, it seemed that reformist impulses within the Russian church enjoyed broad support. But Patriarch Nikon's tyrannical methods and political ambitions soon put him at odds with fellow reformers. Conflict and accusations of heresy also inevitably arose from the process of "correcting" Russian liturgical "abuses." What constituted an "abuse" and what a "correction"? Both Nikon and Aleksei Mikhailovich believed that the service books and ritual practices of the Russian Orthodox Church contained errors, that the models of the Greek church corresponded to true Orthodoxy, and that the Russian errors should be corrected based on old Greek and Slavonic texts. Opponents of Nikon, adhering to the Hundred Chapters, denied the need to change Russian practices and rejected the patriarch's liturgical reforms as "heretical innovations based on 'corrupt' sources." According to the Old Believers, discrepancies between the Greek and Russian service books resulted from changes made by the Greeks following their reconciliation with Catholicism at the Council of Florence (1438–9). The Greeks had introduced heretical errors, while the Muscovites remained true to Orthodoxy. The Greeks, moreover, had paid for their heresy when Constantinople fell to the Ottoman Turks in 1453.[7]

From a modern-day perspective, neither the supporters nor the opponents of Patriarch Nikon's reforms understood historicity and textual criticism. Nikon's opponents did, however, turn out to be correct about the corruption of the patriarch's sources. Modern scholars have determined that the reform of Russian service books relied not on "original" or even old models, but on the Greek *Euchologion* published in Venice in 1602 and on seventeenth-century "Lithuanian" books published in areas of Polish and hence Latinist influence. Nor can the correctors employed by Nikon be described as purely Orthodox in education and orientation.

Among the learned men brought to Muscovy for the important task of translation, Arsenii the Greek stood out for his knowledge of Slavonic, Greek, and Latin. Arsenii came to Moscow in January 1649 in the company of Patriarch Paisios of Jerusalem and remained there to work as a teacher and translator. Soon after Paisios's departure, however, concerns arose over Arsenii's religious affiliations and commitment to Orthodoxy. Rumors of heresy reached Moscow, and in a letter sent to Aleksei Mikhailovich, Paisios accused Arsenii of having been a Muslim and a Uniate (a Catholic of the Eastern Rite). Authorities in Moscow heeded these warnings, and in July the tsar ordered that Arsenii be confined to the Solovki Monastery in Russia's far north. Arsenii remained at Solovki for three years, learning Russian ways. In 1654, apparently forgiven his heresy, the Greek monk became a corrector at the Moscow printing house. In addition, he may have headed a Greek-Latin school, believed by some historians to have operated in Moscow from 1653 to 1655.[8] Twentieth-century scholars question Arsenii's knowledge of Church Slavonic, but to Patriarch Nikon, he seemed an educated man. After Nikon's fall from power in 1658, Arsenii continued to work at the printing house, though by September 1662 his name no longer appeared on the list of official correctors, and he was again exiled to Solovki. Loyalties and qualifications notwithstanding, historians assign Arsenii a significant role in the publication of Russia's new liturgical books.[9]

A second participant in Nikon's reforms, Hieromonk Epifanii (Slavinetskii), also came to Moscow in 1649, at the behest of Aleksei Mikhailovich, who had asked the Metropolitan of Kiev to send two learned monks to prepare a new Slavonic translation of the Greek Bible. Epifanii possessed untainted Orthodox credentials, though his education, like that of so many Kievan churchmen, included Latinist learning. Epifanii began his studies before 1621 at the Slavonic-Greek school of the Kievan Brotherhood and from there advanced to a Latin school probably located in Poland. He then returned to Kiev, became tonsured at the Monastery of the Caves, and by 1642 taught at the Kiev-Mogila College. In Moscow, Epifanii lived and worked at the Chudov Monastery in the Kremlin, where he produced original works and translations from Greek and Latin.[10] His translations included writings of the Eastern Church fathers; the 1663 Moscow Bible, a correction of the 1581 Ostrog Bible and the first complete Bible printed in Russia; selections from

Thucydides and Pliny the Younger; Erasmus's *De civilitate morum puerilium*; and works on anatomy and cosmology, the latter an introduction to the heliocentric theories of Copernicus. Epifanii's sermons are the best known of his original works, but he also composed a philological lexicon and a Greek-Slavonic-Latin dictionary. After Nikon's fall, Epifanii continued the work of translating and correcting Russian liturgical books based on Greek sources.[11]

Nikon, like earlier religious and political leaders in Muscovy, relied on "foreign" correctors and translators because of their superior education and linguistic skills. But in Nikon's time, the implications of this practice for Russian development began to change. The importation of learned men reached a critical mass and occurred in conditions that deepened their cultural impact. From the mid-seventeenth century, the combined force of religious schism in Muscovy and scientific revolution in Europe transformed the dynamics of Russian cultural reception. Muscovite tradition began to face the challenge of emergent European modernity, and strong as the tradition remained, Russian elites increasingly recognized that foreign knowledge had become necessary for Russia's general wellbeing. Both Arsenii and Epifanii appeared to be staunch defenders of Eastern Orthodox Christianity, and both supported reliance on Greek models in reforming the Russian church. As educated men, both also had been exposed to Latinist learning and religious teachings. Although this did not render them less Orthodox, at least not in the eyes of Nikon's supporters, the participation of foreign monks educated in non-Orthodox schools surely made it easier for opponents to associate liturgical innovation with heresy. The Nikonian reforms and subsequent schism showed, moreover, that both the church and monarchy intended to benefit from Latinist learning, the most advanced of the day, even if this meant subjecting Orthodox believers to Catholic and Protestant influences. The dangers of religious contamination remained of vital concern, and perceived heretics continued to be vigorously prosecuted. But fear of heresy did not inhibit the larger process of importing foreign scholars and ideas, regardless of religious affiliation. To the contrary, the Nikonian reforms, with their translation projects and foreign experts, provided a model for subsequent generations of cultural reformers who self-consciously sought to Europeanize Russia.

In addition to correcting service books and liturgical practices, seventeenth-century religious reformers also hoped to raise the moral and educational level of the clergy and laity. Educational institutions barely existed in Muscovy, and although monasteries and government offices sometimes operated informal schools, historians usually trace the beginnings of Russian education to the incorporation of Left-Bank (eastern) Ukraine and the city of Kiev in the mid-seventeenth century. Ukraine gave to Muscovy its first institution of higher learning, the Jesuit-style Kiev Academy, founded in 1631 by Petr Mogila (Ukrainian: Petro Mohyla; Romanian: Petru Movilă). As archimandrite of the Kiev Monastery of the Caves,

Mogila established a Latin-Polish school to teach the liberal arts. In 1632, when Mogila became metropolitan of Kiev, he combined this school with the Slavonic-Greek school of the Kievan Brotherhood to form the Kiev-Mogila College. The college taught the Latin, Polish, Slavonic, and Greek languages together with poetics, rhetoric, dialectic (including scholastic disputation), and philosophy. Although the college did not formally become an academy until 1701, from 1694 the curriculum also included theology. The Kiev-Mogila College offered the most advanced education in all of Muscovy and for generations to come provided the church and monarchy with competent teachers, enlightened intellectuals, and educated bishops. The college also served as the model for the Moscow Slavonic-Greek-Latin school, established around 1685.[12]

Like the translation projects of the seventeenth century, the development of Russian education revealed awareness of the fact that to become learned in the Christian world meant to learn Latin. Following the upheaval of the schism, the monarchy, not the church, took the lead in promoting the assimilation of foreign knowledge. Accusations of heresy receded – the Old Believers had become the heretics – as a steady stream of monks possessing Polish-Latinist, Jesuit-inspired education reached Moscow, welcomed for their European learning by the court, the elite nobility, and at least some church hierarchs.[13] Simeon (Polotskii, 1629–80), poet and teacher at the courts of Aleksei Mikhailovich and Fedor Alekseevich, exemplified the Latinist culture of Kiev that began to transform Muscovy in the second half of the seventeenth century.[14] Simeon came from an Orthodox Belarusian family and graduated from the Kiev-Mogila College in the late 1640s. From Kiev he went to Vilnius, where he probably attended the Jesuit academy until at least 1653. Simeon's spiritual ties to Catholicism remain unclear, though at some point he belonged to the *Ordo Sancti Basilii Magni*, a Catholic order of the Eastern Rite. Needless to say, Simeon's Jesuit education and ties to "Catholicism" did not endear him to ecclesiastical authorities in Moscow. Educated in the seven liberal arts – grammar, rhetoric, dialectic, arithmetic, geometry, astronomy, and music – Simeon reportedly did not master Greek.[15] But Orthodox clergy in Slavic lands often did not learn Greek, and in 1656 Simeon became a monk and teacher at the Orthodox Theophany Monastery in Polotsk. In 1656 in Polotsk, Simeon twice participated in panegyric declamations performed before Aleksei Mikhailovich. He did the same in Moscow in 1660. In 1663 or 1664, Simeon moved to Moscow, and by August 1664 he lived at the Zaikonospasskii Monastery.

Simeon's career in Moscow, like that of Epifanii (Slavinetskii), contributed much to the importation of foreign learning into Russia.[16] In December 1664, the Belarusian monk was called to court to serve as an interpreter. The following April he performed a panegyric oration before Aleksei Mikhailovich and presented him with a collection of poems written to honor the birth of the tsar's third son. Soon thereafter, Simeon became established as Russia's first court poet, and poetic declamation became a regular feature of court life and ceremony. As court poet and tutor to three of Aleksei's children (Aleksei, Fedor, and Sophia), Simeon produced works of religious instruction, polemical writings against Old Belief, sermons, plays, and of course, poetry. In 1665–8 he ran a Latin school to educate government officials, and in 1679 Fedor Alekseevich put him in charge of a palace printing press, independent of church supervision, which operated until 1683. After Simeon's death in 1680, his student Sil'vestr (Medvedev, 1641–91) assumed the responsibilities of court poet, royal tutor, and head of the palace press. Like Simeon, Sil'vestr benefited from the court's support for European learning. Beginning in 1681, he also directed a school, funded by Tsar Fedor and located at the Zaikonospasskii Monastery, where up to 23 students studied Slavonic, Latin, grammar, and rhetoric.

When in the 1650s Patriarch Nikon relied on foreign monks and religious models to reform the Russian church, "foreign" appeared to mean Orthodox but Greek. In reality, Nikon's reforms incorporated Latinist and hence non-Orthodox learning into the framework of Russian Orthodoxy. By the 1680s, Nikon's apparent lack of concern about Latinist contamination had been superseded by serious hier-archical apprehension. Patriarch Ioakim began to associate the foreign knowledge coming into Muscovy with Catholicism and Protestantism and to perceive Latinist learning as a threat to ecclesiastical authority. To counter the Jesuit-inspired education promoted by Simeon and Sil'vestr, Ioakim in 1681 founded a school at the Moscow printing house, where about 30 students, taught by Greek monks, followed a Greek curriculum designed to keep out Latinist influences. The dis-tinction between the "Latin" and "Greek" schools, together with the Eucharistic controversy of the late 1680s, has led historians to speak of a Latinist–Grecophile divide within the court and ecclesiastical elites of the late seventeenth century. It is true that Ioakim, a tireless champion of patriarchal authority, harbored sus-picions about the "Catholic" sympathies of Simeon and Sil'vestr. But Ioakim also opposed independent thinking in matters of faith, holding that church hierarchs should define religious doctrine and that the power of the patriarch should be protected from the secular authorities. While not an opponent of advanced educa-tion, Ioakim equated enlightenment with religious enlightenment and believed in ecclesiastical responsibility for the development of the human mind. Enlighten-ment came to the patriarch from God, passing then to the clergy through priestly consecration and to the laity through the church's teachings. Ioakim's interest in education thus coincided with his belief in church control over religious enlighten-ment. He opposed Sil'vestr not only because of his Latinist orientation, but also because of his school's freedom from patriarchal supervision.

The intellectual influence wielded by Sil'vestr became evident when in 1682 he submitted to Tsar Fedor a plan to establish a Moscow academy modeled after the Kiev-Mogila College. Fedor approved the plan but died later that year. During the *de facto* regency of Sophia, political struggles occupied the court, and the plan to found an academy languished. Meanwhile, Patriarch Ioakim took advantage of the inactivity to ensure that any future academy would be under his control. In 1685 two Greek monks, the brothers Ioannikios and Sophronios Leichoudes, arrived in Moscow, sent by Patriarch Dositheos of Jerusalem in response to Ioakim's request for Orthodox teachers. The Leichoudes brothers set up a Slavonic-Greek school with 40 students at the Epiphany Monastery, and in 1687 their school moved to the Zaikonospasskii Monastery, having absorbed the schools of Sil'vestr and the Moscow printing house. Sil'vestr played no role in the Leichoudes brothers' school, and over the next few years, his position at court deteriorated. Branded a Jesuit or a Uniate by one of Ioakim's associates, he came under attack during the Eucharistic controversy of the late 1680s for taking a Catholic position on the moment of transubstantiation. Then in March 1689, at the urging of Ioakim, Sil'vestr lost his position as corrector at the printing house. By August 1689, his ties to the court of Sophia led to allegations of complicity in a plot to subvert Orthodoxy and overthrow Peter. Ioakim supported Peter in the showdown with Sophia, a mistaken choice given the patriarch's concern about Latinist influences, but one that produced a clear victory over Sil'vestr. After being tried for heresy and conspiracy, Sil'vestr was executed in 1691.

Ioakim died in 1690, and despite his apparent victory the year before, the dissemination of Latinist learning continued unabated. The Greek school founded by the Leichoudes brothers quickly evolved into a Slavonic-Greek-Latin school, the eighteenth-century Moscow Slavonic-Greek-Latin Academy, in which the middle and higher classes were taught grammar, rhetoric, poetics, dialectic, logic, and physics (natural philosophy). The Leichoudes brothers, Greek origins notwithstanding, had studied in Venice and Padua, and their understanding of education included a heavy dose of Latin and Jesuit natural philosophy. A few years after Sil'vestr's demise, they too ran into trouble. For reasons that remain unclear, the Leichoudes were in 1694 removed from their teaching posts at the Moscow school. Historians point to political intrigue and accusations of corruption to explain the change in fortune, but controversy over the direction of education also persisted. Under Ioakim, the religious authorities in Moscow had not yet embraced modern scientific and by definition Latinist learning. Instead, as Ioakim's testament showed, they became fearful of heresy and foreigners. Even so, in Moscow, with church sanction, the Leichoudes brothers offered a relatively advanced form of European education that required knowledge of Latin. They also exposed students to Copernican science and taught a Jesuit version of physics that both preserved geocentricity and allowed for observed astronomical phenomena such as comets and new stars.[17] How Muscovites received this tentative introduction to Europe's new science is not clear. Nor ultimately did it matter. In the year 1694, Tsar Peter I took control of the Russian government. The Leichoudes brothers' interest in scientific subject matter and the distinction they drew between religious belief and secular learning became institutionalized in the state schools subsequently established by Peter. The Jesuit-style education of the Kiev and Moscow academies likewise spread out, providing the model for Russia's ecclesiastical schools into the nineteenth century.

In the process of cultural change evident in Russia from the mid-seventeenth century, Jesuit-style education represented an early, but not the only, source of European influence. Beginning in the 1650s, the monarchy also actively sponsored artistic innovation based on European models.[18] Aleksei Mikhailovich imported foreign artists to train Russians and fulfill commissions, and the Moscow armory became a center of religious and secular painting. An account book for 1667–8 shows 40 secular artists and 27 icon painters working in the armory. For the period from roughly 1660 to 1700, armory records identify about 1,020 painters employed by the monarchy for various projects. Although in painting, as in literature, religious content remained dominant, the secular themes and decorations that appeared in the wall and ceiling paintings of royal palaces provided evidence of openness to change. The secular subject matter included portraits of the royal family, life-size human figures, horses, scroll and ribbon motifs, depictions of heavenly bodies and signs of the Zodiac, and still-life pictures of fruits and flowers. Naturalistic lighting, the use of perspective, and attention to the details of landscape, architecture, interiors, clothing, and facial expression all conveyed an appreciation for the earthly and concrete. Overall, the greater realism in presentation and decoration suggested a willingness to apply foreign techniques. Even icon painters, to the extent allowed by canonical rules and not without controversy, adopted artistic innovations borrowed from Europe. Finally, the development of secular portraiture added to the naturalistic sensibility an interest in the individual person. Already in the sixteenth century, paintings on church and palace walls portrayed contemporary historical figures, though the earliest live portrait of a Russian monarch, an image of the First False Dmitrii (ruled 1605–6), originated in Poland. By the 1620s, royal portraits were being painted in Moscow and from the time of Aleksei Mikhailovich became commonplace. By the 1680s, a small group of private patrons – courtiers, church hierarchs, and foreigners – also began to collect portraits, rendered as easel paintings and engravings.

Alongside painting, the architecture, theater, and music of the late seventeenth century provided evidence of cultural change in a European direction. Architects used classical motifs, storied arrangements, and rich decorative detail to produce a variegated visual effect that blended tradition and innovation. Beginning in the 1680s, the hybrid – some would add overly ornamented, complicated, and fragmented – Moscow baroque style could be found in the homes and churches of elite nobles and merchants, and by the 1690s in the provinces.[19] European theatrical forms also became part of the Muscovite cultural environment. Beginning in the late seventeenth century, Orthodox churchmen brought Jesuit-style school drama to Moscow from Kiev and Polotsk. School drama subsequently became housed in the seminaries spawned by Peter I's Ecclesiastical Regulation and played a role in the development of Russian public theater into the 1770s. Equally significant, the court began to promote theater. After failing in 1660 and again in 1672 to attract foreign actors to Moscow, Aleksei Mikhailovich enlisted a resident Lutheran pastor to write a play based on the biblical story of Esther and to stage it with actors chosen from among the inhabitants of the Foreign Quarter. Written in German and rendered into Russian by translators in the Foreign Affairs Chancellery, the *Artaxerxes Play* was staged at the tsar's Preobrazhenskoe residence outside Moscow on October 17, 1672. Enthusiastically received, this first court performance of a literary play led to the establishment of an acting school and the opening of a second theater inside the Kremlin. Aleksei's court theater employed about 200 actors and craftsmen, and its repertoire treated biblical, hagiographical, historical, and mythological subjects. Derived from the "English tragedies and comedies" popular in the Germanies from the end of the sixteenth century, the court repertoire provided entertainment for the monarch, his family, and courtiers.[20]

Music represented still another form of European entertainment at the Muscovite court. Aleksei Mikhailovich reportedly employed German musicians, and the court theater possessed organs, trumpets, and percussion. Ballet and musical interludes, religious and secular, also made appearances during the performance of plays. Although the accession of Fedor Alekseevich in 1676 ended theatrical and musical performances at court, theater revived in the early years of the eighteenth century. In 1702–3 Peter I established a short-lived public theater on Moscow's Red Square, and his sister Natal'ia Alekseevna presided over court theaters in Preobrazhenskoe and St Petersburg. Music reappeared even sooner. As early as 1686, Ukrainian choristers, famous for their mastery of harmony, performed in the private palace of Sophia's confidant, Prince Vasilii V. Golitsyn. The persistence of European pleasures also is evident from Vasilii Titov's musical rendering of the *Psalter of King David the Prophet*, a Psalter in syllabic verse composed by Simeon (Polotskii) in 1678. In 1687 Sophia received a copy of Titov's musical version of Simeon's *Psalter*.[21] Clearly, the conservatism of Patriarch Ioakim and Tsar Fedor did not halt the process of adapting foreign cultural models to Muscovite needs. To the contrary, Fedor supported Latinist education until his death, and European music found a home at the court of Sophia. It seems that the battle over foreign influences and Latinist learning had ended even before Peter I acceded to the throne. Under Peter, the question of whether or not to embrace European culture all but disappeared. In its place a new question arose: how to become European in the shortest possible time?

——————————— Petrine Cultural Revolution ———————————

When Russia's cultural opening to Europe began in the late seventeenth century, much of Western thought already had become detached from theology and religious dogma, though certainly not from religious belief. In mind, if not yet fully in body – censorship, religious persecution, and absolute monarchy continued to restrict the flow of ideas – European intellectuals enjoyed widespread freedom to produce scientific, philosophical, and literary works without regard to confessional orthodoxy. Increasingly protected from religious sanctions and empowered by Cartesian and Newtonian science, writers and other intellectuals participated in a burgeoning print culture or "republic of letters," where truth could be publicly debated and membership depended on education and intellectual talent rather than birth. In Russia, the institutional and cultural reforms of Tsar Peter I set the stage for similar developments. The Petrine reforms separated church and state by subordinating ecclesiastical administration to the monarchy. Through the creation of clearly delineated spheres of sacred and secular authority, the reforms allowed Russian intellectuals to assimilate and articulate European ideas without fear of being charged with heresy. Although the Orthodox Church remained responsible for ensuring the purity of the faith and the salvation of the faithful, by the end of Peter's reign, church censorship and religious doctrine no longer determined Russian access to European culture.

Of course, as discussed above, for decades prior to the reforms of Peter I, European cultural models seeped into Russia. At the courts of Aleksei, Fedor, and Sophia, European-style education, literature, art, architecture, theater, and music began to take root. The church, by contrast, while in effect promoting the spread of European learning, became under Patriarchs Ioakim and Adrian fiercely opposed to foreign influences.[22] Alarmed by the impact of Polish–Ukrainian–Latinist thinking, church hierarchs increasingly saw in the ways and mores of foreign lands a threat to religious authority and Orthodox belief. Although open conflict between the church and monarchy subsided following the 1666 deposition of Nikon, the potential for trouble remained, becoming evident once again in the reign of Peter. In 1698, while Peter was abroad in England, Patriarch Adrian anathematized a tobacco merchant and his family, even though the merchant engaged in a legal trade based on a concession granted by the government. To Adrian, smoking represented a harmful foreign custom that could not be tolerated. Tsar Peter, on the other hand, had every intention of opening Russia to the full panoply of European ideas and behaviors. The day after Peter returned from the Grand Embassy, on August 26, 1698, he inaugurated the shaving of beards at court. Although both Ioakim and Adrian had pronounced anathemas on shaving, Peter did not hesitate in the pursuit of change. The monarch could conclude, moreover, that Providence blessed his actions. Before any serious confrontation with the church occurred, Peter received "a big gift": Patriarch Adrian died on October 16, 1700.[23] The monarch then managed to put off the appointment of a successor, an indication of the church's already weak political position, and in 1705 settled once and for all the question of beards. A decree of that year ordered "all courtiers and officials in Moscow and all the other towns, as well as leading merchants and other townsmen" to shave their beards and moustaches.[24]

Peter literally beheaded the church, and by the time he replaced the patriarch with a Synod of appointed bishops, in 1721, the lone voice of opposition, that of Stefan (Iavorskii, 1658–1722), represented a cry in the dark.[25] Peter's treatment of the church hierarchy, and his insistence on adopting, even imposing, foreign customs, regardless of Orthodox teachings, exemplified the difference between Muscovite cultural evolution and Petrine cultural revolution. Peter's reforms became broadly transformative not because they departed from the policies of his predecessors, all of whom embraced European culture in some form, but because they introduced European models without hesitation on a massive scale at a rapid pace. Under Peter, quantitative change became qualitative change. Tentative steps in a European direction, here and there, now and then, became the single-minded, unambiguous pursuit of specific goals. Peter enthusiastically embraced the notion that for the immediate future Europe knew better, and Russia must learn from Europe. Russia, he believed, needed to be European in order to be prosperous and strong.

Historians long have noted the utilitarian bent of Peter I's educational and cultural reforms. Peter himself studied the mechanical arts, and in training Russians and importing foreign experts, his policies emphasized practical knowledge capable of producing concrete results. On the face of it, this characterization seems appropriate, especially in light of the paucity of Russian literary works from the early eighteenth century. In reality, however, the practical knowledge acquired from Europe – the techniques of engineering, architecture, painting, literature, medicine, mathematical science, and physics (natural philosophy) – implied and produced much broader cultural change. The Russian reception of European learning, while seemingly eclectic and unsystematic, nonetheless became deeply implanted. The deliberate importation of modern science and philosophy – the effort to understand the material world and human behavior without reference to divine intervention – produced the same liberating effects in eighteenth-century Russia that earlier had been seen in Europe.[26] Peter's interest in European science, a science that blended mathematical calculation and empirical observation with explanatory natural philosophy, informed his two-pronged approach to cultural change. First, Peter aimed to transform the social habits of Russia's elite service classes, so that they would be receptive to the letters, arts, and sciences of contemporary Europe. Second, he sought to build the institutions needed to educate Russians, so that they could master European learning and participate in the progress of modern culture.

Intensive change began with the alphabet reform of 1708–10, which established a civil script, really a type, alongside the Cyrillic script of Church Slavonic. Peter's decision to introduce a civil script stemmed from the need to make available in understandable Russian translations the storehouse of European scientific and technical knowledge. On a deeper level, the alphabet reform represented an effort to address the linguistic confusion of the seventeenth century. From roughly the mid-sixteenth century, Church Slavonic, the language of the liturgy; chancery Russian, the language of the government bureaucracy; and vernacular Russian, the spoken language(s) of the people competed and overlapped in the development of Muscovite literature. By the late seventeenth century, at least some educated clergy began to view the Church Slavonic of their day as inadequate for pastoral duties. Preachers, they believed, needed to use a simpler language understandable to the laity. To that end, such leading church intellectuals as Simeon (Polotskii) and Dimitrii (Rostovskii, 1651–1709) strove to make religious language accessible by writing sermons in a standard Church Slavonic free of rhetorical adornments. In the service of religious enlightenment, both preachers tried to address the listener who lacked learning. The greatest monument to this effort, Dimitrii's four-volume *Lives of Saints*, published in Kiev between 1689 and 1705, enjoyed popularity throughout the eighteenth and nineteenth centuries. But Dimitrii died in 1709, and for the rest of Peter's reign Gavriil (Buzhinskii, ca. 1680–1731), archimandrite of the Trinity-Sergius Monastery, and Feofan (Prokopovich, 1677 or 1681–1736), Bishop of Pskov and Archbishop of Novgorod, carried the banner of linguistic simplification by developing a hybrid language that combined Church Slavonic and vernacular Russian. In Feofan's scheme, Church Slavonic would remain the language of the liturgy, while the "simple speech" promoted by Peter would become the language of scholarship, literature, and government. For sermons, because of the need to quote Scripture and other sacred sources, a hybrid language seemed appropriate.[27]

To present-day readers, the language of Feofan is still heavily Slavonic and not easily understood. But it represented an important step in the development of modern Russian literature. Intellectual luminaries from the reign of Catherine II, individuals fully at home in European Enlightenment culture, praised Feofan's literary achievements. Court poet and father of the Russian Imperial Theater, Aleksandr P. Sumarokov (1717–77), called Feofan "the Russian Cicero." Publisher and leading Moscow Freemason, Nikolai I. Novikov (1744–1818), described him as "the first of our finest writers."[28] According to historian James Cracraft, modern standard Russian dates from the reign of Peter I and resulted directly from the alphabet reform and consequent development of an accessible or "simple" Russian suitable for the people's moral and technical edification.[29] Consistent with Peter's vision, by the mid-eighteenth century, leading churchmen – the likes of Platon (Levshin, 1737–1812), Gavriil (Petrov, 1730–1801), and Gedeon (Krinovskii, ca. 1730–63) – wrote sermons and works of religious instruction in a literary Russian close to the language of the educated laity. Although Church Slavonic remained the language of the liturgy and of much religious writing, from the time of Feofan until the early nineteenth century, the languages of homiletic and secular literature developed as one.[30]

In addition to developing an accessible literary language, the Petrine reforms opened the door to a lexical and informational invasion.[31] Between 1700 and Peter's death in January 1725, Russian presses published 1,312 titles – translations, compilations, and original works – of which 308 were religious in content. Historians estimate that in the period 1695 to 1725, some 5,153 foreign words, including derivations, entered the Russian language from German, Dutch, English, Swedish, French, Italian, Latin, Polish, and Classical Greek. The publication projects of the Petrine government supplied the critical scientific information, technical instruction, and legal regulation needed to build a navy, reform the army and bureaucracy, and turn Russia's service classes, noble and nonnoble, into educated Europeans. Manuals, textbooks, treatises, and legislation covered all the areas of specialized knowledge being imported into Russia: medicine; manufacturing; nautical sciences such as shipbuilding ("naval architecture"), sailing, and navigation; military sciences such as gunnery, siegecraft, fortification ("military architecture"), engineering, artillery, tactics, weaponry, and training; mathematical sciences such as arithmetic, algebra, geometry, and trigonometry; sciences that relied on mathematics such as astronomy, geography, cartography, geodesy, and surveying; and finally, the new physics (natural philosophy) of Europe's scientific revolution, broadly defined to include theoretical and experimental physics, chemistry, botany, and anatomy. In the humanistic sciences, government-sponsored publications encompassed moral philosophy, theology, ethics, etiquette, natural and public law, antiquities, ancient and modern history, music, art, architecture, literature (eloquence), grammar, and lexicography. Never before in the history of Russia had so many publications appeared in so short a period of time. Never before had secular learning been so widely disseminated.

No less than Peter's institutional reforms, the infusion of new knowledge, concepts, images, and words contributed to the emergence of a Europeanized elite that quickly set about the task of producing a modern Russian culture. Feofan (Prokopovich), the architect of Peter's church reform, is best remembered for his sermons, for penning the Ecclesiastical Regulation of 1721, and for his justifications of absolute monarchy based on historical precedent, natural law theory, the Bible, and the writings of Church fathers, Greek and Latin. Feofan's tract *The Right of the Monarch's Will in Designating the Heir to His Realm* appeared in 1722 to defend Peter's decision to abolish the established order of succession. *The Right* employed arguments from reason to demand unquestioning obedience to the monarch and established Feofan's reputation as the primary theoretician of Petrine absolutism. Another advocate for the Russian monarch, Petr P. Shafirov (1669–1739), worked as a translator in the Foreign Affairs Chancellery. Shafirov, the son of a converted Jew who rose to noble status in Muscovite service, wrote an early tract devoted to international law and diplomacy. Published in 1717 as *A Discourse Concerning the Just Reasons Which his Czarish Majesty, Peter I . . . had for beginning the War against the King of Sweden, Charles XII, Anno 1700*, the tract is an effective defense of absolute monarchy and Russian foreign policy.[32] Both Feofan and Shafirov appeared modern in their language and appeals to reason, but they also seemed to linger in the seventeenth-century tradition of panegyric oration.

A different kind of Petrine intellectual emerged in the person of Ivan T. Pososhkov (1652/53–1726), a crown peasant and entrepreneur, who rose to become a merchant and serf owner. Pososhkov came from a family of silver craftsmen attached to the Moscow armory, and his most famous work, *The Book on Poverty and Wealth*, probably did not reach the hands of Peter. Written in 1724, *On Poverty and Wealth* describes the proper organization of society and economy with reference to a divinely ordained order. While clearly a believer in obedience to the monarch, Pososhkov's other writings showed him also to be a supporter of Stefan (Iavorskii, 1658–1722) and a critic of Peter's reforms. Perhaps for that reason, after Peter's death, Pososhkov suffered arrest. He died in prison in February 1726. Pososhkov can be read as a religious traditionalist with a pre-scientific mindset, yet he embraced the notion of material progress and, more importantly, formulated an intellectual viewpoint independent of both court culture and government policy.[33]

The writings of noteworthy intellectuals from the early eighteenth century suggest that the Petrine cultural revolution did not result from ideological originality or radical rejection of the past. It resulted from the massive infusion of European cultural models in literature, architecture, and the visual arts and from the cumulative changes that secured a Russian home for European culture in the social milieu of the court and educated service classes. Peter understood that the transformation he envisioned for Russia required more than book learning and technical expertise. Russia also needed new social mores and customs. So not long after the 1698 shaving of beards at court, Peter decreed that service nobles of all ranks, men and women, wear German clothes and ride in German saddles.[34] Beginning in 1700–1, men were forced to give up their caftans, at least in public, and women were required "to wear dresses, German overskirts, petticoats, hats, and shoes of foreign design."[35] The new dress code also applied to elite merchants, military servicemen, civil servants, and registered townspeople, wives and children included. Peasants who lived and worked in Moscow likewise came under the Petrine sartorial regime. Only farming peasants and clergy, though not the wives of clergy, remained exempt. But to decree is one thing and to enforce another. Historians lack precise information about the spread of European dress. Adoption seems to have been quick at court, though only gradual in the provinces. Whatever the specific patterns of change, by mid-century the physical appearance of the educated service classes showed concretely that a cultural gulf separated them from the massive peasant population.

Of course, public appearances can be deceiving. Petrine subjects who preferred traditional Russian to modern European clothes could in the seclusion of their homes and in distant localities preserve the old habits of dress. They could not, however, retreat indefinitely into the private household. Peter required lifelong service of all noblemen, who consequently spent much time in public view. Among courtiers and the upper service classes of St Petersburg, men and women, polite sociability became a public duty. In the seventeenth century, at court and in noble households, women lived in separate female quarters, the quiet rooms (*pokoi*) or *terem*, and rarely appeared in public. During the *de facto* regency of Sophia, who governed in a public manner that put her person and power on display, practices began to change, at least among royalty. Peter, in his usual fashion, sought to change not only the court but the whole of Russia, and so he ordered all elite women out of the seclusion of the *terem*, requiring them in 1718 to attend French-style assemblies, or evening parties, where they danced, conversed, and mingled with men. Once again, historians possess little information on compliance, though at court, sociability in mixed company is documented as early as 1702. Aleksei Zubov's famous etching of 1712, depicting the celebration of Peter's marriage to Catherine, also shows women in wigs and European court dress seated with men in uniform around a festive table. There is evidence, in addition, that between 1718 and Peter's death in 1725, assemblies took place with some regularity in St Petersburg and in 1722 spread to Moscow.[36] By mid-century, social intercourse in the European manner, both in private homes and public venues, could be found among nobles across Russia.

The abolition of the *terem* and the introduction of assemblies, even if not immediately realized, illustrated the larger trend in Petrine Russia toward development of a public life centered around sites of polite sociability. To encourage polite behavior and European manners, Peter's government also produced Russia's first etiquette manual, *The Honorable Mirror of Youth, or a guide to social conduct gathered from various authors*.[37] Compiled by Gavriil (Buzhinskii) and James Bruce, and translated by a German scholar in St Petersburg, the *Mirror* was published twice in 1717 and subsequently reprinted in 1719, 1723, 1740, 1742, 1745, and 1767. The four Petrine editions of the *Mirror* accounted for 2,478 copies, of which historians believe 1,859 were sold around the time of printing. The *Mirror* is a thoroughly European document, adapted from works such as Erasmus's *De civilitate morum puerilium* (1530), the *Miroir de la jeunesse pour former à bonnes moeurs et civilité de vie* (1539), and the contemporary German manuals *Spiegel für der Bildung* and *Der Goldene Spiegel*. Russian reception of the *Mirror* has not been documented, but the manual's publication history and the absence for several decades of any competing text suggest that if educated Russians read a book of etiquette, they read the *Mirror*. By the 1760s, alternative manuals on how to behave in the *le grand monde* (*svet*) also could be consulted.

Peter's government initiated the development of polite sociability in Russia, and into the nineteenth century participation in public life served the needs of moral education more than political empowerment. In contrast to the situation in Western and Central Europe, sites of polite sociability in Petrine Russia did not institutionalize public opinion or the rise of a public sphere capable of imposing limits on absolute monarchy.[38] The creation of Russian public theater is a case in point. In 1701–2 Peter sent emissaries to Gdansk in search of actors, and by December 1702 the German troupe of Johann Kunst and a Russian troupe trained by Kunst began to stage literary plays before paying audiences in the Lefort palace. At the end of 1703, the German and Russian troupes, now headed by Otto Fürst (Kunst died in early 1703), moved to Russia's first permanent public theater erected on Red Square. The new wooden theater operated until 1706 when, for unknown reasons, Peter dismissed the German actors. Despite the apparent setback, theatrical performances continued at court, and in the last years of Peter's reign, foreign troupes again performed before paying Russian audiences. Not until the 1740s, however, did foreign impresarios receive privileges that allowed them to build permanent theater structures. Russian public theater, organized by private enthusiasts, returned in the late 1740s and became permanently established when Empress Elizabeth founded the Russian Imperial Theater in 1756. Court poet and playwright, Aleksandr P. Sumarokov served as the first director of the theater, and literary historians regard his neoclassical tragedy *Khorev*, published in 1747, as one of Russia's earliest modern plays.[39]

The publication of a printed newspaper, another Petrine endeavor, provided further evidence of Russia's incipient public life.[40] During the seventeenth century, the Foreign Affairs Chancellery produced bulletins of military and political news from Europe, which circulated in manuscript form among government officials. Peter's *News* (*Vedomosti*), published in Moscow from 1702 and in St Petersburg from 1711, marked the birth of Russian journalism. Issues of the *News* sometimes came out on a weekly basis, though data from 1703 to 1724 show fluctuations of one to fifty-six issues per year. Initial press runs ran high, one to two thousand during the first two years of publication, after which the number of printed copies fell to several hundred. On special occasions, in response to the perceived needs of readers, additional copies could be produced. The issue covering the Battle of Poltava in 1709 sold an impressive 2,500 copies. Compared to the Muscovite bulletins, Peter's *News* also offered more varied coverage. In addition to European military and political affairs, domestic Russian, primarily court, events received attention, as did foreign trade and Russian economic development. Finally, as a government publication, the *News* enjoyed a longevity that later eighteenth-century periodicals failed to sustain. From 1728 the Academy of Sciences in St Petersburg assumed responsibility for publishing the *News*, which became known as the *St Petersburg News* (*Sankt-Peterburgskie vedomosti*). The *St Petersburg News* continued publication until 1914. Of course, the publication of one newspaper did not add up to public opinion or indicate the emergence of a public sphere, but once again, a specific Petrine innovation inaugurated a critical element of modern development.

The St Petersburg Academy of Sciences represented yet another Petrine cultural innovation and contribution to the development of Russian public life.[41] Peter's decision to establish the academy resulted from direct experience of European prototypes. In 1697 Peter began to correspond with, and subsequently met on several occasions, the philosopher and father of the Berlin Academy of Sciences, Gottfried W. Leibniz. At some point in their relationship, Leibniz reportedly urged the Russian monarch to found a "college of sciences." Peter visited the Royal Society of London in 1698 and the Paris Academy of Sciences, which elected him an honorary member, in 1717. Finally, in 1719 Peter turned to his personal physician, Lavrentii Bliumentrost, to recruit European scholars prepared to come to St Petersburg to participate in the creation of a Russian academy. In January 1724, Peter approved legislation establishing the St Petersburg Academy of Sciences. The statute called for the creation of a juridical faculty to teach politics, ethics, and natural law; a medical faculty to teach anatomy, chemistry, and botany; and a philosophy faculty to teach logic, metaphysics, general mathematics, general and experimental physics, astronomy, mechanics, eloquence, antiquities, and history. By the time the academy held its first public meeting in December 1725, a group of European scholars had accepted appointments and moved to St Petersburg. The academy's original members included two astronomers, one zoologist and surgeon, three mathematicians, one classical scholar, two natural philosophers specializing in physics and one in chemistry and medicine, and several moral philosophers skilled in law, history, and eloquence. From the outset, the academy performed research, teaching, and public functions, and although not all the legally prescribed subjects could be covered, academicians and professors regularly gave reports and public lectures. In 1727 the total staff of the academy numbered 84: seventeen academicians and professors, nineteen students and apprentices, two teachers, six translators, one master of astronomical instruments, three library assistants, seven printers, seven engravers, two painters, ten clerks, and ten servants. Based on the legislation of 1724, Latin and Russian served as the academy's languages of operation, publication, and teaching.

Within a decade of the academy's founding, its importance for the development of Russian letters, arts, and sciences became evident. In 1733 one of the academy's Russian students, Vasilii E. Adodurov (1709–80), became adjunct in mathematics. By the mid-1740s, the first Russian professors and academicians received academy appointments: Mikhail V. Lomonosov (1711–65) as professor of chemistry in 1745, Vasilii K. Trediakovskii (1703–60) as professor of eloquence in 1745, and Grigorii N. Teplov (1717–79) as academician in botany in 1747. In addition to publishing and teaching, the academy also maintained a library, built on Peter's personal collection and in 1728 numbering over 12,000 volumes. Finally, the academy absorbed Peter's *Kunstkamera* or Cabinet of Curiosities, Russia's first museum, which contained the anatomical collection of Dr Fredrik Ruysch, purchased in Amsterdam in 1717. Together with the military, bureaucracy, and court, the St Petersburg Academy of Sciences provided the institutional framework for the rise of Russia's educated service classes. The academy's publications and meetings, though mainly devoted to scholarship and science, also provided a home for Russian literature and arts. Professors Lomonosov and Trediakovskii are today recognized as canonical figures in the development of modern Russian literature, and in Lomonosov's case, also science. If in the late seventeenth and early eighteenth centuries Russian intellectuals served either the church or the monarchy, within a few decades of the academy's founding, secular intellectuals, outside the church and government, possessed sufficient independence and education to become a voice for Russian society.

Conclusion

Beginning in the seventeenth century, educated Russians looked to Western and Central Europe for models of cultural and institutional change. At the court of Aleksei Mikhailovich, the literary activities of Simeon (Polotskii) and the introduction of theater represented prime examples. In contrast to the court, however, the Muscovite churchmen who dominated Russian high culture and constituted the bulk of the educated classes struggled hard to keep out Latinist influences. Not until the reign of Peter I did the Russian monarchy, supported by growing numbers of educated nobles and servicemen, self-consciously set out to absorb the finest fruits of European letters, arts, and sciences. The gradual penetration of European ideas gave way to frenzied borrowing, as the government focused on such practical needs as educating personnel and building institutions. In historical accounts of Peter's reign, his cultural policies appear dramatic and his methods of implementation utterly ruthless, yet the speed at which Russia's service classes assimilated and embraced European culture suggests that they did not experience the transformation as something traumatic or wrenching.

From the time of Peter's death and continuing to the present day, Russian intellectuals have debated the reality of the Petrine transformation, passing judgment on the content and consequences of the reforms. Peter brought Russia out of backwardness to greatness and international glory. Peter civilized Russia by opening a "window on Europe." Peter made Russia modern and European. Conversely, Peter violated Russian tradition and ignored Russia's past. Peter forced Russia onto an unnatural course of development. Peter established the modern Russian police state, precursor to Soviet totalitarianism. Such varied judgments about Peter's reign are echoed by modern historians. Did the Petrine reforms constitute a radical break with the Muscovite past? Were Peter's policies beneficial or harmful, lasting or transitory, transformative or artificial? Was the price of success, particularly military success, too high? Did the Petrine reforms really make Russia modern and European, or did they act as a brake on progress by strengthening serfdom and absolute monarchy? Finally, did educated Russians actually internalize the European identity they seemed to embrace?

It is true that many Petrine initiatives fell by the wayside and others took root in a distorted and unintended way. It also is true that Peter's vision for changing Russia met opposition at court, among elite nobles, and in church circles.[42] But curiously, whatever the perspective of a particular commentator, current or past, Peter appears in virtually every narrative as a figure of momentous and abiding significance. Regardless of any conclusion reached, Peter's presence is felt, for better or worse. The fact that historians continue to debate whether or not the educated classes of eighteenth-century Russia became genuinely European serves as testimony to the depth of the Petrine transformation. Ambivalence persists concerning the effects of the cultural change. Ambivalence, however, is precisely the point. The ease with which educated Russians assimilated European cultural models and became integrated into European letters, arts, and sciences is not at issue. At issue, perhaps because of the ease and speed of assimilation, is the substance of Russianness and of Russia's relationship with Europe. If the changes wrought by Peter had been fleeting or superficial, their meaning no longer would need to be debated.

Part II

The Building of Society
1725–96

From the time of Tsar Aleksei Mikhailovich and continuing through the reign of his son Peter the Great, the institution of serfdom became firmly established as the social foundation of the Russian service state. In this institutional function, serfdom referred both to the binding of all groups in Russian society and to the arrangements that defined relations between landowners and peasants (whether state, church, crown, or seigniorial). For while specific arrangements showed considerable variation between regions, categories of peasants or landowners, and even individual landed estates, by the time of Peter's death the basic forms of service and obligation had taken shape. The specific forms continued to evolve, and some underwent dramatic change, right down to the final abolition of serfdom in 1861. But during the period from 1725 to 1796, and particularly during the reign of Catherine II, the crucial dynamic in Russian social development moved from the harnessing of resources to meet military and administrative needs to the formation of society as an entity beyond the locality and separate from the government. To that end, policymakers aimed: 1) to build institutions, including civic institutions that extended effective government by addressing the needs of local society; and 2) to educate personnel, including the personnel needed to manage the new institutions. Indeed, the major social innovation of the eighteenth century was the creation of society, or at least the idea of society, as an entity that through civic institutions linked diverse localities, communities, and groups to the central government.

In Western and Central Europe, individuals and social communities had long been part of a corporate constitutional order embodied in institutions of urban self-government, diets, *parlements*, provincial estates, Estates General, and the English Parliament. Linked to central governments and to comparable organizations across "society," Europe's corporate bodies represented the formal institutionalization of both social communities and broader constitutional mechanisms. Over time, in the course of concrete political struggles, the presence of constitutional mechanisms made it possible for diverse social communities to come together as an independent "society" capable of resisting the power of the government. Eighteenth-century Russia lacked a constitutional political tradition, and Russian social communities did not become institutionalized as corporate bodies. Before an independent society could emerge, corporate bodies with formal powers and time-honored linkages to other localities and to the government needed to be created and their relationships "constitutionally" defined. Throughout the age of serfdom, the absence of corporate bodies – bodies that existed beyond the household, family, and immediate community – distinguished Russia from the other great powers of Europe.

Chapter 4
From the Household to Society

In eighteenth-century Russia, as in the Muscovite past, the concept of social order emanated from the moral ideal of the household.[1] Independently of formal status, the household defined a person's immediate social relationships, based on hierarchies of gender, age, and birth. Individuals from all social groups – nobles, clergy, merchants, townspeople, free peasants, and serfs – understood that within the household, elders or superiors looked after the spiritual and material needs of their dependents, who in return remained obedient even in the face of abuse. The average Russian subject, during the course of his or her life, most likely filled the shoes of both authority figure and subordinate. In the context of different relationships, many individuals played both roles simultaneously. The wife of a peasant patriarch might lord it over her daughter-in-law at the same time that she suffered beatings and abuse at the hands of her husband. In all families, moreover, among lowly serfs and elite nobles, children grew up to become spouses, parents, and household heads. Beyond the household, in civic society and public life, similar dichotomies arose. A poor noble might enjoy absolute power over his handful of serfs, but find his ability to marry and the progress of his career dependent on the whims of a commander. Commanders too, in military and civil service, remained subject to superiors, and even the monarch answered to God.

Consistent with the requirements of social hierarchy, works of religious instruction taught all Russians that, in the household, obedience derived from love and punishment from magnanimity. The combination of love and magnanimity ensured that each person fulfilled his or her obligations not only to God and monarch, but also to other human beings. Religion also taught that the mutual obligations found in the household extended into society, where relations between parents and children were replicated time and again: in relations between teachers and students, commanders and subordinates, clergy and congregants, masters and slaves, husbands and wives, and even rich and poor.[2] The *Short Catechism for the Instruction of Young Children*, composed by future Metropolitan of Moscow Platon (Levshin) and first published in 1766, admonished readers to treat their fellow human beings with tenderness, courtesy, tolerance, generosity, and kindness; to feed the hungry and thirsty, clothe the naked, visit the sick and prisoners, welcome the stranger, and defend others from insult and injury. The catechism also encouraged spiritual acts of charity such as leading others away from sin, instructing the ignorant in God's law and in piety, giving good advice, patiently enduring and even forgiving the insults of others, and praying for the salvation of every individual soul.[3] In the private household and in public life, personal relationships ruled the day, and social order depended on the moral qualities of individuals. Everyone, whether superior or subordinate, needed to live up to his or her obligations.

To guide social relationships outside the household, government pronouncements regularly invoked patriarchal principles of obedience, duty, and mutual obligation. In Russian judicial reasoning, the common wisdom taught that a good commander brought blessings to his subordinates, who responded with loyalty and zealous service, whereas a bad commander brought arbitrariness and abuse, which led subordinates into disobedience and rebellion. Although the personal qualities needed to make the moral order of the household a social reality could never be universally or even broadly guaranteed, the government's desire to apply patriarchal principles to large-scale social and political arrangements persisted, sustained by utopian assumptions about the moral perfectibility of the individual human being. Lacking strong legal institutions, the Russian government had no choice but to rely on the personal authority of individual servicemen to achieve social order. At the same time, the reliance on personal authority, on the personal qualities of those who wielded power in a particular situation, encouraged arbitrariness and unpredictability. Precisely because individual servicemen could not be counted on to carry out their moral duties, formal institutional controls needed to be developed.

Through the definition of social categories, each associated with specific privileges and obligations, the Russian government sought not only to mobilize resources, but also to regulate social relationships. The basic categories of Russian society, rooted in the 1649 Law Code and agglomerated during the course of the Petrine reforms, did not change in the eighteenth century. Individuals, families, and entire communities continued to belong to one or another peasant category, to the townspeople or merchants, or to educated groups such as the clergy and nobility. Alongside these primary categories, the Russian government also created subgroups identified by distinctive occupational functions, service obligations, and legal privileges. Among the most significant and persistent of these subgroups, the category of the *raznochintsy* (literally "people of various ranks" or "people of diverse origins") appeared early in the eighteenth century and usually referred to outsiders or nonmembers of a given social category or community – for example, nonnobles or town residents who did not belong to the official urban community (the *posad*). In other usages, the *raznochintsy* constituted an umbrella category encompassing various proto-professionals and lesser servicemen: low-ranking civil servants and unranked administrative employees, retired soldiers, children of senior military officers born before a father's ennoblement, children of personal (non-hereditary) nobles, nonnoble students in state schools, technical specialists, scholars, artists, and performers. Throughout Russia's age of serfdom, resource mobilization, the growth of the military and bureaucracy, and the spread of education gave rise to new social groups that fell outside established social categories. The category of the *raznochintsy* allowed the government to regulate these groups and integrate them into the official structure of society.[4]

The history of the *raznochintsy* shows that Russian policymakers worked hard to reconcile legal definitions with concrete reality. But service requirements, the spread of education, and the play of economic necessity and "market forces" frequently hindered effective government control. Regardless of how the law defined the economic and occupational functions of specific social categories, people did what was necessary to survive, thrive, and develop. In conditions of local economic self-sufficiency, preindustrial technologies, and limited market integration, individuals at all levels of the social hierarchy improvised and adapted in response to immediate circumstances. Nonnobles exploited serf labor by concluding illicit deals with economically needy nobles. Peasants, lesser servicemen, and nobles alike violated prohibitions on their participation in urban trades. Even serfs, with the consent of their masters, sometimes managed to become successful entrepreneurs or accomplished actors, musicians, architects, sculptors, and painters. Time and again, material necessity and individual talent transcended the boundaries of official society.[5]

On occasion, the effort to construct and regulate a legally defined society produced more overt challenges to government authority. The educated service classes, a group that played a critical role in state building, eventually reached the numerical dimensions and degree of cultural sophistication that made the emergence of diverse outlooks and opinions inevitable. By the 1790s, intellectual dissent could be glimpsed among Russia's educated nobles and servicemen. Popular rebellion likewise revealed the limits to social harmony and administrative control. The Pugachev Rebellion of 1773–4 erupted in the Southern Urals region among Iaik Cossacks facing encroachments by the Russian government and the loss of traditional autonomy. The rebellion quickly spread to Urals factory workers suffering from the harsh conditions of early industrialism and to minority peoples – Bashkirs, Tatars, Votiaks, Chuvash, Mordvinians, and Kazakhs – feeling the pressure of Russian settlement and more intensive bureaucratic regulation. Toward the end of the rebellion, in the summer of 1774, Russian peasants, upset over increased obligations imposed by the government and serf owners, also joined the rebels.[6] By November 1774, the great Pugachev Rebellion had been effectively repressed. But it remained a reminder of how fragile good order could be in the face of concrete reality and the government's own social and political policies.

The Nobility

As had been the case since the reign of Peter I, the nobility remained the most privileged and tightly regulated group in eighteenth-century Russian society. In a telling characterization of the Russian nobility, the prerevolutionary historian and liberal politician Pavel N. Miliukov wrote that 'never and nowhere did the privileges of a noble estate rise so quickly, exist for so short a time, and crumble so completely as with us.'[7] The quick rise of the "noble estate" describes developments, or apparent developments, in the eighteenth century, when following the humiliations and obligations imposed by Peter I, Russian nobles benefited from steady improvements in their legal status, economic privileges, standard of living, and access to education and the rewards of service. Peter I agglomerated the noble ranks of Muscovy into a single hereditary noble "estate" and introduced new marks of noble distinction. The landed property of nobles became fully inheritable patrimony, and nobles did not have to pay the capitation. But Peter also subjected male nobles to harsh obligations that included the acquisition of education, usually obtained at home or through private instruction, and lifelong service, starting in the lower ranks alongside commoners. Peter aimed not to degrade noble status, but to ensure that the nobility provided Russia with a "qualified elite" capable of leading the army and bureaucracy in accordance with the common good.[8] Throughout the eighteenth century, nobles and policymakers assumed that men born into the nobility would dominate the officer corps and higher levels of government, based on both qualifications and preferential treatment in service appointments and promotions.

Preferential treatment for nobles, which remained largely informal in the reign of Peter I, became institutionalized following his death. In 1732 the Noble Cadet Corps opened its doors to literate sons of nobles, and from that time onward the Russian monarchy made a special effort to establish schools that gave nobles the education they needed to succeed in service. The Cadet Corps trained officers for the land forces, and its graduates entered military service as either non-commissioned or senior officers, avoiding the need to rise through the ranks.[9] Nor did less privileged nobles such as Andrei T. Bolotov (1738–1833), who began service as a common soldier, serve in the manner of peasant recruits. In his memoirs, Bolotov describes how in 1748, just a few months before his tenth birthday, he was enrolled as a soldier in his father's regiment. During Bolotov's first year of "service," his "commander" promoted him to corporal, subensign, and quartermaster sergeant. By 1750, thanks to the favor of a passing general, Bolotov held the noncommissioned rank of sergeant, and although he did not really begin active service until March 1755, already in 1760 he reached the rank of lieutenant (rank 12 in the Table of Ranks).[10] The nobility's obligation to serve surely represented an onerous burden, but it also brought rewards in the form of social recognition, promotion to higher rank, and sometimes also grants of landed property and serfs. From the 1760s, legislation clearly specified that nobles receive preference over nonnobles in both civil and military appointments.[11] Even at its harshest, the noble burden of service could not be compared to that of the common soldier conscripted from the peasants or townspeople. Nonnoble conscripts served for life until 1793, when the term of service was reduced to twenty-five years, a term already granted to nobles in 1736.

Even if the legislation regulating service had not explicitly favored nobles over nonnobles, the educational opportunities available to nobles would have given them a decided advantage in service appointments and promotions. As time passed, and as Russia's educated classes grew, technical qualifications came to play an ever greater role in defining the obligations and rewards of service. But because Russia's educated classes remained so small relative to the overall population, government-sponsored meritocracy continued to bolster rather than challenge noble privilege. Throughout the eighteenth century, the nobility remained the most reliable source of educated servicemen. By the 1760s, the availability of qualified servicemen and the attractiveness of both military and civil service made it possible to free the nobility from the obligation to serve. The 1762 emancipation of the nobility from compulsory service constituted the height of noble privilege. Although the emancipation manifesto assumed that nobles would continue to serve, and even insisted that they had a moral obligation to do so, for the first time in Russian history, noble status, including the right to own serfs, did not depend on service to the monarch. Nobles remained nobles and retained all noble privileges, regardless of whether or not they served. To serve became a choice freely made because of the advantages it brought to the individual noble. The freedom not to serve became a noble privilege that increased the already significant distance between the nobility and other social groups.[12]

Nobles generally welcomed the 1762 emancipation and saw in it official recognition of their dignity and status. Between 1762 and 1771, close to 48 percent of Russian military officers obtained full retirement.[13] But not all nobles could take advantage of their newly acquired freedom. Among servicemen who entered civil service after retiring from the military, also during the years 1762–71, close to 64 percent were nobles who owned no serfs.[14] In socioeconomic terms, the Russian nobility was a highly stratified class, and many nobles relied on service to supplement the meager income from their hereditary estates. Data from 1719–27 show that small landowners with fewer than 100 serfs (males) made up 91 percent of nobles, but owned only 41 percent of serfs. By contrast, the mere .8 percent of nobles who owned more than 500 serfs accounted for 26 percent of all serfs.[15] According to the 1762 poll-tax census (third revision), 51 percent of landowners (heads of households) owned fewer than 21 serfs, 31 percent owned 21–100, 15 percent owned 101–500, and 3 percent owned over 500.[16] Landless nobles depended entirely on service for their economic survival, and the preference they received in service appointments and promotions represented a crucial attribute distinguishing them from commoners. But because clergy, nonnoble civil servants, and other commoners from the *raznochintsy* also enjoyed exemption from the capitation, and might very well possess superior levels of education, in the case of poor nobles the concrete advantages of the 1762 emancipation appeared ambiguous. Only through service could these nobles hope to attain a measure of social recognition. Not surprisingly, then, historians characterize the 1762 emancipation as both the emancipation of the nobility from obligatory service and the emancipation of the state from any obligation to protect the interests of the nobility.[17]

The emancipation also yielded ambiguous results with respect to noble privileges. Nobles remained subject to corporal punishment, and the government retained the authority to confiscate noble estates. Guarantees of the noble's person and property came later, in the reforms of Catherine II. In charters to the nobility, towns, and state peasants (the last never promulgated), Catherine attempted to define and secure the "rights" of her subjects within the framework of the legally distinct and hierarchically arranged Petrine social categories.[18] For nobles, Catherine's provincial administrative reforms (1775 and 1778) and Charter to the Nobility (1785) established institutions and relationships that, according to some historians, consolidated the nobility's status as a "ruling class."[19] Even before the Catherinian legislation, powerful noble families used networks of patronage to influence access to office and the rewards of service. Catherine's reforms further enhanced the power of the "ruling class" in local administration. New civic institutions came into being, and newly created noble assemblies acquired the authority to elect some local officials and to determine whether or not individual nobles were eligible for membership and participation. The assemblies constituted both a corporate organ of the provincial nobility, responsible for managing local noble affairs, and an arm of the central bureaucracy, responsible for supporting educational and social institutions.

Historians have barely begun to investigate the activities of noble assemblies before the mid-nineteenth century. The assemblies seem mainly to have worked with government officials to police the behavior of local nobles. The limited research available suggests that in their deliberations, noble assemblies addressed a range of important social problems: inheritance and bequests, family disputes, trusteeship of estates belonging to widows and orphans, and sequestration of estates due to mismanagement or the abuse of serfs.[20] Like peasant communes, noble assemblies appear to have functioned as institutions of local self-government, with the addition of access to and supervision by provincial governors and powerful officials in St Petersburg. At no time did the assemblies possess legislative powers, and only in the 1850s, on the eve of the emancipation of the serfs, did they begin to acquire a political voice or behave as the corporate embodiment of noble class interests. Nor is there evidence that before the era of the Great Reforms, nobles viewed participation in local elective offices as anything other than a form of government service.

Other features of the Catherinian reforms carried more immediate appeal. The Charter to the Nobility exempted nobles from corporal punishment and granted them full property rights over their estates. Because the Charter recognized the nobility as a propertied class rather than a service class, it allowed landowners to develop the resources on their estates for any economic purpose. In addition, nobles could not be deprived of their privileges or property except as a consequence of formal judicial proceedings. To the extent that any Russian subject enjoyed legal security, the reforms of Catherine II went a long way toward ensuring legal security for nobles.

But this legal security should not be exaggerated or held up as evidence of a golden age of noble privilege and domination. Not until the liberal judicial reform of 1864 did Russian subjects receive guarantees against arbitrary search and arrest. Moreover, in contrast to nobles in England, France, the German states, and even the empire's own Baltic provinces, Russian nobles lacked proprietary claims to judicial and administrative authority outside the boundaries of their private estates. No Russian noble possessed a right to office, and the monarch could with the stroke of a pen mandate new obligations, restrict the powers of elected officials and judges, and change the relationship of noble assemblies to the government bureaucracy. However beneficial the terms of the Charter to the Nobility may have been, the charter should not be seen as a "bilateral contract" comparable to the English Magna Carta. The Catherinian charter, like all grants of "rights" and privileges in eighteenth-century Russia, was a "unilateral grant" that could be rescinded or altered at any time.[21]

Given the extent of economic differentiation within the Russian nobility, legal privileges comprised the most broad-based characteristics of the group. But nobles also enjoyed a host of economic privileges which set them apart from other social categories. In 1711 Russian nobles gained the right to trade as long as they were not in active service. In 1755 the government limited this privilege to the whole-sale marketing of goods produced on noble estates, but then restored it in 1807 by allowing nobles to register in merchant guilds. Laws of 1716 and 1765 also assigned to nobles the exclusive right to distill spirits, and a law of 1754 granted them a monopoly on the sale of liquor to government contractors.[22] By far the most significant economic privilege enjoyed by nobles was the right to exploit serf labor through the ownership of populated estates and individual serfs. Laws of 1730, 1743, and 1746 restricted the possession of serfs by nonnobles, and serf ownership became an exclusive noble right based on decrees of 1754, 1758, and 1760. By 1785 the Senate strictly and consistently interpreted all prohibitions against the possession of serfs by nonnobles. Even so, in practice, the noble right to own serfs never amounted to a monopoly on the use of serf labor. Throughout Russia's age of serfdom, through deception and illegal arrangements, and sometimes with active noble collusion, commoners continued to acquire serfs.[23]

The question of serf ownership suggests that despite definite improvements in the legal status of Russian nobles following the death of Peter I, the social meaning of nobility remained ambiguous. Historians offer two images of the eighteenth-century nobility: one describes a landed gentry, grounded in the agrarian economy and rural environment, and the other a rootless educated service class, disjoined from life in the countryside and oriented toward the career and cultural amenities of urban centers such as Moscow, St Petersburg, and Riga. Both images tell part of the story.[24] In Sergei Aksakov's 1856 novel *A Russian Gentleman*, the patriarch Bagrov is a traditional nobleman of ancient lineage and limited education.[25] Untouched by European culture and indifferent to material comfort, Bagrov rules his household as a tyrant, inspiring fear in all his dependents. The patriarch's authority over his serfs is similarly absolute, yet his lifestyle, clothing, and personal taste blend imperceptibly into peasant folkways. Close to the land and steeped in custom, Bagrov is a man virtually unchanged by the Petrine cultural revolution. His boorish habits stand in stark contrast to the refined manners and cultural sophistication of his daughter-in-law, Sophia (Wisdom). Sophia's family represents the post-Petrine service nobility, at home in European culture and urban sociability. Sophia's father owes his noble status to service and based on the possession of European education considers himself superior to Bagrov. In Sophia and her family, the reader sees a newer type of Russian noble, one who values foreign learning and material comfort over Russian customs and ancient lineage.

In reality, such a clear dichotomy between "old" and "new" nobles did not exist in eighteenth-century Russia. Already in Muscovy, "nobles" became stratified into ranks, and distinctions of wealth appeared no less pronounced than in later times. The policies of Peter I reinforced the nobility's obligations to the monarchy and established the possession of European culture as a mark of nobility and of elite status more generally. By century's end, Russia's educated service classes, noble and nonnoble, had absorbed European learning and made it their own. The difference between the Muscovite and Imperial Russian elites resulted directly from the cultural reforms of Peter I. But the result was less to divide nobles into "old" and "new" than to divide Russian society into, on the one hand, Europeanized educated elites, composed mainly of nobles but also of *raznochintsy* and wealthy merchants, and on the other hand, masses of peasants and townspeople, barely touched by European culture. Of course, not all nobles became suddenly Europeanized; like Bagrov, many remained unrefined, uneducated, and bound to Muscovite traditions. On the whole, however, eighteenth-century Russian nobles comprised an educated service class, engaged with the cosmopolitan Enlightenment culture of contemporary Europe. If not all nobles changed in the aftermath of the Petrine reforms, then those who failed to change lagged behind in access to social recognition and the rewards of service. Although the cruel, pretentious, and superficially Frenchified landowners of the late eighteenth-century Russian stage – the likes of Mrs Prostakova (Simpleton) in Denis Fonvizin's 1783 comedy *The Minor* – surely failed to understand the substantive meaning of Enlightenment ideas, their claim to have assimilated European culture could not have been more striking.[26]

A second division in eighteenth-century Russian society, one that affected but was not limited to the nobility, was the emergence of a class of civil servants who identified above all with the monarchy and state. The appearance of officials who took pride in standing above the interests of any social group began with the Petrine reforms, or even earlier in the Muscovite chancelleries, though not until the 1762 emancipation of the nobility did a permanent divide arise between landowning nobles and noble bureaucrats. Over time, particularly in the early nineteenth century, noble bureaucrats became increasingly professional and detached from serfdom, while landowning nobles became increasingly absorbed in rural life. The separation of the landowning nobility from the noble bureaucracy represented a long-term pattern of change that had only just begun in the late eighteenth century. Throughout the entire Imperial period, moreover, a core of elite noble families continued to combine lineage, landed wealth, European education, and high office.[27] No complete separation of landowning nobles and noble bureaucrats ever occurred. Even so, the 1762 emancipation did make possible the building of "gentry nests" in the Russian countryside. Freed from the obligation to serve, interested nobles with sufficient means could focus their time and energy on developing their estates.

The life of Andrei T. Bolotov, who left military service soon after the 1762 emancipation, illustrates the lingering blend of land ownership, service, and European culture. Often short of resources, and from 1774 returned to service as an administrator of crown villages, Bolotov nonetheless found in the family estate of Dvorianinovo the epicenter of his mature life. At the same time that Bolotov participated in the larger world of Enlightenment culture – in 1766 he became a member of the Free Economic Society – the landowner in him enjoyed being close to nature and took pride in contributing to the development of Russian agronomy. A noble of modest means, Bolotov embodied the multiple characteristics of the post-Petrine nobility: home schooling, military and civil service, estate management, the assimilation of European culture, and the production of Russian letters. Bolotov embraced all these activities with equal aplomb, yet he was neither alienated from agrarian society nor confined to its structures. His material life remained simple, though not uncomfortable; his spiritual life combined Russian Orthodoxy and European philosophy; and his intellectual life encompassed science, scholarship, and literature. There was in Bolotov no sense of old versus new; there was the old and the new seamlessly interwoven in diverse forms of Russian expression.[28]

Like landowners and masters across the globe, eighteenth-century Russian nobles did not for the most part live like their peasants or share the everyday concerns of peasant families. The economic condition of noble estates did, however, depend on peasant labor and methods of production. Continued reliance on grain production and on the three-field system of crop rotation meant that the estate economy of nobles for the most part mirrored the communal economy of peasants. Although beginning in the 1760s a few enlightened landowners introduced advanced systems of crop rotation, for the vast majority, estate management focused not on production, which the peasants controlled, but on administration.[29] Russian nobles collected dues from their serfs, induced them to work, and on occasion adjudicated their disputes and punished their transgressions. In times of hardship, nobles might be able to provide material or medical assistance. Nobles and peasants also regularly came together to observe the rites and festivals of the Russian Orthodox Church. Even so, nobles and peasants lived in separate cultural worlds. In this sense, eighteenth-century nobles did become "alienated" from agrarian society, though to contemporaries this alienation appeared "natural." Nor, aside from the limited and infrequent activities of noble assemblies, did eighteenth-century nobles participate in a local political life. Nobles manned local offices, but these offices were not linked to corporate bodies possessing time-honored "rights" and engaged in a politics of open contestation. Russian government remained highly centralized, and all legal-administrative mandates came from the top down. The government in St Petersburg created local institutions and offices that nobles then were called upon to bring to life. Russian nobles, regardless of ties to their estates and neighbors, remained servicemen beholden to the monarch.

Serfdom

Following the 1762 emancipation of the nobility from compulsory service, the traditional justification for serfdom disappeared: the need to provide support for nobles so that they could in turn serve the monarchy. No longer did the monarch need the services of all his nobles in order to operate the armed forces and bureaucracy. He did, however, continue to rely on nobles to govern the countryside, not just as government officials, but as serf masters. Although the eighteenth century represented a time of relative success in building institutions and mobilizing personnel, government administration, much less actual control, hardly reached beyond the district capital. Of course, troops could be called in when necessary, but in general, it fell to peasant communes and noble landowners to maintain order at the village level.

At the time of the 1762 emancipation, also the year of the third poll-tax census, the total male population of Russia numbered 8,507,901. Out of this total, the number of peasants reached 7,971,834 or 93.7 percent. Within the peasantry, the number of state peasants totaled 2,029,585 (25.46 percent), church peasants 1,026,930 (12.88 percent), and crown peasants 493,307 (6.19 percent). In 1762–4 the government secularized church lands, and church peasants, now called economic peasants, became a category of state peasants. Serfs remained the largest peasant category with 4,422,021 males or 55.47 percent of the peasant population.[30] Given that serfs were ruled directly by noble landowners, the very size of the serf population meant that serfdom functioned as a major institution of government and serf owners as major enforcers of legal-administrative authority.

As in the Muscovite and Petrine eras, the peasant commune provided the link between the village and the noble estate or government bureaucracy. The commune might correspond to a single village, or it might encompass multiple villages or parts of villages. Regardless of geographic boundaries, the commune, through its elected or appointed officials, was responsible for administering communal lands and determining household obligations to the landowner and government. Based on the principle of collective responsibility, the commune divided the burden of taxation, dues in money or kind (*obrok*), and labor services (*barshchina*) among member households. Depending on the financial burden carried by each household and on the number of husband–wife labor teams it contained, the commune also distributed allotments of arable land. Although each household farmed its own allotment, the commune regulated crop rotations, the annual cycles of planting and harvesting, and the use of common resources such as pastures, meadows, forests, ponds, and mills. Finally, the commune exercised undefined police and judicial powers over its members, organized the selection of military recruits from among young adult males, and provided economic assistance to destitute households, widows, orphans, the aged, and the disabled. In general, it was the responsibility of the household to remain economically viable; however, the commune had an interest in distributing burdens and resources so that the maximum number of households could do just that. To ensure viability, communes adopted a variety of "welfare" measures, including the exemption of only sons from military conscription, the provision of mutual aid, and the organization of cooperative labor. Focused above all on preserving member households, the commune tried "to establish distributive mechanisms which reduced risk in an uncertain environment and limited the numbers of those most vulnerable to crisis by providing more equal access to productive assets."[31]

Because of the commitment to household survival, almost any description of the Russian peasant commune appears consistent with the egalitarian images propagated by nineteenth-century socialist intellectuals. But life is never so simple. Although the individual peasant household might strive at all costs to preserve its socioeconomic integrity, the commune was not necessarily committed to the preservation of every household. Poor households could become a burden, and from the commune's point of view, it might be preferable to send the head of such a household off to the army. Broad generalizations about intracommunal relations are difficult to assess. One recent study of monastery villages in the 1720s suggests that communal assemblies garnered widespread participation and made decisions in an orderly and democratic manner.[32] But other historians, working on the late eighteenth and early nineteenth centuries, describe the commune in harsher terms.[33] Based on the records of seigniorial estates, these studies show that individual households competed for the favor of village oligarchs who cooperated with landowners to impose social control. In this scenario, the position of a given household depended on ties of kinship, patron–client relationships, or membership in a village faction. Corruption and hierarchy overshadowed egalitarianism and collectivism as defining features of peasant society.

Both "democratic" and oligarchic forms of intracommunal relations surely could be found among state, church, crown, and seigniorial peasants. Given the current state of empirical research, it is impossible to say which type of communal administration dominated at a given moment among a particular peasant category in a specific geographic region. Perhaps the truth lies somewhere in between these two poles or across a broad spectrum of possibilities. That a variety of conditions could coexist within near universal patterns remained a truism of Russian peasant life. In either situation, moreover, the goal of "providing more equal access to productive assets" could be preserved.[34]

Nor is it likely, given the size of the Russian empire and the fragmentary nature of the available documentation, that historians ever will complete a sufficient number of concrete microstudies to allow for definitive generalizations about peasant life. The study of monastery villages mentioned above is based on a mere forty communal decisions made in the years 1721–3 by peasants from the Joseph Volokolamsk Monastery.[35] The other studies mentioned are based on the records of no more than a handful of privately owned villages or noble estates composed of several villages. The best option for the historian is to describe the variety of possible patterns characteristic of peasant society. The basic principles of peasant social organization appear to have been broadly based; however, the effective impact of these principles depended on local conditions and on the personal qualities of peasant patriarchs, communal and estate officials, and landowners of all stripes.

As noted previously, inadequate legal institutions, and in the case of rural villages the well-nigh complete absence of a government presence, meant reliance on the personal behavior of the individuals who wielded power.

In addition to authority relationships, historians of eighteenth-century peasant Russia pay close attention to the role of environmental factors in determining patterns of social control and economic exploitation. Their most important insight is to show that while little changed in the methods of Russian agricultural production, agrarian society nonetheless developed empirically in response to concrete conditions and needs. Across the Russian empire, production expanded during the eighteenth century, but not because of an "agricultural revolution" or the adoption of more intensive methods of production. Peasants responded to population growth and landowners to rising prices and market opportunities by bringing additional lands under cultivation. Extensification substituted for intensification, the former made possible both by the availability of land in European Russia and by the spread of Russian settlement into Siberia and into the non-Russian steppes of the Mid-Volga, Southern Urals, and Lower Volga and Don regions.[36]

Even after the 1762 emancipation of the nobility from compulsory service brought landowners home to develop their estates, little changed with respect to agricultural production. Enlightened landowners who composed instructions regarding estate management – instructions issued by about twenty families have been identified for the period 1750–1830 – understood the economic condition of peasants in moral and administrative terms. Through the use of instructions modeled after government regulations, landowners sought to check the arbitrary behavior of communal officials and hired stewards and to establish an economic framework that, by freeing peasants from poverty, would allow virtue to reign.[37] These instructions do indeed reveal an interest in economic problems and a desire to increase estate revenues through greater peasant wellbeing. But landowners did little or nothing to improve methods of agricultural production or to determine which crops might be more profitable to grow. There is no evidence that in Russian estate management, landowners made any attempt to calculate the expenses associated with production. Basic cost accounting seems not to have entered their thinking. When landowners sold grain and other estate products, they viewed the price of the sale as an independent variable, indeed as a profit, unrelated to the cost of production.

Russian landowners, like Russian peasants, remained risk averse in their approach to farming. Rather than risk disruption by experimenting with more complicated systems of crop rotation, both landowners and peasants strove to maintain economic equilibrium by relying on production methods that had worked in the past. Nor did landowners see a reason to invest in agricultural improvements, even if they possessed sufficient money to do so. Most, moreover, did not have the resources that would have been needed to achieve fundamental structural change. Like farming systems across the globe, Russian agriculture remained vulnerable to climatic and environmental fluctuations. Such are the laws of nature, then and now. Even so, in eighteenth-century Russia, peasants and landowners generally got what they needed, or expected, out of the economic arrangements they knew. The irony is that while landowners lorded it over peasants, their own understanding of the estate economy derived from the peasants' way of organizing agriculture.[38]

Historians divide Russian agrarian society into economic regions based on the prevailing forms and relations of production. In the less fertile Central Non-Black Earth region, which in the nineteenth century became the commercial-industrial center of European Russia, serfs were more likely to pay landowners monetary dues and thus enjoyed greater freedom to participate in nonagricultural activities such as wage labor, trade, handicraft production, and manufacturing. In the Central Black Earth and Mid-Volga regions, where the soil was more fertile and farming more profitable, landowners tended to require labor services on the demesne in order to produce grain for sale. Peasants in these regions likewise relied primarily on agriculture to meet their own needs and consequently were less involved in the nonagricultural economy. But these general patterns were not universal. Decisions about whether to impose monetary dues or labor services depended on local conditions and access to markets: the quality of the land, the amount of trade turnover, and the location of a particular estate relative to ports. In the Northwest and Central Non-Black Earth regions, peasants on estates close to St Petersburg and Moscow, or with access to Baltic ports, frequently worked the landowner's demesne; closeness to markets made the production of grain for sale a profitable enterprise. Estates in the Central Black Earth region benefited from access to the Oka and Volga rivers, though in the more remote province of Voronezh, landowners preferred to collect monetary dues. Landowners who lacked adequate reserves of land also required their serfs to pay dues, and these peasants, like their counterparts in the Northwest and Central Non-Black Earth regions, were more heavily involved in nonagricultural pursuits. Over time, the number of peasants required both to pay dues and to perform labor services increased.[39] Detailed study of specific villages and estates suggests that the regional patterns may have been less significant than immediate decisions made because of practical needs and concrete opportunities.

Throughout the age of serfdom, Russia's agricultural economy appeared remarkably uniform in its emphasis on grain production. But uniformity in the main product grown masked the variety of foodstuffs produced for consumption and the wide range of nonagricultural activities found in peasant villages. Although economic data from the eighteenth century are highly unreliable, a study by economist B. F. J. Hermann, published in 1790, suggests that prior to the early nineteenth century historical images of a "grain monoculture" may be off the mark.[40] In 1788 cereals and cereal products, including vodka, accounted for only 14.5 percent of gross economic product and the net harvest before processing for only

7.4 percent. Estimates of per capita food consumption indicate that bread comprised only about 3.7 percent (based on value) of total consumption and cereal products as a whole about 19 percent. Historians and contemporary European observers agree that in the 1780s the average Russian enjoyed a plentiful and wholesome diet, consisting of vegetables, fruits, sweets, dairy products, and above all "flesh" – fish, beef, and mutton – about one-third (based on value) of total food consumption.

Alongside foodstuffs and clothing for household consumption, peasants also made a significant contribution to the production of nonagricultural goods. Still, no historian has been able to measure the macroeconomic significance of peasant trade, handicraft production, and manufacturing. Almost all that Russia produced in the eighteenth century – roughly 94 percent of gross economic product in 1788 – involved the direct provisioning of households. Only 6 percent of gross economic product "passed through the market place."[41] Peasants entered the realm of market relations in a variety of ways, including work as hired laborers. Serfs, for example, might hire themselves out to other serfs to perform labor services owed to the landowner. Serfs who worked the landowner's demesne directly might by default participate in commercial grain production for shipment to markets and consumers. Towns, the armed forces, grain deficit areas, state and noble distilleries, and exporters to foreign countries all needed supplies of grain.[42] Peasants also worked on a seasonal basis in handicraft production, manufacturing, trade, and transport. At the turn of the nineteenth century, in the Central Non-Black Earth province of Kostroma, peasants on the Lieven family's estate of Baki maintained self-sufficiency in grain production, but also worked as timber and horse traders, craftsmen, fishermen, and wage laborers. In addition, Baki peasants hosted a weekly fair where fish and baked goods could be purchased. An 1806 report compiled by an estate steward on the Sheremetev family's Central Black-Earth estate of Rastorg in Kursk province shows that serfs grew hemp to sell in raw form or as woven sackcloth. During the winter months, Rastorg serfs further supplemented their incomes by working in transport.[43] Clearly, by the end of the eighteenth century, the agricultural economy had begun to represent something more than a means to provide household subsistence.

Although most peasant traders engaged in petty commerce by traveling to local towns and bazaars, a handful became big-time merchants and manufacturers, able to abandon farming altogether. Until the emancipation of the serfs in 1861, these peasants occupied ambiguous legal terrain. Serfs possessed no property rights – whatever they "owned" legally belonged to the landowner – and the business operations of all peasant entrepreneurs required passports and permissions from landowners or government officials. Still, the most successful peasant entrepreneurs engaged in "protoindustrial" mass production for translocal markets. During the eighteenth century, peasant handicraft production and manufacturing for distant markets could be found in the Central Non-Black Earth and Central Black Earth regions. Already in the late seventeenth and early eighteenth centuries, peasants from Central Non-Black Earth villages in the Vladimir region produced and peddled icons for mass consumption. One of these, the monastery village of Mstera, the property of the Panin family from 1744, long remained a center of icon painting and also developed a linen-weaving industry that in the late eighteenth century employed over 400 peasants. By that time, Mstera was just one of 44 major industrial villages in Vladimir province.[44]

In the Central Non-Black Earth villages of Ivanovo (Vladimir province) and Pavlovo (Nizhnii Novgorod province), both the property of the Sheremetev family, capitalist manufacturing enterprises renowned for their use of serf labor developed. The metalworking industry of Pavlovo originated in the seventeenth century and by the late eighteenth and early nineteenth centuries "specialized in locks, knives and scissors, and surgical instruments." Already by 1700, the peasants of Pavlovo preserved few ties to agriculture.[45] In Ivanovo, linen weaving developed in the seventeenth century, followed by cotton and linen printing in the eighteenth. Statistics vary, but by 1789 Ivanovo contained about 188 printing workshops and 20 factories. Among the peasants of Ivanovo, independent printers thrived alongside large-scale manufacturers from families such as the Grachevs, Garelins, and Butrimovs. The large-scale peasant entrepreneurs "put out" cotton and linen weaving to domestic producers, but also operated factories where production took place on the premises. In 1789 the seven largest factories in Ivanovo employed 107 workers, all peasants who paid monetary dues to the landowner while working for serf employers.[46] The economic specialization and stratification found in protoindustrial villages such as Ivanovo and Pavlovo testify to the dynamic development that could be achieved within the parameters of Russian serfdom. Although in the late eighteenth century Russian policymakers and intellectuals began to question the moral basis for serfdom and to focus attention on the abuses it engendered, they proved unable or unwilling to move against an institution so full of economic life and so essential to policing the countryside.

Nor was late eighteenth-century Russia on the verge of an economic breakthrough that might have undermined the effectiveness of serf labor. The commercialization and mechanization of production that from the 1780s began to transform societies in Western Europe did not seriously affect Russia until after the 1861 emancipation of the serfs. Agricultural and industrial production increased steadily in eighteenth-century Russia, and peasants who paid monetary dues increasingly were drawn into capitalist market relations. Rural trade intensified in response to the formation of translocal markets and the growing demand for agricultural and manufactured products. Networks of urban markets and of local, regional, and national fairs kept traders on the move for much of the year.[47] But significant technological change did not occur, and by 1800 Russia reached an economic ceiling beyond which it could not advance "unless the structure of its organic economy were subsequently to be transformed."[48]

Russia's combination of economic growth and adherence to time-honored methods of production fits well the concept of an "industrious revolution" that preceded the mechanization of production known as the "industrial revolution." Historians of the industrious revolution point to changes in household patterns of resource distribution, time allocation, and consumption to explain the transformation of agricultural and industrial production that began in late eighteenth-century Europe. Prior to the intensification of production brought on by the industrial revolution, changes in household tastes and aspirations increased demand for marketed goods and labor. Instead of treating demand as a consequence of changes in production, historians of the industrious revolution see production as a consequence of changes in demand. Servicing and perhaps also generating the intensification of demand, Europe's cities became connected "in systems of commercial interaction" that established "a framework for regional economic development in which industrial growth could occur." Rather than being a product of industrialization, Europe's urban networks and consumer markets created the economic environment that helped to ignite and sustain a long-term process of industrial transformation.[49]

In late eighteenth-century Russia, despite the rapid growth of internal trade and the development of urban networks, the transformative effects of household consumption remained circumscribed.[50] Only the nobility and urban classes, less than 10 percent of the male population throughout the eighteenth century, became significant consumers of marketed goods. Peasants consumed also, and following an economic downturn in the reign of Peter I, their standard of living improved steadily for the remainder of the century, the result of a near five-fold increase in Russian national income between 1718/22 and 1788.[51] But peasants also produced much of what they consumed, and while statistical measures are hard to find, diversity in the exchange of goods and limited specialization continued to be characteristic of trade fairs throughout the eighteenth century. Developments in Mstera, Pavlovo, and Ivanovo showed that specialized production for distant markets did take root; however, the absence of a monopolistic guild system also meant that large numbers of peasant producers-consumers continued to manufacture decorative, household, and religious objects for personal and local use. Unrestricted handicraft production, local self-sufficiency, and a sustained need for agricultural labor kept peasants on the land and restricted the demand for marketed goods. Meager consumer demand, combined with geography and especially transportation costs, blocked economies of scale in production and distribution. Scarcity of capital – there were no private banks in eighteenth-century Russia – and high transportation costs created volatile market conditions which encouraged entrepreneurs, including merchants, to spread out economic risk by avoiding specialization.[52] The success and dominance of diversified small-scale production blurred the boundaries between the agrarian and manufacturing economies, between subsistence and commercial production, and between the peasants and townspeople. Peasant households met their subsistence and consumer needs in dynamic and inventive ways, but in ways that did not require qualitative economic change.

Towns and Townspeople

In 1762 European Russia's officially recognized town dwellers constituted only 2.8 percent of the registered population. Close to a century later, in 1858, the proportion of inhabitants registered in towns reached 7.3 percent.[53] Throughout the age of serfdom, Russia remained, by any measure, a country of peasants. Urbanization proceeded at a slow pace that barely affected the overall organization of society. Yet towns were dynamic places of economic, social, and cultural activity. Based on the Law Code of 1649, townspeople paid taxes and fulfilled service obligations to the government as members of an official urban community (*posad* or *posadskaia obshchina*). Registered townspeople enjoyed the right to engage in trade and manufacturing, to maintain shops, and in general to conduct business within the territory of the town. Townspeople also participated in institutions of local self-government and justice. Legislation from the reign of Peter I divided townspeople (called *posadskie* or *kuptsy*) into three guilds, defined according to wealth and occupation. In addition, Peter's government established craft organizations (*tsekhi*) to regulate artisans and incorporate them into the official urban community. In the reign of Catherine II, administrative reforms and the Charter to the Towns recognized important legal distinctions between merchants (*kuptsy*) and ordinary townspeople (now called *meshchane* or *posadskie*), suggesting that a more stratified urban population had emerged. Membership in the new merchant category depended not on heredity or territory-based citizenship, but on the possession of capital and the ability to pay an annual fee. Simply put, merchants bought the legal privileges that separated them from the mass of hereditary townspeople. The Catherinian legislation divided merchants into three guilds, again based on the amount of capital they possessed, and further secured their privileged status by exempting the members of all three guilds from the capitation and those of the first and second guilds from conscription and corporal punishment.[54]

The legal status of townspeople and merchants is important for understanding how they fit into the larger framework of Russian society. But as the case of peasants also shows, legal-administrative definitions did not necessarily correspond to socioeconomic realities. The capital cities of Moscow and St Petersburg were bustling centers of economic exchange and production; military, civil, and religious administration; and print and performance culture. At the same time, in towns across Russia, registered urban citizens enjoyed access to plots of city land, which they could buy, sell, rent, and swap. Families grew crops for their own use and for sale, and sometimes they gathered hay and wood in community fields and forests.[55] Some towns retained an agrarian or semi-agrarian character. Nor did towns necessarily arise because of economic activity; towns also could be designated for administrative purposes by policymakers and officials. The number of officially recognized towns fluctuated during the eighteenth century: 339 in 1708, 280 in 1719, 342 in 1727, 269 in 1738, and 337 in the 1760s. Catherine II's provincial reforms sought to impose greater administrative symmetry and as a result downgraded some established towns to villages and elevated mere settlements to district centers. In the period 1775–96, 271 rural settlements became towns, and the total number of towns reached 673.[56]

As might be expected given the amorphousness of Russian towns, registered townspeople and merchants at no time monopolized the urban economy. Townspeople made a living as merchants, shopkeepers, petty traders, hawkers of second-hand goods, artisans, transport and factory workers, casual laborers, and domestic servants. Some also farmed, cultivated gardens, raised livestock, and fished. The economic possibilities available to townspeople were numerous and diverse. Yet in any of these occupations, despite legal restrictions, peasants and *raznochintsy* also could be found. Clearly, the government failed to prevent people who did not belong to the townspeople and merchants from gaining access to the urban economy. During the eighteenth century, over 50 percent of the people living in towns fell outside the official urban classes.[57] Instructions to the Legislative Commission of 1767–8 revealed the broad range of social groups participating in urban trades, often with the permission of the government: nobles, state officials, ecclesiastical ranks and churchmen, military servicemen (retired and active) and their wives, single householders, coachmen, plowing soldiers (former musketeers and gunners), peasants, farriers, artisans who were not enrolled in craft organizations, ethnic and religious minorities, and townspeople from other cities. Among the economic activities pursued by these groups, the instructions mentioned trade and transport, including the ownership of ships; the manufacture of leather, soap, and tallow; and the ownership of retail stores, warehouses, storerooms, cellars, bakeries, offices, fishermen's cabins, inns, and eating houses.[58] The presence of so many urban entrepreneurs who did not belong to the official townspeople or merchants bears witness to the inventiveness of the Russian people and the dynamism of the preindustrial Russian economy.

The diversified and minimally specialized economies of eighteenth-century Russian towns complemented and reinforced peasant involvement in nonagricultural activities. Peasants and townspeople crossed economic, social, and geographic boundaries with relative ease, despite being bound to a place of residence and a

legally defined social category. Official society provided a framework for the development of socioeconomic relationships, but it could not contain those relationships.
Undifferentiated, dynamic, and porous, the structures of society and economy
allowed individuals to make a living in myriad ways. Still, survival and even success did not mean security. Prior to the mid-nineteenth century, it was difficult
to discern in Russia a solid middle class or commercial-industrial elite. Few of
the great merchant families of the seventeenth century preserved their status beyond
the reign of Peter I.[59] Although a core of successful business dynasties remained
active over several generations from the early eighteenth century into the twentieth,
for most Russian entrepreneurs the eighteenth century was a time of rapidly
rising and falling fortunes. Among first-guild merchants registered in Moscow
in 1748, only 26 of 382 families remained on the rolls at the end of the century;
of the 235 families registered in 1766–7, only 10 remained. Similarly, among the
merchants registered to trade through the port of St Petersburg in the years 1772
to 1804, only 10 of 289 families remained regular participants in foreign trade.
Of the 42 families active in 1804, only 20 appeared in earlier records.[60] Because
registration as a merchant depended on annual payments, and because the conditions in which Russians conducted business could be so volatile, the composition of the commercial elite changed continually.

The life of Fedor V. Karzhavin (1745–1812) illustrated what it meant to be a
prosperous first-guild merchant engaged in European trade. Educated in France
with practical training in medicine and architecture, Karzhavin moved easily between
a variety of occupations. Employed during his career in Europe, the Americas,
and Russia, Karzhavin worked as a translator, author, diplomat, teacher, private
schoolmaster, architect's assistant, pharmaceutical assistant, field surgeon, tobac-
conist, and purveyor of books, pictures, and curiosities. Despite elite merchant
origins, Karzhavin occupied an uncertain social status punctuated with economic
failures and repeated changes in employment.[61] The instability of Karzhavin's
career(s) helps to explain why observers in the reign of Catherine II connected
what they considered Russian economic backwardness to a lack of urban development. In their view, proof of limited urban development could be found in the
absence of a European-style "third estate" or middle sort of people. Whereas in
earlier decades the Russian government had focused attention on expanding the
ranks of educated servicemen, officials now also recognized the need to encourage the development of a middle estate. Catherine and her advisors associated
the middle estate with sound morals, industriousness, and hard work, and they
included in the category individuals involved in the arts, sciences, navigation, trade,
and crafts. Graduates of church and state schools, children of low-ranking civil
servants, and children of unranked administrative employees also belonged to the
middle estate.[62] Although by the time of Catherine's reign educated nonnobles
had achieved a significant presence in towns and cultural institutions across the land,

Russia still lacked established free professions comparable to those in Western and Central Europe. Russia's proto-professionals or semi-professionals almost always belonged to the hierarchy of service classes employed by the government. Nor did Russia's merchants and manufacturers coalesce into a politically organized class or become consumers of a distinctive middle class culture.

Economic insecurity surely weakened Russia's urban elite, but this did not mean that men of merchant rank were completely absent from public life. In the seventeenth century and continuing into the reign of Peter I, trading men served as advisors to the monarch. In the period following Peter's death, merchants participated in various commissions, including the Legislative Commission of 1767–8, where they were given the opportunity to discuss their needs and consult with the government about policies affecting their interests. Eighteenth-century businessmen also served in elected city offices and on the exchange committee of St Petersburg, established in 1703. Finally, there is much evidence that prosperous merchants enthusiastically supported the development of social and cultural institutions. The St Petersburg Mercantile Society, founded in 1784, offered merchants an arena for sharing economic information and a site for friendly sociability. By 1786 the Moscow Merchant Club hosted balls, literary evenings, and card games, where wealthy families socialized and conversed. Nor were Russia's civic-minded merchants found only in the capitals. At the end of the eighteenth century, wealthy merchants in Tula and Moscow participated in educational, cultural, philanthropic, and social activities. Literary theater, popular among the urban classes, also developed in provincial towns. The founding of the Russian Imperial Theater in 1756 was in part the work of Iaroslavl merchant Fedor G. Volkov (1728–63), whose troupe was summoned to give performances in St Petersburg beginning in 1752.[63] A few decades later, on Russia's Arctic Circle, Arkhangel'sk merchant Vasilii V. Krestinin (1720–95) became a corresponding member of the Academy of Sciences and in 1792 published *A Short History of the City of Arkhangel'sk*, a work suffused with Enlightenment ideas about public engagement, civic duty, and social responsibility.[64] Throughout the eighteenth century, merchants became involved in the social and cultural life of Russia's towns, and on occasion even in a national political discourse. Merchants did not, however, constitute a translocal politically organized or even institutionally linked socioeconomic class. In the sea of peasants that was Russian society, townspeople and merchants, like government officials, represented just another drop in the ocean.

Civic Life and the Formation of Society

Throughout the eighteenth century, the vast majority of Russians remained socially and economically atomized in households, local communities, and networks of patronage or family relationships. Social experience remained small-scale, despite the growth of translocal institutions and market integration. In the imperial bureaucracy and armed forces, nobles and nonnobles served together. In the marketplaces of towns and commercial fairs, merchants and petty traders effectively breached the barriers intrinsic to serfdom. Legal prescriptions and definitions integrated diverse populations into an all-encompassing framework, and virtually every Russian identified with the Orthodox Church, defined less as an institution than a community of believers. The sources of shared social experience were indeed significant, yet there were no social institutions that linked the people of a given socioeconomic class horizontally or those of a given geographic region vertically. The links that bound people tended to be legal-administrative, determined by the government; personal, based on kinship or patronage; or universal and hence also abstract, based on Christian belief.

From the mid-eighteenth century, and particularly in the reigns of Elizabeth and Catherine II, Russians took some tentative steps away from the highly individualized organization of social relationships. In a range of cultural and institutional settings, they began both to imagine themselves and to behave as members of a larger social collective.[65] Within the framework of the noble assemblies and boards of public welfare established by the administrative reforms of the 1770s–80s, nobles began to participate in civic organizations and institutions devoted to culture, education, and philanthropy. There were as yet no formal links between the noble assemblies of different provinces, but within each province a noble "society" could be glimpsed. In the towns of Russia, in the performing arts, and in the growing print culture associated with literature, science, and scholarship, an even broader public or society emerged, one that reached beyond the nobility to include merchants, clergy, and *raznochintsy*. Nobles remained the primary producers and consumers of the printed word, especially the bourgeoning Russian literature of the mid to late eighteenth century. But in painting, architecture, and the performing arts, both producers and consumers came from a variety of social backgrounds, including foreigners and serfs.

Unlike the many noble servicemen who wrote poetry and plays, merchants rarely produced literature or art. Vasilii V. Krestinin represented a notable exception. Yet merchants too were eager to be part of *le grand monde* – to participate in the sociability and cultural activities of local elites, to dress fashionably, to maintain elegant homes, and to provide formal education for their children. Merchant involvement in high culture and civic life sometimes became excessive, leading to debt and economic ruin.[66] Nobles also could get in over their heads when they tried to live as modern Europeans.[67] The socioeconomic foundations of *le grand monde* were far from stable, yet regardless of social origins and practical means, educated Russians aspired to be part of the open sociability and Enlightenment culture of contemporary Europe. They embraced the cosmopolitanism of Enlightenment thought, the modern science that Enlightenment thinkers sought to popularize, and the latest cultural models emanating from Europe. Their joy at being counted among the civilized peoples of the world revealed a genuine openness to cultural change through learning.

Love of learning could not, however, change the fact that the purveyors of Russian enlightenment and cultural refinement comprised a miniscule group in a large and populous country. Historian Boris Mironov estimates that in European Russia overall literacy among inhabitants over the age of nine reached a mere 6.9 percent in 1797. Among the urban population, literacy rates were significantly higher: 21 percent, including 28.6 percent among males and 12 percent among females.[68] In France, already in 1686–90, literacy rates roughly matched the rates found in urban Russia at the end of the eighteenth century: 29 percent for adult men and 14 percent for adult women. A century later, in 1786–90, French men had achieved a literacy rate of 48 percent and women of 27 percent. Literacy rates in England were even higher: 60 percent among adult men and 35–40 percent among adult women in the mid-eighteenth century.[69] Clearly, late eighteenth-century Russia did not possess a sufficient number of readers, estimated at several thousand in the 1760s and 1770s, or a sufficiently commercialized market for cultural goods to sustain either an autonomous public or independent classes of writers, artists, and performers.[70] Russia's reading public and consumers of high culture remained more or less equivalent to the educated service classes, dominated by the nobility and dependent on the government.

But noble domination of cultural institutions did not mean that Russian literary culture was specifically noble. Eighteenth-century publishers promoted both the broad-based religious teachings of Eastern Orthodox Christianity and the more elite secular learning of modern European science and philosophy. Whether refined or raucous, urban sociability in the form of assemblies, clubs, and public theater attracted and engaged persons of diverse social origins. The educated commoners who enjoyed Russia's cultural fruits did not necessarily seek to enter an exclusive noble world. To the contrary, they partook of a shared Russian contribution to a cosmopolitan pan-European culture. In theater, literature, scholarship, and journalism, educated Russians participated in a conversation about moral principles, good government, and social organization. Despite institutional fragmentation and social atomization, they became part of a larger public or society, constructed around the discussion of ideas and the representation of social and political relationships. Grounded in artistic creation and the printed word, the "society" of eighteenth-century Russia played no formal institutional or political role, and it did not yet constitute a vigorous consumer market. But identification with society brought growing numbers of Russians – primarily noble, educated, and/or urban – out of familism, localism, and parochialism.[71] By the start of the nineteenth century, those Russians who produced and consumed print culture, bought tickets

to public theaters, and supported institutions of sociability and public welfare provided the basis for a new social group: a "civil society of the educated" composed
of educated Russians who were "neither agents of the government (*pravitel'stvo*)
nor, in the traditional sense, its subjects (*narod*)."[72] In the main capitals and provincial towns of late eighteenth-century Russia, a new form of society began to emerge
– a society in which civic relationships and Russian culture, rather than serfdom
and service, represented the characteristic qualities.

Chapter 5
From Service State to Government by Moral Means

Over roughly thirty years the personality and policies of Tsar Peter I bore down on the people of Russia like a force of nature. When the emperor died in January 1725, he left an enormous vacuum at the apex of the Russian political order. For decades to come, Peter's successors found it hard to fill his shoes. High drama unfolded around the political struggles that dominated life at court. Intrigue, disgrace, exile, imprisonment, and even death threatened legitimate monarchs and the favorites who sought power through closeness to the throne. Among courtiers and elite nobles, personal insecurity spread, as landed property and service rank became political tools used by rulers to consolidate support and punish opposition. On more than one occasion political crisis threatened to undermine the personal absolutism forged so skillfully by the tsar reformer. It is indicative of Peter's success, and of Russia's readiness for the transformation he commanded, that chronic political instability did not change the basic direction of government policy. Peter's successors, regardless of which political grouping brought them to the throne, embraced his vision of European progress and modernity. When subsequent monarchs modified Petrine policies, they sought not to alter the course of development, but to address concrete problems and perhaps also to ease the burdens placed on the Russian people. Throughout the eighteenth century, Russia's military forces, government institutions, and educated classes continued to evolve along the lines mapped out by Peter. Within a political framework characterized by absolute monarchy, subordination of the nobility and church, limited administrative control, and imperial rather than national monarchy, Russia emerged from relative obscurity to become one of the great powers of the modern world.

─────────────────   The Advance of Empire   ─────────────────

By the end of the eighteenth century, Russia's educated service classes shared the sense of living in a country on the move. From the perspective of the governing elite, theirs was a time of stunning progress – if not for the many, then at least for the few – and this progress was nowhere more evident than in the combined successes of foreign policy and imperial expansion. Russia's initial march to great-power status grew out of the need to secure frontiers against dangerous and frequently predatory enemies. In the south and southeast, the nomadic societies of the steppe long had threatened Russian towns and settlements. The goal of defending against and eventually subjugating the steppe peoples occupied the monarchy from the sixteenth into the mid-nineteenth century. In the Caucasus, southwest, and west, Russia pursued a more aggressive expansionist strategy already in the reign of Peter I. The Great Northern War against Sweden established Russian power in the Baltic, and the Persian campaign of 1722 revealed offensive intentions in Transcaucasia. Based on a peace treaty of 1723, Russia acquired the southwestern and southern shores of the Caspian Sea, including the cities of Baku and Derbent. But the Caspian territories could not be pacified, and in treaties of 1732 and 1735 Russia returned them to Persia. The empire's southward advance seemed to be checked, yet Russian intentions had not changed. Although expansion into the Caucasus did not seriously get under way until the early nineteenth century, the absorption of eastern Georgia began in 1783, when the Kingdom of Kartli Kakheti came under Russian protection. Russian troops left Georgia in 1791, and the resurgence of Persia led to a period of uncertainty about the kingdom's status. That ended in 1800–1, when Russia removed the Bagratid dynasty and formally annexed Georgia.[1]

Russian forward movement in Transcaucasia, Crimea, and Ukraine invariably came up against the interests and power of the Ottoman Empire, arguably the most troublesome of Russia's enemies. Wars against the Ottomans took place in 1695, 1696, 1711, 1736–9, 1768–74, and 1787–91. Peter I's conquest of Azov proved illusory, and not until the war of 1735–9 did Russia reoccupy the port. At that time, Russia also gained access to the Black Sea, though on the condition that her Black Sea trade be conducted in Turkish ships. While not insignificant, these early successes seem marginal when compared to the achievements of Catherine II's Russo-Turkish wars. Under Catherine (ruled 1762–96), the Zaporozhian Cossack region, Crimea, the Kuban steppe, the Taman peninsula, and Kabarda in the Caucasus all became part of the Russian empire. In the Caucasus, the boundary of the Russian empire reached the Kuban, and perhaps more important, Russia gained the right of free navigation in the Black Sea and straits. Following Catherine's Turkish wars, one last attempt by the Swedes to reassert power in the Baltic (war of 1788–90), and the partitions of the Polish-Lithuanian Commonwealth (1772, 1793, and 1795), Russia controlled an impressive swathe of territory stretching from the Baltic to the Black Sea and maintained a visible naval presence in both regions. Peter I's territorial gains against Sweden, combined with Catherine II's gains against the Ottoman Empire and the Polish-Lithuanian Commonwealth, gave to Russia unprecedented status in world affairs. Never before had Russian borders reached so far, and never before had Russian power in Europe and Asia appeared so impregnable.

In the process of pursuing territorial expansion against traditional enemies, Russia also became one of the largest multiethnic empires in the modern world. Following the disintegration of the Golden Horde in the 1430s and 1440s, successor states and tribal confederations vied for domination on the Eurasian steppe. From the mid-sixteenth century, Muscovy actively joined the struggle for the Mongol legacy. Between 1552 and 1580, the Khanates of Kazan, Astrakhan, and Siberia fell to the military forces of Tsar Ivan IV, and while the Khanate of Crimea remained independent under the protection of the Ottoman Empire, it too became part of Russia in 1783. The conquests of Ivan brought a large Muslim Tatar population into Muscovy and opened the Volga region to Russian settlement. In the early seventeenth century, the Muscovites crossed Siberia from the Ural Mountains to the Pacific. During these early phases of territorial expansion, Russia also came into contact with a succession of nomadic peoples who occupied the steppe in the centuries after the breakup of the Golden Horde. Pressing upon each other and upon the settled agricultural societies of Qing China, Persia, the Ottoman Empire, and Russia, the nomads belonged to tribal groups organized into loose political confederations headed by hereditary or elected khans claiming lineage from the Chinggisid dynasty. For the most part Muslim, the nomads moved across a range of seasonal pasturelands, living off their herds and off the booty seized in destructive military raids.

The steppe region of the former Russian empire is divided today between the countries of Moldova, Ukraine, Russia, and Kazakhstan. In the days of the empire, the geographical boundaries of the steppe ran from the Danube River in the west to Lake Balkhash in the east. The forest zone of European Russia defined the region's northern edge, and the foothills of the North Caucasus and the northern shores of the Black and Caspian Seas its southern perimeter. For centuries, the frontiers that separated the steppe peoples from surrounding sedentary societies remained dangerous and porous. As nomads moved closer to areas of Russian settlement, and as Russian settlers and troops began to spread out and contest the nomads' freedom of movement, the Russians had no choice but to deal with each of the steppe peoples in turn. Following the conquests of Kazan (1552) and Astrakhan (1554), efforts to subjugate the Nogay Tatars and Bashkirs defined Russia's relations with the steppe. In the 1630s, the Kalmyks moved into the region, and in the eighteenth century, the Kazakhs became the dominant group in Russian–steppe relations. Russia did not effectively subdue the peoples of the steppe before the early nineteenth century, and only in the 1860s did the Kazakhs become fully integrated into the empire.[2]

The absorption of the steppe into the Russian empire was a complicated and protracted process. Steppe peoples readily fragmented into separate political entities and departed to new geographical locations. Nor did those who submitted to Russian authority necessarily respect Russian sovereignty. In one set of circumstances the nomads might join together or with the Ottomans and Crimeans against Russia, and in another they might join with Russia against each other. Shifting alliances and internal struggles make it difficult for historians to disentangle the threads of steppe politics. The important point is that in the seventeenth and eighteenth centuries the nomadic peoples of the steppe and Crimea continued to threaten the settled territories of Russia proper. Wherever Russian settlement abutted tribal pasturelands, Russian towns and villages suffered destructive raids at the hands of nomadic horsemen. Long after Russian muskets and cannon made it impossible for the steppe peoples to conquer and occupy Russian territory, the nomads still could wreak havoc by razing towns and villages to the ground and by carrying away booty and captives. Well into the eighteenth century, nomads captured thousands of Russian men, women, and children to be redeemed for ransom or sold into slavery in Constantinople and Central Asia.

Russia faced the threat from the steppe in flexible and pragmatic ways, always assuming, however, that the "backward" nomads eventually would become settled agriculturalists and subjects of the tsar. In almost every case, Russian officials and commanders envisioned a relationship in which cooperation and submission to the Russian monarch would open the door to administrative and military integration, to be followed after many years by assimilation into the "superior" Russian way of life, both agricultural and Christian. The process began with an oath of allegiance taken by nobles or a friendly khan, after which the Russian authorities tried to ensure that future khans also favored cooperation with Russia. Political conflict within the steppe societies and lavish gift giving by the Russians, backed also by occasional troop movements, usually brought success, though the Russians might be forced to retreat or compromise along the way. Problems repeatedly arose because allied khans proved unable or unwilling to control their subjects. After the signing of many a treaty and the taking of many an oath, raids and resistance to Russian encroachments continued, leading eventually to military pacification. The effective imposition of military control usually followed the spread of fortification lines, which the Russians started to build in the late sixteenth century. The extension or completion of a defensive line allowed additional territories to be claimed, secured by troops, and opened to Russian settlement. But here too, even after the Russians achieved military dominance over an area of the steppe, losses of control were likely to continue. Not surprisingly, policy toward the nomads remained variable and gradualist. Settlement, trade, and conversion to Christianity always were encouraged, though for the most part not forced. Consistent with steppe tradition, Russian officials governed through native elites and allowed subject societies to preserve their own legal and cultural institutions. Only after decades of Russian rule and local resistance could these institutions be linked through courts and administrative offices to the central government in St Petersburg.

Russian expansion into the steppe, at least before the nineteenth century, has long been described as an "organic" process of colonization, spearheaded by the government for geopolitical rather than economic reasons. Changeable relations between Russia and the steppe peoples, even after oaths of allegiance were supposedly taken, supports the view of early colonization (ca. 1500–1800) as a "defensive" effort "to secure and stabilize the empire's southern borderlands."[3] It is worth noting, moreover, that Russia's interactions with the steppe societies hinged also on the nomads' relations with China, Persia, and the Ottoman Empire. All the great empires used the steppe peoples against enemies, while also seeking to protect their own populations from nomadic incursions. Defensive strategies surely informed Russian policy; like China's great wall, Russia's lines of settlement and military fortification represented a response to the nomads' destructive freedom of movement. But in the Russian case, the promise of economic gain and feelings of superiority based on Christianity and European culture also encouraged more modern forms of imperialist aggression. Already in the earliest stages of Russian expansion, lands belonging to native peoples were seized, and both the lands and their peoples forcibly incorporated into the Russian empire, all in the name of Russia's civilizing mission. Historian John P. LeDonne describes Russia as a Eurasian state in search of hegemony from the Elbe River to eastern Siberia.[4] No less than defense of an unstable frontier, Russian policy toward the steppe aimed to command resources, human and material, and to impose political sovereignty over foreign peoples.

A closer look at Russia's relations with the Bashkirs and Kalmyks illustrates the dynamic interplay between defensive and imperialist colonization. After the conquest of Kazan, Muscovy came into contact with the Bashkirs, a Turkic-speaking Muslim people living in the southern Ural Mountains between the Kama and Iaik (Ural) Rivers.[5] Some Bashkirs lived as hunters, fisherman, beekeepers, and even farmers, but most remained nomadic or semi-nomadic. Although the Muscovites established the fortress of Ufa on Bashkir lands as early as 1586, only in the late seventeenth century did the government begin systematically to impose tax and service obligations. Growing numbers of Russians and minority peoples (Tatars, Mordvinians, Chuvash, and Cheremis) also occupied and farmed Bashkir lands. The Bashkirs responded to these encroachments with armed rebellions in

1662–4, 1676–82, and 1705–10. Real military subjugation at the hands of the Russians followed in the 1730s. In 1730–1 the Kama fortification line separated the Bashkirs from Kazan, and in 1736 the building of Orenburg marked the completion of another defensive line spreading out from Samara on the Volga River. The new line blocked Bashkir access to the southern steppe, with the result that armed rebellion again erupted in 1735–40. This led in turn to brutal suppression but still not to final pacification. The Bashkirs revolted once more in 1750, and they were among the earliest supporters of the Pugachev rebellion in 1773–4. Not until 1798, after more than a century of intermittent bloodletting, were the Bashkirs at last organized into irregular military units similar to Cossack hosts and subject to Russian authority.[6]

Russian policy toward the Kalmyks followed a similar pattern of cooperation, confinement, and eventual subjugation.[7] Tibetan Buddhists from western Mongolia, the Kalmyks moved into the Caspian steppe in the early seventeenth century because of pressure from tribes in eastern Mongolia and from the Muslim Kazakhs. Once the Muscovites understood that the Kalmyks could not be pushed back to the east, they tried to enlist the nomads' help against the Khanate of Crimea. An alliance took shape, and in 1655 the Kalmyk tayishis (nobles belonging to the ruling dynasty) swore allegiance to the Muscovite tsar. In return, the Russians promised to stop Bashkir raids and to allow the Kalmyks unrestricted access to pasturelands along the Volga and Akhtuba Rivers. The agreement held out some hope for stability, but also allowed for divergent interpretations. In 1657, after receiving payments from Crimea, the Kalmyks attacked the Russian provinces of Kazan and Ufa. The Crimean khan even declared that the Kalmyks had become his subjects. In subsequent years, the Kalmyks again cooperated with Russia against Crimea, though efforts to transform the nomads into an irregular military force remained ineffective. In the 1680s, Kalmyk horsemen once more decimated Kazan and Ufa provinces. Finally, based on a treaty of 1697, cooperation revived. The Russians for a second time agreed not to restrict the boundaries of Kalmyk pasturelands and promised to stop Bashkir and Cossack raids.

At the beginning of the eighteenth century, the Russians and Kalmyks seemed to have reached an uneasy accommodation. The Volga River marked the eastern boundary of Kalmyk movement, not because of Russian defenses, but because the territory east of the river remained vulnerable to Kazakh attacks. Cossack communities along the Don River formed the western boundary, and in the south the Nogay Tatars dominated the steppe of the North Caucasus. But then in 1718, Russia completed the Tsaritsyn fortification line connecting the Volga and Don Rivers, and Russian troops began to prevent the Kalmyks from moving north into their summer pastures. The Kalmyks had become encircled, and by 1724 the Russians were able to influence the selection of the new Kalmyk khan. Russian political interference again intensified after completion of the Mozdok line along the Terek River further restricted Kalmyk migration to the south. Hemmed in with no place to go and increasingly vulnerable to Russian intrusions, 30,000 Kalmyk households (more than 150,000 people) left the Caspian steppe for Jungaria in January 1771. Only about a third of the migrants reached China, the rest falling victim to winter snows, thirst, and Kazakh depredations. Those who survived the journey eventually became incorporated into the military system of the Qing dynasty, and those who remained on the Volga immediately became subjects of the Russian monarchy. In 1771 the Kalmyk khanate ceased to exist, and the 11,000 households remaining in Russia were placed under the authority of officials in Orenburg. In subsequent decades, Russian settlement in the south accelerated, and in 1825 full administrative integration was achieved, marked by the transfer of responsibility for relations with the Kalmyks from the Ministry of Foreign Affairs to the Ministry of Internal Affairs.

During the centuries of expansion into the steppe, Russian policymakers and intellectuals always assumed that subjugation of the nomads brought the benefits of civilization to wild and barbarous peoples. At the same time, however, the Russian government's concrete actions revealed a pragmatic, tentative, and even defensive approach to empire building. The same can be said of relations with the Ottoman Empire and with the Ottomans' vassals, the Crimean Tatars. A strong state and formidable military foe, the Crimean Khanate of the sixteenth and seventeenth centuries repeatedly laid waste to Muscovite and Polish-Lithuanian lands. During the *de facto* regency of Sophia (1682–9), Prince V. V. Golitsyn twice led military campaigns designed to overpower the Crimean Tatars and end their incursions into Russia. Although militarily unsuccessful, Golitsyn's campaigns marked the onset of offensive Russian expansion against the Khanate of Crimea.

The offensive posture continued in the reign of Peter I, who hoped to replicate his successes in the Baltic region by also establishing a Russian foothold on the Black Sea. Peter achieved only limited results against the Ottomans, but Russian policy did not change in the decades following his death. During the Russo-Turkish War of 1735–9, Russia at last defeated the Tatars and briefly occupied part of the Crimean peninsula, including the capital Bakhchisarai. Permanent gains came only in the Russo-Turkish War of 1768–74, when Russian troops drove the Ottomans from the northern shore of the Black Sea and established a protectorate over Crimea. Although technically the Khanate became free and independent, in practice Russia appointed Crimean khans and directed their policies. In 1783, following a rebellion by Tatar nobles, the Russian government removed the last autonomous khan and placed the Khanate under the authority of a Russian governor. These successes proved lasting, yet Russian treatment of the Tatars remained pragmatic and gradualist. The government recognized the landed property and privileges of Tatar nobles, the free status of Tatar peasants, and the religious authority and economic resources of Muslim leaders. Such tolerance notwithstanding, many Crimean Tatars emigrated to the Ottoman Empire. The emigration continued for decades, accompanied by Slavic colonization and the settlement of foreign colonists in Crimea. Deprived of lands and driven from towns, the Tatars constituted a minority of the peninsula's population by the mid-nineteenth century.[8] Although tolerated in their homeland, at least until the deportations of World War II, the Crimean Tatars could not be allowed to thwart Russian power. The strategic importance of Crimea was far too great for the territory and its people to escape full military and administrative incorporation into Russia.

Equally important for the consolidation of Russia's position on the Black Sea were the territories of present-day Ukraine.[9] Ukraine lay at the center of the medieval "Russian" state, Kievan Rus, the legacy of which can be claimed equally by Russians, Ukrainians, and Belarusians. Ukraine's incorporation into the Russian empire began in 1654, when the Zaporozhian Cossacks exchanged Polish for Russian protection. This led to the Thirteen Years' War between Russia and Poland, brought to a close by the Truce of Andrusovo (1667), which recognized Russian control over Left-Bank (eastern) Ukraine, Kiev, and Smolensk. Andrusovo effectively partitioned Ukraine, divided the Cossacks, and unleashed a period of foreign intervention and Ukrainian civil war that continued until 1686. By end of the seventeenth century, the Cossacks had splintered into three groups: the Hetmanate of Left-Bank Ukraine fell under tenuous Muscovite control, the Polish-Lithuanian Commonwealth retained authority in Right-Bank Ukraine, and the Zaporozhian Sich on the lower Dnieper preserved its autonomy, sometimes allying with Crimea and the Ottoman Empire, though theoretically under combined Russian and Polish protection.

The establishment of Russian authority in the Hetmanate proceeded with modest speed during the eighteenth century. The Left-Bank elite consisted of landed nobles (*szlachta*) and Cossack officers who until the 1760s governed through separate administrative, fiscal, and judicial institutions. Nobles enjoyed the right to own landed estates, demand labor from peasants, serve in civil and military posts, and participate in councils that advised the hetman, the chief administrative and military leader elected for life.[10] Despite these privileges, Ukrainian nobles were not equated with their Russian counterparts: the officials and military officers of the Hetmanate did not come under the Table of Ranks, and the Russian government did not recognize all noble claimants as *szlachta*. Ordinary Cossacks likewise experienced downward mobility under Russian rule. Although Cossacks participated in local self-government, served in the army, remained exempt from taxes, and possessed the right to own land, distill liquor, and trade specified commodities, they eventually suffered economic decline, lost the right to elect their officers, and ceased to sit in official councils.

In Ukraine, as in the steppe, the Russian government sought to foster cooperation with local elites while maintaining an effective military presence. Military control could not, however, be negotiated. Following Hetman Ivan Mazepa's betrayal of Peter I in the war against Sweden, interference in Cossack affairs intensified, though on the whole, Russian policy remained gradualist. Local officials continued in their posts, and although successive monarchs forbade the election of a hetman, the office did not permanently disappear. In 1722–7 the Little Russian College, established by Peter I and attached to the Senate, governed the Hetmanate, but then in 1727 the office of hetman was revived. Beginning in 1734, a collegial board composed of Ukrainians and Russians ruled the Hetmanate. In 1747 Empress Elizabeth (ruled 1741–61) again allowed the election of a hetman, one closely associated with the court, but kept the Hetmanate under Senate supervision. Finally, in 1764 Catherine II abolished the office of hetman altogether. The cautious but steady introduction of Russian legal and military practices began, and within a few years, the erosion of local independence could not be denied. At the Legislative Commission of 1767–8, Ukrainian nobles, Cossacks, clergy, and townspeople closed ranks in a failed attempt to defend their traditional autonomy against the centralizing policies of the Russian government.

During the 1760s and 1770s, Russian intrusions and social conflict created an explosive situation in the seemingly secured southwest. Rebellions throughout Ukraine targeted Polish and Russian authority, as well as noble landowners and Cossack officers. Similar revolts against the imposition of tax and service obligations, administrative interference, and Russian settlement broke out in the Southern Urals and Volga regions among Iaik Cossacks and non-Christian subjects of the empire. Such widespread instability, culminating in the great Pugachev rebellion of 1773–4, led to decisive Russian action. In 1774 the government subordinated all Cossack hosts to Russian command and in 1775 abolished the Zaporozhian Sich, steps made possible by Russian success in the Russo-Turkish War of 1768–74. Over the next decade, between 1779 and 1789, the Russian authorities set out to make Ukraine into a region of the Russian empire. Catherine II's provincial reforms began to replace Ukrainian self-government, and the Cossacks of the former Hetmanate became subject to regular conscription into the Russian army. Formal serfdom arrived in 1783, marked by the introduction of the capitation and a complete ban on peasant movement from private estates. The secularization of church lands followed in 1786, bringing Ukrainian religious autonomy to an end and leading to the transformation of Ukrainian monastic peasants into Russian state peasants. Although by the 1820s Russian policymakers and intellectuals demonstrated awareness of a Ukrainian national culture, they would, from the time of military and administrative incorporation in the late eighteenth century until the revolutions of the early twentieth century, continue to deny the nationhood of Ukrainians, treating them instead as "Little Russians."

Further Russian expansion into Ukraine resulted from the partitions of the Polish-Lithuanian Commonwealth, carried out by Russia and Prussia in 1772, 1793, and

1795, with the participation of Austria in the first and third partitions. The formation of the Commonwealth dated from a dynastic union of 1386, followed by combination into a single state under a monarch and Diet in 1569. Although elected for life, the Polish king remained weak and the nobility strong, at a time when other European monarchs embraced, and to varying degrees succeeded in implementing, absolutist political principles. To a present-day observer, Poland's noble "republic" looks remarkably democratic. But over time, Polish freedom gave way to political chaos and military vulnerability. During the second half of the seventeenth century, "the requirement of unanimity in passing laws in the Polish Diet" came "to mean that if even one deputy [in the name of his entire district] raised an objection (*liberum veto*) to any proposed legislation, the Diet was regarded as dissolved."[11] Political arrangements of this sort did little to encourage compromise and stability. The nobility's insistence on preserving traditional liberties repeatedly led to conflict with their Saxon kings, who hoped to reform the Polish political system by establishing hereditary monarchy. More ominous for the Commonwealth, internal dissension opened the door to foreign intervention. For decades, Russia and Prussia cooperated to protect the liberties of Polish nobles and to prevent significant political change precisely in order to keep the Commonwealth weak. Already in 1733–6, in cooperation with Austria, and again in 1764, in cooperation with Prussia, the presence of Russian troops helped to determine the outcome of elections to the Polish throne.

Success in controlling elections to the Polish throne did not, however, produce a compliant client state. Nor could the competing interests of the neighboring great powers always be reconciled. For monarchs concerned to preserve the balance of power in Europe, dismemberment of the Polish-Lithuanian Commonwealth became an attractive option, especially in light of the potential for French intervention on behalf of the Poles. Indeed, the complete destruction of Polish independence did not come until Napoleon's defeat in 1815 and the consequent subordination of Congress Poland (also known as the Kingdom of Poland) to the Russian crown. But already in the partitions of 1772–95, the Russian empire acquired Right-Bank Ukraine, eastern Belarus, and Lithuania, an area referred to from the early nineteenth century as the western provinces.[12] In these territories, a Catholic Polish *szlachta* (nobility) – numbering about 600,000 men, women, and children – dominated a mass of Lithuanian, Belarusian, and Ukrainian peasants, many of whom worshiped in the Uniate or Eastern Rite Church.[13] Significant numbers of Jews also resided in the region, making the Russian empire, after the partition of 1793, home to the world's largest Jewish population.[14] Jews lived in self-governing religious communities, and Polish nobles, 60 percent of whom were landless at the end of the eighteenth century, participated in the election and deliberations of local dietines. Despite the introduction of Russian courts, institutions, and culture – the capitation and conscription into the Russian army arrived in

1773 and the 1775 provincial reform in 1778 – substantial autonomy remained. Polish civil law operated alongside Russian law, Polish nobles occupied judicial and administrative offices, Catholic schools taught Polish children, and the Catholic Church lost none of its authority. The Russian approach to administrative incorporation remained gradualist, based on cooperation with local elites and tolerance of indigenous cultures. Only after the rebellion of 1830–1 did Russification and repression become hallmarks of Russian policy in the western borderlands. From that time onward, Polish patriots refused to reconcile with Russian rule, seeking instead to restore the independent statehood of the Polish nation.

The Russian government's pluralistic approach to the incorporation of new territories worked especially well in the Baltic region, where established elites enjoyed rights beyond those of their Russian counterparts and where local institutions provided models for Russian development.[15] Estonia and Livonia came under Russian rule already in 1710, at which time Peter I confirmed the traditional privileges and autonomy of the German nobles and burghers, who constituted a minority elite in a sea of Estonian and Latvian peasants. Joined by Courland following the third partition of Poland in 1795, the Baltic territories fit easily into the Russian imperial framework, but also retained independent Lutheran churches and local German administration and justice. The Treaty of Nystad (1721) established two Baltic provinces, guaranteed religious freedom for non-Lutherans, and subordinated the region's German courts to Russia's Justice College and Senate. At once subjugated and autonomous, the Baltic German elite soon began to supply Russian society and government with significant numbers of servicemen, scholars, and professionals.[16] Successive Russian monarchs recognized the rights of the Baltic German nobles and burghers, left their traditional social position undisturbed, and until 1881 never failed to confirm their privileges. Still, the very act of confirmation rendered these rights ambiguous, implying temporality and the possibility of revocation.

Already in the reign of Catherine II, it became evident that Russian policymakers intended to subject all the peoples and regions of the empire to uniform laws and administrative structures. Although in the Baltic provinces German remained the language of administration, introduction of the capitation and the Catherinian provincial reform in 1783, followed by the Charters to the Nobility and the Towns in 1785, temporarily required that the corporate bodies of the nobility and the towns operate within the framework of Russian institutions. Tsar Paul rescinded the changes imposed by his mother, though he preserved the capitation and also established regular military conscription. Encroachments by the Russian government did not end. But community autonomy and noble power survived, and the Baltic German "myth of contractually secured rights" continued to provide the Russian monarchy with cooperative local elites.[17] Not until the mid-1860s did policies of Russification and bureaucratic interference from St Petersburg begin to undermine the loyalty of nobles and burghers in the Baltic provinces.

Britain may have "*had* an empire, but Russia *was* an empire," and by the end of the eighteenth century, Great Russians comprised "only about half the subjects of the Tsar."[18] Clearly, no work devoted to any aspect of Russian history can ignore the fact that the Russian polity contained numerous ethnic and religious minorities. Although successive Russian governments treated minorities as members of distinct communities, governed by their own laws, social hierarchies, and institutions, the goal of administrative incorporation and its implications for local autonomy also became obvious at an early date. Unable to impose either administrative uniformity or full social control over its immense territorial domains, the Russian government's policies toward borderlands and minorities remained pragmatic, malleable, and differentiated. Yet in every case, minority communities were expected to support Russian state power by paying taxes, performing service, and remaining loyal. In Russia, state and empire building were combined in a single geographical space, so that the history of Russia became 'the history of a country in the process of being colonized.'[19] While present-day historians see in Russian empire building a more imperialistic orientation, there is no question but that efforts to administer borderlands and minorities ran parallel to and overlapped with similar efforts to build institutions of regular government in Russia proper.

The Problem of the Succession

The need to engage simultaneously in state and empire building made it difficult for Russian rulers to achieve the Petrine goal of regular government. Different territories and minority peoples required different strategies of incorporation and subjugation. Ongoing expansion ensured that institutions, legal prescriptions, and administrative structures remained fluid and changeable. No less noteworthy, the stunning success of eighteenth-century Russia's imperial advance occurred in conditions of chronic political instability. From the death of Peter I until the promulgation of the succession law of 1797, the question of who would rule Russia remained problematic, occupying the time, energy, and thoughts of the elite nobility. Peter himself triggered the problem when he departed this world without clearly designating a successor. Already in 1718, the monarch violated the time-honored principle of seniority by removing from the succession his elder son, Aleksei Petrovich, and replacing him with Peter Petrovich (d. 1719). In 1722 Peter took an even more drastic step and decreed that the reigning monarch should choose a successor from whomever he pleases. Although Peter neglected to identify his choice in a clear and unequivocal manner, in May 1724 he came close to naming a successor when he staged a coronation ceremony in Moscow for his second wife, Catherine Alekseevna.

Catherine was by birth a commoner, and her life story before becoming Peter's mistress in 1703 remains obscure. The couple married only in 1712, after which Catherine gained renown for the courage and physical endurance she displayed while accompanying her husband on military campaigns. Of the eight children Catherine bore for Peter, only two daughters survived: the future Empress Elizabeth (ruled 1741–61) and Anna Petrovna (d. 1728), wife of the Duke of Holstein-Gottorp and mother of the future Emperor Peter III (ruled 1761–2). Peter I also was survived by a grandson, son of the unfortunate Aleksei, the future Emperor Peter II (ruled 1727–30). Finally, Peter I had three nieces, daughters of his former co-ruler Ivan V (d. 1696). Anna Ivanovna became empress of Russia in 1730, and her sister Catherine's infant grandson "ruled" as Ivan VI in 1740–1. At the time of Peter's death, however, only his wife Catherine and his grandson Peter Alekseevich emerged as contenders for the throne, each supported by groupings within the St Petersburg elite. Given the Muscovite tradition of succession from father to son, a tradition never fixed by law, Peter Alekseevich appeared the more likely heir. But Peter I's law on the succession made all members of the Romanov dynasty legal candidates for the throne. Based on the coronation of 1724, Catherine's candidacy prevailed in a peaceful transfer of power spearheaded by Peter's long-time favorite Alexandr D. Menshikov (1673–1729).[20]

Timely distribution of monetary rewards, immediate declaration of an amnesty, support of the Guard regiments stationed in the capital, and the hard work of Menshikov ensured the accession of Empress Catherine I (ruled 1725–7). Catherine's candidacy also received support from the Senate, church hierarchy, *generalitet* (holders of the top four ranks in the Table of Ranks), and upper bureaucracy (for example, the presidents of the colleges). Not everyone applauded the choice, but open expressions of discontent could be easily suppressed. In any event, the succession proceeded without violence, and Empress Catherine I introduced no significant changes to her husband's policies. A weak ruler from the start, she remained under the influence of Menshikov, who, as always, sought to increase his already extraordinary wealth and power. But although Menshikov dominated Catherine, he could not completely control her actions or manage the entire government. To coordinate administration and keep the wheels of government turning, the empress in February 1726 established the Supreme Privy Council (*Verkhovnyi Tainyi sovet*) with six appointed members, including Menshikov and Dmitrii M. Golitsyn (1665–1737), who had supported the candidacy of Peter Alekseevich.[21] Described as 'a purely absolutist organ,' the Council imposed no legal limits on the power of the monarch.[22] The Senate, established by Peter I to integrate policy and supervise administration, became subordinate to the Council, which stood above the government's regular structure of command. Enormous power therefore became concentrated in the hands of the few individuals who controlled the Supreme Privy Council.

The personal weakness of Catherine I notwithstanding, the absolutist power of the monarchy remained. High-level officials and commanders continued to exercise authority solely in the name of the empress, and no one could take significant action without her consent. But Catherine was not Peter, and unlike Peter, she failed to have her way either in foreign policy or in the matter of the succession. The concrete limits to her power first became evident in connection with Holstein's claim to Schleswig, which had been acquired by Denmark in a 1720 treaty with Sweden. Anna Petrovna married the Duke of Holstein in 1725, and because Catherine understood foreign policy in dynastic terms, she hoped to go to war against Denmark, in order to make good her son-in-law's claim to Schleswig. No military campaign ever materialized, in large measure because of Menshikov's opposition and the inaction or lukewarm response of other members of Catherine's government. Similarly indicative of the empress's limited power, Menshikov blocked her plans for the succession. Catherine wanted the throne to pass to her daughters, Anna and Elizabeth, but much of the St Petersburg elite expected Peter Alekseevich to ascend the throne. Menshikov agreed and already in late 1726 began to concoct a plan to marry his daughter to Peter and make himself regent. As Catherine lay on her deathbed, Menshikov took steps to arrest and exile opponents and to ensure that the Guard regiments received their pay. By manipulating events at court during the empress's dying days, he seemed to prevail. Still, Catherine's testament, of which there are competing versions, did not hand Menshikov a clear victory. The empress accepted that Peter would inherit the throne, but she also established a regency composed of Anna, Elizabeth, the Duke of Holstein, and the members of the Supreme Privy Council.

Menshikov did not lose heart and early in the reign of Peter II came close to realizing his dynastic ambitions. At age eleven, the emperor-to-be showed little aptitude for government. Instead, he preferred to spend his time hunting around Moscow, which temporarily replaced St Petersburg as the political center of Russia. Menshikov kept close watch over Peter and even succeeded in having the church sanction his daughter's betrothal to the monarch. Other developments also seemed to favor Menshikov: the absence of Anna and Elizabeth from the Supreme Privy Council, the departure of Anna and her husband for Holstein, the abolition of the monarch's personal Cabinet (*Kabinet*), and Menshikov's control of court resources, which allowed him to distribute estates to supporters. But while Peter II was the third Russian monarch to accord Menshikov special favor, and while the favorite had been an able administrator since the reign of Peter I, his actions betrayed boundless greed and ambition. With hindsight it seems clear that Menshikov did more to pursue his own enrichment and power than to serve his patrons. The favorite consistently abused power, which multiplied the number of his enemies and at the time of Peter I's death left him under investigation for corruption. During the summer of 1727, after a period of illness, Menshikov at last began to lose out to competitors within the governing elite. Leading the charge were Andrei I. Osterman (1687–1747), a fellow member of the Supreme Privy Council, and courtiers from the Dolgorukov family, Aleksei Grigor'evich (d. 1734) and Ivan Alekseevich (1708–39), father and son. In mid-August, Peter II began to live separately from Menshikov and in early September asserted monarchical authority over the Guard regiments and Supreme Privy Council. The regency came to an end. Alexander Menshikov, deprived of titles, ranks, and orders, was sent into exile, and his clients were removed from official posts.

With the fall of Menshikov, the Dolgorukovs, especially Aleksei and his son Ivan, became the handlers of Peter II. Ivan entertained Peter with hunting parties, while Aleksei and another family member, Vasilii L. Dolgorukov (d. 1739), sat in the Supreme Privy Council. The Dolgorukovs not only managed the daily life of the young emperor, they also possessed the power to grant appointments and military orders (*otlichiia*). But unlike Menshikov, they did not seek to dominate the entire government. Osterman ran foreign policy, and all shared power within the Council. Thus while the Dolgorukovs kept busy trying to control Peter and secure the position of their family, the Council actually governed, regularly hearing reports from the Senate, the Main Chancellery of the Court, and the War, Admiralty, and Foreign Affairs Colleges. The Council also received communiqués from ambassadors and some military commanders. Peter II's indifference to government, together with the Dolgorukovs' focus on their private interests, brought a semblance of stability to the Council. Except in the cultural sphere, where church censorship and restrictions on book publishing increased, the government of Peter II followed that of Catherine I in trying to ease the economic and administrative pressure placed on society and officialdom. As before, no one in the government sought to overturn the reforms of Peter I.

The personal absolutism institutionalized by Peter I likewise remained strong. Although Peter II was not actively involved in affairs of government, the Supreme Privy Council wielded power in his name. Even in the absence of a functioning ruler, political power continued to derive directly from the person of the monarch. As the fate of Menshikov showed, members of the governing elite held their official and court positions only so long as they enjoyed the confidence of the ruler. No matter how politically disengaged Peter II might be, once his support was withdrawn, even the most powerful grandee lost all authority. Personal politics ruled the day, and in order to satisfy individual and family interests, members of the elite sought the favor of the monarch. Rather than act on behalf of a noble class, governing oligarchy, time-honored institution, controversial policy, or set of ideological principles, Russia's powerbrokers practiced an archaic form of patronage politics in the pursuit of private gain. The Dolgorukovs, while not as tyrannical as Menshikov, nonetheless followed his political cue. They too sought to secure the private position of their family by marrying Ekaterina Dolgorukova (1712–45), daughter of Aleksei and sister of Ivan, to Peter II. The betrothal took place on November 30, 1729, but on the night of January 18–19, 1730, Peter died of small-pox. The result was another succession crisis, more complicated and consequential than those that had preceded it, and another "struggle for the tsar's favors."[23]

With the death of Peter II, the male line of the Romanov dynasty came to an end. The Supreme Privy Council moved quickly to fill the power vacuum and to ensure its own position by changing the Russian political order. This effort and the events it unleashed constitute one of the most intriguing episodes in Russian political history. If the Council, or rather those members of the Council who supported the proposed changes, had been successful, the Russian monarchy might have become limited and contractual. The drama began when the Council ignored the testa-ment of Catherine I and offered the crown to Anna Ivanovna, widowed Duchess of Courland and daughter of Ivan V. The Council also placed conditions on Anna, and at least initially, the empress-elect accepted the proposed limits to her power. The conditions called for a permanent eight-member Council (at the time the Supreme Privy Council numbered seven) and specified that without the Council's agreement the empress could not make war, conclude peace, impose new taxes, grant promotions above the rank of colonel in state or military service, appoint Russians or foreigners to court ranks, distribute estates and villages, spend state revenues, or deprive nobles of their property without a court proceeding. In addi-tion, the childless Anna agreed not to marry or designate an heir, and she promised "to hold all her faithful subjects in irrevocable favor (*neotmennaia milost*')."[24] If Anna violated the conditions, she would be deprived of the Russian crown.

Historians have long debated whether the actions of the Supreme Privy Council represented a step toward oligarchy or constitutionalism. There is no clear answer to this question. On January 25, 1730, a delegation sent by the Supreme Privy Council reached Courland with the conditions in hand. Anna departed for Moscow on January 30, and arrived two weeks later. In the interim, nobles who had gathered in Moscow to celebrate the wedding of Peter II waited uneasily for Anna to appear. Rumors of the conditions spread, and groups of nobles responded by preparing their own projects for the reform of government. Like the conditions drawn up by the Supreme Privy Council, the meaning of the noble projects and the intentions of their authors remain obscure. Some participants in the political discussions focused on correcting the abuses of previous reigns, especially the domination by favorites and their families. Others articulated potentially sophisticated ideas about alternative and more consultative forms of government, including constitutional or limited monarchy. Still others wanted nothing more than to ensure the preservation of their own personal power and privileges. In the end, Anna renounced the conditions, abolished the Supreme Privy Council, and restored personal absolutism – all without eliciting a hint of organized political opposition. Although one should take seriously the ideas developed in the various projects for political reform, support for these projects clearly ran shallow.

Historians identify a total of seven noble projects dating from 1730. The most important and representative of these, "project 364" and "project 15," named after the number of their signatories, were submitted to the Supreme Privy Council during the first week of February. Consistent in their social demands, the projects called for a defined term of noble service, a more orderly system of promotion for nobles, an end to the requirement that nobles serve as common soldiers or sailors, abolition of the 1714 law on single inheritance, and amelioration of the condition of clergy and townspeople. In their desire to restore Muscovite inheritance practices and ease the service burdens imposed by the Petrine state, the nobles' social demands seem traditional and moderate. The political demands put forth in the 1730 projects are more difficult to decipher, appearing both more innovative and potentially more radical. Project 364 clearly opposed the Supreme Privy Council, whereas project 15 did not. Both projects envisioned a supreme governing body to pass laws and make policy. Both associated the composition of this body with the *generalitet* and nobility, and both envisioned a role for elections in determining its make-up and possibly also the choice of high-level officials such as senators, governors, and presidents of colleges. But the noble projects did not make clear how the elective mechanism would work, who would participate in the assemblies of electors, or to whom the electors would be accountable. Nor did the projects mention the monarch or articulate principles about the nature and sources of political power.

During the period of uncertainty prior to Anna's arrival, the Supreme Privy Council responded to the noble projects and continued to discuss political reform. A plan worked out in late January and early February preserved the Council's control over the government, including the subordination of the Senate, and treated elections as an internal matter to be handled by the Council and Senate. The plan also specified that candidates for election to the Council, Senate, and office of college president come from eminent families and from persons holding the top four ranks in the Table of Ranks (the *generalitet*). In response to the social demands articulated in the noble projects, the grandees sitting in the Supreme Privy Council said nothing. All of the plans and projects, moreover, indicated that only a small number of nobles would participate directly in elections to the supreme governing body or be eligible for elective posts. The *generalitet* of 1730 included about 166 nobles, and the noble projects mentioned electoral assemblies of no more than 100 persons.[25] The motivations and goals embodied in the noble projects seem myriad and ill-defined, yet all the projects sought to prevent further abuses at the hands of favorites. The Council's plan, by contrast, aimed to preserve its dominant position while broadening somewhat the circle of powerbrokers.

Whatever the goals of the various "projectors," they failed both to speak with a unified voice and to articulate a coherent set of political ideas. Awareness of limited monarchy in Britain or Sweden combined with vague calls for elections or for limits on the power of the monarch did not a constitution or a constitutional movement make. After being confronted with repeated expressions of support for Anna and for the Russian tradition of absolute monarchy, the Supreme Privy Council lost its resolve. Some Council members opposed the conditions from the start, and the Council never enjoyed the confidence of nobles outside the inner circle of the government. Anna, by contrast, once she arrived on the outskirts of Moscow, gained the trust of company commanders and soldiers in the Guard regiments, especially the Preobrazhenskii Regiment responsible for her security. Already on February 12, Anna began to grant promotions to Guard officers and soldiers, followed by distributions of monetary rewards and salaries. Days of discussion and maneuvering culminated on February 25 in a gathering of 166 nobles and persons of unspecified rank at court. The gathering petitioned Anna to restore the autocracy (*samoderzhavstvo*) and rule as her ancestors had done.

Within days of receiving her subjects' petition, Anna abolished the Supreme Privy Council and revived the Senate with 21 appointed members, this despite the request by the petitioners of February 25 that the nobility elect senators and governors. The restoration of personal absolutism could not have been swifter. What began as an opportunity to place legal limits on the power of the monarch ended with an unequivocal affirmation of absolute monarchy, presented as time-honored and grounded in Russian tradition. Historians have long noted that a majority of the nobles present during the events of 1730 distrusted and feared the grandees associated with the Supreme Privy Council. For this reason, the argument goes, they preferred absolute monarchy to the possibility of tyranny at the hands of an aristocratic oligarchy. But the less elite nobles also repeatedly expressed a desire to incorporate elections into the selection of high-level officials. Why, aside from the restoration of absolute monarchy, did these demands have no effective impact on the outcome of the crisis? How is it that Anna Ivanovna could so easily ignore the political ideas of the nobles who brought her to power?

An answer lies in the political culture of 1730. Both the grandees and the less elite nobles gathered in Moscow lacked a developed political language or a common way of thinking about political relationships. Consequently, as events unfolded, both groups proved unable to formulate a coherent program for the reform of government or to mobilize social support for change. Echoes of shared political assumptions could be heard in the plans of the Council and in the noble projects, but no unifying set of ideological principles emerged. Instead, the political ideas and aspirations of 1730 came together in "a motley fusion of statements and moods with variation in the very level of comprehending the problem."[26] Russia's educated service classes were only just beginning to develop a social voice independent of the church and monarchy, only just beginning to articulate ideas about the burning questions of the day. In the end, people chose the familiar because they feared the unknown and lacked the conceptual vocabulary needed to imagine an alternative.

The reign of Anna Ivanovna often is described as the *bironovshchina*, after the empress's most trusted advisor, Ernst Johann Biron (1690–1772). Denounced as a time of terror, tyranny, and rule by Germans, the years under Anna, while harsh in the treatment of political opponents, also produced a functioning government and political structure (one nearly destroyed by her immediate successors). Biron wielded great power, and official reports submitted to Anna passed through his hands. But Biron did not abuse his power, at least not immediately. Devoted to the empress and her interests, which he equated with the interests of Russia, Biron's relationship with Anna represented the fulfillment of Petrine personal absolutism. Under Anna, a Cabinet composed of three appointed ministers supervised the Senate and all other important government offices. Biron did not sit in the Cabinet, which was dominated by Andrei I. Osterman, a member of the Supreme Privy Council since its creation in 1726. Osterman had conveniently absented himself during the succession crisis of 1730, and his political sympathies remained opaque. But Anna needed his foreign policy expertise. That Osterman could become "the soul" of Anna's Cabinet testified to an important development in the organization of Russian government.[27] Chaotic rule *by* favorites, which characterized the reigns of Catherine I and Peter II, had given way to a workable version of the Petrine system: the personal rule of an absolute monarch *through* favorites and qualified officials.

Anna Ivanovna's government continued the process of ordering and adapting the institutions and policies inaugurated by Peter I, and when the empress died in October 1740, the succession appeared also to proceed according to the Petrine law of succession. Anna chose as her heir Ivan VI, the infant son of Prince Anthony Ulrich of Brunswick-Bevern-Luneburg and Anna Leopoldovna (Anne of Mecklenburg, 1718–46), daughter of the empress's sister Catherine. After some hesitation Anna also appointed Biron to be regent, assigning him absolute political authority until Ivan reached age seventeen. It looked as if the empress had secured the throne for the descendants of her father: if Anna Ivanovna's appointed successor died without issue, the crown would pass in order of seniority to the other (as yet unborn) male children of Anna Leopoldovna and Anthony Ulrich. The house of Brunswick might even replace the house of Romanov as the ruling dynasty of Russia.

Immediately following Anna Ivanovna's death, Biron assumed the role of regent in what appeared to be a smooth transfer of power. But appearances are deceiving, and at the eighteenth-century Russian court, the best laid plans repeatedly came to naught. Biron's regency lasted a mere 22 days. From the start Anna

Leopoldovna believed that she should be regent and refused to accept the legit-imacy of Biron's appointment. For his part, Biron failed to secure support from the Guard regiments, and his apparent dynastic ambitions aroused suspicion and fear among the broader St Petersburg elite. Toward the end of Anna Ivanovna's reign, Biron had tried to arrange a marriage between Anna Leopoldovna and his son, once the boy grew up. Although the plan evaporated when Anna married Anthony Ulrich, Biron's role as regent encouraged stories about schemes to marry his son to Elizabeth and his daughter to the future Peter III. Biron's beha-vior recalled the power grabs of Menshikov and the Dolgorukovs. His fate soon resembled theirs as well.

On the night of November 8–9, 1740, Biron was arrested by a contingent of Guard soldiers and officers led by Fieldmarshal Burchard Christoph Münnich (1683–1767). Anna Leopoldovna became regent, and Biron and his family were sent into exile in Siberia. Biron's fall did not result from any public outcry, institu-tional action, or judicial process. Although from the outset some within the gov-erning elite questioned the concentration of power in the regent's hands, Biron self-consciously identified with the policies of Peter I and probably would have been a more capable steward of government than Anna Leopoldovna proved to be. Equally important, based on Empress Anna Ivanovna's decision, Biron was in fact a legal regent. His overthrow thus constituted the first palace coup carried out by Guard officers and soldiers under a high-level military commander. Portrayed as a dangerous threat to the wellbeing of the empire, Biron became the victim of violent action by the political elite and Guard regiments of St Petersburg.[28] Direct political intervention by the Guard represented a significant development to be repeated in the years ahead.

Following the removal of Biron, Fieldmarshal Münnich headed the govern-ment, but his power also proved short-lived. Impolitic and eager to command, Münnich aroused opposition among the governing elite and in March 1741 "received permission" to retire. In the meantime, some effort had been made to organize a functioning government. Already in January, the Cabinet had been divided into departments or areas of responsibility entrusted to individual mem-bers: Osterman managed foreign affairs; Münnich and, following his retirement, Anthony Ulrich commanded the military domain; and together Aleksei M. Cherkasskii (1680–1742) and Mikhail G. Golovkin (1699–1754) handled domestic policy. The result, however, was not greater regularity in administration. Instead, incompetence and disorganization spread to the highest levels of government. Although initially Anna Leopoldovna seemed to understand the need for energetic governance, her actions repeatedly violated established practices – for example, she ignored seniority in granting appointments and promotions – and policy tended to drift both at home and abroad. Simply put, the regent Anna did not know how to govern, and increasingly she withdrew into private life. The members of Anna's Cabinet were likewise incapable of integrating the government and implementing a consistent policy. Unlike other rulers since the death of Peter I, Anna failed to entrust power to a "minister" or favorite who could govern in her place. Petrine personal absolutism could survive without a hands-on emperor, but someone had to function as the point of integration for the system of government. It was this point of integration, the nucleus of supreme authority, which disappeared during the regency of Anna Leopoldovna.

The brief reign of Ivan VI came to an end on November 25, 1741. Elizabeth, the sole surviving child of Peter I, acceded to the throne following a palace coup planned and implemented by the officers of the grenadier company of the Preobrazhenskii Guard Regiment. Anna Leopoldovna and her circle offered no resistance, as Russia's military and civil leaders quickly fell into line behind Elizabeth. Confiscations and arrests, including the arrest of the year-old emperor and his parents, quickly ensued, together with the usual monetary rewards, grants of estates, and promotions for supporters. In 1742 alone, Empress Elizabeth received 2,000 petitions and during her entire reign distributed some 200,000 peasants.[29] Elizabeth based her claim to the throne on Catherine I's testament, which if honored following the death of Peter II would have given the crown either to her or to the offspring of her sister Anna Petrovna (d. 1728). The reign of Anna Ivanovna was therefore declared illegal, and steps were taken to erase the image of Ivan VI from public memory. On the day of the coup, Elizabeth also took command of the four Guard regiments and began to justify her rule through identification with Peter I. The propaganda effort even reached the free press of Holland, where newspaper publishers received payments and pensions to ensure favorable coverage of Elizabeth's accession. Over the next two decades, bishops, poets, and government officials joined in a chorus of praise for Elizabeth, associating her reign with idealized representations of her father and denouncing the period from 1725 to 1741 as a time of domination by foreigners. Through elaborate spectacle and reasonably good government, the empress achieved a measure of political stability and effectively secured the throne for the Petrine line of the Romanov dynasty.

Throughout Elizabeth's reign, the policies of Peter I served as models for emulation. Soon after taking power the empress declared a restoration of Petrine institutions, particularly the Senate, though she also maintained a personal Cabinet and appointed a Council with eleven members to oversee the government. In 1756 the Conference, established in connection with preparations for Russia's entry into the Seven Years' War (1756–63), became the highest administrative body. The juxtaposition of the Senate and Conference illustrates how Elizabeth controlled the government by dispersing power between the regular bureaucracy and irregular bodies that lay outside (or above) the established chain of command. Like her predecessors, the empress avoided innovation, choosing instead to adapt Petrine policies to changing conditions and needs. Her most striking contribution to the Petrine legacy came in the building of cultural institutions. Moscow University (1755), the Russian Imperial Theater (1756), and the Academy of Fine Arts (1757) all opened their doors in Elizabeth's reign, heralding Russia's full participation in the world of European letters, arts, and sciences (see chapter 6). Under Elizabeth, limited innovation, the furtherance of Petrine precedents, and a more detached style of personal rule encouraged stability, if not also regular government.

Elizabeth's successor, Peter III, criticized her reign for being chaotic and disorderly. Yet precisely because the empress did not meddle in everyday matters of government, the bureaucracy could function separately from the court and monarch. The Russian archival record becomes appreciably more ordered in the 1740s, suggesting that a measure of consistent and effective administration had been achieved. Legislation from 1743 revived the town magistracies of the Petrine era, and by placing them firmly under the authority of the central government, connected local urban institutions to the empire's larger administrative structure. The modernization of church administration and the development of a network of seminaries, both also central to the Petrine legacy, benefited from the creation of ecclesiastical consistories attached to the eparchies governed by bishops. The treatment of Old Believers, sectarians, and non-Orthodox religious minorities became harsher under Elizabeth, as did the tax burden placed on the Russian people. After temporary reductions in 1742 and 1743, the capitation was raised by 10–15 kopecks in 1745. Of particular importance for the political future of the monarchy, Elizabeth also improved discipline in the Guard regiments. The empress insisted on receiving regular reports from commanders, and she presided over changes in recruitment that undercut the noble character and corporate spirit of the Guard. Over the next few decades, the Guard regiments became hierarchical military units, with soldiers drawn increasingly from the regular army and the Russian lower classes and with officers coming from better educated and wealthier segments of the nobility. Social regulation, achieved through tighter administration and moderation in the use of power, became the hallmark of Elizabeth's reign.

Elizabeth's personnel policies also encouraged greater stability, at least in the upper ranks of society and government. The basic pattern of rewarding support and punishing disloyalty did not change, but fewer repressions, removals, and transfers of high-level officials occurred. During the reign of Anna Ivanovna, 13 percent of governors and 22 percent of the heads of central administrative offices suffered arrest, judicial prosecution, and exile. In the reign of Elizabeth, the corresponding figures reached only 8 percent and 12 percent. The social status of higher officialdom also rose under Elizabeth: 79 percent of governors and 70 percent of college and chancellery heads held ranks III–V. Under Anna the corresponding figures equaled 71 and 58 percent.[30] The apparent calm of Elizabeth's reign did not, however, reduce the government's vigilance in prosecuting political crimes. In the reign of Anna Ivanovna, the Secret Chancellery investigated an average of 161 cases per year; in Elizabeth's reign, the average number reached 277.[31] Elizabeth, no less than her predecessors, refused to tolerate the slightest hint of political opposition. Even so, after the chaos of 1730 and 1740–1, greater social regulation, insistence on decorous behavior in church, and ongoing rotations of officials seemed mild and indicative of good order.

The atmosphere of moderation achieved under Elizabeth endured beyond her reign, but not before another succession crisis wrought havoc within the governing elite. Elizabeth upheld the succession law of her father and the testament of her mother, when in February 1742 she brought to the Russian court her nephew, Karl Peter Ulrich, Prince of Holstein-Gottorp, son of Anna Petrovna, and grandson of Peter I. In November, following conversion to Orthodoxy, the prince, renamed Peter Fedorovich, became heir to the Russian throne. In February 1744, Peter's future wife arrived in St Petersburg: Sophie Friederike Auguste, Princess of Anhalt-Zerbst and future Empress Catherine II. Converted to Orthodoxy as Catherine Alekseevna, the princess married Peter in 1745 and years later, in 1754, gave birth to Tsarevich Paul. The Petrine line at last seemed secure; however, even before Elizabeth's death, the question of the succession produced conflict at court and among the elite nobility. The problem of Ivan VI also hung over Elizabeth: left to rot in prison, the deposed emperor remained a potential catalyst for discontent and rebellion. Equally important, it appeared inevitable that once Peter Fedorovich acceded to the throne, a battle over the direction of Russian foreign policy would erupt.

The looming conflict over foreign policy concerned Russia's relations with the newest great power in Europe, the kingdom of Prussia. European diplomacy suffered a severe shock when Frederick II, King of Prussia, occupied Austrian Silesia in December 1740. For much of Elizabeth's reign Russia enjoyed good relations with both Austria and Britain, while growing ever more suspicious of Prussia. France, Austria's traditional rival, also drew closer to the Habsburgs in response to the Prussian threat. A veritable revolution in European diplomacy thus unfolded as "Prussia left its alliance with France for one with Britain, and Austria left its alliance with Britain for one with France."[32] The realignment of diplomatic forces culminated in the Seven Years' War, pitting Austria, France, and Russia against the rising power of Prussia. Prussia's ally Britain stood somewhat to the side, though in exchange for the protection of English interests in Hanover, the British did provide subsidies to Frederick II. Russia, while maintaining the all-important trade relationship with Britain, took an active stand against Prussia. Allied with Austria and France, Russia agreed to remain in the war until Austria recovered Silesia, and in return received subsidies from Austria and the promise of territorial gains in eastern Prussia. As stated by the Conference, the Prussian territories could then be exchanged for border adjustments with Poland so as to ensure Russian control of the Baltic–Black Sea corridor.[33] Although Russia's war aims were achieved in 1758, Elizabeth honored her commitment to the Habsburgs, sending Russian troops to participate in Austrian-planned campaigns in 1759, 1760, and 1761.

Perhaps Elizabeth had overly committed Russia to the defense of Austrian interests. But this was not really the issue that divided the Russian court and threatened the succession. From the outset, Peter Fedorovich made no secret of his support for Prussia, and already in May 1757 he had to be removed from the Conference. Peter's behavior represented an open challenge to Elizabeth, and rumors arose that the empress intended to transfer the succession to Tsarevich Paul with Catherine Alekseevna as regent. Nothing came of the rumors, and when Elizabeth died in December 1761, Catherine supported her husband's accession. But Catherine's support did not last long. Emperor Peter III ruled just a few short months, from December 25, 1761 until June 28, 1762. He was overthrown in yet another palace coup, carried out by Guard officers and soldiers with the active participation of Catherine. Peter gave up his throne without any active resistance and died a few days later, most likely murdered by Aleksei G. Orlov (1737–1808), a Guard officer and one of Empress Catherine II's co-conspirators.

The overthrow of Peter III made clear that even a legitimate monarch and direct descendant of Peter I enjoyed little security, if he antagonized the upper ranks of the military and bureaucracy. Yet Peter correctly understood his power to be absolute, and he aspired to follow in the footsteps of his grandfather by becoming a tsar reformer. Like his more immediate predecessors, Peter preserved important instruments of personal rule: he left the Senate weak, divided his Cabinet into an economic department and a private chancellery, and replaced Elizabeth's Conference with an Imperial Council responsible for coordinating administration. The emperor also enacted some of the most important legislation of the eighteenth century: the emancipation of the nobility from compulsory service and the secularization of church and monastery lands, including the transfer of church and monastery peasants to a College of Economy. Based on unrealized plans initiated under Elizabeth, the secularization did not actually become reality until 1764; however, it showed Peter III's most noteworthy policies to be in line with those of his predecessor and successor. Equally consistent with the thinking of Elizabeth and Catherine II, Peter downgraded the Secret Chancellery to a department (*ekspeditsiia*) of the Senate and abolished the legal principle of "the Sovereign's word and deed" (*slovo i delo Gosudarevo*), which treated as treason any unauthorized conversation about the monarch. Under Elizabeth, Peter III, and Catherine II *together*, Russian subjects acquired unprecedented "freedom" of expression and broad access to European culture. Ironically, the greater cultural freedom, not to be confused with tolerance of political opposition, made it easier for the conspirators of June 1762 to move against the unpopular Peter.

Peter III's personal habits did nothing to endear him to the courtiers, Guard officers, and high-level officials who ultimately decided his fate. The emperor disliked court ceremony and etiquette, openly carried on an affair with Elizaveta Vorontsova, publicly insulted his wife, and appeared indifferent, if not hostile, toward the Russian Orthodox Church. Catherine Alekseevna, while no paragon of domestic virtue, presented a dignified public persona, took seriously the religious authority and rites of the church, and knew how to cultivate support and loyalty among her subjects.[34] In contrast to Peter, who could not control his top officials and generals, Catherine brought together different groups of conspirators, whose motivations varied and who were not necessarily aware of each other's existence. Nikita I. Panin (1718–83), a respected diplomat and tutor to Tsarevich Paul, hoped for a coup in favor of the heir with Catherine as regent, whereas the Guard officers who organized and carried out the actual seizure of power always intended for Catherine to rule. None of these differences, however, produced open competition or conflict. Throughout the period of preparation leading up to the coup, the opponents of Peter III looked to Catherine as the immediate alternative, and at no time did anyone one openly press for the establishment of a regency.

The organized support of Guard officers able to control their subordinates (during Elizabeth's coup Guard soldiers acted independently of their officers) was key to Catherine's success and to the preservation of her position once she seized the throne. Peter, by contrast, antagonized the Guard and opposed Russia's established international position. Upon taking power, the emperor quickly pulled Russia out of the war against Prussia, ignoring treaty obligations to Austria and handing Frederick II a crucial victory in Europe. This action in itself might not have been sufficient to turn Russia's military and civil leadership against Peter, for all parties to the war needed peace. Russia's financial problems had become severe, and the Russian governing elite had become divided over the question of European alliances. But Peter's plans did not end with withdrawal from a costly and divisive war. Playing the part of a petty German duke rather than the ruler of a great empire, Peter ordered the Russian military to prepare for war against Denmark.

The aim of this war, which Peter effectively declared on May 21, was to restore Schleswig to the emperor's native Holstein. Peter's own Imperial Council immediately protested the move: the army could not be made ready for a summer campaign, the military's financial resources had been exhausted, and the troops lacked provisions and forage. Peter was not deterred. He commanded officials to search out funds in every corner of the government, ordering that monies be taken from places such as the Tula Provincial Chancellery and the resources allocated to Tsarevich Paul. The Synod received instructions to scour its estates and deliver horses suitable for military service. On June 8, Peter also reached an agreement with Frederick II, who promised to send 15,000 Prussian troops to fight with Russia against Denmark. Although the pledge of aid failed to persuade Russia's governing elite that the war was either feasible or desirable, the stage seemed set for a summer campaign. The impending campaign was not, however, the only issue at hand. Peter also began to impose unpopular reforms on the Guard regiments garrisoned in the capital. Frequent training exercises prepared the regiments for parade-ground marches, and officers were required to purchase costly new uniforms. Finally, on June 25, Peter ordered a contingent of Guard troops to march out from the capital. Just days later, on June 28, the emperor lost his throne when the officers and soldiers of the Izmailovskii and Semenovskii Guard Regiments pledged allegiance to Catherine. The remaining regiments in St Petersburg, the military leadership, and the upper bureaucracy quickly followed suit. By July 5 Peter was dead.

Empress Catherine II declared her accession to be an act of Providence welcomed by the Russian people and by the ecclesiastical, military, and civil ranks of the empire. Yet her reign began in an atmosphere of uncertainty. Following the coup, a crime wave hit St Petersburg, and in the Preobrazhenskii and Semenovskii Guard Regiments, sympathy for the dead Peter lingered. Catherine responded to the threat of opposition with generous grants of money and serfs. Russian scholar I. V. Kurukin describes Catherine's coup as the most expensive of the eighteenth century, estimating that from July through December 1762, the empress spent 1.5 million rubles to win over supporters. For the eight-month period from July 1762 to March 1763, Catherine also gave away 21,423 male souls, in contrast to the 8,546 souls Peter had distributed during the six months of his reign.[35] Gifts and promotions may have satisfied the elite, but in the popular mind, Peter's stature as a good tsar continued to grow. Beginning in 1764, a series of pretenders claimed to be the deceased monarch, and rumors persisted of plans to overthrow Catherine in favor of Paul or Ivan VI. There is no evidence of any serious or feasible plot to remove the empress; however, she was sufficiently concerned to confirm an earlier order of Peter III that Ivan be put to death if anyone tried to free him from prison. On the night of July 4–5, 1764, the disaffected military officer Vasilii Ia. Mirovich did just that, and Ivan was promptly killed by his guards.

After the death of Ivan, Catherine's political position stabilized, as she quickly and effectively set about the task of governing. Although the empress's only legal claim to the Russian throne derived from her status as the mother of Paul, she managed until her death in 1796 to keep the tsarevich and his entourage under control. Catherine also successfully dominated her favorites, courtiers, top officials, and military commanders. With but a few isolated exceptions, Russia's entire governing elite, including the church hierarchy, seemed to fall in line behind her policies. The one great social rebellion of Catherine's reign, led by the Cossack pretender Emelian Pugachev in 1773–4, took place in the Southern Urals and Volga regions, far from both the center of political power and the heartland of Russian serfdom. The rebellion, while massive and brutal, remained a borderland event that in no way threatened the security of Catherine's government. Nobles took small comfort from the rebellion's relatively quick suppression, yet the aura surrounding the person of Catherine and the accomplishments of her reign continued to grow. Modern historians consistently rate Catherine one of Russia's greatest rulers, comparable in stature and achievements to Peter I, the mythologized creator of modern Russia, and to Alexander II, the liberal monarch who emancipated the serfs and presided over the Great Reforms.[36]

By almost any standard the reign of Catherine II (the Great) is indeed a wonder to behold. How did a woman ruler, also a foreigner and a convert with no legitimate claim to the Russian throne, govern such a vast empire in an age of chronic political instability? The governing elite's deep disdain for Peter III is part of the answer. But what of Tsarevich Paul, who once he came of age stood patiently, or not so patiently, waiting in the wings? Given the technical illegality of Catherine's rule, and the presence of a legitimate and competent heir, the only plausible answer lies in Catherine's personal qualities and capabilities. More than any of Peter I's eighteenth-century successors, Catherine realized his vision of regular government, military might, and cultural advancement. Catherine ruled as an absolute monarch, and she continued to rely on personal favorites and trusted servicemen to carry out her policies. But Catherine also did much to regularize the functions of government, to integrate the localities into the central administrative apparatus, and to win the battle for the hearts and minds of her subjects. Catherine did nothing to alleviate the hardships of serfdom or to limit its spread into non-Russian borderlands; however, she did give peasants and townspeople access to reformed courts, and she encouraged nobles and other educated Russians to discuss Enlightenment ideas and participate in a pan-European "republic of letters." Although Catherine countenanced no opposition or uninvited societal initiative, she allowed meaningful public conversation about important social and political problems. Peter I gave to Russia a modern body, so the cliché goes, and Catherine II gave to Russia a modern soul.

The Search for Regular Government

In July 1787, students at the Tver Noble School performed a drama with ballet before Catherine II's grandsons, the future emperor Alexander I and his brother Constantine. Throughout the drama, published in 1790 under the title *Appreciation of Good Works*, Catherine appears as the goddess Minerva (the Roman goddess of wisdom and the arts, also identified with the Greek goddess of war, Athena) and the spiritual successor to Peter the Great. As the play's action draws to a close, Peter himself declares that Catherine's greatness has surpassed his own. Plans that he could only imagine, the empress has brought to pass. Thanks to her wise policies, noble intentions, and personal virtue, Catherine has made possible the happiness and goodness of her subjects.[37] *Appreciation of Good Works* was just one of the many literary creations in which poets sang the praises of Catherine II and identified her policies with those of Peter I. Most modern-day historians agree, moreover, that she was a reformer in the Petrine mode. Yet despite a shared vision of Russian greatness and European progress, Peter and Catherine possessed distinctive personalities, and as absolute monarchs, they wielded power in very different ways.

In the words of Princess Ekaterina R. Dashkova, aristocrat, courtier, and co-conspirator of Catherine, Peter I, for all his "genius, energy, and zeal for improvement," lacked an adequate education and consequently allowed "unbridled passions" to influence his reason. "Quick-tempered, brutal, and despotic, he treated all people without distinction as slaves who must bear with everything." Nor, in Dashkova's opinion, could the suffering caused by Peter's brutality be regarded as a necessary accompaniment to progress: "his ignorance did not allow him to see that many reforms introduced by him through violence were being introduced quietly and peacefully by trade, exchange, the passage of time, and the example of other nations." Peter, Dashkova went on to explain, "almost entirely abolished the freedom and privileges" of the nobility, and "he introduced a military form of government which is certainly the most despotic of all governments." Equally harmful, Peter's eagerness to change the laws, including his own laws, had the effect of undermining "the power of the law and the respect which is due to it."[38]

Dashkova's harsh judgment of Peter, whose greatness she nonetheless recognized, stood in stark contrast to her praise of Catherine. The princess described Catherine as "easy of access, but never at the cost of her own dignity, so that the respect with which she was approached was untinged with servility or fear." Indeed, Catherine's "presence inspired religious veneration and a respect deeply felt and quickened by love and gratitude. Gracious and full of charm and gaiety, she wanted her rank to be forgotten in private life." Of course, even Catherine's closest associates could not overlook her rank or the absolutist power she possessed, though had this been possible to do, "the generally felt conviction of her natural superiority would still have remained to inspire a pious respect inseparable from her person and every thought of her."[39] Clearly, there was much in Catherine's moral character and style of rule to distinguish her from the heavy-handed Peter. At the same time, the stuff of which Russia was made, the "raw material" with which Catherine could work, also had changed significantly since the early eighteenth century. When Catherine set out to renew the process of reform begun by Peter, she did so in international and domestic conditions much more favorable to Russia and to her (and her predecessor's) goals.

The decades between the death of Peter (1725) and the accession of Catherine (1762) were by default years of limited government. Succession struggles dominated the political landscape, and successive governments suffered shortages of money and manpower. Preoccupied with political conflict, military might, and cultural progress at the top of society, Peter's successors shied away from rapid change and broad social transformation. They adhered to the basic goals of the Petrine reforms, working hard to maintain Russia's great-power status, catch up to Europe in the arts and sciences, build central institutions of government and culture, and train the personnel needed to manage those institutions. But post-Petrine governments also tended to leave local communities and officials to their own economic and administrative devices. As long as the Russian people remained peaceable, delivered recruits, and paid taxes, more or less, their superiors and commanders preferred to let things be in the countryside and provincial towns.

Truth to tell, Peter's successors had no choice but to abandon his program of "social engineering." Already during the brief reign of Catherine I, fiscal crisis forced reductions in government spending and led to the realization that the administrative and economic pressures of the Petrine era could not be sustained. Catherine I reduced the capitation by four kopecks and cut in half the number of board members at the head of each college. Unranked officials (those below the Table of Ranks) in the Colleges of Justice and Patrimonial Estates (*Votchinnaia kollegiia*) ceased to receive salaries and were instead compelled to collect fees from petitioners. The problem of meager resources continued in the reign of Peter II, leading to a shortage of administrative clerks (*pod'iachie*) in the provinces and to the closing of local offices attached to the central colleges. After the relentless intrusions of the Petrine era, the downsizing of government may have brought relief to the Russian people. Less regulation of domestic and foreign trade benefited nobles and townspeople, and legislation of 1729 introduced bills of exchange, which encouraged commerce. But the government's limited administrative reach carried another set of problems. Outside the capitals and most important provincial towns, eighteenth-century Russia remained a vast undergoverned land. Policymakers may have wanted to believe that Russia possessed a surplus of officials; however, in 1725 the empire supported only one official for every 10,000 inhabitants. Prussia, during the reign of Frederick William I (ruled 1713–40), had one official for every 1,500 inhabitants.[40] Government declarations notwithstanding, a calculus of scarcity prevented the Russian monarchy from maintaining an adequate administrative apparatus, which in turn made it difficult to collect taxes, manage state monies, and enforce laws.

Fiscal crisis and shortages of administrative employees to keep records, implement policy, and collect accurate information about resources continued in the reign of Anna Ivanovna. Anna's government tried to account for revenues and expenditures by requiring reports, conducting inspections, and prosecuting corruption. But such measures had little effect. The small number of officials assigned to local offices meant too little supervision, which gave the few officials present broad discretionary authority and opened the door to arbitrariness and abuse. The enormous geographic distances of the Russian empire and the primitive system of communications only added to the problem. Local "autonomy," or rather the absence of effective government in the localities, at once bolstered the institutional weight of serfdom and allowed a significant degree of community self-government. Although community self-government (not to be confused with democratic self-government) might seem a beneficial state of affairs, the limited power of the central government proved to be a double-edged sword. The "freedom" given to individuals and communities allowed them to live on the basis of pragmatic decisions and mutual understandings; however, the "freedom" given to local officials, noble landowners, regimental commanders, and even village elders also permitted egregious abuses of power. The freedom to elude authority and the freedom to exercise discretionary authority, while not comparable to a state of lawlessness, nonetheless prevented the realization of regular government and the rule of law.

The problem of undergovernment and the corruption it permitted plagued the Russian provinces throughout the age of serfdom. Yet haltingly in the reign of Elizabeth, and with unprecedented vigor in that of Catherine II, more orderly patterns of social and institutional development began to take root. Elizabeth's policies brought greater regulation to the countryside by connecting city government to the central bureaucracy and by strengthening the authority of bishops over the clergy and laity. In a similar but more pernicious vein, Elizabeth also increased the power of serf owners when she forbade runaway serfs to join the army, a practice Peter I had allowed, and denied all serfs a civic identity by having masters take the oath of allegiance in their place. Serious discussion of government reform and legal codification also revived under Elizabeth, though nothing concrete emerged from the meetings of successive legislative commissions. Still, Elizabeth's government did create important cultural and educational institutions, and the empress herself actively encouraged the process of Europeanization begun by her father. Indeed, the most noteworthy development of Elizabeth's reign may have been the rise to maturity of educated service classes, noble and non-noble, committed to modern science and scholarship, secular Russian literature, and the Petrine goal of regular government.

The search for regular government is a constant refrain in eighteenth-century Russian sources. In the tradition of the well-ordered police state, regular government meant the ability both to order social relationships and to mobilize human and material resources to serve the common good.[41] In Russia, the common good developed as an official concept focused on the construction and maintenance of instrumentalities of government and national defense. The Russian state became the guardian of the common good, and generations of policymakers viewed change through legislation and official regulation as the best means for its realization. Not surprisingly then, efforts to write a new law code to replace the Muscovite *Ulozhenie* of 1649 appeared on the agenda of successive Russian governments already from the time of Peter I. Little came of these efforts before the reign of Catherine II, and even then the job remained unfinished until 1832. Still, from the late 1750s onward, members of Russia's governing elite became convinced that "fundamental laws" (not to be confused with modern constitutions) offered the best guarantee of regular government.[42] Fundamental laws, policymakers assumed, would ensure legality (*zakonnost'*) in judicial proceedings, state administration, and social relationships.

Catherine II made her initial contribution to the formulation of fundamental laws, and to the reform of government more broadly, by calling yet another legislative commission to write a new code of laws[43] Composed of deputies sent by social communities from across the empire, the Legislative Commission of 1767–8 appeared at once traditional and innovative. The Law Code (*Ulozhenie*) of 1649 had been approved by a gathering of representatives from society, the Assembly of the Land, convened by Muscovite tsars to consult on important social, political, and diplomatic issues. The Catherinian Legislative Commission represented a significantly broader range of social groups and localities, but it too was a consultative assembly brought together by the monarch. When the Commission assembled in Moscow in July 1767, it consisted of 29 deputies from government institutions, 142 from the nobility, 209 from the towns, and about 200 from the state peasants and other social communities, including 54 from the empire's non-Russian peoples. The deputies arrived with instructions (*nakazy*), or more accurately petitions, drawn up by their constituents to describe local conditions and convey concrete grievances and demands.[44] After the official opening of the assembly, the deputies heard a reading of Catherine's own Instruction or *Nakaz*, which together with the local instructions was supposed to guide their deliberations.[45]

In 20 chapters and 526 articles, Catherine's Instruction set forth "a mixture of statements about what Russia is, what it ought to be, and how society in general ought to be organized."[46] Written originally in French, then translated into Russian with corrections made by the empress herself, the Instruction is widely seen as a bold, if not entirely original, pronouncement of progressive Enlightenment ideas. Drawn largely from *The Spirit of the Laws* (1748), a monumental work of political theory by Charles Louis de Secondat, Baron de Montesquieu, with points taken also from Cesare Beccaria's *On Crimes and Punishments* (1764) and Jacob Friedrich Bielfeld's *Institutions politiques* (1765), Catherine's Instruction revealed a commitment to absolute monarchy tempered by an Enlightenment conception of fundamental laws and an appreciation for the diversity of customs and circumstances found in human societies. Although Catherine rejected Montesquieu's classification of Russia as a despotism, she nonetheless insisted that "such a large state could only be governed in accordance with a system in which the sovereign rules alone but subject to the fundamental laws, the limitations of which he voluntarily accepts."[47] Alongside broad theoretical points, the Instruction also elaborated specific principles of government. The empress rejected the use of torture; defined crime, including political crime, as a matter of deeds, not words; and declared that only through formal judicial proceedings should "citizens" be deprived of life, liberty, or property. Consistent with Catherine's absolutist political beliefs, she also called on judges to apply the law in the strictest possible fashion. Laws should be clearly formulated and easily understood (an elusive goal in eighteenth-century Russia), so that judges would not be tempted to interpret the law. Only the monarch possessed the authority to make laws and interpret their meaning. Catherine's Instruction showed familiarity with the liberal tenets of Enlightenment thought, but also made clear that the empress intended to preserve, and indeed enhance, the personal absolutism of Peter I.

The Legislative Commission never completed its appointed task, and when war broke out with the Ottoman Empire in October 1768, Catherine disbanded the assembly and sent the deputies home (or to their military posts). Although subcommissions continued to meet into the early 1770s, they too failed to produce a new code of laws. From the start, moreover, the Commission lacked any regular institutional status; it was an *ad hoc* gathering summarily created and eliminated by the empress. Not surprisingly, some historians see in the entire enterprise nothing more than Enlightenment hypocrisy and Catherinian propaganda. But in convening the Legislative Commission, Catherine made a sincere effort to consult her subjects on important matters of state. In presenting the deputies with her Instruction, the empress also initiated, within the categories of Enlightenment thought, a public discussion about law, justice, civic relationships, and the organization of government. Before condemning Catherine as a hypocrite, it is therefore instructive to remember that: 1) she repeated a longstanding Muscovite tradition whereby the monarch sought advice from his subjects, and 2) the Commission incorporated broad social representation from across the Russian empire. No comparably representative body would meet again in Russia before the election of the Duma following the Revolution of 1905. Even more important, the instructions submitted by the deputies, filled as they were with complaints about legal-administrative abuses, government inefficiency, and economic hardship, provided Catherine and her advisors with much valuable information, at least some of which found its way into major legislative acts of the 1770s and 1780s.[48]

Despite the limited achievements of the Legislative Commission, the process proved instructive, and Catherine soon emerged as an effective institutional reformer. Beginning with the 1775 reform of provincial administration and culminating in the 1785 Charters to the Nobility and the Towns, Catherinian legislation brought unprecedented effectiveness and social participation to local government.[49] Between 1775 and 1785, a reform of territorial divisions transformed the empire's 25 megaprovinces (*gubernii*) into 41 smaller ones (also called *gubernii*), each headed by an appointed governor. Two or three provinces were combined to make up a governor generalship, commanded by a governor general who personally reported to the empress, Senate, and procurator general. The reform sought to deconcentrate administrative power without giving up central control, and the governors general provided the link between the localities and the center. When in the capitals, governors general attended sessions of the Senate and sat in the departments where matters of concern to their provinces were being discussed. As a consequence of the reform, provincial bureaucracy and local officialdom grew enormously. At the time of the empress's death in 1796, the number of provinces reached 50, including those carved out of recently acquired territories in Crimea and Poland. Each province was further divided into districts (*uezdy*), the number of which rose from 169 in 1775 to 493 in 1796. Although the ratio of ranked officials to inhabitants did not improve in the reign of Catherine, the absolute number of these officials rose from 12,000 in 1755 to 21,300 in 1796, and all received salaries from the state.[50] In addition, as the empire's borders expanded and as administration in the borderlands evolved, new provinces continued to be formed and the boundaries of old ones reformed. The basic territorial structure established by Catherine proved adaptable and for this reason survived until the end of the monarchy in 1917.

Catherinian legislation also set up a system of local courts that would not be fundamentally altered before the liberal judicial reform of 1864.[51] Prior to Catherine's reign, local officials and provincial governors served as "judges" for the populations under their authority. The organization of judicial authority fell along *soslovie* lines, and there was no separation of judicial and administrative powers. The Catherinian reforms upheld the *soslovie* principle in local government but also attempted to separate administration, finance, and justice. Although at the district level these functions tended to overlap, the reforms did establish separate courts for nobles, townspeople, and state and crown peasants.[52] The local courts consisted of judges and assessors, some appointed and others elected by the social groups they served. Assessors did not actually decide cases, but rather advised the judge or judges who presided over the court. The governor or governor general confirmed in office all elected judges and assessors, and the provincial administration appointed judges to the peasant courts. Although the inequities of *soslovie* differentiation meant that nobles and townspeople enjoyed broader electoral rights than peasants, it remains significant that free (that is, non-seigniorial) peasants to some degree participated in elective courts. For the first time in Russian history, local communities across society became integrated into a regular system of justice with channels of appeal reaching the Senate and monarch in St Petersburg.

Closely tied to the local courts were the boards of public welfare (*prikazy obshchestvennogo prizreniia*), established in each province to oversee schools, orphanages, hospitals, insane asylums, almshouses, workhouses, and houses of correction. The boards of public welfare also supported local theaters and encouraged the development of state-regulated private philanthropy. Governors, together with assessors from the noble, town, and peasant courts, served on the boards, which tied these bodies to the government bureaucracy and enhanced the significance of local elections. Elections played an even greater role in the noble assemblies. Based on the reform of provincial administration and the Charter to the Nobility, the noble landowners of each district and province formed a noble assembly which met every three years to elect local noble officials, including judges, assessors, and marshals of the nobility, all subject to confirmation by the governor or governor general. Each district assembly elected a marshal of the nobility, and from this group the provincial assembly chose two candidates, one of whom the governor or governor general confirmed as provincial marshal of the nobility. The district and provincial marshals convened meetings of the noble assemblies, and the provincial marshals headed trusteeships responsible for the care of noble widows and orphans. The assemblies also enjoyed the right directly to petition the governor, the Senate, and even the monarch. Finally, the assemblies and elected marshals compiled the genealogical books of each province's nobles and hence also determined who possessed noble status. Like the boards of public welfare, the noble assemblies functioned both as sites of societal initiative and as extensions of the government bureaucracy. Linked to the courts and various administrative offices, the assemblies blurred the distinction between noble control of local government and bureaucratic control of noble affairs.

The Charter to the Towns produced similar ambiguities in a very different social setting. Like the Charter to the Nobility, the Charter to the Towns reinforced *soslovie* difference by strengthening distinctions between the categories of official urban "citizens," particularly merchants and ordinary townspeople, and between the town's citizens and legal or illegal residents. Like the Law Code of 1649, the charter defined economic functions, service obligations, and legal privileges based on membership in an official social category. Although, as in previous reigns, the effort to restrict participation in the town economy to official citizens and legal residents failed, the charter effectively established a representative structure for city government and an institutional framework for the emergence of urban political elites. An elected council of six members, one chosen from each of the six social categories participating in the general town council (*duma*), managed the town's economy, infrastructure, financial resources, welfare and educational institutions, obligations to the central government, and relations with other communities. Like the noble assembly, the council of six members also enjoyed the right to petition the governor regarding the needs of the town. Implementation of the Charter to the Towns remained far from uniform or complete; however, the Catherinian structure proved adaptable to the circumstances of particular communities and to future economic development. It survived without significant alteration until the 1870 reform of city government.[53]

Clearly, the concrete provisions of the Catherinian charters did not always become reality. Diverse local conditions repeatedly produced idiosyncratic applications of the law. Sometimes facts on the ground prevented the requirements of the law from being met; sometimes officials and their subordinate populations chose to ignore the law; and sometimes, especially in borderlands, minority and other social categories, Cossacks for instance, lived in separate "societies" under distinct legal-administrative regimes – that is, the law did not apply. Yet despite the perennial Russian gap between legal prescriptions and everyday life, the charters remained important not only for their specific effects, but also as expressions of the impulse to devise comprehensive laws that could be enforced uniformly across the empire. It is in this sense that the Charters to the Nobility and the Towns and the unpromulgated Charter to the State Peasants have been described in terms of a corporate "constitutional" order.[54] The charters applied to all members of a given social category, and within the confines of each category, Empress Catherine II hoped both to equalize the "rights" of her subjects and to bring a greater measure of security and predictability to their lives, or at least to their interactions with the government and fellow "citizens."

Decades earlier, Tsar Peter I had put forth a vision of regular government grounded in legal regulation, bureaucratic rationality, and obligatory service. Catherine II added to that vision a conception of government by moral means – a government built upon social engagement, legally regulated but free of coercion. In addition to defining social categories and guaranteeing their "rights," the Catherinian reforms sought to enlist local elites in the service of civic progress and regular government. At the time of Catherine's accession, the most coercive aspects of the Petrine service state had been dismantled, though only with respect to the nobility. A decade later, Russian literary culture began to treat noble service as a moral obligation and to associate the common good with civic duties rather than service obligations. Understanding of the common good remained oriented toward government needs, but also implied moral commitment and social responsibility. The monarch and nobles alike emerged as moral beings, and moral worthiness became a criterion of social status, legitimate authority, and the right to rule.[55] Worthiness to rule was hardly a new concept. Peter I institutionalized merit as a basis for noble status and in depriving Tsarevich Aleksei of the throne decried his lack of merit. Catherine II and her supporters likewise denounced Peter III for his personal moral failings. Repeatedly in the eighteenth century, legal monarchs and successors to the throne were deemed unworthy and removed from power. After the many irregularities surrounding the succession – irregularities that required immediate and long-term justification – political power came to represent the ability to assert not only military might and bureaucratic control but also moral authority. Although in Russia and abroad moral authority had long been central to Christian kingship, Catherine II relied on moral authority in a way that previous eighteenth-century rulers had not.[56]

The justification, assertion, and exercise of political power by moral means may have helped Empress Catherine II to feel comfortable on her illegally seized throne. But the reliance on moral authority also exposed the limits to regular government. In eighteenth-century Russia, the politics of moral authority substituted both for openly contested politics, hardly possible in absolutist Russia, and for strong civic institutions grounded in the rule of law. Since the mid-seventeenth century, Russia had made significant progress in state building, military mobilization, and the spread of European culture. This progress encouraged the development of (modern) legal-administrative forms of authority in which political relationships were impersonal, codified, and institution-based. But at the same time, the Russian government continued to rely on (medieval) personal-moral forms of authority to achieve its goals. Both the vastness of the Russian empire and the legal consciousness of policymakers militated against bureaucratic regularity. Distances and primitive communications left much decision making in local hands, while changeable conditions on the ground rendered irrelevant or inapplicable many legislative prescriptions emanating from the center. To keep a town functioning or a military regiment under arms required constant improvisation by officials and commanders. Improvisation affected judicial practice as well: if technical adherence to the law prevented justice from being rendered or duty from being fulfilled, authorities readily forgave violations of the law.

For physical and intellectual reasons, eighteenth-century Russia remained undergoverned and underinstitutionalized. Lacking the services of technically trained jurists (professional legal education became available only in 1835), Russia's governing elite looked to moral progress for solutions to legal-administrative problems.[57] The moral qualities of officials and subordinate populations hardly represented a reliable basis for regular government. Despite the good intentions of some officials, administrative corruption and abuse remained widespread. Plays such as Ivan Ia. Sokolov's *The Judge's Nameday* (1781), Vasilii V. Kapnist's *Chicanery* (1798), and Nikolai V. Gogol's *The Government Inspector* (1834) depict

Russian life as an endless stream of thievery, deception, and cruelty. Clearly, the goal of regular government proved elusive. Yet signs of civic progress also abounded. Toward the end of Catherine's reign local "societies" of the sort rarely seen outside Moscow and St Petersburg began to appear. Theater and public sociability, a national periodical press, and growing numbers of educated commoners and specialists could be seen in provincial towns across the land. The concrete achievements of Russian government surely fell short of literary and legislative ideals, but this did not preclude the emergence of reasonably effective civic institutions. After decades of uncertainty, political arrangements stabilized, allowing the government to bring a measure of material and cultural progress to people in the provinces.

Chapter 6

Russian Enlightenment Culture: A Moral Voice for Society

In the decades following the reforms of Tsar Peter I, European cultural models and Enlightenment ideas continued to pour into Russia. The empire's new cultural institutions developed at a rapid pace, and the educated classes became able contributors to a prepolitical literary public sphere.[1] To present-day observers, the literary, artistic, and scientific products of eighteenth-century Russia often seem artificial, derivative, and unoriginal. But Russia's educated classes achieved a noticeable presence in European society, and the cultural models they borrowed quickly filled with Russian content and meaning. Having adopted European manners, languages, and categories of thought, they began to take pride in their own cultural creations and to count themselves among the enlightened peoples of Europe. Hopeful and enthusiastic in the pursuit of knowledge, they embraced the fruits of European civilization, unencumbered by the idea that the Russian nation possessed a unique cultural heritage in need of preservation. Their love for the fatherland notwithstanding, educated Russians conceived morality, society, and politics in broad humanistic (or universal Christian) terms. They recognized cultural difference, but attributed such difference to concrete historical and environmental conditions, not to essentialist ethnic traits. Educated Russians also embraced rationalistic thinking and Enlightenment principles of earthly progress, natural equality, and the dignity of the individual human person, though they did not necessarily conclude that these principles required the elimination of absolute monarchy, noble privilege, or even the institution of serfdom. In their understanding, progress hinged as much on moral as on material or scientific development. Belief in equality and in the dignity of the individual meant that every human being possessed the same God-given capacity for moral goodness and that each person should be respected and recognized for his or her moral worth. In eighteenth-century Russia, the Enlightenment represented a moral philosophy, not a political or social movement.

——————   The Rise of Russian Enlightenment Culture   ——————

The moral impulses of the Russian Enlightenment blended easily with Orthodox religious beliefs, so it is not surprising that throughout the eighteenth century, religion retained a powerful hold over the Russian mind and imagination. But the church no longer defined the moral universe of the educated classes or the parameters of artistic expression. By the mid-eighteenth century, Russia possessed an elite secular culture independent of the church and closely associated with the monarchy. Following the lead of the court, Russia's predominantly noble, educated service classes provided the audience, patronage, and talent needed to sustain the development of modern letters, arts, and sciences. Church hierarchs, though members of a separate community, also belonged to the educated classes, and leading prelates such as Gedeon (Krinovskii, 1726–63), Gavriil (Petrov, 1730– 1801), and Platon (Levshin, 1737–1812) worked hard to integrate Orthodox teachings into the Enlightenment milieu of the court and nobility. When in 1778 future Bishop of Arkhangel'sk Apollos (Baibakov, 1737–1801) published a "sacred tragedy" based on the biblical story of Jephthah (*Judges* 11–12:7), he proclaimed a desire to show that alongside classical and contemporary European literature, biblical stories also could provide compelling subject matter for the theater.[2] As Apollos's play suggests, for a brief period lasting from the mid-eighteenth to the early nineteenth century, church, monarchy, and educated society all seemed to embrace the same European ideas and artistic forms. Their cooperation and like-mindedness produced the early fruits of modern Russian culture.

Contributions from the educated clergy and service classes notwithstanding, the monarchy remained the central player in the process of reflective cultural adaptation that had begun with Peter I. We have seen that Tsar Peter established Russia's first printed newspaper, first public theater, and first French-style evening parties. Peter also founded state schools and an Academy of Sciences with a *gymnasium* and university. In the post-Petrine era, the monarchy continued to create educational institutions and foster the spread of European art, architecture, and entertainment. By the 1730s, Italian actors, musicians, and singers performed at court, and from 1735 to the mid-1760s the "Italian company," a large ensemble of comedy, opera, and ballet artists, functioned as the permanent production center for court theater. German acting troupes also made appearances at court in 1738 and 1740, and French comedy arrived in 1742.[3] The monarchy became Russia's undisputed leader in the promotion of theater based on literary texts. Another creation of the monarchy, the St Petersburg Academy of Sciences, carried on the scholarly and scientific mission envisioned by founder Peter I. Beginning in the 1730s and 1740s, educated Russians, including Russian students of the academy, received appointments as adjuncts, professors, and academicians.

Throughout the eighteenth century, foreigners continued to occupy high-level academic positions, but increasingly, the academy's role as a European learned body stemmed not from the national origins of faculty, but from the international recognition accorded the science and scholarship of Imperial Russia.

In the reign of Empress Elizabeth, when political uncertainty temporarily abated and Russia's educated elite reached the critical mass necessary to become a voice for society, another formidable burst of government-sponsored cultural development occurred. Peter I's Academy of Sciences had included an art department, which in 1747 became part of the reorganized Academy of Sciences and Arts. Elizabeth then founded a separate Academy of Fine Arts in 1757. Based on legislation of 1764, the academy maintained a boarding school to identify talented youth and prepare them for advanced study in art, architecture, and sculpture. The Academy of Fine Arts remained Russia's premier art institution until the demise of the monarchy in 1917.[4] Moscow University, established in 1755, represented the empire's first fully operative Russian university.[5] The brainchild of Elizabeth's favorite, Ivan I. Shuvalov (1727–97), and the renowned poet and scientist, Mikhail V. Lomonosov (1711–65), the university housed three faculties (jurisprudence, medicine, and philosophy) and two *gymnasiums*, one for nobles and one for nonnobles, from which students could advance to higher education. The faculty of jurisprudence taught general jurisprudence, Russian jurisprudence, and politics; the medical faculty taught chemistry, natural history, and anatomy; and the philosophy faculty taught logic, metaphysics, moral philosophy (*nravouchenie*), experimental and theoretical physics, oratory and poetics (*krasnorechie*), general and Russian history, antiquities, and heraldry. Because both Russian and Latin served as languages of instruction and public discourse at the university, the preparatory *gymnasiums*, each consisting of four "schools," offered Russian in the first school and Latin in the second. The curriculum of the third school covered arithmetic, geometry, geography, and a short course in philosophy, while the fourth school taught Greek and the European languages that had become necessary for the mastery of modern learning (French, German, Italian, and English). Although decades would pass before the university adequately met its curricular obligations, the goal of establishing a European standard of higher education for Russia arose immediately.

From the outset, Moscow University also did more than educate young Russians. The university operated a printing press beginning in 1756, published the *Moscow News*, also from 1756, and provided a home for the public theater of Italian impresario Giovanni-Battista Locatelli from 1759 until his bankruptcy in 1762.[6] Under Locatelli's direction, university students staged contemporary European plays in Russian translation together with the tragedies and comedies of Russia's first celebrated playwright, Aleksandr P. Sumarokov (1717–77). Support for Locatelli stemmed from a broader government effort to promote public theater that had begun with the opening of the Russian Imperial Theater in 1756.[7] Located in St Petersburg, the Russian Theater benefited from direct government financing and quickly overshadowed the productions of private managers and educational institutions. Almost immediately, the theater began to offer regular performances on Mondays and Thursdays. In 1759 the Russian Theater became a professional troupe under court administration, comparable to the already existing French and Italian troupes, and part of the growing network of imperial theaters. Imperial status provided the theater with trained performers, set and costume designers, and musicians, but also undercut its public character. Only when the court left St Petersburg could the paying public attend performances. During the period 1767 to 1783, the imperial theaters gave 1,261 performances, of which 555 were open to "private viewers."

Convinced that theater brought moral and cultural benefits to society, Empress Catherine II tried to increase public access by sponsoring free performances in St Petersburg and Moscow. In 1765 the Moscow theater on the Devich'e field and the St Petersburg theater on Brumberg Square staged performances free of charge before diverse audiences of nobles and commoners. Free public theater proved fleeting, however, as the government could not long finance productions that generated no revenues through ticket sales. Instead, the authorities continued the practice of granting privileges to impresarios. Few of them, however, achieved lasting success. One after the other, and sometimes in pairs, Russian and foreign theater managers suffered financial losses that forced them to close down operations. In 1780 one of the more successful managers, the English tightrope-walker Michael Maddox, obtained a monopoly to put on plays and various entertainments in Moscow. Maddox's productions continued for roughly two decades and included the building of a permanent theater, the Petrovskii. But Maddox also never got out of debt. Eventually, the Moscow Foundling Home took over his theater and debts, and in 1806 the Directorate of Imperial Theaters in St Petersburg began to manage all public theater in the empire's second capital.

In St Petersburg, direct government control of public theater appeared even sooner. Legislation of 1783 designated two "city theaters" for the paying public, and for a time impresarios received privileges and leased theaters from the Directorate. But like their Moscow counterparts, the St Petersburg theater managers also had trouble making ends meet. The network of imperial theaters, by contrast, grew and solidified. In 1800 the Directorate maintained five city and five suburban theaters in St Petersburg and its environs. By 1827, and continuing until 1882, the Russian Imperial Theater held a monopoly on theater productions in both capitals. Only in the provinces, thanks to local energy and resources, did independent theater manage to survive. The provincial organizers of theatrical performances included governors and boards of public welfare working with contracted actors, wealthy nobles who trained and maintained troupes of serf actors, private impresarios, and amateur performers who also could be nobles. Provincial theater developed unevenly and never attained the cachet of imperial performances, but still made a significant cultural contribution. Already in 1752, the formation of the Russian Imperial Theater had begun with the summoning to St Petersburg of an acting troupe from Iaroslavl, headed by the merchant's son and factory owner Fedor G. Volkov (1729–63).

Although the staffing and financial problems of Russian cultural institutions continued into the nineteenth century, the policies of Peter I and his daughter Elizabeth established the foundations for sustained development. Catherine II continued these efforts and in 1783 founded the Imperial Russian Academy for the study of the Russian language. The academy operated as a separate institution until 1841, when it became the Second Section of the Academy of Sciences.[8] Like her predecessors, Catherine believed that Russia belonged to the world of European culture and should adopt the intellectual and artistic models emanating from Europe. But her approach to cultural progress reached beyond the building of institutions and the education of personnel. Catherine also actively cultivated the creative and spiritual capacities of her subjects. Because the number of educated Russians remained small, the empress acted as a kind of grand *salonnière* eager to engage in polite conversation. She contributed to the conversation by authoring memoirs, political theory, plays (in French and Russian), fairy tales, and primers (*azbuki*), including one written for her grandson, the future Alexander I. Catherine also corresponded with Enlightenment intellectuals such as Voltaire, Denis Diderot, Jean Le Rond d'Alembert, and Baron Melchior von Grimm. Above all, the empress encouraged her subjects to read, think, and write. Princess Ekaterina R. Dashkova (1743–1810) reports that in 1786 Catherine persuaded her to write a play for the court's Hermitage Theater. The empress understood from personal experience the pleasure that writing could bring, and so Dashkova spent several days writing the comedy *Mr This-and-That*.[9] Alongside churchmen, professors, academicians, and court poets, a substantial number of educated individuals, noble and nonnoble, tried their hand at composing literary, scientific, and philosophical works. They, together with their readers and the products of their pens, made up Russia's prepolitical literary public sphere, a cultural space for the debate of social, political, and moral issues.

As early as the 1730s, Russian authors and translators began to read their compositions in literary circles and salons.[10] Yet for decades to come, the periodicals published by official cultural institutions remained the most effective means for fostering debate and informing the public about scientific and artistic developments.[11] Between 1728 and 1742, the Academy of Sciences produced a supplement to the *St Petersburg News* that published literary works and translations alongside articles devoted to history, geography, ethnography, mathematics, and science. From 1755 through 1764, the academy published another literary-scientific journal,

Monthly Compositions (*Ezhemesiachnye sochineniia*), which in an effort to provide society with useful information covered subjects such as history, geography, statistics, ethnography, economics, commerce, philosophy, and literature. Finally, in 1756 Moscow University began to issue the *Moscow News*, patterned after the *St Petersburg News*, which also could be described as an institutional periodical for the broad reading public. In the decades following Peter's death, Russian authorities recognized that the educated classes needed up-to-date information. They also assumed that official publications should play a role in spreading European cultural models among the reading and writing public.

Just as official and unofficial cultural products could be one and the same in eighteenth-century Russia, author and audience could be difficult to distinguish. Most authors were either amateur writers unfettered by romantic notions of individual artistic genius or talented writers who also held appointments in military or civil service. The makers of Russia's modern literary culture, whether at court, in service, or at home on a country estate, basically talked among themselves. The readership for literary publications remained miniscule by European standards, and no private printing presses operated before the 1770s. Individuals could rent government presses for private projects, but only briefly, between 1783 and 1796, did the law allow independent presses, subject to police supervision, to operate freely.[12] Censorship also affected the content of literary culture, though it had not yet become systematized in a special administrative apparatus. The church oversaw religious publications, and institutions that operated printing presses employed in-house censors to identify material opposed to existing laws, the government, the church, or standards of decency and good manners. Censorship lacked consistency and in practice often seemed equivalent to attentive editing. But censorship also could hit like a bolt out of the blue and be imposed in an arbitrary manner. Woe to the author or publisher who willfully or accidentally aroused the monarch's suspicions, incurring his or her personal disfavor. Self-censorship represented an essential (and historically unmeasureable) skill that Russian intellectuals had better master.

Unfortunately, historians possess little concrete understanding of how censorship impacted the progress of letters, arts, and sciences in eighteenth-century Russia. That the effects tended to be intermittent is suggested by the appearance of unofficial literary journals as early as 1759. Though short-lived and also printed at government presses, journals such as *The Industrious Bee* (*Trudoliubivaia pchela*), produced in 1759 by Aleksandr P. Sumarokov, and *Idle Time Used Well* (*Prazdnoe vremia, v pol'zu upotreblennoe*), issued in 1759–60 by teachers and students at the Noble Cadet Corps, showcased the literary labors of Russia's emerging intellectual elite. *The Industrious Bee* published moral philosophy, Russian poetry, and the works of Sumarokov, whose views on the development of Russian literature the journal promoted. Sumarokov soon ran into trouble with literary rival Mikhail V.

Lomonosov and with censors at the Academy of Sciences. *The Industrious Bee* was closed, and in 1760 the poet moved his activities to *Idle Time Used Well*, which continued the publication of his compositions alongside works, predominantly translations, devoted to moral philosophy, ancient history and culture, economics, and education. Both journals also published translations of classical and European literature and showed a special interest in satire. At roughly the same time, Moscow University brought out a series of literary journals, edited by poet, playwright, novelist, and Freemason Mikhail M. Kheraskov (1733–1807). Historians describe *Useful Entertainment* (*Poleznoe uveselenie*, 1760–62), *Idle Hours* (*Svobodnye chasy*, 1763), and *Good Intention* (*Dobroe namerenie*, 1764) as the first Russian journals devoted solely to artistic literature and particularly to poetry. Through Kheraskov's publications and with the help of his personal patronage, the likes of Vasilii I. Maikov (1728–78), Ippolit F. Bogdanovich (1743–1803), and Denis I. Fonvizin (1744 or 1745–92) launched literary careers.

Both Sumarokov and Kheraskov occupied official positions at leading cultural institutions, and both therefore embodied the lack of a clear distinction between official and intellectual elites in eighteenth-century Russia. Sumarokov served as the first director of the Russian Imperial Theater until 1761, and Kheraskov served in various posts at Moscow University from the time of its founding in 1755. Both men became towering literary figures, and because of their literary talents, both also are seen by historians as representing the emergence of a Russian educated elite separate from the government. But a firm boundary between educated servicemen and independent intellectuals had not yet developed in Russia, and so in journalism, as in theater, the monarchy continued to play a critical and fruitful role. Indeed, under the stewardship of Empress Catherine II, the periodical press became more than a means to promote literary trends or disseminate useful information. Catherine used the press to draw her subjects into serious intellectual discussion, and she deserves credit for nurturing their efforts.

The empress's direct sponsorship of the periodical press began in 1769–70 with the publication of a satirical journal, *All Sorts of Things* (*Vsiakaia vsiachina*), devoted to the eradication of vice and the unmasking of corruption and abuse in Russian society. Catherine's precise role in the journal's publication remains unclear, though historians agree that she followed the progress of its production and that her voice is heard in its pages. Echoing the empress's desire to spread enlightenment, the editor of *All Sorts of Things* sought to elicit reader reaction by urging the public to participate in journalistic debate. Several journals emerged in response, and in the case of *The Drone* (*Truten'*), published by Nikolai I. Novikov (1744–1818) in 1769–70, direct exchanges with the editor of *All Sorts* ensued.[13] A leading Freemason and private publisher, Novikov continued to produce satirical journals for several years, publishing *The Tatler* (*Pustomelia*) in 1770; *The Painter* (*Zhivopisets*), with financial assistance from Catherine, in 1772–3; and *The Purse*

(*Koshelek*) in 1774. Other literary figures who in 1769–70 answered the call to publish satirical journals included Fedor A. Emin (1735–70), Mikhail D. Chulkov (ca. 1742/1743–92), and Vasilii I. Maikov.[14]

In each of the satirical journals, contributors responded to *All Sorts of Things*, engaged the content of competing publications, and provided moral commentary that sought to define the appropriate parameters of satire and to expose the vices of individuals and social groups. The satirical approach can be seen as a salutary antidote to the ferocious polemics and personal attacks that dominated the careers of such literary icons as Sumarokov, Lomonosov, and especially the unjustly mocked "fool" of Russia's "new literature," Vasilii K. Trediakovskii.[15] By assuming a humorous rather than accusatory tone, the editors of satirical journals hoped to improve behavior, prevent abuses, and limit exploitation. Equally important for the development of modern Russian culture, the flurry of activity initiated by Catherine established Russian literary journals, modeled after the moral weeklies of Europe, as a vibrant forum for public debate.

Empress Catherine II also promoted public debate by supporting the establishment of Russia's first learned societies. The Free Economic Society for the Encouragement in Russia of Agriculture and Domestic Economy, created in 1765, remained prominent until the end of the monarchy in 1917.[16] The society began as a self-governing organization composed of fifteen founder members, one of whom drew up its regulatory statute. Catherine approved the statute, and with her protection and financial support, the Free Economic Society set about collecting useful information which it disseminated through the publication of *Transactions* (*Trudy*). During the first twenty-five years of the society's existence, it had close to 300 members, whose relations, according to the founding statute, rested on concrete knowledge and practical skills rather than social origin and service rank. That the Free Economic Society did indeed foster critical thinking and egalitarian social intercourse is evident from the famous essay competition it held in 1766–8.

The question posed in the essay competition concerned the usefulness to society of granting property rights to peasants.[17] Given the centrality of serfdom in Russia, the question carried a powerful political message. The winning essay, written by Beardé de l'Abbaye of Aachen, a French member of the Dijon Academy, concluded that while emancipation required long-term preparation, peasant freedom and ownership of land would benefit both the government and landowners. Such implicit criticism of Russian society did not at all disturb Catherine. The empress viewed serfdom as a morally harmful institution that eventually would be abolished. There is even evidence to suggest that she or other "influential persons" orchestrated the submission of the essay in order to counter a more radical response written by Voltaire.[18] When asked if Beardé de l'Abbaye's essay should be translated and published, Catherine approved the idea. But she also left the final decision about publication in the hands of the society. After some hesitation, members voted fifteen to thirteen to publish, and a Russian translation of the essay appeared in the *Transactions* of 1768. Why, despite the empress's advice (and possible participation), the question of publication divided the society's membership remains unclear. Some members may have feared political repression (perhaps in the future) or social disorder. Others may have thought that such sensitive issues should not be publicly debated or that ideas about the abolition of serfdom should not be disseminated beyond a narrow circle of trustworthy specialists. Still others may have believed in the legitimacy of the institution. The motivations behind individual votes no doubt varied, yet on the whole, the disagreement revealed an ability to think independently even in the shadow of the empress.

The debate over publication did not change the fact that in general the Free Economic Society seemed content to follow Catherine's lead, and lead the empress did. In 1768 Catherine established a society to promote the development of the Russian language, the Society for the Translation of Foreign Books, which in 1783 became part of the newly created Imperial Russian Academy for the study of the Russian language. By that time, the society had published 112 translations and prepared another 129, a substantial contribution to the overall growth of publishing in Catherine's reign.[19] Concern for the progress of Russian literature produced similar associations at Moscow University.[20] The idea for the Free Russian Assembly of Lovers of the Russian Language dated to 1757, though only in 1771 did the assembly begin to pursue the goal of enriching the Russian language by publishing original and translated literature. In a gesture to the public, the assembly invited the participation of "all lovers of the sciences," whether or not they enjoyed university affiliation. The Free Russian Assembly closed in 1787, also superseded by the Imperial Russian Academy, but the group left a corpus of publications and documentary collections related to the preparation of Russian, church, and geographical dictionaries. In addition, the assembly encouraged the development of other groups among students and professors at the university. Beginning in 1781, the Assembly of University Pupils, formed under the supervision of Professor and active Freemason Johann Georg Schwarz (1751–84), held literary readings and discussions for current and former students. In 1789 the supervisor (*kurator*) of the university founded the Society of Lovers of Learnedness (*uchenost'*), which he hoped would promote the enlightenment of the mind (*razum*), the improvement of the heart, good taste, and happiness. In keeping with this goal, the society immediately sponsored an essay competition devoted to a classically eighteenth-century question: "With which sciences should the enlightenment of a person begin – with those that concern the heart and morality or with those that belong to the mind (*razum*) and keenness (*ostrota*)?" The conflation of morality and science stood at the core of Russian Enlightenment culture.

The operations of Russia's learned societies, like those of public theater and the periodical press, retained a semi-official status into the nineteenth century. The Free Economic Society, Catherine's translation society, and the various assemblies at Moscow University all emanated from persons occupying official positions in the government. Not surprisingly, these bodies did not become autonomous, politically organized civic organizations. But they did represent a modern form of voluntary association. Members came together in self-governing collectives to pursue an activity in which they shared a common interest. The societies of the Catherinian era also did more than promote moral education and the development of Russian literature and science. They instilled habits of critical thinking and debate. As sites of social intercourse grounded in Enlightenment principles of equality and intellectual achievement, they encouraged ideological independence and implicit disregard for established social hierarchies. In this respect, they not only brought Europe's republic of letters to Russia; they also set the stage for the transformation of Russia's prepolitical literary public sphere into the more truly independent learned societies, philanthropic organizations, secret societies, and intellectual circles of the early nineteenth century.

──────────── Voices of the Russian Enlightenment ────────────

If the modern Russian state "took off" in the reign of Peter I, modern Russian culture "took off" in the reign of Catherine II. That Catherine's subjects responded to her cultural leadership with energy and aplomb is evident from the rapid progress of Russian letters, arts, and sciences in the later eighteenth century. Of course, well before Catherine's reign, individual Russians began to make their mark in the world of European culture. Antiokh D. Kantemir (1708–44), the son of a Moldavian prince who entered the service of Peter I, is described as "arguably Russia's first indigenous Enlightenment man of letters."[21] Kantemir studied Greek, Latin, Italian, and Russian from an early age; briefly attended the Moscow Slavonic-Greek-Latin Academy; and completed his formal education at the St Petersburg Academy of Sciences, where he also began to learn French. Literary historians remember him for translations of classical and European literature, for poetry written in syllabic verse, and especially for verse satires directed against ignorance, hypocrisy, and corruption.[22] Kantemir was sent to Britain for diplomatic service in 1732, and remained abroad until his death, but before leaving Russia, he collaborated with Feofan (Prokopovich) and Vasilii N. Tatishchev to edit documents and write historical works that glorified the deeds of Peter I. Out of this "learned guard" (*uchenaia druzhina*), an informal circle of intellectuals organized by Feofan, Vasilii N. Tatishchev (1688–1750) emerged to become "the first Russian to publish a documented history of Russia." Tatishchev wrote his *Russian History* in the 1730s and 1740s, and it was "published in successive parts or books in 1768, 1769, 1773, 1774, 1784, and 1848."[23] The *History* remains the most admired Russian historical work to come out of the eighteenth century.

Following in the footsteps of Kantemir and Tatishchev, three founders of Russia's modern literary language also achieved international recognition in the decades prior to the accession of Catherine II. Vasilii K. Trediakovskii (1703–69), Mikhail V. Lomonosov (1711–65), and Aleksandr P. Sumarokov (1717–77) repeatedly clashed with each other in heated and often vicious literary debates, yet together they elevated Russian literature to a position of prominence in contemporary Europe.[24] In 1745 both Trediakovskii, the son of a priest, and Lomonosov, the son of a prosperous ship-owner and state peasant, became the first Russian professors at the Academy of Sciences in St Petersburg. Trediakovskii received an appointment as Professor of Latin and Russian Eloquence and Lomonosov as Professor of Chemistry. Trediakovskii's work covered a broad range of literary genres, and he is today admired for contributions to poetry, versification, literary theory, and linguistics. Also an able and scholarly translator, he looked to ancient Greek for models of versification and to Church Slavonic for vocabulary to enrich the Russian literary language. Trediakovskii struggled heroically to develop a poetic style that would be distinct from everyday speech, but instead of garnering praise, he ended up being ridiculed by generations of literary polemicists. In his own lifetime, Trediakovskii also experienced profound professional disappointment. He became isolated from colleagues and former collaborators, stopped attending the academy in 1757, suffered dismissal in 1759, and died in poverty in 1769. In more recent times, Trediakovskii's reputation has revived, as scholars have come to appreciate his serious literary accomplishments.

The conflicting images of Trediakovskii stand in stark contrast to the esteem and adoration long enjoyed by his colleague, sometime collaborator, and literary opponent, Mikhail V. Lomonosov. Beginning in the eighteenth century and continuing to the present day, Lomonosov has been rightly beloved for his poetic talent and intellectual genius. Known as "the first Russian chemist and physicist," Lomonosov regarded his scientific achievements as the most important of his life.[25] But he also made lasting contributions to linguistics and history, and he played a pivotal role in the founding of Moscow University, which now bears his name. During a variegated and illustrious literary career, Lomonosov defined the characteristics of Russian solemn ode, collaborated with Trediakovskii to reform Russian versification and formulate the principles of syllabo-tonic meter, and in 1755 completed his *Russian Grammar* (published in 1757), "the first published grammar of the Russian language written in Russian."[26] Although also an expert in mining, metallurgy, the art of mosaics, chemistry, and physics, Lomonosov is best remembered for his poetry, particularly the use of iambic tetrameter and rhymed verse, and for his mythological status as "the father of Russian literature."[27]

The third giant of eighteenth-century Russian literature, Aleksandr P. Sumarokov, an associate and rival of both Trediakovskii and Lomonosov, achieved renown among contemporaries as the Russian Boileau, the Russian Racine, the Russian Molière, the Russian La Fontaine, and the Russian Voltaire.[28] Present-day readers value Sumarokov for his clear and precise literary style, which implanted in Russia the rules of European neoclassicism. In addition to directing the Russian Imperial Theater and helping to develop the periodical press, Sumarokov produced models of Russian literature in almost "every current European poetic and dramatic genre": fable, song, sonnet, elegy, satire, eclogue, idyll, epigram, ballad, madrigal, rondeau, folktale, ode, tragedy, comedy, opera, and ballet. Sumarokov also carries the title of Russia's "first professional writer," due to his status as court poet and director of the Russian Imperial Theater, able after 1756 to devote all his time to literary pursuits.[29] In the words of Nikolai I. Novikov, who published Sumarokov's collected works in 1781–2, the poet 'achieved great and immortal fame for himself via works in a variety of poetic and prose genres, not only from Russians but from foreign Academies and from the most famous European writers.'[30]

Among readers and literary scholars of today, Trediakovskii, Lomonosov, and Sumarokov are appreciated more for their historical importance than for the artistic pleasure they provide. This is no surprise, given the technical and aesthetic distance separating the ornate Slavonic style of Feofan (Prokopovich) from the elegant classicism of Sumarokov. Change came quickly to the Russian language, and in contrast to the early masters of Russian literature, individuals who sought to establish normative rules of composition and who viewed their creative work as the fulfillment of a service obligation, the writers of the later eighteenth century, those who rose to prominence or began literary careers in the reign of Catherine II, are both more numerous and more intellectually and stylistically diverse. Equally important, audiences from the eighteenth century to the present have continued to enjoy their works. The comedies of Denis I. Fonvizin, the most admired artifacts of the eighteenth-century Russian stage, elicit outright laughter with their depictions of moral corruption and social vice. Despite Fonvizin's use of stilted moralistic prose, plays such as *The Brigadier* (1769) and *The Minor* (1783) retain their power both to entertain and to evoke moral outrage over the abuses of serfdom, the injustices of social hierarchy, and the personal degradation caused by unbridled ambition. In Fonvizin's comedies, one finds the quintessential realization of Enlightenment literature's effort to teach and be socially useful without overburdening the human mind.

To Fonvizin's use of satire to deliver social criticism and moral instruction, Nikolai M. Karamzin (1766–1826) added sentimentalist prose and verse.[31] An active translator, journalist, historian, and poet (and possibly also a Freemason), Karamzin is acclaimed for the epistolary travelogue, *Letters of a Russian Traveler* (1797–1801), and for sentimentalist tales such as "Poor Liza" (1792) and "Natal'ia, the Boyar's

Daughter" (1792). Both the *Letters* and the tales assume a close relationship between the reader and a narrator who shares his personal emotions, thoughts, and experiences. Karamzin also claims credit for devoting serious attention to women readers and for holding up female sensibilities and virtues as models for all authors to follow. Scholars see in his prose and poetry, which today can sound overwrought and melodramatic, an accessible language and an original emotive style that by feminizing Russian literature brought it to a higher level of artistic achievement. Karamzin's twelve-volume *History of the Russian State* (1816–29) became a monument not only in the field of modern Russian history but also in the history of modern Russian literature. His sentimentalist aesthetics, which emphasized feeling and imagination as sources of knowledge and self-understanding, anticipated the broad appeal of the naturalist orientation in Russian literature and the literary genius attributed to subsequent generations of Russian writers. But Karamzin also remained a product of the Catherinian era, and his *Memoir on Ancient and Modern Russia* (1811) showed him to be a statesman, political theorist, and conservative defender of serfdom and absolute monarchy.[32] The perfect synthesis of loyal serviceman and European man of letters, Karamzin epitomized the harmonious blend of morality, culture, and politics that defined the Russian Enlightenment.

Like Karamzin, Ivan A. Krylov (1769–1844) formed a bridge between the culture building of the eighteenth century and the full flowering of modern Russian literature in the nineteenth.[33] By the end of Catherine II's reign, Krylov enjoyed a solid literary reputation based on his work as a journalist, playwright, and satirist. Soon after the accession of Alexander I, he turned his attention to the writing of fables. It is as a fabulist that he is most familiar to readers of today. The son of a poor military officer who had risen from the ranks, Krylov's ascent to literary greatness began already in his lifetime. Under the patronage of Aleksei N. Olenin (1763–1843), who in 1811 became director of the Imperial Public Library, he obtained a library post and became a not infrequent guest at court. In 1838, to commemorate Krylov's seventieth birthday, a medal was minted in his honor and a scholarship established in his name. Ironically, despite the official recognition accorded to Krylov, cultural historians connect his biting satire to the libertine literature of eighteenth-century Europe. Highlighted most famously in studies of political libels and "forbidden bestsellers" popular in the period leading up to the French Revolution, libertine literature used erotic and pornographic themes to encourage political dissent.[34] Whether or not Krylov intended to promote freethinking or the desacralization of the monarchy, he represented an early Russian version of the celebrity author and person of literary genius eager to the push the limits of acceptable speech. Recognition of Krylov's artistic talent and reverence for his bold irreverence endure in the twenty-first century.

Although often uninspiring and clumsy, the products of eighteenth-century Russian culture seem remarkable when one considers the limited intellectual offerings of the Petrine era. In numerous areas of literary, artistic, and scientific endeavor, native Russians made significant contributions which today are considered foundational works in the development of modern Russian culture.[35] Russian scholarship, like Russian literature, began to appear by the mid-eighteenth century and then "took off" in the reign of Catherine II. At Moscow University, during a time when Germans dominated the professoriate, Nikolai N. Popovskii (1730–60), a student of Lomonosov and Professor of Eloquence and Philosophy from 1755, taught the university's first philosophy course in Russian. Semen E. Desnitskii (ca. 1740–89) and Ivan A. Tret'iakov (1735–76), both regarded as followers of Adam Smith, became Russia's first Professors of Law, after studying at Glasgow University in 1761–7. The philosopher and mathematician, Dmitrii S. Anichkov (1733–88), also a professor at Moscow University from 1771, attained notoriety as a "freethinker" following the presentation of his 1769 dissertation *Discourse from Natural Theology on the Origin and Occurrence of Natural Worship of God*. In St Petersburg, Grigorii N. Teplov (1717–79) provided Russian readers with a handbook on European philosophy (1751), and Iakov P. Kozel'skii (1728–after 1793) published *Philosophical Propositions* (1768), another popular account that examined philosophy from a scientific perspective. One could mention numerous other Russian scholars from the ecclesiastical and secular elites, together with architects, painters, and sculptors from the serf and free classes.[36] Yet only a handful of individuals emerged from the intellectual melting pot of the Russian Enlightenment to become canonical cultural figures. For this reason, the eighteenth century seems less important for the works and achievements of gifted artists, writers, and scholars than for the cumulative progress that produced Europeanized educated classes and a Russian version of modern European culture.

Indeed, during the period from the mid-eighteenth to the mid-nineteenth century, educated Russians collectively developed social relationships and creative talents that turned the government-led cultural borrowing of Peter I and his successors into letters, arts, and sciences that became distinctively Russian in content, form, and meaning. An especially poignant site of cultural Russianness arose in the institution of serfdom, which outside the imperial court provided the most effective support for artistic development.[37] Although church hierarchs and merchants also required the services of architects and painters, noble serf owners became the most visible patrons of the arts. Nobles could educate their human property and force serf architects, painters, and laborers to build and decorate their palaces. They also could force serf actors, musicians, dancers, and singers to entertain the residents and guests of those palaces. Serf choirs, orchestras, and musical ensembles, being relatively cheap to train and maintain, became especially numerous. Historians estimate that in the late eighteenth century, over one thousand serf musicians provided music for up to fifty monthly balls in Moscow.[38]

Serf theaters required greater resources and tended to be the preserve of the wealthiest nobles. Historians identify a total of 155 serf theaters that operated between the 1760s and the 1840s; another 18 that are mentioned in contemporary reports remain uncorroborated. A majority of the serf theaters (103) were located in 14 towns, and of these, 40 operated in the eighteenth century, 31 in eighteenth-century Moscow. Rural estates in 23 provinces maintained 53 serf theaters, of which 24 are dated to the eighteenth century.[39] The aristocratic Sheremetev family established the most acclaimed serf theater, which from 1779 until 1797 gave performances in Moscow, Kuskovo, Markovo, and Ostankino. Father and son, Petr B. (1713–88) and Nikolai P. (1751–1809) Sheremetev, employed an international array of artists, masters, architects, and composers, and their theater produced a varied repertoire of French, Italian, German, and Russian works, including operas, comedies, and ballets.[40] Out of these artistic endeavors, there also emerged a real-life drama, the marriage of Nikolai to his serf actress, Praskov'ia Kovaleva (Zhemchugova, 1768–1803), who after giving her husband a son and heir, died tragically from the combined effects of childbirth and tuberculosis.

In addition to providing pleasure for the master, serf painters, architects, and performers became prized economic assets. Skilled individuals sold for a high price, and serf performances sometimes turned into commercial operations. At the turn of the nineteenth century, in the provincial town of Nizhnii Novgorod, the serf theater of Prince Nikolai G. Shakhovskoi (d. 1824) evolved into commercialized public theater. Shakhovskoi, who spent winters in Moscow and summers on his estate in Nizhnii Novgorod province, reportedly maintained a household with about 300 servants, including an ensemble of musicians, singers, actors, and actresses. In 1798, with assistance from local nobles, his serf troupe became the Nizhnii Novgorod public theater. Decades later, in 1827, two local residents, a government official and a first-guild merchant, purchased the theater on condition that the serf actors and actresses – 96 persons, including children – be freed. Shakhovskoi's commercialized serf theater thus became a privately operated commercial theater where hired performers entertained a paying public.[41] The apparently happy fate of Shakhovskoi's troupe should not obscure the more general suffering endured by serf painters, architects, actors, and musicians who, more often than not, wallowed away their lives in personal subjugation. The experience of artistic awareness combined with unrealized opportunity led many an individual to alcoholism and/or suicide.[42] It is an all too fitting irony of Russian history that private serf owners, living like absolute monarchs, commanded troupes of "court" performers, whose exploitation, at times cruel and inhuman, contributed much to the creation of artistic life in the empire's capitals and provincial towns.

Serf theater, despite significant artistic achievements, represented a pernicious form of private cultural patronage. Private publishing, on the other hand, brought more genuine public benefits that grew to unprecedented dimensions in the reign of Catherine II.[43] Before the legalization of private publishing in 1783, a handful of individuals successfully petitioned for permission to open presses. The most renowned of these, Nikolai I. Novikov (1744–1818), acquired a ten-year lease on the Moscow University Typography in 1778. Beginning in 1783, the government also allowed private publishers to purchase and operate printing presses without first obtaining a privilege. The privately owned presses had to be registered with the local police, who then became responsible for ensuring that content inimical to church, government, or decency did not get published. Based on the 1783 law, Novikov added to his publishing operations the Rosicrucian Press, established in 1783, and the Typographical Company, established in 1784. Both presses depended for financial support on Novikov's ties to Freemason circles, literary collaborators, and rich patrons, and both drained his economic resources. Still, despite the financial uncertainty, the presses produced over 350 publications between 1783 and 1792. Together with the Moscow University Typography, Novikov's presses accounted for close to 40 percent of Russian-language publications in the years 1785 to 1789.[44]

Impressive as these numbers seem, the growth of private publishing under Catherine II proved transitory. In economic terms, the Russian reading public remained too small to sustain a publishing industry. More important, in the early 1790s, the empress's long-term cultivation of intellectual life gave way to visible repression. In 1790 Aleksandr N. Radishchev (1749–1802) published *Journey from Petersburg to Moscow*, which condemned tyranny, serfdom, and censorship in the name of natural liberty. Just days after seeing Radishchev's book, Catherine ordered his arrest, and within a month he had been convicted by a criminal court and sentenced to death. Radishchev awaited his demise for over a year, until Catherine decided to commute the sentence to ten years' exile in the remote Siberian town of Ilimsk (about 330 miles north of Irkutsk).[45] Soon thereafter, in 1792, Nikolai I. Novikov, who had personally collaborated with the empress to produce satirical journals, suffered a similar fate: arrest, conviction, and incarceration in the Schlüsselburg Fortress for publishing and distributing banned books. Finally, in 1796 the empress ordered the closure of all privately owned printing presses.

Over time, Catherine II's commitment to private publishing succumbed to the instincts of the absolute monarch. Censorship grew more bureaucratic, regulative, and intrusive, as suspicions aroused by Freemasonry, the French Revolution, and the appearance of dissidence, or perceived dissidence, among leading Russian intellectuals took their toll. The construction of a modern censorship apparatus began with a Catherinian decree of 1796, subsequently confirmed by Emperor Paul, and continued under Alexander I, who in 1804 instituted Russia's first systematic censorship law requiring prepublication review of all books and compositions. Clearly, the monarchy intended to impose control over the written word. In practice, however, the effective reach of the censors remained limited, and Alexander actually encouraged the spread of print culture by lifting the ban on private presses. Radishchev achieved lasting recognition as one of Russia's first dissident intellectuals, and Novikov's legacy endured to inspire later generations. Private publishing revived very quickly in the reign of Alexander I, becoming an unstoppable torrent by the mid-nineteenth century.

A similar pattern of societal initiative, government repression, and subsequent upsurge also characterized the development of secret, philanthropic, and cultural societies that arose outside the orbit of the court and official institutions. The process began with the development of Freemasonry during the later eighteenth century. Freemasonry originated in seventeenth-century England and Scotland among master stonemasons who had developed legends and rituals highlighting their role as builders of palaces and churches. Over time, the myths and ceremonies of the stonemasons attracted the attention of individuals interested in science and esoteric philosophy, and by the eighteenth century the guilds evolved into fraternal lodges which opened their membership to outsiders. Freemasonry came to be seen as a means to gain "access to the wisdom and secrets of the ancients."[46] Masons modeled their lodges on the biblical Temple of Solomon – "the only perfect edifice ever known, built by divine wisdom but later destroyed" – which they also sought to rebuild.[47] The lodges functioned in secret, usually as brotherhoods, bound together by rites, constitutions, mysteries, and degrees of access to a carefully guarded body of knowledge. At its height in 1766–70, Freemasonry in England encompassed 184 London and 200 provincial lodges.

In the second quarter of the eighteenth century, Freemasonry spread out from Britain across the European continent, carried by geographically mobile merchants who made up a significant proportion of the membership.[48] In the 1730s and 1740s, Englishmen, Scotsmen, and Russians who had lived abroad brought Freemasonry to Russia.[49] Russian Masons came mainly from the noble service classes, though a sizeable contingent of merchants, manufacturers, nonnoble officials, professionals, artisans, performers, artists, and clergy also joined the lodges. Even a handful of former serfs, including Andrei N. Voronikhin (1760–1814), a noted architect freed by his master and probably father, Count Aleksandr S. Stroganov (1733–1811), became initiated into Masonic degrees.[50] Over the course of the eighteenth century, more than 140 Masonic lodges appeared in roughly 40 cities and towns of the Russian empire. The peak of activity occurred between 1770 and 1790, when the number of active lodges increased from under 14 at the end of the 1760s to around 90 at the end of the 1780s. The largest concentrations formed in Moscow and St Petersburg, with Moscow superseding St Petersburg as the center of Russian Freemasonry during the 1780s.

Most emblematic of Moscow Freemasonry was the Rosicrucian circle of Nikolai I. Novikov, which in the early 1780s began to acquire a public face.[51] In the words of Novikov, the goal of the brothers of the Golden-Rose Cross was to attain 'an understanding of God through awareness of nature and oneself, following the teachings of Christian morals.'[52] Rosicrucians worked for the establishment of God's kingdom on earth, which they conceived as a condition of universal harmony based on humanity's reunification with God and nature. Individually and collectively, they embarked upon a spiritual journey leading to ever-higher degrees of knowledge and moral self-perfection. Because the Rosicrucians also strove to be "monks in the world," they grounded their search for communion with God in religious faith, which they understood as something experienced in everyday life. Organized under the umbrella of the Friendly Learned Society, founded in 1782 by Moscow University Professor Johann Georg Schwarz, and the Typographical Company, established in 1784 by Novikov, the Rosicrucians sought in their worldly mission to promote education and spread enlightenment in Russian society. To that end, the Friendly Learned Society supported students at the university (under the auspices of the Assembly of University Pupils), published educational books, and encouraged the acquisition of ancient and scientific learning. The Typographical Company directed the circle's broader publishing program, the Rosicrucians' preferred method for spreading enlightenment, which made available an eclectic array of ideas taken from Freemasonry, Hermeticism, cabala, alchemy, theosophy, Paracelsianism, and the spiritualist and mystical traditions of Catholic, Protestant, and Orthodox Christianity. Through the spread of spiritualist thought and esoteric knowledge, the Rosicrucians hoped to provide a model of ethical behavior for a new human being who would be capable of constructing a just society here on earth.

The aspirations of the Moscow Rosicrucians were not inherently political, oppositionist, or radical, but they were utopian, and they did envision the spiritual and material reconstruction of human society. One could say that Orthodox Christianity envisioned the same. Still, the Rosicrucians, and Russian Masons in general, even though they adhered to the teachings and rites of Russian Orthodoxy, operated outside the institutional boundaries of the official church. Similarly, while many Masons served in the bureaucracy or military, their circles and lodges functioned in secret, independently of the monarchy and government. Masons also maintained ties to associations in Europe and so placed themselves under the authority of foreign masters and rules. For these organizational reasons, as much as for the content of their publications, Novikov and his associates ran into trouble.

The troubles began in 1785, when a commission headed by Archbishop of Moscow and Kaluga Platon (Levshin) investigated Novikov's publishing activities and religious beliefs. The commission examined 461 titles published by Novikov. Of these, 12 were criticized for Masonic or Encyclopédist (referring to the *Encyclopédie* of Diderot and d'Alembert) content, but only 6 were banned.[53] With regard to Novikov's religious beliefs, Platon reported to Catherine, 'I pray to all-generous God that there should be Christians like Novikov not only in the literary congregation but in the whole world.'[54] Despite these favorable conclusions, persecution of Novikov continued. Perhaps due to the concerns of other church hierarchs and government officials, Catherine remained suspicious and in 1787 ordered raids on bookshops across the empire. In Moscow, authorities seized 313 titles (142,000 volumes), including 166 titles published by Novikov. In the end, only 14 titles were banned, and the rest returned to their owners. Novikov's publishing operations again survived, but the repeated disruptions further weakened his already shaky finances. Nor did the government let the matter rest. In 1788 Novikov received notice that Catherine would not renew his privilege for the Moscow University Typography, set to expire the following year. The final blow came in 1792, when Novikov was arrested, convicted, and sentenced to fifteen years' imprisonment for violating a 1787 law that repeated previous bans on the publication and sale of religious books not produced at official church presses.[55] Masonic lodges also began to close, though no wholesale repression occurred. Freemasonry revived quickly following the death of Catherine, only to be fully prohibited in 1822.

Freemasonry enjoyed a relatively brief lifespan in Russia; however, the goals of the lodges and individual Masons became emblematic of the moral voice that the educated classes began to acquire in the reign of Catherine II. Societies, clubs, and salons could be traced back to the assemblies introduced by Peter I, and in the later decades of the eighteenth century, the number of such gatherings grew substantially. Their activities responded to a broad range of needs and provided venues for the pursuit of variegated interests: acquisition of Russian and foreign news, discussion of business affairs, organization of burials, study of history, reading of literature, performance of music and plays, and finally, entertainment in the form of dining, dancing, card games, and even debauchery.[56] The meetings of Russian Masons, including Novikov's Rosicrucian circle, also appealed to the desire for sociability, cultural refinement, and moral or intellectual edification. But the Masons aimed for much more than the satisfaction of private interests and personal needs. They reflectively practiced social engagement. Through publishing programs, support for education, and the pursuit of moral self-perfection, they sought to participate in the construction of a new social order based on universalistic human principles. Theirs was not a narrow particularistic vision, nor a vision of social revolution and political change. Theirs was a moral vision that gave voice to an emergent and still miniscule "society," poised to become, in the decades ahead, a self-defined entity independent of the church and government.

Russia's Age of Enlightenment: An Appraisal

The reign of Empress Catherine II surely deserves the appellation "Russia's age of enlightenment," though there is abundant ambiguity in the naming. Of course, across Europe and North America, the Enlightenment represented an intellectual orientation full of contradiction and potentiality. While popular accounts tend to connect Enlightenment ideas to the birth of liberal democracy and the capitalist market economy, historians long have noted that no single political ideology or set of socioeconomic policies defined "the Enlightenment." In Imperial Russia, where absolute monarchy survived until 1906 and reigned unchallenged until the Decembrist Rebellion of 1825, the Enlightenment became associated with the thinking and cosmopolitan culture of the empire's small educated classes. Russian Enlightenment thought, inspired by universalistic principles of natural equality and human goodness, emphasized moral education, the cultivation of reason, the fulfillment of duty, and deference to God-given natural order, including the established social and political order. Enlightened Russians also embraced the possibility of earthly progress, despite keen awareness of human shortcomings, and with rare exceptions, they remained reconciled to hierarchy and authority, even as they denounced the inequities and injustices associated with patriarchy, judicial corruption, and the institution of serfdom. Perhaps not surprisingly, historians question whether or not Russia's educated classes understood the Enlightenment principles they professed. Did they really believe in the underlying equality and moral worth of all human beings, the efficacy of properly cultivated human reason, or the ability of governments and human beings to reform and improve society? Given the gap between stated principles and concrete actions, scholars frequently ask if Russia even had an Enlightenment. In the words of Viktor Zhivov, "the Russian Enlightenment was a Petersburg mirage."[57]

But to call the Russian Enlightenment a mirage misses the point. Like Enlightenments across Europe, the Russian Enlightenment "was forever hesitating on the road to progress."[58] Enlightened Russians did not produce ideologies of political opposition or movements of social reform. Instead, they focused on the practice and lived experience of the Enlightenment – on how to lead an enlightened, morally purposeful, and spiritually uplifting life and on how to foster enlightenment through education, sociability, and public discussion. In Russian Enlightenment thought, the individual human being, constructed on a moral rather than a legal or political basis, held the key to social progress. Through the pursuit of personal perfectibility, not the remaking of social and political institutions, progress would be achieved.

Among Russia's educated classes, the emphasis on moral self-perfection bolstered cognitive acceptance of absolute monarchy, noble privilege, and the institution of serfdom. A noble serf owner could be a good master, and a bad master could be reformed or deprived of his or her property. Similarly, the personal power of a virtuous monarch offered the best guarantee of good government. That a particular ruler might be a person in need of moral reformation did not undermine God-given monarchical authority, though it might lead to the removal from power of an unworthy individual. In 1785, when the Moscow governor-general recommended that performances of Nikolai P. Nikolev's (1758– 1815) tragedy *Sorena and Zamir* be prohibited because it contained verses harmful to the monarchy, Catherine II's response epitomized the relationship that she hoped to cultivate with her subjects. Catherine reportedly told her loyal serviceman that the lines critical of monarchy 'have nothing to do with your Empress. The author challenges the despotism of tyrants, whereas you call Catherine a mother.'[59] In Nikolev's play, as in so many literary depictions – whether of parents, spouses, serf owners, officials, or monarchs – criticism of abuses referred to immoral individuals and did not appear to attack established institutions. Indeed, for most of the eighteenth century, authors could decry injustice without appearing oppositionist.

But just a few years after the Nikolev incident, Russia's cultural climate had changed, and Catherine sang a different tune. The exile of Aleksandr N. Radishchev (1791) and the imprisonment of Nikolai I. Novikov (1792) showed that neither societal independence nor concrete criticism of serfdom would be tolerated. Historians disagree as to whether or not the likes of Radishchev and Novikov actually sought to remake social and political arrangements. Neither of them developed a political program or belonged to a political organization. Both, however, came to be seen as threats to Catherine's personal authority. The pattern of repression continued in 1793, when to the surprise of contemporaries, the empress banned Iakov B. Kniazhnin's (1740–91) tragedy *Vadim the Novgorodian* and berated Princess Ekaterina R. Dashkova for allowing its publication.[60] Although no one went to prison over the incident, it confirmed the limits to freedom of thought in Catherinian Russia.

Kniazhnin's play recounts the rebellion of a legendary Slavic prince, Vadim of Novgorod, who returns from war to find the Varangian Riurik in control of the city. Riurik had been invited to Novgorod to end civil disorder, and because his reign is based on virtue and his power is accepted by the people, he easily defeats Vadim. Riurik then seeks reconciliation, but Vadim remains defiant in the name of freedom, preferring death to the acceptance of a good monarch loved by his subjects. According to Princess Dashkova, Kniazhnin's tragedy affirmed monarchy and in its representation of rebellion seemed less dangerous than many French tragedies performed in the Hermitage and public theaters. But Kniazhnin's character also refused to submit to a worthy ruler and thus stood in sharp contrast to the Vadim depicted by Catherine II in the historical play *From the Life of Riurik* (1786). In Catherine's version of the story, Riurik grants clemency to the rebellious Vadim, who responds with expressions of eternal loyalty and becomes the monarch's trusted serviceman. When juxtaposed to Catherine's Vadim, the Vadim of Kniazhnin denied the need to reconcile his individual conscience with the legitimate authority of his monarch.

There is no evidence that Kniazhnin penned his play as a response to Catherine. Nor do historians know what specifically aroused the empress's ire. Clearly, though, Catherine did not want to conduct a conversation about monarchical legitimacy. As one Novgorodian leader reminds the Catherinian Vadim, there is no need for debate when a subject is supposed to carry out the will of the ruler. Indeed, the relationship between the will of the ruler and the need for debate lay at the heart of the monarchy's role in the emergence of modern Russian culture. From the time of Peter I onward, Russia's rulers understood that the formulation of good policies required professional knowledge and informed discussion. But the will of the ruler also remained essential to Russian intellectual life, and the will of the ruler fluctuated, often without apparent cause. By the 1790s, the will of the ruler became more of a hindrance than a help in the process of cultural development. Encouragement of debate (and creativity) gave way to control over the terms of debate, and after 1800 the effort to control led increasingly to disaffection. The limits to personal liberty and pluralistic speech, while still negotiable, precisely because of the role played by an absolute monarch, could easily be reached. In such conditions, the monarchy came to be seen as an obstacle to progress, and the Enlightenment focus on moral reformation of the self became a source of rebellion. Educated society's reconciliation with authority rested on unstable foundations.

Part III

Government and People in Old Regime Russia 1796–1861

Already in the late seventeenth century, Russia began to confront the challenges of European modernity, specifically Europe's military power, technological achievements, and broad cultural appeal. For much of the eighteenth century, the Russian government and educated elites met the European challenge with little or no cultural conflict. The monarchy successfully maintained its military forces and extended the territory of the empire. The educated service classes embraced the cosmopolitan, confessionally more tolerant culture of the European Enlightenment, and high-level churchmen such as Moscow Metropolitan Platon (Levshin) approached errant Russian laity, including even Old Believers, with a pedagogical spirit. Russian scientists, poets, and philosophers – the likes of Mikhail Lomonosov, Aleksandr Sumarokov, Denis Fonvizin, and Empress Catherine II – produced works of enduring value that received recognition abroad. Among educated Russians, there was no broadly perceived conflict between European enlightenment and Russian Orthodox traditions. Nor did patriotic expressions of Russian or Slavic pride conflict with the transnational outlook or experience of being European. For educated Russians who avoided the perils of palace coups and political dissent, the eighteenth century represented a time of unprecedented promise and possibility. Through the development of literature and the arts, these Russians joined the ranks of "enlightened peoples."

By the end of the eighteenth century, the comfort of military and cultural achievement within a European framework gave way to the anxiety of new challenges represented by political revolution in France and industrial transformation in England. As the economic, social, and political consequences of European modernity became apparent – consequences such as the factory system, urbanization, the class society, the capitalist market economy, and the mass politics of liberalism, socialism, nationalism, and conservatism – Russian attitudes toward the process of Europeanization became increasingly diversified and ambivalent. A significant number of educated Russians, both officials and individuals outside of government, elaborated moral critiques of European "progress." In terms of concrete development, Russian social and political institutions began increasingly to diverge from those found in the more democratic, urbanized, and industrialized societies of nineteenth-century Europe. The persistence of serfdom and the absence of a politically organized civil society help to explain the Russian divergence, but an equally important factor can be found in the strength of Russian political culture. The elevation of necessity, morality, and justice over strict adherence to the law; the emphasis on individual moral solutions to social and political problems – an emphasis embodied in the cultural ideal of personal perfectibility; and the persistent understanding of political power as the ability to assert moral authority – these aspects of Russian political culture provided the filter through which Russia participated in the world of contemporary Europe.

Chapter 7

The Emergence of
Independent Society

In the eighteenth century, the Russian monarchy seemed always to be pushing and dragging the empire's subjects along the road to great-power status and European modernity. By the nineteenth century, the roles of initiator and follower often appeared to be in the reverse. Whether in the pursuit of economic profit, literary acclaim, social progress, or political reform, the people of Russia, especially the educated among them, tended to go beyond the intentions of their increasingly conservative government. In the decades following the 1815 defeat of Napoleon, the monarchy focused above all on preserving the social and political arrangements that had brought military glory and great-power status to the empire. Instead of fostering social change in the name of the common good, policymakers struggled to maintain established order and to contain the dynamism of socio-economic relationships. Russia's defeat in the Crimean War (1853–6) led to a revival of government-sponsored social change, heralded by the emancipation of the serfs in 1861. But already in the decades leading up to the emancipation, Russian society developed in directions barely imaginable in the eighteenth century. The traditional *soslovie* distinctions built around serfdom and service to the monarchy remained, but new social groups also took shape. The appearance of factory workers, commercial-industrial elites, urban middle classes, and professional classes suggested that economic and cultural development had outpaced the social policies defined by Peter I's Table of Ranks and Catherine II's Charters to the Nobility and the Towns. Not only did the sociological configuration of Russian society appear altered, innovative ways of thinking about social relationships also emerged. By the 1860s, sociocultural concepts such as the public (*publika*), society (*obshchestvo*), the people or nation (*narod*), and the intelligentsia (*intelligentsiia*) became integral to social and political discourse. Although absolute monarchy remained the lynchpin of social and political arrangements, independent society also began to play a significant public role.

Economic Development and the Emergence of Independent Society

Historians of the industrial revolution in Europe look to demographic increase to explain the onset of economic modernity, the formation of capitalist market relations, and the sustained growth of agriculture, manufacturing, and trade.[1] In Russia, population growth, including significant increases in the urban population, likewise stimulated economic development. Historians estimate that in the late eighteenth and early nineteenth centuries the average per capita demand for manufactured goods in Russia increased 34 times, largely due to rural consumption.[2] Based on official censuses, which did not include all the territories of the Russian empire, the male population grew from 7,791,063 in 1719 to 18,617,650 in 1795. Although about a third of the recorded increase resulted from the acquisition of new territories, indicating that the population grew unevenly, from the late 1790s steady growth occurred. Census data for the years 1795 to 1811 show a population increase of about 14 percent, and by 1860–4 the total population of the empire, excluding only Finland, Khiva, and Bukhara, reached 74 million.[3] But population density remained low, and much of the economic growth resulted from the expansion of production rather than higher productivity achieved through the application of new technologies. Russia's industrial "take-off" did not begin before the 1880s, a century after Britain led Europe into the industrial revolution, and even in places where Russian producers developed ties to urban, regional, and foreign markets, methods of production in agriculture and manufacturing changed very little. Clearly, limited technological change represented a drag on economic modernization, but it did not indicate economic stagnation. In the late eighteenth and early nineteenth centuries, the Russian economy displayed unprecedented dynamism, which gave rise to new economic classes and to ever-higher levels of participation in production for the capitalist market.

Before the coming of railways in the mid-nineteenth century, the transport of goods and people around Russia depended on rivers, which could be frozen or unusable for up to half the year, and on overland haulage, which also could be blocked by snow drifts or spring mud. For this reason, markets tended to be local or regional, production diversified within regions rather than specialized between them, and peasant communities and noble estates pragmatically self-sufficient. At the same time, despite local self-sufficiency and difficult communications, entrepreneurial activity appeared at every turn. Both domestic and foreign trade grew robustly. The value of exports tripled between 1762 and 1793, and by 1793, manufactured goods accounted for 45 percent of exports. In the early nineteenth century, grain and animal products became increasingly important export items, and the relative weight of manufactured goods declined. But based on yearly averages, from 1826–30 to 1856–60, the value of imports and exports grew about two and a half times. Comparable levels of growth also occurred in the domestic marketplace, where commercial activity centered on periodic fairs and bazaars; permanent urban markets composed of stores, stalls, and commodity exchanges; and itinerant trade conducted by peddlers. The number of domestic trading centers jumped from around 608 in the 1750s to 2,571 at century's end. Rural markets also grew in importance, a sure sign of more effective economic integration. Already in 1760, villages on noble estates hosted 36 percent of periodic trade fairs, and by 1800 the figure stood at 51 percent. In the 1790s, the number of village fairs topped 3,000. Difficult conditions notwithstanding, by 1860 Russia boasted "a hierarchical and time-sequenced network" of 5,653 periodic fairs "that permitted the exchange of goods between the most remote parts of the empire."[4]

Although historians describe market integration in the late eighteenth and early nineteenth centuries as regional rather than national, and although technological advances proceeded very slowly, "society" overall became more economically interconnected as nobles, peasants, merchants, and townspeople developed deeper ties to the market. Rising consumer demand stimulated greater involvement in commercial production. In the reign of Peter I, nobles acquired the legal right to engage in trade and distill spirits. In 1754 they obtained a monopoly on the sale of liquor to government contractors, and although in 1755 the nobles' right to trade was limited to the wholesale marketing of goods produced on their estates, in 1807 the old freedom to engage in any type of trade was restored.[5] Noble landowners in the age of serfdom did not generally become capitalist entrepreneurs or even plantation-style producers for the market – they remained above all the monarch's servicemen – but they did benefit from access to raw materials and to free labor for production and transport. By the 1750s, noble estates became sites of significant commercial manufacturing that ranged across a wide array of food processing, textile, and metalworking industries.[6]

In the peasant economy, off-farm work, handicraft production, and trade encouraged ongoing participation in the capitalist market. Off-farm work became well established by the late eighteenth century, especially among serfs who did not perform labor on the landowner's demesne. Off the farm, peasants could work in trade, transport, and manufacturing, sometimes as hired laborers and sometimes as small-scale producers and sellers. For the most part seasonal, this work did not require separation from farming. To the contrary, off-farm work became integrated into both local estate and larger regional economies. In Kursk province, for example, peasants on the Sheremetev family's Rastorg estate grew hemp to sell either in raw form or as woven sackcloth. During the winter months, Rastorg peasants also earned wages as transport workers. Peasants on the Lieven family's Baki estate in Kostroma province were even more heavily involved in off-farm occupations, working as timber and horse traders, craftsmen, fishermen, and wage laborers. In addition, the Baki peasants hosted a weekly fair where fish and baked goods were sold, all the while remaining self-sufficient in grain production.[7]

Peasant handicraft production represented another source of vital ties to the market. Village households produced a variety of agricultural goods suitable for commercial sale: food products such as milled grain, beer, butter and dairy produce, and vegetable oil extracted from flax, hemp, and sunflower seeds; tallow from animal fat, which could be used to make soap and candles; tanned hides to make footwear, harnesses, and other leather goods; sheepskin coats; yarn spun from flax and hemp fibers and from fleeces; woven linen, canvas, and woolen cloth; and additional textile items such as rope, sacks, clothes, hats, and felt boots.[8] Peasants also manufactured decorative, household, and religious objects, with the result that individual artisans and even entire villages achieved renown for the beauty and quality of their work. Some peasants made luxury goods for the homes and palaces of wealthy nobles, while others produced objects that drew them into wide-ranging market relations. The villages of Mstera, Palekh, and Kholui in Vladimir province made icons that a special class of peddlers traded throughout Russia. The trade in icons dated from the mid-seventeenth century, when these villages belonged to a monastery and icon painting became the main occupation of the local peasants. The icon trade also affected neighboring villages, where peasants serviced the icon painters and their customers by producing brushes, shrines, and wooden boards. By the mid-nineteenth century, the production of icons in Vladimir province reached mass proportions. Kholui painters alone turned out 1.5 to 2 million icons per year. In Mstera, where other forms of manufacturing also appeared – a linen-weaving industry developed in the eighteenth century, an illustrating business began operations in 1844, and a lithography shop opened in 1858 – diversification and modernization did not undermine the tradition of producing religious objects. Demand for Mstera's icons continued into the twentieth century.[9]

Much peasant and estate manufacturing remained small-scale, rudimentary, and oriented toward local or regional markets. But in some noteworthy cases, rural manufacturing achieved economies of scale and evolved into modern industrial production. In Nizhnii Novgorod province during the 1850s, over 15,000 peasants on two Sheremetev estates worked in metalworking enterprises that manufactured locks, knives, scissors, surgical instruments, and metal parts for agricultural tools. In four districts of Vladimir and Kostroma provinces, rural enterprises devoted to cotton weaving and dyeing employed over 135,000 peasants in the mid-1850s. In 1857 the Sheremetevs' textile village of Ivanovo in Vladimir province "contained

135 mills and factories, with 10,300 workers, and an annual output worth 5.8 million rubles."[10] Textile production dotted the Russian countryside, most notably in the central provinces of Moscow, Vladimir, Kostroma, Tver, Nizhnii Novgorod, and Iaroslav, and displayed a range of organizational forms. Individual households worked in every stage of flax production and linen weaving. Cotton and silk weaving, by contrast, became associated with more advanced capitalist structures such as the importation of raw materials, the use of wage labor, and factory-related cottage production, referred to as the "putting out" system. In the putting out system, rural producers gave up independent access to the market in both the purchase of raw materials and the sale of their products. Instead, they worked at home for merchant and peasant entrepreneurs who provided them with raw materials and then picked up finished goods for distribution to the market. From the 1830s through the 1850s, the number of domestic weavers tied to spinning factories or dyeing works ballooned in central Russia. Based on one estimate for the 1850s, cottage production in the Central Non-Black Earth provinces accounted for 23 percent of Russia's total industrial output.[11]

Although Russian textile manufacturing developed overwhelmingly in response to the peasant market, military needs and consumption at the court also created demand that stimulated production. Government-oriented industrial production represented a distinctive line of development less tied to overall market integration or to the emergence of an entrepreneurial elite from among the merchants and peasants. The production of iron and armaments in Russia dated back to the seventeenth century, when the need for cannon, church bells, and religious ornaments encouraged manufacturing in towns such as Moscow, Tver, Iaroslavl, and Tula. Tsar Peter I deepened the government's focus on military needs and became the first ruler systematically to promote large-scale industrial development. When the Great Northern War with Sweden cut off foreign supplies of iron, Peter ordered the establishment of new industrial enterprises that could satisfy military demands: metallurgical and armaments plants; works to produce ships, sailcloth, and rope; and factories for the manufacture of wool, linen, and leather to meet the clothing needs of the growing army and navy. Peter's policies led to the founding of both state and private factories, with the most significant development centered in St Petersburg and the Ural Mountains. The government also guaranteed the new enterprises a labor force by assigning state peasants to work in factories and allowing factory owners to purchase serfs.[12] St Petersburg's naval shipbuilding complex, the Admiralty, became the largest industrial operation in eighteenth-century Russia. Equally impressive, the Urals iron industry used local sources of iron ore and timber to produce a high-grade metal that made Russia a major exporter of iron in the second half of the eighteenth century.[13]

By the end of Peter I's reign, over 200 manufacturing enterprises had been established, and gains in the production of iron and armaments proved sufficient to supply an army of roughly 220,000 men. By 1720 the annual output of military muskets exceeded 20,000. Petrine industries also built and equipped a navy on the Baltic and Caspian Seas, and Russian textile manufacturing supplied all the empire's sailcloth and a significant share of the cloth needed for the army.[14] This unprecedented industrial growth continued in subsequent decades. By the 1790s, the number of iron works had expanded from Peter's original twelve to 165. For the year 1767, historians identify a total of 663 large-scale industrial enterprises in Russia, and at the end of the eighteenth century 1,200 with a labor force of 200,000.[15] By the second quarter of the nineteenth century, real progress toward a modern factory system became evident. Serfdom would not be abolished until 1861, but already in the 1830s wage labor began to replace servile labor in factory production, and legislation of 1835 recognized factory workers as a distinct group whose relations with employers required regulation. At mid-century, more than half a million workers labored in 10,000 manufacturing establishments. Russia possessed fully developed metallurgical and textile industries, and large mechanized factories could be found in urban and rural locations.[16]

By the mid-nineteenth century, regional industrial geographies also became discernible. The Urals metallurgical industry remained important, but continued to rely on charcoal for fuel at a time when England introduced coke smelting, the puddling of iron, and rolling mills. By 1800 technological backwardness and high transportation costs made the Urals iron industry less profitable and less economically noteworthy. In St Petersburg, by contrast, manufacturing developed in new directions. Although production for military needs remained central, by the 1840s and 1850s the economic initiatives of private entrepreneurs overshadowed those of the government. During the nineteenth century, large-scale textile, metallurgy, and machine construction factories defined the industrial physiognomy of St Petersburg. The Moscow region displayed comparable dynamism, and already in the 1820s Moscow became established as a center of textile manufacturing. Cotton production led the way not only in Moscow, but also in St Petersburg and the serf "village" of Ivanovo (Vladimir province). By 1850 "Russia had become the world's fifth largest producer of cotton goods."[17]

Alongside traditional centers of Russian manufacturing, new industrial regions located on the empire's peripheries also arose during the first half of the nineteenth century. In the 1820s and 1830s, the Kingdom of Poland emerged as a major supplier of textile and metallurgical products. Government-owned enterprises played a significant role in the Kingdom's development, but at the same time an independent commercial-industrial elite formed from the ranks of nobles, merchants, and Jews. By the 1860s, factories in the Baltic city of Riga (Livonia) manufactured textiles, sugar, and tobacco, and private banks began to finance railroad construction. In another Baltic city, Narva in Estonia, entrepreneurs from Moscow and St Petersburg established a huge cotton-spinning and weaving factory in 1857.

Finally, in the south, the Baku oil industry began to develop in the 1860s.[18] Across the empire, economic growth kept up an impressive pace, but growth does not an industrial revolution make, and Russia's industrial revolution remained decades away.

The social changes associated with mechanized production and transportation, urbanization, and the concentration of workers in large factories barely touched Russian society in the final decades of serfdom. That said, already in the reign of Peter I economic growth began to produce new entrepreneurial elites. Emblematic of this development was Nikita D. Demidov (1656–1725), a state peasant by birth, whose father had worked in Tula as a blacksmith. Demidov also began his career as a simple blacksmith and crafter of weapons, but soon became a major arms supplier to Peter I. Demidov's mining and metallurgical operations originated in the Tula area and rapidly spread to the Ural Mountains, where he founded industrial enterprises employing thousands of workers. Granted noble status in 1720, Demidov's career showed that even in an age of serfdom economic success could bring rapid social mobility.[19]

But Demidov's story was truly exceptional. Although Russian business empires sometimes survived over several generations, even reaching into the early twentieth century, most merchant fortunes came and went with unsettling rapidity. Data for the cities of Arkhangel'sk, St Petersburg, and Moscow reveal significant instability in the composition of the entrepreneurial elite. In Moscow, only 26 of the 382 first-guild merchant families registered in 1748 remained at the end of the century. Historians estimate that during the first half of the nineteenth century, membership in the merchant guilds of St Petersburg, Moscow, and other cities changed by 54 percent each year. Data from 1873 show that 108 of 623 first-guild Moscow merchants came from eighteenth-century merchant families, whereas 185 descended from individuals who entered the guild between 1800 and 1861. Not surprisingly, given the fluctuations in the composition of the merchant category, the perception arose among government officials and subsequent generations of historians that Russia lacked an energetic middle class capable of leading the country toward economic and cultural modernity.[20]

Russia's uneven conformity to European patterns of development should not, however, be blamed on the absence of vibrant middle classes. Russia possessed considerable entrepreneurial talent, and Russian entrepreneurs did not shy away from risk. But throughout the eighteenth century, Russia did lack a stable and predictable business environment. Economic ruin came easily, as merchants suffered repeated financial losses. The transport and preservation of merchandise could be expensive and uncertain due to administrative corruption, attacks by bandits, climatic conditions, and navigational problems. The failure to meet contractual obligations also plagued the conduct of business. Serf entrepreneurs by definition lacked civic rights (Russians as a whole lacked civil rights), and for all entrepreneurs, the limited development of property, bankruptcy, and contract law made it difficult to take legal action when loans went unpaid or goods were not delivered. In the absence of modern banking and credit institutions, poor book-keeping and personal deal making dominated the business landscape.[21] Lacking insurance and reliable credit, entrepreneurs adhered to the practices of earlier generations and stayed afloat by investing "in many different kinds of activity in widely separate parts of the country."[22] Conditions improved somewhat in the first half of the nineteenth century, after legislation of 1805, 1807, and 1836 established rules for company registration and limited liability for investors in joint-stock companies. Not until the 1860s, however, did the presence of modern banks and corporations produce the sort of stable business environment that allowed standardized practices and concentrated investment to supersede hidden deals and the dispersion of resources.[23]

Clearly, by the time of the emancipation settlement of 1861, the notion that Russia lacked viable middle classes or a mature commercial-industrial elite no longer conformed to social reality. The perception persisted, however, because of the unusual origins of Russia's modern capitalist class. The indigenous core of this class descended from Old Believers and peasants, including serfs, who built up large-scale business operations in the late eighteenth and early nineteenth cen-turies. Old Believers belonged to a venerable and vulnerable religious minority, and as social outsiders, they tended to preserve ties to traditional community life. As a result, the successful entrepreneurs among them did not immediately assume the social attributes or participate in the cultural activities of Russia's educated urban classes.[24]

Serf entrepreneurs likewise occupied an outsider status and displayed similar sociocultural characteristics, though not necessarily for the same reasons.[25] Among the serfs who became large-scale factory owners, the Sheremetev peasant Ivan Grachev (b. 1706) founded Ivanovo's first linen mill in 1748 and went on to accumulate a substantial fortune. In 1795 his son Efim (1743–1819) paid 135,000 rubles to become a free man. In the mid-nineteenth century, I. G. Zav'ialov, a peasant from the Sheremetevs' village of Vorsma, operated the largest metalworking business in the Pavlovo area. Although historians make no mention of Zav'ialov having bought his freedom, he owned five workshops which employed 100 hired laborers and put out work to another 500 peasants. The founder of the Morozov textile empire, the Old Believer serf Savva V. Morozov (1770–1862), became the owner of a silk-weaving enterprise in the village of Zuevo in Moscow province. In 1820 Morozov paid 17,000 rubles to Nikolai G. Riumin for his and his four sons' freedom.[26] In terms of production, Russia's most successful serf entrepreneurs appear to have been modern industrialists, but they remained in the untenable position of not legally owning their property or capital. Although noble masters surely had a stake in protecting the economic interests of their serfs, until serfs became free men, they were better off avoiding the lifestyle of prosperous merchants. The cost of freedom was high in Russia, and the best way to reduce that cost was to hide wealth and live like an ordinary peasant.[27] Once again, the perception that Russia lacked a significant commercial-industrial elite resulted from invisibility and dispersion rather than real absence.

Indeed, once wealthy peasants and Old Believers became legally recognized Russian merchants, they participated in the same social, cultural, and philanthropic activities as Europeanized nobles and educated servicemen. In the late eighteenth century, the Moscow Merchant Club sponsored balls, literary readings, and card games in settings where privileged families met to converse and share information. Merchants reportedly paid by the hour to read Aleksandr N. Radishchev's *Journey from Petersburg to Moscow*, published in 1790 and banned by Catherine II for depicting the abuses of serfdom. In the reign of Nicholas I (ruled 1825–55), successful entrepreneurs could be found associating with exiled Decembrists, a group of elite military officers who had rebelled against the monarchy in December 1825. Writing from Siberia, the Decembrist Aleksandr N. Murav'ev (1792–1864) praised the elegance and cultural accomplishments of the Irkutsk merchant Vasilii N. Basnin (1800–76) and described the local merchant elite as an "aristocracy in education and manners."[28] Historians also describe a later generation of Moscow entrepreneurs, born between the 1830s and 1850s, whose social qualities combined economic success with philanthropy, patronage of the arts and sciences, and participation in local government. Born to humble parents, including serfs, who also appeared Europeanized in their dress, manners, and hygiene, and in the forms of entertainment they enjoyed, the young Moscow entrepreneurs attended secondary schools in Russia and studied business practices and technology in Europe.[29]

Russia's commercial-industrial elite in no way constituted a politically organized class or interest group, yet throughout the age of serfdom, entrepreneurs participated in official discussions about economic policy. By the late 1850s and early 1860s, they publicly campaigned for higher tariffs, private railroad construction, and government support for industrial development. Merchants organized banquets in support of the emancipation of the serfs, and they provided financial backing for Slavophile periodicals that criticized bureaucratic interference in the economy. Russian entrepreneurs also served in elected city offices and on the exchange committees of St Petersburg (established in 1703), Moscow (established in 1839), and Nizhnii Novgorod (established in 1848).[30] Unlike the nobility and educated service classes, Russia's commercial-industrial elite produced only a handful of acclaimed literary figures or nationally recognized disseminators of Enlightenment culture. Entrepreneurs did, however, become consumers and patrons of Russian literature and the arts, and their presence in the empire's capitals and provincial towns contributed much to the social and cultural dynamism of the early nineteenth century. Clearly, Russia's commercial-industrial elite aspired to more than economic success. In their eyes, status honor required not only wealth, but also cultural sophistication and service to society.

Cultural Development and the Emergence of Independent Society

Economic development represented one source of social change in Imperial Russia, and cultural development another. Government-directed cultural development accelerated in the reign of Peter I, largely in response to the need for educated servicemen. Peter required nobles to educate their sons at home or by other private means, but he also sent Russians abroad to acquire the latest technical skills and to study in European universities, policies that continued under his successors. Between 1698 and 1810, 768 Russian subjects, including 302 Germans, attended German universities, and in the period 1811–49, 336 students did the same.[31] In addition, throughout the eighteenth and early nineteenth centuries, the government employed home-grown translators and foreign specialists to transmit European knowledge of the arts and sciences to Russians. Finally, also beginning in Peter's reign, state schools provided general and specialized education to a range of social groups, not just to nobles. By the mid-eighteenth century, the spread of Russian education and the importation of European learning gave to the empire significant cadres of educated servicemen, composed of military officers, civil servants, clergy, translators, writers, artists, architects, engineers, scholars, scientists, physicians, and technical specialists.

In the eighteenth century, military officers and civil servants born into the nobility made up the bulk of Russia's educated service classes. But the service classes also included sufficient numbers of nonnobles to create awareness of a "middle sort of people" (*srednii rod liudei*) wedged between the nobility and peasantry. Catherine II's Instruction to the Legislative Commission defined the middle sort as free persons occupied in the arts, sciences, navigation, trade, and crafts. Characterized as individuals of sound behavior, industry, and hard work, the middle sort encompassed a wide array of occupations: white (non-monastic married) clergy, scholars, nonnoble civil servants (ranked and unranked), artists, technical specialists, merchants, factory owners, ship owners, navigators, artisans, freedmen, employees in shops and service establishments, purveyors of prepared food, and stewards who worked for merchants. More easily defined in negative than in positive terms, the middle sort consisted of free social groups, for the most part living in towns, but not monastic clergy, nobles, military servicemen, or peasants.[32]

The Catherinian understanding of the middle sort conflated economic, administrative, cultural, and technical classes. But while Russia's commercial-industrial elite arose primarily from spontaneous market forces, the non-economic middle represented the fruits of official policy, particularly of efforts to mobilize human and material resources for purposes of state building and national defense. Beginning in the reign of Peter I, service obligations became Russia's most important source of both educational opportunity and upward social mobility. Appropriately, given the military impetus for so many policies, the common soldier, conscripted from the lowliest serfs, state peasants, and townspeople, emerged as one of the most striking examples of the relationship between service, education, and mobility. Upon induction into military service, conscripts became legally free and consequently emancipated from the authority of the landlord or local community. Soldiers' wives also became free, as did any children, including from the early nineteenth century illegitimate children, born to soldiers or soldiers' wives after the former entered service. Although Russia's long term of service meant that the legal freedom of soldiers and soldiers' sons might never be realized, they nonetheless became candidates for social and cultural advancement.[33]

Special schools for soldiers' sons operated from 1719 until the end of the Crimean War in 1856, at which time the military domain laid claim to 378,000 soldiers' sons. Most became common soldiers or noncommissioned officers, and only a handful advanced to officer rank. But others learned crafts, worked as copyists, or acquired special technical and administrative skills needed by the military and bureaucracy. During the eighteenth century, when *soslovie* boundaries remained porous and the channels of social mobility relatively open, considerable numbers of soldiers' sons also became academicians, scientists, and artists. In the period 1755 to 1770, sons of soldiers and noncommissioned officers comprised a sizeable contingent among students and professors at the Academy of Sciences University and Moscow University. In the early nineteenth century, although the requirements for promotion in service became more stringent, the range of specialists trained in military schools continued to grow. Among the proto-professional groups that soldiers' sons could join, government sources identified judicial officials, laboratory assistants, gunpowder technicians, gymnastics and fencing monitors, topographical workers, engravers, surveyors, architects, clerks, engineering and construction personnel, teachers and teaching assistants for military schools, feldshers (medical orderlies), pharmaceutical assistants, navigators, telegraph signalers, drummers, musicians, and instructors in foreign languages such as German, Armenian, Farsi, Turkish, and Kalmyk. For the capable and the lucky among the sons of Russia's soldiers, opportunities to acquire specialized skills and proto-professional status arose with some regularity.[34]

The schools for soldiers' sons passed through several incarnations – garrison schools, military orphanages, and cantonist battalions – that throughout the eighteenth and early nineteenth centuries provided religious instruction, general education, and specialized training. Equally important, until the reign of Catherine II, the military schools represented the only national network of state schools. The cipher schools, established in provincial towns by Peter I, briefly served children of nobles, townspeople, clergy, civil servants, and military servicemen, though almost immediately the pool of willing attendees became limited to children of civil servants and military servicemen. In 1744, when the cipher schools were merged with the garrison schools, most of the students already were soldiers' sons. Fortunately for Russia, Peter's failed experiment in public primary education did not undermine the continued existence of informal parish schools, where from the seventeenth century local clergy taught reading and writing.[35] But parish schools offered only the most basic education and could not adequately prepare students to acquire the technical skills needed by the government. Official interest in the spread of public education continued to grow, leading in 1782–6 to the first fruitful attempt to develop an integrated system of state-sponsored primary schools.[36]

The popular schools (*narodnye shkoly*) established in the reign of Catherine II gave to Russia an educational infrastructure that developed curriculum materials, prepared students for higher education, and trained teachers and lesser officials. Modeled on the Austrian "normal schools," the Catherinian schools included two-year lower schools (*malye*) in district towns and four-year main (*glavnye*) schools in provincial capitals.[37] A special commission that reported to the empress supervised the schools and directed the preparation of teachers and learning materials. Provincial governors assumed responsibility for the actual creation and administration of the schools, and the boards of public welfare provided facilities and funding. Not surprisingly, given the lack of direct government support, development was uneven, resources limited, and the local reception, both official and public, less than enthusiastic. Intended to be free of charge and open to students from any social group, the schools ended up serving a primarily urban population, though one that encompassed both nobles and serfs. In 1800, 790 teachers taught 18,128 male and 1,787 female students in 315 popular schools; 176,730 students reportedly passed through their halls during the period 1782 to 1800. The majority of teachers were sons of clergy who, even if they had attended ecclesiastical seminaries, received additional training in the main schools or the St Petersburg Teachers Seminary, Russia's first pedagogical institution.[38]

The Catherinian schools represented a serious but nonetheless disappointing start to the development of public education in Imperial Russia. Although public schools open to persons from all social groups became a permanent feature of some district and provincial towns, the actual number of schools and students remained miniscule. Much more effective progress occurred in the first half of the nineteenth century. During the reigns of Alexander I (ruled 1801–25) and Nicholas I (ruled 1825–55), the Russian government preserved its longstanding commitment to technical education, which since the seventeenth century generally came under the specific military or administrative department in need of trained personnel. In the decades leading up to the Great Reforms, new and reformed schools prepared specialists for work in forestry, agriculture, veterinary medicine, transportation, commercial navigation, engineering, artillery, mining, mechanics, chemistry, surveying, architecture, pedagogy, medicine, and jurisprudence. As in the past, the specialized schools also provided general education. But specialized schools had long been a mainstay of Russian education, and officials could build upon the many concrete achievements of the eighteenth century. A more ambitious educational reform, initiated under Alexander I and elaborated under Nicholas I, aimed to create an integrated system of public education extending from the parish school, which taught basic literacy, to the university, which provided higher education in the European mold.[39]

The process of reform began in 1802, when a reorganization of central administration replaced the Petrine colleges with eight ministries, including a Ministry of Popular Enlightenment (see chapter 8). The following year, the Russian government created six educational regions, each crowned by a university that supervised and provided teachers for the lower schools in its territory. Students began their studies in one-year parish schools (not to be confused with church-run parish schools) and then moved on to district (*uezd*) schools which offered two additional years of instruction. At the next level, secondary schools or *gymnasiums* located in provincial capitals offered a four-year curriculum designed to prepare students for admission to a university. In addition to the empire's three existing universities, located in Moscow, Vilnius (a Polish university dating from 1578), and Dorpat (a German university dating from 1632), new Russian universities opened in Kazan and Khar'kov, and in 1819 the St Petersburg Pedagogical Institute (heir to the Catherinian Teachers Seminary) became St Petersburg University.[40] The entire pyramid of public schools and universities was in theory state-supported and open to all social groups. Details are sparse, but even after fees were introduced in the St Petersburg educational region in 1819, orphans and the poor continued to study free of charge. The reform clearly showed that the Russian government had committed itself to the development of broad-based public education. Still, official attention continued to focus on secondary schools and universities. Once again the financing of primary schools was left dependent on local resources, and little progress occurred outside urban areas.

The data on schools are incomplete and unreliable; however, the trend of overall growth is not disputed. At the end of Alexander I's reign, the Russian system of education included, in addition to specialized schools, 6 universities, 3 elite lycées, 57 *gymnasiums*, 370 district schools, 349 parish schools (located mainly in towns), 600 private schools, and 3 main schools (the name assigned to the Catherinian provincial schools). Based on one estimate, in 1824 the educational reach of the Ministry of Popular Enlightenment encompassed 69,452 students in 1,410 schools, compared to the Catherinian network which in 1800 had covered

19,915 students in 315 schools.[41] Growth continued in subsequent decades, so that 3,551 students studied in universities and 17,827 in *gymnasiums* by 1854.[42] Equally important, in the reign of Nicholas I the government seemed to make progress in establishing village schools. Official data for 1836 identified 661 parish schools; by 1841 their number rose to 1,021 and by 1858 to 1,129 with 53,659 students. Outside the domain of the Ministry of Popular Enlightenment, primary schools also appeared in state and crown villages in 1830 and 1832 respectively. By 1842 the Ministry of State Domains reported 1,884 schools with 89,163 students and by 1853 it reported 2,795 schools with 153,117 students. The purpose of these schools was to provide moral education and train copyists for work in village administration. Primary schools on crown estates likewise grew, numbering 44 with 750 students in 1835 and 204 with 7,477 students in 1853. Finally, in addition to state-sponsored village schools and informal schools that sometimes were registered as state schools and counted in official statistics, church schools continued to provide primary education. Officials reported 2,000 church-run parish schools with 19,000 students in 1839 and 7,907 with 133,600 students in 1860.[43]

Whether or not further study can produce more reliable statistics, when measured against the size and population of the Russian empire, the achievements of public primary education in the age of serfdom do not impress. Government attention and resources almost always rested at the top of the social and cultural pyramid, among nobles and ranked civil servants and in elite institutions such as the Academy of Sciences, Academy of Fine Arts, and Moscow University. But official statistics surely also underestimated the reach of elementary schooling, especially in light of unofficial schools and already established educational networks in Baltic German, Ukrainian, Polish, and Finnish areas.[44] More important than the actual numbers, the government's need for technically competent specialists, officials, and military servicemen did not subside, but rather sustained a long-term effort to establish state schools that reached diverse social groups. As a practical matter, the growth of state schools meant that nobles, who already enjoyed easier access to education and patronage, acquired even more privileges and benefits. But state schools also provided nonnobles with greater opportunities to obtain education, benefit from the rewards of service, and rise into the middle or noble classes.

Education surely spawned social mobility, but social mobility did not become a goal of official policy. To the contrary, in the first half of the nineteenth century, the rules of promotion in service showed that the government intended to make the attainment of hereditary nobility more difficult. From the outset of their careers, hereditary nobles possessed advantages over commoners, who entered service at lower ranks and served longer terms before being promoted. To limit the growth of the nobility, the government also raised the ranks at which ennoblement occurred. From 1845, ennoblement in civil service occurred at rank 5 instead of rank 8, and in military service at rank 8 instead of rank 14. In 1856 the ranks granting ennoblement again rose, to 4 in civil service and 6 in military service.[45] At the same time that noble status became less accessible, however, the nobility's claim to the benefits of service also became more dependent on education. The advantages of simply being educated grew in importance. The university statutes of 1804 automatically conferred on graduates rank 12 in the Table of Ranks, regardless of social origin, and the educational requirements for advancement in service became more rigorous for nobles and nonnobles alike. Beginning in 1809, the government required candidates for promotion to rank 8 in civil service to pass an examination, a requirement that when eventually implemented gave decided advantages to graduates of state schools. The military developed similar testing requirements in the reign of Nicholas I.[46] The ongoing need for educated servicemen and the growing importance of education for success in service meant that despite new restrictions on ennoblement, larger numbers of nonnobles moved into the educated service classes, and the educated classes as a whole became less noble in composition.

Throughout the early nineteenth century, Russia's educated classes, both noble and nonnoble, remained relatively small. But they nonetheless reached the critical mass needed to become an ideologically diversified force for social change (see chapter 9). Historians of the period speak not merely of educated service classes, but of educated classes in the broad sense. Although most educated Russians continued to serve the monarchy, sufficient numbers worked outside the government to sustain independent cultural and professional activity. By the 1830s, artists, performers, and writers – as opposed to itinerant purveyors of popular culture – could settle down, most likely in towns, and support themselves by producing for wealthy clients and the periodical press. Less recognized but no less significant, private medical practitioners, informal legal experts, and unlicensed teachers also could live by providing services for the empire's subjects. By the 1840s, in addition to educated nobles, Russia's educated classes included 15–20,000 nonnobles employed as teachers, physicians, midwives, medical orderlies, civil servants, statisticians, agronomists, veterinarians, architects, engineers, scholars, scientists, artists, musicians, writers, and performers. From these groups, the professional classes of modern Russia eventually emerged, though not until after 1864, when the establishment of locally elected *zemstvo* assemblies created substantial opportunities for employment outside the government.[47] Only then could professional work become a form of service to the people rather than service to the state.[48]

Decades earlier, however, beginning in the late eighteenth century, collective concepts such as the "public" (*publika*) and "society" (*obshchestvo*) arose to describe cultural and social relationships separate from the church and government. Aleksandr P. Sumarokov (1717–77), poet, playwright, and father of the Russian Imperial Theater, defined the public as people of taste and knowledge, whether or not they were nobles. Sumarokov distinguished people of taste from the dark uncultivated masses (the *chern'*, literally "black"), but also insisted that not all nobles belonged to the worthy public. In the understanding of Sumarokov and other late eighteenth-century literary figures, the public constituted both an abstract concept and a social body composed of patrons, fellow writers, critics, readers, and theater audiences.[49] Like the public, "society" (*obshchestvo*) represented another elite group distinguished by culture rather than social origin. Based on the literature and journalism of the late eighteenth and early nineteenth centuries, the concept of society encompassed: 1) *le grand monde* or *svet* (literally, "the world"), understood as fashionable, polite, or high society; 2) the civil society of the educated, associated, according to Marc Raeff, with a yearning for autonomy and privacy; and 3) the society of educated Russians who were "neither agents of the government (*pravitel'stvo*) nor in the traditional sense its subjects (*narod*)."[50] Although nobles remained the most visible group in society, from the outset, membership required not elite social origins but education, moral refinement, and the possession of European culture. Both the public and society can be seen as forms of collective sociocultural identity and as expressions of a desire for independence from the government. Neither concept, however, implied adherence to any concrete ideological program.

The same can be said of the intelligentsia, a more assertive form of sociocultural identity embraced by educated Russians who sought to define for themselves a recognized public role.[51] Historians situate the origins of the intelligentsia in a range of social milieus: 1) the educated and increasingly disaffected service nobles of the late eighteenth century; 2) the idealist philosophical circles that formed around the universities, salons, and periodical press of the 1830s and 1840s; and 3) the radical nonnobles and nihilists who rose to cultural prominence in the 1860s. One historian counts over 60 definitions of the intelligentsia in the scholarship of the former Soviet Union, and while no single definition seems likely to prevail, among nineteenth-century *intelligenty* (sing., *intelligent*), membership in the intelligentsia required very definite social and moral qualities.[52] To warrant inclusion in the intelligentsia, a person needed to display a critical mind, a secular code of ethics, a commitment to social justice, a belief in the dignity of the individual, and if not the cultural refinement of the Europeanized social elite, then at least a distinctive lifestyle, as in the case of the nihilists. Possessed of social conscience and political awareness, the *intelligent*, or member of the intelligentsia, adopted a sociocultural ideal that defined personal morality and personal interests in social terms. The *intelligent* worked for the betterment of society, whether or not this effort met the immediate needs of his or her family and community. Although the intelligentsia identity assumed neither social radicalism nor political opposition, it did imply a critical attitude toward conditions in society and government. More important, it indicated a desire to change those conditions.[53]

By the 1860s, Russia's educated classes comprised a socially, professionally, and intellectually diverse group, organized around print culture, polite sociability, and sociocultural concepts such as the public, society, and the intelligentsia. Ironically, however, social diversity did not immediately produce cultural pluralism. The educated service classes of the eighteenth century articulated a uniform brand of Enlightenment thought barely distinguishable from that of the government.[54] In the first decades of the nineteenth century, print culture and public theater spread rapidly in the Russian provinces, and educated classes of more varied ideological hues began to emerge. Still, the Enlightenment culture of the eighteenth century continued to define principles of justice, equality, and progress. Although by the 1820s new cultural credos and organized political opposition appeared, the government and educated classes still employed common categories of thought and action. Irrespective of political ideology, educated Russians evaluated their society in relation to contemporary Europe, which they chose either to reject or to emulate. In addition, following the lead of the eighteenth-century monarchy, self-identified members of the public, society, and the intelligentsia also posed as carriers of civilization and enlightenment to a presumably backward and benighted Russian people. Insofar as Russia's educated classes identified with a broader society, they claimed to embody its essential aspirations and beliefs. Social progress corresponded to their understanding of social progress, not to government policy or to broad-based participation in civic institutions.

In the mid-nineteenth century, Russia's educated classes remained culturally closer to the court and officialdom than to the common people; however, their ties to the people reached beyond those of the eighteenth-century educated service classes. Early in the century, a "parting of ways" between the government and educated classes began to change Russia's social and political landscape. Educated Russians claimed to represent the voice of the people or nation, and their identification with the public or society came to imply moral autonomy, social criticism, and borderline rejection of the government.[55] The Decembrist Rebellion of 1825 made clear that society's independence of mind could on occasion lead to open political opposition. By the 1860s, the self-conscious arrival of the intelligentsia showed that the "parting of ways" also had produced a distinctive sociocultural identity. In contrast to members of the public or society, who readily served in the military and bureaucracy, members of the intelligentsia declared their separation from the service classes and began consciously to repudiate the government, even if they sometimes occupied official positions. At a time when Russia's social, cultural, and professional elites continued to be denied fundamental civil liberties or the opportunity to participate in a politically organized civil society, identification with the public, society, or the intelligentsia provided a meaningful substitute for legally recognized, institution-based autonomy.

—   Government and the Emergence of Independent Society   —

Over the centuries, European philosophers and politicians have defined society in a variety of ways. Whatever the definition, the concept of civil society generally implies the integration of society and government (the social and political spheres) through institutions that link competing interests, localities, and groups. In the seventeenth and eighteenth centuries, theorists such as John Locke, Adam Ferguson, Adam Smith, and various French Enlightenment figures concerned with the problem of making society civil used civil society as a synonym for the political state. In the nineteenth century, G. W. F. Hegel defined civil society as the realm of free market relations beyond the family and distinct from the government. Our present-day understanding of civil society envisions a sphere of voluntary association and effective social action independent of the government and market. Not only does civil society give voice to public opinion(s), it also possesses the political power and organizational strength to influence public policy.

Consistent with current understandings of civil society, historians of Russia who look at eighteenth-century Western and Central Europe cannot help but notice the presence of longstanding legal prerogatives possessed by corporate bodies such as diets, provincial estates, *parlements*, Estates General, the English Parliament, and institutions of urban self-government. Although the English Parliament is the only traditional corporate body that evolved into a democratic representative assembly, increasingly in the eighteenth century the activities of corporate bodies combined with popular street action in the form of demonstrations and outright rebellions to produce a new politics of open contestation grounded in the public sphere. In the public sphere, situated between the private sphere of the household and the sphere of political authority represented by the state, the freedom and openness of relationships within the private household spread out into the sphere of political authority. Through popular mobilization, the activities of autonomous civic organizations, the commercialization of print culture, and the formation of communities structured around sites of sociability, the public sphere began to limit the "absolute" power of the monarchy. Over time, political contestation gained wide acceptance, and political authority became the common domain of society and government. In the process, the public sphere became the seedbed for modern civil society, organizationally autonomous and consciously independent of the government.[56]

In broad outline, the development of Russian civil society followed the familiar European pattern. In the late eighteenth and early nineteenth centuries, Russian society emerged as an entity *distinct* from the government. But prior to the Great Reform era of the 1860s, it would be misleading to speak of a politically organized civil society *independent* of the government. A realm of free market relations

(Hegel's civil society) did exist, though often illicitly and without legal protections (remember the serf entrepreneurs), as did a prepolitical literary public sphere (the public or society discussed above) grounded in print culture, learned societies, philanthropic organizations, social clubs, commercial associations, and Masonic lodges.[57] Not before the 1860s, however, did Russian society become organized into corporate bodies that functioned as forums for political debate and institutional posturing. Except for the Russian Orthodox Church, which the reforms of Peter I separated from the sphere of state power, and the Catherinian noble assemblies, which operated at the district and provincial levels, no social institution represented anything more than a mechanism for ordering local community relationships. Lordship in Russia carried no administrative or judicial powers beyond the boundaries of the individual landowner's private estate, and the self-government of peasants and townspeople did not link up with any territorial or national body beyond the village or town. Nor did local customs become codified as customary law on the model of the provincial *coutumes* in France.[58] In Russia, local communities and individual subjects dealt with the government not through corporate institutions that embodied competing interests, but directly, face to face, and in isolation from one another.

Because Russian society lacked corporate bodies, historically sanctioned and legally constituted, that could compete with the monarchy for social and political authority, the building of civic institutions became a process initiated by the government and carried out by the educated service classes in the name of the common good. Efforts to encourage engagement with civic institutions (for example, the courts and boards of public welfare established by Catherine II) aimed not to protect the prerogatives of society, but to enhance the power of the government. The Russian monarchy treated civic institutions as tools of administration, and before the era of the Great Reforms, society did little to challenge the official position. There is no evidence of peasants, townspeople, merchants, or nobles being eager to serve in local courts and administrative bodies. Nor is there evidence that they used the institutions available to them for anything other than the defense of private interests. Popular engagement with the government tended to be reactive rather than interactive. Petitions, judicial proceedings, nonpayment of taxes, evasion of service obligations, flight, and even rebellion may have constituted autonomous social action. But to carve out a social space that protected private interests did not add up to politically organized civil society. To the contrary, such acts of social assertion, whether carried out by individuals, households, or communities, represented discrete episodes and produced discrete outcomes.

In the absence of corporate bodies engaged in a politics of open contestation, educated Russians focused on individual moral virtue as the solution to social and political problems. In literature, legislation, and judicial practice, the individual –

the individual constructed on a moral rather than a political basis – became the key to social progress. By reconciling the satisfaction of personal desire with adherence to duty, the individual attained freedom and became integrated into society and polity. Freedom represented a moral, not a political, concept; and human progress hinged more upon the cultivation of personal perfectibility than the remaking of civic institutions. Although good institutions might encourage the cultivation of virtue, without virtuous individuals, institutions easily became a source of injustice rather than rightful order. In Russian political culture, personal relationships invariably trumped institutional ones, creating a tension between justice achieved through the moral improvement of the individual and justice achieved through the remaking of institutions.

Not before the Decembrist Rebellion of 1825 did representatives of Russian society attempt to revamp institutions through political contestation.[59] Unlike the noble "constitutionalists" of 1730, the Decembrists claimed to speak for all of Russian society, and while the Decembrist leadership came from the elite officer corps, the movement also took in nonnoble soldiers from the Guard regiments. Equally significant, the Decembrists articulated a broad program of radical social and political change that called for an end to absolute monarchy, the abolition of serfdom, and the creation of a new system of government. The Decembrist Rebellion evoked no response in the general population and garnered little concrete support among the educated classes, yet it showed that organized political opposition had arrived in Russia and that society had begun to replace absolute monarchy as the harbinger of modernity and the motive force of change.

The Decembrist Rebellion shocked the government and dramatized the presence of political disaffection among the educated classes, though with hindsight it appears to have been an isolated incident. Politically speaking, Russian society did not really come of age until the onset of the Great Reforms. As the age of serfdom came to an end, the landed nobility began to play a translocal political role, not as in the past, by serving in the military and bureaucracy, but by representing the interests of noble landowners in relation to the government and other social groups. The turning point came in 1858, when at the behest of the central government, provincial committees of nobles met to draw up projects for the impending emancipation of the serfs.[60] The projects were locally conceived and generally nonpolitical; however, the landed nobility appeared largely united in refusing to endorse the government's vision of the emancipation settlement. Not surprisingly, officials in St Petersburg roundly rejected the noble projects, a move that led some provincial assemblies to demand open debate and societal representation in an ongoing process of reform. Calls for political change entered the public sphere, not in a Decembrist-like act of blind rebellion, but as part of a government-initiated process of reform. The government consulted with noble representatives on a matter of national importance, but then completely ignored their views and silenced their voices, opting instead for reform by bureaucratic fiat. Relations between the landed nobility and the government changed forever. Noble landowners coalesced into a distinct social and political interest group, separate from the government and the educated service classes. Russia's pre-political public and society, grounded in print culture and polite sociability, gave way to a politically conscious noble society, grounded in legally and historically constituted institutions. The collective articulation of noble interests in opposition to official policy heralded the birth of Russian civil society independent of the government.

By the time of emancipation in 1861, Russian society seemed well on the way to modernity. The educated service classes of the eighteenth century had morphed into socially differentiated and ideologically diversified groups. New social classes also had arisen with distinctive functions, identities, and interests. Sociocultural concepts such as the public and society remained, but they now overlapped with sociological entities such as the landed nobility and professional classes. Commercial-industrial elites had begun to prosper in the capitalist marketplace, giving them the means and the desire to participate in the high culture previously dominated by the court and educated service classes. In the 1860s, the stage seemed set for the development of a modern civil society in which commercial-industrial associations, elected *zemstvo* assemblies, and professional organizations would effectively limit the power of the government, not by disengaging from or opposing constituted authority, but by sharing in its exercise, and if need be challenging specific policies, from a position of institutional autonomy.

Such an outcome did not materialize, and an account of the reasons lies beyond the chronological boundaries of this book. Suffice it to say, that while Russian society in the 1860s possessed the potential to become modern and liberal, Russian government remained traditional and authoritarian (see chapter 8). Nor did Russia's modern commercial-industrial and professional elites assume leadership over the educated classes. The leadership role fell to the intelligentsia, a group that originated in the absence of autonomous social institutions, but then evolved into a hodgepodge of ideologically radical and politically fragmented movements, united both by their failure to develop deep ties to the Russian people and by their refusal to cooperate with the Russian government. In the decades ahead, as Russia's nascent civil society struggled to strike roots among the people and secure institutional independence from the government, destructive revolutionary movements came and went. By 1917 the combination of government intransigence, intelligentsia implacability, and revolutionary violence would destroy the potential for liberal democratic solutions to the problems of European modernity in Russia.

Chapter 8

The Limits to Bureaucratic Government

Generations of historians have depicted Russia's eighteenth century as a time of progress and reform initiated from above by the government and educated service classes. When historians turn to the nineteenth century, however, a decidedly different picture emerges. Although reform efforts in the vein of the eighteenth century continued, the historiography focuses more on the limitations and lost potential of these efforts than on their successes. In place of the coercive progress of Peter I and the enlightened absolutism of Catherine II, historians stress the tyrannical arbitrariness of Paul (ruled 1796–1801), the unreliable reformism of Alexander I (ruled 1801–25), and the "police-state" repressiveness of Nicholas I (ruled 1825–55). Indeed, in the Russian monarchy's ongoing search for regular government, the reforms of Catherine II opened up two possible paths of development: the path of civil society and the path of bureaucratic monarchy. The possibilities for societal initiative created by local elective offices and noble self-government, both significant features of the Catherinian reforms, persisted in the early nineteenth century. But so too did longstanding traditions of absolute monarchy and bureaucratic regulation. At court and in the bureaucracy, state power remained the overriding concern in both domestic and international affairs.

Following the death of Catherine II, Russia's monarchs continued to modify Petrine institutions. But like their predecessors, they also insisted on maintaining personal control over the process of reform. For although early nineteenth-century rulers operated in a more stable political environment – the succession law of 1797 ended much of the uncertainty of the eighteenth century – they nonetheless faced more autonomous and potentially hostile educated classes. The combination of personal rulership and an independent-minded educated society meant that instead of encouraging Russia's elites to take the lead in the cause of economic, social, and cultural progress, government policy tended to stymie societal initiative, intellectual freedom, and liberal plans for political reform. Historians are well aware that in the decades leading up to the emancipation of 1861, active and judicious reformism, usually hidden from public view, inspired enlightened officials at the highest levels of the bureaucracy. But because no fundamental change occurred, and because the educated classes, or at least the disaffected among them, appeared ever more critical of Russia's social and political institutions, the "prereform period" is often associated with conservatism, militarism, and repression. Rather than being recognized for their efforts to render more effective the Petrine service state, the rulers of the time emerge as remote figures, attentive to military and administrative power, but detached from the needs of the Russian people – the people who paid for that power, and for the cultural splendors of Moscow and St Petersburg, with servile labor and death in battle.

War, Diplomacy, and Empire

The conservatism of the Russian government should come as no surprise, given the empire's military and diplomatic stature in the first half of the nineteenth century. Russia emerged from the French Revolutionary and Napoleonic wars as leader of the military victory against France and defender of the old regime in Europe.[1] Russian action against revolutionary France began at the end of the eighteenth century, when Emperor Paul joined a military coalition consisting of Britain, Austria, the Ottoman Empire, and the Kingdom of Naples. During the months of negotiation leading up to the formation of the Second Coalition (1798–1802), Russia sent a naval squadron to support British operations along the Dutch coast (July 1798) and cooperated with the Ottomans to occupy the Ionian Islands (September–November 1798).[2] In February 1799, soon after the coalition took effect, the Russians captured Corfu, and Field Marshal Aleksandr V. Suvorov (1729–1800) became commander of a joint Austro-Russian army.[3] During the spring and summer of 1799, Suvorov scored significant victories in northern Italy, but instead of seizing the opportunity to march on Paris, the field marshal's superiors ordered him to cross the Alps into Switzerland. There he was supposed to join up with General Aleksandr M. Rimskii-Korsakov (1753–1840), whose corps was advancing from the Rhine valley. In late September, however, Rimskii-Korsakov and the Austrians suffered defeat near Zurich. Although Suvorov managed to extricate his troops from impending disaster, in the face of unchecked French power, the coalition began to unravel. In January 1800, Emperor Paul ordered Suvorov and his army back to Russia. In June French troops defeated the Austrians in the Battle of Marengo and then again in December in the Battle of Hohenlinden. Following Hohenlinden, the Austrian military effort collapsed.

The War of the Second Coalition marked the onset of one of the most dramatic periods in the history of European warfare. In November 1799, French general Napoleon Bonaparte became First Consul and head of a military dictatorship known as the Consulate.[4] For the next fifteen years, until Emperor Napoleon's defeat at Waterloo in March 1815, Europe's monarchies faced the double-edged sword of revolution and military aggression. Napoleon sought nothing less than the complete domination of Europe, and during the years of bloody conquest, intermittent peace, and shifting alliances, Russia and Britain remained the main obstacles to his success. Napoleon counted few friends among the monarchs of Europe, but the forces aligned against him had difficulty uniting for action. Each government tended to pursue its own interests and strategic goals. More often than not, Napoleon's enemies abandoned allies, hoping to avoid further territorial losses or to conclude illusory alliances with France. Although on occasion the need to protect commercial interests, freedom of the seas, and established thrones produced a measure of unity, alliances repeatedly crumbled in the face of French military success. The Second Coalition evaporated within a few years, as France reached separate agreements with coalition partners: rapprochement with Russia (1800), the Treaty of Lunéville with Austria (February 1801), and the Treaty of Amiens with Britain (March 1802). Thanks to these agreements, the defeated allies recouped territorial losses and even made some gains. Europe as a whole enjoyed general peace for the first time in a decade. But French aggression did not subside, and peace did not endure. Napoleon did not abandon efforts to undermine British control of the seas, and by May 1803 Britain and France again went to war. Less than two years later, in March 1805, Napoleon launched a plan to invade England. This led to the formation of the Third Coalition (April 1805), and months later, to the stunning naval victory of Admiral Horatio Nelson off Cape Trafalgar (October 21, 1805).

The Third Coalition (1805–7) pitted Britain, Sweden, Russia, and Austria against France. Britain escaped invasion and preserved naval superiority, while Russia and Austria experienced humiliating losses that opened the door to French domination of the Germanies and Poland. In late August 1805, Napoleon's Grand Army marched eastward from Boulogne, and a few days later the Austrians invaded Bavaria. At about the same time, a Russian army moved westward to join up with the Austrians. Before the allies could meet, however, the French defeated the Austrians at Ulm in Bavaria (October 17), clearing the way for an invasion of Austria. Although at Dürenstein (November 11) and Hollabrünn (November 15–16) Russian forces effectively delayed the French advance, they proved unable to prevent the occupation of Vienna. Greater losses appeared in the offing. Some two weeks after Vienna fell, on December 2, Russian and Austrian armies met the full force of French military might and suffered painful defeat at Austerlitz in Moravia. After Austerlitz, the Russians again abandoned their coalition partners and retreated into Poland. The Austrians surrendered unconditionally and on December 26 signed the Treaty of Pressburg. A few weeks later, in February 1806, Prussia agreed to an alliance with France, and in July fifteen German states joined the Confederation of the Rhine under French control. Over the next year, Napoleon became master of Western and Central Europe.

Following the collapse of the Russo-Austrian military effort at Austerlitz, the monarchs of Europe entertained few illusions about Napoleon's ultimate intentions. In July 1806, Russia and Prussia began to cooperate in preparation for further military hostilities. By October war between Prussia and France appeared inevitable, and before the Russians could make good on any commitments France defeated Prussia simultaneously at Jena and Auerstadt (October 14, 1806). French troops then occupied Berlin, and the Prussian king fled to the east. Only at the end of 1806 did Russian forces begin to pick up the slack, engaging the French in limited actions in Poland. In February 1807, the Russian and French armies met head on in the indecisive Battle of Eylau. A few months later, on June 14, the Russians suffered defeat at Friedland. In July Alexander I of Russia and Frederick William III of Prussia signed the Treaties of Tilsit.

Based on the Treaty of Tilsit (1807) and the Erfurt Convention (1808), Russia accepted the French domination of Western and Central Europe embodied in the Confederation of the Rhine and the Grand Duchy of Warsaw, the latter formed from Prussia's Polish provinces without the Belostok district. Russia also promised to declare war on Britain and to close the empire's Baltic ports to British trade, unless the British accepted French demands to respect freedom of the seas and to give up French, Spanish, and Dutch colonies conquered after 1805. Finally, Russia promised to hand over the Ionian Islands to France and to withdraw Russian ships from the Adriatic Sea. In return for these concessions, Napoleon agreed to mediate the war between Russia and the Ottoman Empire which had broken out in 1806 and, if mediation failed, to support Russia against the Ottomans. In addition, France would recognize Russian control over the Ottoman Empire's European provinces of Moldavia and Wallachia. Momentarily assuaged by the rhetoric of alliance and the displays of friendship between Alexander and Napoleon, the Russian and French governments pledged "to fight side by side in any European war, to the limit of their resources."[5]

Under the terms of Tilsit and Erfurt, the Russian and French emperors each seemed to get what he wanted without really giving up anything at all. In reality, the peace of 1807–12 delivered little more than an uneasy breathing spell. Napoleon's plan to use the alliance with Russia to break the economic power of Britain came to naught. The Russo-British commercial relationship had been strong and mutually beneficial since the sixteenth century. Although at Tilsit Alexander I agreed to adhere to the Continental System, established in 1806 to strangle the British economy, he failed to enforce the ban on trade. Russia did sever diplomatic relations with Britain in November 1807, but then never directly pursued war. Nor did the French uphold their end of the bargain, though one should remember that Napoleon had been the victor in 1807. Even so, Napoleon mocked the alliance by blatantly challenging Russian interests in Poland. In 1809 the French emperor incorporated into the Grand Duchy of Warsaw Polish territories (Western Galicia) taken from Austria. The Polish question could not have been more sensitive for Russia. The partitions of Poland represented the crowning achievement of Catherine II's foreign policy, and the last thing her grandson wanted to see was a strong and independent Poland on Russia's western border.

Problematic from the start, relations between Alexander I and Napoleon further deteriorated in 1810 and 1811. French expansionism continued in July 1810, when Napoleon annexed the Kingdom of Holland. In December 1810 and January 1811, he added the Hanseatic cities of Hamburg, Bremen, and Lübeck together with the Duchy of Oldenburg. Alexander's sister Catherine was married to the heir apparent of Oldenburg, and the integrity of the duchy had been specifically guaranteed by the Treaty of Tilsit. Such were the aggressions of Napoleon. On the Russian side, Alexander proved equally indifferent to French interests. The Russian emperor refused to accept the Trianon Tariff; neglected to close Russian ports to neutral ships, which regularly carried British goods; withdrew from the Continental System in December 1810; and imposed duties on products, primarily French in origin, brought to Russia by land.[6] No less offensive, Alexander responded tepidly to Napoleon's proposal of marriage to his sister, Anna Pavlovna. Alexander did not directly refuse Napoleon, but rather suggested a postponement due to the girl's young age.[7] Clearly, both parties to Tilsit violated the alliance's spirit and provisions. It is not surprising, therefore, that during 1811 and continuing into the early part of 1812, officials in Russia and France openly discussed the possibility of war. More ominously, the Russian and French emperors prepared for conflict.

The showdown came in the War of 1812, which to this day remains one of the most monumental events in the history of Imperial Russia. The beginning of the end for Napoleon, for the Russian people, the terrible and ultimately victorious war symbolized both their rightful stature among the nations of modern Europe and their unique legacy, culture, and world historical mission. Emperor Alexander I saw in the defeat of Napoleon the hand of Providence and the call for Russia to lead the world in the establishment of the universal Christian republic.[8] Given the frightful circumstances of 1812, Alexander can be forgiven his grandiose messianic vision.

On June 24, Napoleon's Grand Army, "one of the largest armies the world had ever seen," crossed the Niemen River into Russia.[9] Napoleon led a force of 368,000 infantry, 80,000 cavalry, and over 1,000 guns. From the start, Russian commanders avoided giving battle, and in mid-August the French reached Smolensk.

A two-day French assault ensued, compelling the Russians to set the city ablaze and leave it to the enemy. Lacking shelter and provisions – the Grand Army carried supplies for only 24 days – Napoleon pressed onward to Moscow. On September 5–7, a Russian force of 125,000 met 135,000 French troops near the village of Borodino, 120 kilometers west of Moscow. One of the most vicious battles of the Napoleonic wars, Borodino proved indecisive, though the Russians gave the French a nominal victory by again withdrawing. More indicative of the nature of the struggle, the dead and wounded on both sides reached staggering proportions: 58,000 Russians and 50,000 French.[10]

After Borodino, the road to Moscow lay open, and on September 14 Napoleon occupied Russia's venerable old capital. Most of Moscow's 300,000 inhabitants had been evacuated, so the French entered a ghost town rather than a vibrant city. Fires also soon broke out, destroying the noble homes where French troops might have quartered and the stores of grain, gunpowder, and ammunition that Napoleon might have used to supply his men. Before the fires could be brought under control, between one-half and two-thirds of the city burned to the ground.[11] The occupation and destruction of Moscow constituted a blow to the Russian spirit, but the loss did not mean the end of Russia. Alexander I's stubbornness stood him in good stead, as he repeatedly ignored offers of peace proffered by Napoleon. On October 19, unable to obtain supplies, the French began to withdraw. On October 24–5, at Maloiaroslavets, Napoleon tried and failed to destroy the main Russian army commanded by Fieldmarshal Mikhail I. Kutuzov (1745–1813). From that point onward, the French retreat became a catastrophe. All along the devastated route back to Smolensk, and then west of Smolensk, on both sides of the Berezina River, Russian troops and partisans kept up attacks on the retreating French soldiers. Of the roughly 100,000 men under Napoleon's command at the start of the retreat, 60,000 reached Smolensk, and only 40,000 survived to leave the Russian Empire.[12]

Once the French army had fled Russia, more than a year passed before the allies occupied Paris and removed Napoleon from power. During the spring and summer of 1813, Russia, Prussia, Britain, Sweden, and Austria formed yet another alliance. Hostilities began in August, and in mid-October, following the Battle of the Nations at Leipzig, Napoleon's reconstituted army retreated across the Rhine River. Over the next several months, the French suffered a series of setbacks. The Confederation of the Rhine collapsed, the Dutch provinces rose up in revolt, the Austrians scored military victories in northern Italy, and French losses at the hands of the British continued in Spain.[13] At the beginning of 1814, allied armies crossed the Rhine, and on March 31, 1814, Alexander I and Frederick William III entered Paris. In April Napoleon abdicated and departed for Elba. The Bourbons reclaimed their throne as constitutional monarchs, and Louis XVIII, brother of the guillotined Louis XVI, became king of France. But Napoleon's ambitions did not die easily. In March 1815, the defeated emperor returned to power after successfully raising an army and rallying supporters. Fortunately for Europe, the so-called Hundred Days passed quickly. In June 1815, a combined force of Belgian, Dutch, German, and British troops under the command of the Duke of Wellington, who earlier had led successful actions against the French in Spain, routed Napoleon at Waterloo. On June 21, Napoleon abdicated for a second time and on July 15 departed for his final exile on the island of St Helena. The age of the French Revolution came to an end, and although Europe would never again be the same, the continent's most notable monarchies survived.

The Russian monarchy did more than survive. In September 1814, the Congress of Vienna assembled to redraw the map of Europe. Meetings and private discussions continued until June 1815, dominated by Europe's five "great powers": Britain, Russia, Austria, Prussia, and France. The participants sought above all to restore a balance of power among the sovereign states of Europe that would ensure future peace and prevent any single country or ruler from becoming dominant on the continent. The effort failed, and instead of preserving the balance of power, the Vienna settlement "proved the possibility and salutary uses of hegemony."[14] Historian Paul W. Schroeder argues that between 1763 and 1787, diplomatic efforts to achieve a balance of power actually did little to "promote equilibrium, limit conflict, and preserve the independence of essential actors." Instead, "balancing practices and techniques" produced "imbalance, hegemony, and systemic conflict." After 1815, by contrast, an effective Concert of Europe "reconciled great-power demands for influence and control with small-power requirements for independence," balanced "the needs of the international community against the needs and claims of individual states," and finally, "secured and legitimized international rights while also allowing room for international change."[15]

More than any other factor, the reality of British and Russian hegemony determined the international arrangements that emerged in post-Napoleonic Europe. Britain ruled the seas, and Russia emerged from the Congress of Vienna in control of a reorganized Poland, Congress Poland, which pushed the empire's boundaries 417 kilometers further west. The Congress also recognized Russia's previous acquisition of Finland and Bessarabia. Indeed, throughout the upheavals of the French Revolutionary and Napoleonic wars, the Russian empire continued to encroach on European, Ottoman, and Persian territories. Following Tilsit, Napoleon encouraged Russian ambitions in Finland, and in February 1808, tsarist troops occupied the Swedish territory. Guerilla warfare against the Russians began in the summer of 1808, and only in September 1809 did Sweden agree to cede the Åland Islands and Finland. The incorporation of Bessarabia followed the Russo-Turkish war of 1806–12. Based on the Treaty of Bucharest (May 1812), the Ottomans gave up Bessarabia; Russia abandoned claims to Moldavia and Wallachia, which in theory remained autonomous under Ottoman suzerainty; and the Caucasian frontier, which the Ottoman government believed had been restored to its pre-war border, remained in dispute. Against the Persians, who claimed suzerainty over the Caucasian kingdom of Georgia, Russia had even greater success. Emperor Paul annexed Georgia in 1800–1, and Alexander I affirmed the act in September 1801. The incorporation of Georgia led to sporadic fighting with local rulers and eventually to a victorious war against Persia (1804–13). The Treaty of Gulistan (October 1813) allowed Russia to maintain a naval fleet in the Caspian Sea and recognized Russian sovereignty over Georgia, northern Azerbaijan, and Daghestan in the North Caucasus.[16] Despite enormous military outlays and the very real threat to national survival represented by the Napoleonic wars, Russian empire building proceeded apace.

After 1815 Russia continued to challenge Ottoman and Persian interests, and from the 1860s the empire added significant territories in Central Asia and the Far East.[17] At the same time, in Europe, Russia defended monarchical legitimacy and established social order. When the Greeks revolted against the Ottomans in 1821, Alexander I avoided involvement. But Russia had other longstanding claims against the Ottomans and eventually became embroiled in the conflict. In 1828 Nicholas I declared war, and Russian troops once again occupied Moldavia and Wallachia. The Treaty of Adrianople, signed in September 1829, further strengthened Russia's international position. The empire gained control over the mouth of the Danube River and the eastern coast of the Black Sea. Serbia, Moldavia, and Wallachia became autonomous, and the independence of Greece followed in 1832.[18] Finally, Adrianople guaranteed that the Black Sea Straits would be open to the commercial ships of all governments at peace with the Ottomans.[19] Russia had given up on Catherine II's "Greek project," the idea of restoring a Christian empire in Constantinople, recognizing instead the importance of the Ottoman Empire as a counterweight to the power of Britain, Austria, and France.

In addition to gains against the Ottomans, the army of Nicholas I advanced at Persian expense in Transcaucasia (the South Caucasus) and also did much to consolidate Russian rule in the North Caucasus. In June 1826, Persia renounced the Treaty of Gulistan and sent troops across the Russian border. After some early Russian losses, the tide turned, and in 1827 the fighting moved to Persian soil. In October Russian troops took Erevan and marched toward Teheran. The Treaty of Turkmanchai ended the war in February 1828. The treaty affirmed Russia's right to keep a fleet in the Caspian Sea and added the provinces of Nakhichevan and Erevan to the empire's South Caucasian territories. In the North Caucasus, Russian expansion proceeded with greater difficulty. There Russia did not face a powerful state or fight a concentrated war, but found it difficult to subdue the region's staunchly independent Muslim peoples. Full subjugation of the Caucasus did not come until 1864, and then, only after fifty years of costly struggle.

In the period from the end of the Napoleonic wars to the Crimean War (1853–6), ongoing expansion and peace in Europe lent to the Russian Empire an air of stability and strength. But dramatic changes had begun, and hidden weaknesses soon became apparent. During the first half of the nineteenth century, Russia's educated classes became sufficiently large, articulate, and diversified to make felt the presence of "public opinion(s)." The empire's bureaucracy became ever more educated and professional, but also increasingly divided into reformist and conservative camps. Calls to abolish serfdom became acceptable to Nicholas and his enlightened officials, who could not, however, openly discuss the possibility of reform for fear of arousing peasant unrest and noble opposition. Finally, although Europe did not directly threaten Russia, repeated revolutions in 1830 and 1848, including the Polish Rebellion of 1830–1, showed that political liberalism and social radicalism continued to spread. The Russian monarchy confronted no serious domestic opposition after the Decembrist Rebellion of 1825, yet at home and abroad the Crimean War exposed serious vulnerabilities.

Russia's humiliating performance in the Crimean War brought to an end the unassailable power that the empire had enjoyed since the victory over Napoleon. Already in the period leading up to the war, the unresolved "eastern question" encouraged European challenges to the empire's international position. Broadly defined as "the aggregate of all the problems connected with the withdrawal of the Ottoman Empire from the areas which it had conquered since 1354 in Europe, Africa, and Asia," the eastern question dominated European diplomacy from "the 1820s until the aftermath of the First World War."[20] The issues at stake included: 1) the future of the Ottoman Empire's European (and eventually West Asian) territories; 2) the protection of Christians, Catholic and Orthodox, under Ottoman rule; and 3) the balance of power in Europe and the Mediterranean, in light of the perceived decline of Ottoman power. Not unlike the situation that emerged after World War II, in post-Napoleonic Europe, the other great powers – Britain, Austria, Prussia, and France – remained fearful of Russian power and suspicious of Russian intentions.

From Russia's point of view, actions taken in the period leading up to the Crimean War represented the continuation of policies pursued since the reign of Peter I and brought to fruition under Catherine II. Russian foreign policy long had sought to return Christians to Christian rule, to extend the empire's borders into Ottoman territories, and to secure Russia's economic and military position on the Black Sea. The Crimean War showed, however, that in a diplomatic environment governed by the 1815 Vienna settlement and increasingly aggressive European imperialism, Russia's traditional ambitions had become more broadly explosive. Open conflict began after Russian troops once again occupied Moldavia and Wallachia (July 2, 1853), and the Ottoman Empire declared war on Russia (October 4). Britain and France, their fleets positioned at the entrance to the Dardanelles since June

1853, demanded in February 1854 that Russia withdraw from the Danubian principalities. Russia responded by sending troops across the Danube into Bulgaria, turning the war against the Ottomans into a wider European conflict.

Although the Anglo-French coalition remained just that, with the addition of the Kingdom of Sardinia, the allies' power proved sufficient to defeat Russia. Prussia remained neutral throughout the war, and Austria did not directly join the hostilities. But Franz Joseph did much to undermine Russia's international position and ensure a coalition victory. An early sign of Russian weakness appeared in August and September 1854, when Russia withdrew from Moldavia and Wallachia in response to the concentration of Austrian troops across the border. At about the same time, a combined French, British, and Ottoman force landed in the Crimea, and in October the allies began to bombard Sevastopol. The garrison and people of Sevastopol resisted heroically, hoping that the siege would be lifted, but no breakthrough occurred. In November Nicholas I agreed to negotiations based on four points put forth by Britain, France, and Austria. The four points called for: 1) the replacement of Russia's protectorate over Moldavia, Wallachia, and Serbia with a European guarantee; 2) free navigation on the Danube; 3) revision of the 1841 treaty forbidding the passage of warships through the Straits as long as the Ottoman Empire remained at peace, an arrangement that ensured Russian domination of the Black Sea; and 4) the replacement of Russia's claim to protect Orthodox Christians in the Ottoman Empire with a collective European guarantee for all Christians regardless of denomination. Emperor Nicholas I seemed to capitulate, but still peace did not come. Negotiations dragged on in Vienna until June 1855 (Nicholas died in February), and hostilities continued after Sevastopol fell on September 9. In November Russian forces even achieved a victory in the protracted siege of the Ottoman fortress at Kars. Finally, in December Austria threatened military action, if Russia did not return to peace negotiations based on the four points. On January 16, 1856, Alexander II (ruled 1855–81) agreed not only to negotiate, but also to accept a border change in favor of Moldavia and the right of the European powers to submit additional demands at the peace conference.

Based on the Treaty of Paris (March 1856), all territories occupied during the Crimean War returned to their status before the start of hostilities. In addition, Russia ceded to Moldavia southern Bessarabia, including the mouth of Danube, and accepted the internationalization of the river. Russia also lost any claim to a protectorate over Moldavia, Wallachia, and Serbia (all declared autonomous by the 1829 Treaty of Adrianople) and recognized the neutralization of the Black Sea with the stipulation that no fortresses be built on its shores.[21] The terms of the peace clearly weakened Russia's international power and prestige, but the condition and performance of the Russian military should not be unduly criticized. Both the Russian and allied armies suffered from mismanagement and inadequate logistical support, and troops on both sides absorbed significant losses from exposure, disease, and hunger. The fighting could not have been fiercer, and for all parties the military effort proved difficult to sustain. Ultimately, however, Russia succumbed to the superior technological capability of Britain and France.

Toward the end of the eighteenth century, beginning in Britain, Western Europe entered a period of "industrial revolution." Consequently, by the time the Crimean War began, British and French ships of the line "completely outclassed" Russia's Black Sea fleet, which contained "ten small paddle-wheelers." Lagging behind in the transition from sail to steam power, the Russian navy had obtained its first steamship only in 1848. Nor could the smoothbore muskets and cannon used by the Russians at Sevastopol match the rifles and modern ordnance of the enemy. British and French guns fired farther and more quickly than Russian ones, and the allies possessed abundant stores of ammunition. During the siege of Sevastopol, the British and French "fired at least 400,000 more shells . . . than the Russians were able to fire back."[22] Additional impediments to Russian military success included shortages of manpower, the absence of railway connections, and the poor quality of roads. Throughout the war, the seafaring British had an easier time getting troops to the battlefield than did the Russians. As late as 1860, Russia possessed no more than 1,600 kilometers of railway, and in 1870 still only 8,056 kilometers of paved military roads.[23] Unable to maintain a large military reserve, because conscription brought legal freedom to serfs; unable to equal allied firepower or move troops effectively by land or sea, because of technological inferiority; and finally, unable because of a financial crisis to pay for the Petrine standing army, the Russian government became convinced of the need for change.[24]

Reform with Order

Prior to Russia's defeat in the Crimean War, few of the empire's subjects took seriously the possibility of fundamental social or political reform. The liberal achievements of the French Revolution – equality before the law, constitutional guarantees of civil rights, elected representative government, and the removal of family relations from church control – barely resonated in early nineteenth-century Russia. Russian intellectuals defended the dignity of the individual, clamored for greater autonomy, and pushed the boundaries of free expression. Some even advocated the abolition of serfdom or called for a thoroughgoing reformation of society. But educated Russians also tended to think in moral rather than political terms (social reformation depended on the moral self-reformation of the individual), and except for the Decembrist Rebellion of 1825, no organized political opposition emerged. Indeed, throughout the first half of the nineteenth century, plans for political reform continued to emanate primarily from official circles, where reform meant not liberal democracy or legal equality, but limited civil liberties and, above all, more rational and effective government.

Russia's search for regular government made good, if intermittent, progress beginning with the reforms of Peter I and continuing through the reign of Catherine II. During the reign of Emperor Paul, the limits to Russian regular government became painfully evident. Although Paul ended the political uncertainty of the eighteenth century by establishing a clear order of succession to the Russian throne, after only a few years in power, he too succumbed to a murderous overthrow, tacitly approved by his son and heir, Alexander I. Paul also bolstered the status of the nobility by accelerating military promotions for nobles, increasing service requirements for the promotion of nonnobles, and allowing subjects to petition him directly. Still, among courtiers and elite servicemen, his reign became associated with misfortune and despotism. In the words of Princess Ekaterina R. Dashkova, "whoever was not personally a victim of Pavel I's despotic tyranny had the fate of a friend, a relation, of someone near and dear to bewail." The princess condemned Paul as "a coward by nature," noting that he "acted by spasms, his every action dictated by the whim of the moment, all too often, alas, violent and cruel." In recalling Paul's demise, Dashkova unabashedly gave thanks to God: "Providence allowed the Emperor's existence to be brought to a close, and with it all the public and private disasters, for taxation and persecution were growing and multiplying with every day that passed."[25]

Historical judgment tends to echo the opinions of Paul's contemporary detractors, though with more nuanced attention to the monarch's personal character flaws and emotional instability, attributable in part to the trauma of early separation from his parents, his father's assassination, and long-term estrangement from his mother. Historians also recognize that Paul enacted significant legislation, in addition to the 1797 succession law which instituted primogeniture in the male line.[26] Like his mother, Paul seemed to want to ameliorate the condition of the serfs. But also like his mother, he ended up extending the institution of serfdom. During the emperor's very brief reign, he distributed some 600,000 peasants to noble servicemen and in 1796 introduced serfdom to New Russia and the Don Cossack region. Following the lead of Peter I, Paul also permitted merchants to purchase peasants, with or without land, for work in factories.[27] Paul showed no inclination to abolish serfdom, though he did seek to regulate the institution and to eliminate abuses by placing restrictions on noble landowners. A law of February 1797 banned the sale by auction of house serfs and landless peasants, and in 1798 the sale of peasants without land became illegal in Left-Bank Ukraine. Of greater consequence, a manifesto of April 1797, in keeping with God's law, forbade landowners to require serfs to perform labor services on Sunday and suggested that three days of labor services per week should suffice to meet the economic needs of the master. The Law Code of 1649 already had established the ban on Sunday work as a legal norm, and historians are justifiably skeptical about the enforcement of Paul's measures. But regardless of concrete results, the 1832 *Digest of Laws of the Russian Empire* upheld both the ban on Sunday work and the three-day limit on labor services. There is evidence, moreover, that in 1853 the Minister of Internal Affairs ordered governors and marshals of the nobility to enforce the three-day limit.[28]

In hindsight, Paul's most important legislative acts seem consistent with eighteenth-century patterns of reform and administration; however, his treatment of the governing elite caused serious disaffection. Paul viewed nobles as servants of the crown, and although he did not rescind the 1785 Charter to the Nobility or the nobility's freedom from obligatory service, he did insist that nobles listed on regimental rolls appear for inspection and show proficiency in the Prussian-style drill and tactics practiced in the Russian army.[29] In addition, Paul levied taxes on nobles to support provincial administration, barred nobles not in service from participating in noble elections or holding elective office, and abolished provincial level noble assemblies. The district assemblies remained, though in general, governors asserted greater control over the nobility's corporate institutions. Paul's penchant to legislate revealed a penchant to regulate and a desire to reconcentrate the administrative power deconcentrated by his mother. The process of reconcentration led to the dismantling of numerous local bodies and the restoration of centralized colleges. In the provinces, governors general (*namestniki*), boards of public welfare, city councils, class-based urban institutions, and various lower courts all disappeared. At the center of political power, the Senate's importance as the empire's highest judicial organ increased, and administrative colleges abolished by Catherine II in the 1780s reappeared, headed by a single director instead of a collegial board. Catherine had reduced the number of colleges to three: War, Admiralty, and Foreign Affairs. Paul restored the Colleges of Mines, Manufactories, Commerce, and State Revenues; granted the title minister to the director of the College of Commerce; and created a Department of Appanages, headed by a minister and responsible for the lands belonging to the royal family.

The policies of Emperor Paul cannot be called coherent, but neither do they appear illogical or completely arbitrary. Although Paul seemed eager to disregard his mother's legacy, he did not seek to undo her work altogether. Above all, he wanted to instill order and morality into government. But Paul equated order with regimentation, and he remained unable to understand government apart from the principles of service and duty to his person. At a time when Russia's educated classes, including the educated service classes, displayed a growing desire for individual autonomy, his policies aroused hostility in the governing elite. To powerful, educated Russians, proud of the empire's cultural and military achievements, the personal rulership that had dominated the eighteenth century looked increasingly despotic and dysfunctional. To educated servicemen more specifically, personal rulership also seemed less effective, as the size and professionalism of the military and bureaucracy grew and as the tasks of government became increasingly complex.

For much of the eighteenth century, Russian government lacked a central institution capable of integrating policy and administration. The Senate of Peter I initially played this role, though without denying the monarch the right to intervene in routine matters of government. After Peter's death, successive oligarchic councils dominated the government, downgrading the Senate and undermining its integrative function. Under Catherine II, the Senate became the empire's highest judicial body, and the empress ruled through the procurator general of the Senate, the Council Attached to Her Majesty's Court (*Sovet pri vysochaishem dvore*), and an increasingly important personal chancery or secretariat. Emperor Paul, despite his interest in bolstering centralized power, likewise neglected to provide Russian government with a point of integration other than his person. From December 1800, the Council ceased to meet, and Paul began to rely on a personal chancery to exercise monarchical prerogatives. The procurator general became a kind of prime minister, combining in his hands the functions associated with ministers of justice, finance, and internal affairs.

Not until the reign of Alexander I did Russia's rulers begin to transform the Petrine service state into a modern bureaucratic government. They did this, however, not by changing political arrangements, but by reorganizing central administration and fostering a more educated officialdom. In the eighteenth century, patronage relationships, court intrigue, and palace coups dominated the political process. Successful reformers such as Peter I and Catherine II imposed their will by force of personality and talent. After 1801 monarchs sat more or less securely on the throne, and while court intrigue did not disappear, "coups" took place in the bureaucracy, not the palace. Removal of top officials replaced removal of sitting monarchs as the primary means for changing the balance of political forces. Although policymakers of the early nineteenth century possessed sufficient intellectual talent to address the problems of the day, increasingly the government divided into reformist and conservative camps, and even the most powerful official could not make anything happen without the support of the ruler. An educated, reform-minded official such as Mikhail M. Speranskii (1772–1839) could at a given moment wield enormous political influence; however, he remained the monarch's favorite, dependent on his royal patron for both personal security and the ability to act. The monarch made all policy decisions, and successive rulers, while able to envision the abolition of serfdom, a crucial step toward modern socioeconomic development, remained unable to imagine fundamental political change.

Emperor Alexander I is a case in point. Early in his reign, Alexander kept company with a small group of "young friends" who embraced the possibility of political reform and met regularly to discuss "constitutional" principles.[30] Known collectively as the Unofficial Committee, the friends in 1801 debated a draft Charter to the Russian People, believed by historians to be the work of Mikhail M. Speranskii, Aleksandr N. Radishchev (1749–1802), and the Vorontsov brothers, Aleksandr R. (1741–1805) and Simon R. (1744–1832). The Charter confirmed the emancipation of the nobility from obligatory service and the Catherinian Charters to the Nobility and the Towns. It called for security of person and property, freedom from arbitrary arrest (the English principle of *habeas corpus*), and the right of merchants and townspeople to travel abroad and change their place of residence. The Charter also promised to address the empire's need for better laws, a reference to plans for legal codification, and declared that "every Russian subject shall enjoy unhindered freedom of thought, creed or religion, worship, speech, writing, and action, to the extent that these are not contrary to the laws of the state and not damaging to anyone else."[31] By the end of August 1801, Alexander I appeared ready to accept the Charter, which subsequently received approval from the Permanent Council, a body established in April to consider government affairs and decrees. But the monarch never promulgated the Charter, and it passed quietly into oblivion.[32]

The passing of the Charter did not end the constitutional question. During 1801 and 1802, members of the Unofficial Committee produced additional plans for political reform, which called for legal recognition of the rights of the nation, including security of property and "the freedom to do anything with it that does not harm others." The Committee seemed mainly interested in the elimination of arbitrariness in government, and in the establishment of legal safeguards to counter the harm caused by unworthy rulers. "The Constitution is the law which regulates the method to be observed in the making of administrative rules. Requiring modification and interpretation, these rules must, of necessity, undergo changes in a known, fixed, and invariable manner, in order to close the door to all *arbitrariness* and, consequently, decrease the evil which may result from the difference in talent of those who are at the head of the state."[33] The Unofficial Committee said nothing about abolishing serfdom or limiting absolute monarchy, though its pronouncements did specify that the condition of the peasants be improved through definition of their status and property rights.

The plans and projects of the Unofficial Committee utilized a language of rights and constitutions familiar to the citizens of modern Western-style democracies. But assimilation of the language of rights did not mean that Alexander's reform-minded friends endorsed parliamentary democracy or elected representative government. Rather, they understood constitutional principles as legal guarantees, capable of containing arbitrary actions by tyrannical rulers such as Paul appeared to have been. Alexander I shared his friends' desire that Russian government be grounded in legal prescriptions, that it be a government of laws, and that persons in positions of authority, including the monarch, uphold the law and respect its provisions. But not unlike the eighteenth-century idea of regular government, the nineteenth-century idea of a *Rechtsstaat*, a law-based state, in no way limited the monarch's ability to change the law as he deemed fit. Although "methods" for changing "administrative rules" did become legally established, the law did not restrict the monarch's power to overturn official decisions. In the thinking of officialdom, and of most Russian subjects of the day, affirmation of the monarch's absolute right to enact legislation, dispense justice, and intervene in decision making represented their best guarantee of security and satisfaction.

So instead of constitutional reform, Alexander I implemented a reform of central administration that gave to Russian government a more modern face. The reorganization of central administration began in 1802 with reform of the Senate and the creation of ministries and a Committee of Ministers.[34] Legislation defined the Senate as "the supreme office (*mesto*)" of the empire, limited in its power only by the power of the emperor. The Senate supervised the monarchy's administrative edifice; received annual reports from the ministers, though not for long; and as "guardian of the laws," watched over the observance of justice (*pravosudie*). Of greater potential import, the Senate briefly acquired the right, lost in 1803, to comment on imperial decrees and to suggest reconsideration of new laws that contradicted existing ones. In practice, the reform of the Senate did not lead to greater coherence in government. The Senate possessed only nominal authority over the eight ministries established to carry out the tasks of administration: war, navy, foreign affairs, internal affairs, commerce, finance, popular enlightenment (education), and justice.[35] For a time, moreover, in some cases lasting into the reign of Nicholas I, colleges continued to operate within the ministries. Not until 1810–11 did additional reforms firmly establish the principle of unified ministerial command (*edinonachalie*).

The General Statute on Ministries (June 25, 1811) introduced a standardized structure of organization and record keeping for all ministries, and spelled out the mutual relations between their constituent offices and between the ministries and other institutions. At the head of each ministry stood a minister, aided by an assistant minister, a chancery, and a council. The apparatus of the ministry consisted of departments, divided into sections, which were further divided into desks. Department directors answered to the minister, section heads to department directors, and desk heads to section heads. The emperor appointed the ministers, who answered only to him (not to the Senate). The Committee of Ministers crowned the ministerial edifice, bringing together ministers, heads of main administrations with the rights of ministers, and individuals appointed by the monarch. The Committee provided general supervision over administration and official personnel, discussed legislative projects, and reviewed cases that individual ministers could not decide because of inadequate laws or because the interests of other departments were at stake. For the ministries and related offices, though not for the entire government, the Committee represented an effective point of bureaucratic integration.

The reforms of 1802–11 surely promoted the modernization of central administration in Russia, but they did not address the constitutional principles elaborated in the Unofficial Committee. A more concrete plan for constitutional reform issued from the pen of State Secretary Mikhail M. Speranskii, the son of a village priest, who made a brilliant career in the Ministry of Internal Affairs.[36] Between 1807 and 1812, Speranskii functioned as a *de facto* prime minister with responsibility for a range of policy issues. His activities encompassed the reform of seminary education, the establishment of the lycée at Tsarskoe Selo to train sons of elite nobles for government service, and the introduction of a testing requirement for promotion to rank 8 in civil service. In addition to these assignments, Alexander I put Speranskii in charge of restoring state finances and writing a new law code. In the latter capacity, Speranskii in 1809 produced a plan for political reform that aimed to reorganize Russian government on the basis of "immutable laws" and to establish popular participation in a legislative assembly. According to the plan, the monarchy would become limited "by the intrinsic and essential power of institutions" and by the establishment of "a sovereign power based on law not only in words but in deeds. . . ."[37]

Although arguably indicative of liberal aspirations, Speranskii's plan fell short of calling for constitutional monarchy. The plan restricted political rights to men of property, who participated in elections to township, district, and provincial assemblies called dumas and to a legislative assembly called the State Duma. The State Duma organized legislative commissions to discuss "matters submitted in the name of the sovereign power by one of the Ministers or members of the Council of State." The plan left legislative initiative in the hands of the government, but also allowed Duma members to submit "representations" on state needs, neglect of duty, and "measures violating the fundamental laws of the state."[38] The Council of State, composed of officials appointed by the monarch, reviewed all legislative projects, which could not be implemented, however, without imperial confirmation. In effect, Speranskii's plan envisioned the creation of an institutional mechanism for consulting with representatives of society in the making of laws. The plan in no way limited the legislative or judicial authority of the monarch, but conceived a regularized process of legislative review. The monarch still made the law, though he did so after *consulting* his subjects and highest officials within an established institutional framework. Lest there be any doubt about Alexander's commitment to absolute monarchy, in 1812 the emperor removed Speranskii from power and sent him into exile, first in Nizhnii Novgorod and later in Perm. Speranskii remained out of favor until 1816, when he returned to service as governor of Penza province. The only substantive change to come out of the 1809 plan remained the State Council, established in 1810 to act as a clearing house for new legislation and to reconcile the work of legislative, executive, and judicial authorities.

Speranskii's fall dealt a blow to Russian "constitutionalism," yet the possibility of political reform remained. In 1818–20, Alexander I initiated one last burst of liberal activity in connection with the promulgation of the Polish Constitution of November 15/27, 1815. The Polish constitution united Congress Poland and Russia through the person of the Russian emperor, who as king of Poland possessed the authority to call, prorogue, and dismiss the bicameral Polish Diet.[39] Composed of an elected lower house, the *Sejm*, and an appointed upper house, the Senate, the Diet passed laws by majority vote, but lacked the authority to initiate legislation. Alexander also could veto any of its resolutions. In addition, although the constitution specified that the Diet meet every two years, only four sessions took place between 1815 and 1830.[40] The Polish Constitution placed serious limitations on the authority of the Diet; however, it established representative government on a relatively broad basis: between 106,000 and 116,000 landed nobles and urban property owners qualified to participate in elections.[41] The constitution also recognized rights of *habeas corpus*, freedom of religion and the press, and a separate Polish army (not to be used outside the kingdom). In addition, only Poles could hold government posts, though Alexander's brother Constantine became commander-in-chief of the army, and the Polish language achieved recognition as the official language of the kingdom.[42]

In a speech given at the opening of the Polish Diet in 1818, Alexander I hinted at a desire to extend the benefits of constitutional government to Russia. Soon thereafter, he secretly commissioned one of the "young friends," Nikolai N. Novosil'tsev (1761–1836), to produce a constitutional charter for the empire.[43] The draft charter envisioned a federal structure that divided the empire into twelve lieutenancies (*namestnichestva*) each with a bicameral legislative duma (*seim*).[44] The appointed upper house of a lieutenancy duma consisted of the St Petersburg or Moscow department of the Senate, which temporarily moved to the capital of the lieutenancy. Nobles and residents of district towns, except for Jews and lesser townspeople with no immovable property, elected the lower house. Lieutenancy dumas then elected delegates from whom the monarch chose the members of the lower house of the State Duma (*Seim*). The Senate functioned as the State Duma's upper house, and both houses approved or rejected legislation submitted by the monarch. The State Duma could not initiate legislation, though according to some historians, the right to reject legislative projects amounted to veto power. But the charter also held that if the monarch did not confirm a legislative project approved by both houses, the project stood annulled, for "the Sovereign is the sole source of all authority in the Empire: civil, political, legislative, and military."[45] While vague and contradictory on the question of legislative prerogatives, the charter clearly envisioned the establishment of *habeas corpus*, freedom from arbitrary arrest, the inviolability of property rights, and equal protection from the law.[46]

Like previous plans for political reform, Novosil'tsev's charter did not see the light of day, and historians disagree as to whether or not it meant to impose meaningful limits on the power of the monarch. The historiographic confusion is telling. Alexander I's intentions and those of his officials remain unclear. Perhaps they did not fully understand Western principles of liberalism or the language of rights and constitutions they seemed to embrace. Russian scholar Sergei V. Mironenko explains the confusion by pointing to a distinction made in the charter between laws (*zakony*), which he believes the State Duma could veto, and 'regulations (*ustavy*), statutes (*uchrezhdeniia*), ukases (*ukazy*), rescripts (*reskripty*), and rules (*postanovleniia*),' which the monarch could enact without Duma approval.[47] But based on the *Complete Collection of Laws of the Russian Empire* (1830) and the *Digest of Laws of the Russian Empire* (1832), all legal-administrative acts sanctioned by the monarch's "so be it" constituted "the laws" (*zakony*) and carried equal weight as law. Indeed, much of the legislation included in the *Complete Collection of Laws* consists of judicial or administrative decisions confirmed by the monarch and thereby enacted into law. Nor did the language of the charter precisely define the legal significance of the distinction being made between the various forms of legislation. One fact, moreover, remains indisputable: constitutional monarchy would not be realized in Russia until the creation of the Duma in 1906, a concession reluctantly granted by Emperor Nicholas II (ruled 1894–1917) during the Revolution of 1905.

The meaning of constitutionalism in the reign of Alexander I, like the emperor's religious mysticism and enigmatic personality, is difficult for historians to penetrate. Reform of the peasantry, though more straightforward in terms of legislative output, seems similarly ambiguous and contradictory. Throughout Alexander's reign and continuing into that of his successor, Nicholas I, the Russian government made piecemeal changes to the institution of serfdom without, however, undertaking fundamental reform.[48] Legislation from 1801 allowed nonnobles (merchants, townspeople, and state peasants) to purchase unpopulated lands, and a law of 1803 permitted landowners to emancipate peasant villages based on mutual agreements. In return for a monetary payment, serfs acquired personal freedom and ownership of land. Known as "free agriculturalists," the former serfs became part of the state peasantry. Although by 1855 only 114,000 male souls had become free agriculturalists, the law nonetheless established two key principles of peasant reform: emancipation with land and payment for the land by emancipated serfs.

The government of Alexander I also drafted plans for the abolition of serfdom, though only in the Baltic provinces (Estonia, Livonia, and Courland) did these plans lead to action. In Estonia and Livonia, the Russian authorities began in 1804 to regulate relations between landowners and serfs, based on registers of allotments and obligations introduced by the Swedes before the Baltic territories became part of the empire. The reform gave serfs an hereditary right to cultivate their allotments and defined their obligations according to the amount and productivity of the land. But both peasants and nobles objected to the reform, leading the Russian government to undertake full emancipation in 1816–19. Although this first attempt at general emancipation proved harmful to the peasants, it taught the Russian government an important lesson. The emancipation deprived peasants of any hereditary right to cultivate a piece of land and established "voluntary agreements" between peasants and landowners to define allotments and obligations. The resultant decline in the peasants' economic condition led to serious disturbances and further reform. From 1849 in Livonia and 1856 in Estonia, peasants became eligible to buy part of their allotment land, though at prices set by the landowner. Peasants still did not have guaranteed access to land, and in 1858 disturbances again erupted. Serfdom came to an end in the Baltic provinces, but at great economic and social cost. Russian policymakers learned from the experience that any general emancipation had better include a right to land.

Interest in general reform of the peasantry intensified during the reign of Emperor Nicholas I, who convened no fewer than ten secret committees to consider the question. The work of the committees did not produce fundamental change; however, the information officials collected and the principles of reform they worked out provided a solid foundation for the 1861 emancipation settlement. Even piecemeal and ineffective legislation called for study of conditions in the countryside and alerted officials to problems and realities on the ground. Already in the first years of Nicholas's reign, policymakers assumed that peasants should be entitled to a minimum amount of land. A law of 1827 forbade landowners to sell or mortgage lands from their estates, if to do so would leave peasants with less than 12 acres of land for every male serf. Beginning in 1842, a law on "obligated peasants" allowed landowners and serfs to conclude contracts that defined the latter's allotments and obligations. Like the "voluntary agreements" introduced in the Baltic provinces, the contracts proved unpopular. Landowners retained ownership of the land as well as police and judicial powers over the peasants. They also were freed from the obligation, dating back to the early eighteenth century, to help peasants in case of crop failure. Not surprisingly, by 1858 only 27,000 male serfs had become "obligated peasants." Even fewer peasants, less than 1,000, took advantage of an 1847 law that allowed serfs to buy mortgaged estates put up for auction. If peasants living on an estate could raise the necessary money, they became legal owners of the land and free men within the state peasantry. But most peasants lacked the means to purchase bankrupt estates, and landowners opposed the law, fearing their serfs would deliberately try to ruin them by refusing to fulfill obligations. Sensitive to the nobility's concerns, the government revised the law in 1847: landowners first had to give their permission before serfs could buy their estates.

Nicholas I, like Alexander I, refused to impose compulsory emancipation on the Russian nobility. He did, however, try to regulate the power of noble landowners. As early as 1719, Peter I ordered military governors to intervene to prevent the physical abuse of peasants. Decades later, in the reign of Catherine II, the 1775 reform of provincial administration permitted governors to prosecute landowners who subjected serfs to cruel treatment or excessive obligations. Governors could sequestrate and place under guardianship the estates of such landowners.[49] Under Nicholas I, thanks to improved administrative procedures introduced in 1817 and the late 1820s, official efforts to stop abuses "acquired some bite." Information is fragmentary, and there is no evidence of rigorous enforcement; however, Nicholas's government brought to trial a few thousand landowners and convicted a few hundred.[50] In addition, the penal code of 1845 limited the punishments landowners could impose on serfs to four months of imprisonment or 40 blows with the rod. Landowners still could send peasants to the army or to exile in Siberia, and in both cases they continued to receive recruit quittances for the banished individuals.[51] But clearly, fair treatment had become a recognized legal principle.

Another reform that aimed to tighten controls on landowners took place in Right-Bank Ukraine (provinces of Kiev, Volhynia, and Podolia) in 1847–8. In this region, Polish nobles ruled over Ukrainian peasants, and the Russian government, eager to restrict the nobles' power, introduced measures to guarantee for serfs the perpetual use of land allotments and to define in inventories their obligations to landowners. Similar to the 1804 reform in the Baltic provinces, the reform in Right-Bank Ukraine also built upon estate inventories that had recorded peasant allotments and obligations before the eighteenth-century partitions of Poland. Progressive on the face of it, the reform of 1847–8 did nothing to ensure sufficient land for peasants, and neither they nor their masters supported its provisions. As a result, the Russian government abandoned plans to extend the reform to Lithuania and Belarus.

Reform of appanage and state peasants turned out to be more successful, perhaps because officials had no need to accommodate noble landowners.[52] The 1829 reform of appanage peasants, 5–6 percent of the peasantry in the early nineteenth century, based dues on the value of land allotments (a proposal originally put forth by Emperor Paul), required peasant villages to stock reserves of grain, promoted the improvement of farming methods by introducing better quality livestock and more productive crops such as the potato, and addressed the problem of land shortage by resettling peasants on state lands in the Mid-Volga region. Although the reform aroused peasant suspicion and provoked disturbances, its basic features became part of a more ambitious reform of state peasants implemented in the late 1830s and 1840s.

State peasants comprised about half the peasantry, and from 1838 they came under the authority of a new Ministry of State Domains, headed by Count Pavel D. Kiselev (1788–1872). The ministry oversaw an administrative structure that extended from St Petersburg down through multiple levels to the self-governing peasant commune. Concerned with the moral and material condition of the peasants, Kiselev's reforms included a wide range of policy initiatives: measures to discourage drunkenness, the opening of primary schools for peasant children, the introduction of a lottery system to ensure a more equitable distribution of the military service obligation, and efforts to address the problem of corrupt administration, a major cause of peasant disturbances, by appointing competent officials who would be paid decent salaries. To encourage agricultural improvements and help peasants meet their official obligations, the reforms also established agricultural colleges and model farms, introduced better breeds of livestock and crops such as the potato, upgraded famine relief, countered land shortages by granting state lands (mainly forest) to peasant villages and by resettling peasants on vacant lands, and tried, unsuccessfully, to establish norms for household allotments. Finally, beginning in 1842 the Ministry of State Domains assessed peasant obligations based on land values and income from nonagricultural activities. Although historians disagree as to whether or not the reforms brought concrete benefits to state peasants, Minister of State Domains Kiselev clearly viewed his policies as "the start of a general reform of the entire peasantry."[53]

By the mid-nineteenth century, an enlightened group of Russian officials not only recognized the need for general reform of the peasantry, they also understood general reform to mean the eventual abolition of serfdom.[54] But to achieve their goal would be difficult. Before Russia's defeat in the Crimean War, reform efforts stalled because of the government's inability to reconcile two competing commitments: 1) that peasants be guaranteed a minimum allotment of land, and 2) that emancipation not be imposed by force on the nobility. For this reason, general reform came only after Emperor Alexander II ordered that emancipation indeed be imposed from above by the government and that a portion of the nobility's landed property be assigned to and purchased by village communes, to which individual peasants remained legally bound and obligated. The emancipation settlement of 1861 gave peasants personal freedom, guaranteed access to communal lands, and a system of peasant courts and administrative institutions, linked to the traditional commune, that eventually freed them from the direct authority of landowners. From the outset, the terms of the emancipation alienated the nobility and failed to satisfy the peasants. From the historian's perspective, by contrast, the emancipation settlement appears to have been a serious and sincere effort, undertaken on a colossal scale, to meet the challenges of European modernity by restructuring socioeconomic and legal relationships in a peaceful and equitable manner.

The Great Reforms of the 1860s, including the implementation and consequences of the 1861 emancipation, belong to another story and time period. As ruler and reformer, Nicholas I stood in the tradition of Peter I, not Alexander II. Nicholas's reputation as militaristic and repressive, while one-sided, is not completely undeserved. Nicholas acceded to the throne amid the Decembrist Rebellion of 1825, and as monarch, he faced the Polish Rebellion of 1830–1. Nicholas also witnessed revolutionary upheavals in Europe in 1830 and 1848. It is not surprising, therefore, that his domestic policies sought to bolster government authority and social order. For the first time in the history of Imperial Russia, leading officials and intellectuals actively promoted a conservative ideology, dubbed by historians "official nationality," that celebrated the principles of Orthodoxy, autocracy, and nationality. The brainchild of Count Sergei S. Uvarov (1786–1855), Minister of Education from 1833 to 1849, official nationality represented a Russian response to the challenges of European modernity. Citing the "rapid downfall of religious and civic institutions in Europe," Uvarov set out to define "sustaining principles" that could both guide Russia toward further progress and protect the empire from revolution. Russia, in the words of Uvarov, needed 'a *Russian system* and a *European education.*'[55] Uvarov's "Russian system" called for adherence to the Russian Orthodox Church, belief in the teachings of Eastern Orthodox Christianity, and preservation of absolute monarchy and the Romanov dynasty. The "Russian system" also assumed avoidance of the capitalist economic transformation that had led to social crisis in the cities and factories of Western and Central Europe. But avoidance of rapid industrialization did not preclude economic, social, and cultural progress. For the foreseeable future, the pursuit of scientific and technological development appeared consistent with the ways and mores of the Russian people. Russians, according to Uvarov, continued to need "European education," by which he meant assimilation of the most advanced European learning and participation in the full panoply of the modern European (and now also Russian) arts.

As cultural metaphor and political idea, official nationality seemed to represent the perfect synthesis of Russian tradition and European progress. But the synthesis did not hold up in practice. The tripartite formula of Orthodoxy, autocracy, and nationality also revealed the deeply conservative impulses of the Russian government. Nicholas I continued the search for regular government begun by Peter I and modified by Catherine II; however, he abandoned the constitutionalist path tentatively articulated by Alexander I. To ensure regular government – understood by Nicholas as social control, bureaucratic regulation, and administrative effectiveness – the monarch allowed Mikhail Speranskii and a team of associates to move forward with the work of legal codification. Completed and published in 1832, the *Digest of Laws of the Russian Empire* became "the sole authoritative source" for determining which laws remained in effect and applied in concrete situations.[56] Regarded by historians of jurisprudence as technically and conceptually deficient, Speranskii's codification nonetheless brought greater stability and predictability to official decision making. It did not, however, touch the power of the monarch or his ability to change the law at will. Nor did it institutionalize a legislative role for society. Codification made clear that regular government meant the preservation of order through tighter bureaucratic control, not consultation with the monarch's subjects.

Consistent with the Russian government's focus on bureaucratic control, censorship under Nicholas I became more systematic, comprehensive, and intrusive. Never before had censors exercised such broad-based institutionalized power. Nor did bureaucratic censorship preclude direct intervention by the monarch. In 1826 Nicholas himself assumed the role of personal censor to Russia's beloved national poet Aleksandr S. Pushkin (1799–1832).[57] Nicholas's government also tried to use education to control minds and social change. Higher tuition costs and efforts to tie the content of curriculum to social origin aimed both to increase the proportion of nobles in state schools and to restrict access to secondary and higher education for students from the lower classes. Nobles did indeed begin to enter gymnasiums, universities, and specialized schools in ever greater numbers; however, the social and intellectual diversity of Russia's educated population also continued to grow.[58] Larger numbers of educated Russians, pursuing variegated professions and occupations, produced a diversity of experience, thought, and dissent that led in turn to official concern about the mood and activities of the empire's subjects. In June 1826, Nicholas established Russia's modern secret police or gendarmerie, the Third Section of His Majesty's Personal Chancery, "to act as the moral and political guardian of all Russia."[59] Nicholas instructed officials of the Third Section to gather information on events across the empire, to arrest and exile "dangerous and suspicious persons," and to conduct surveillance to protect the country from internal threats and sedition.[60] Nicholas understood, it seems, that the loyalty of his subjects no longer could be taken for granted.

Until Russia's defeat in the Crimean War, however, evidence of popular discontent remained minimal. The empire continued to enjoy great power status, while preserving social order and avoiding the consequences of economic modernization. The prevention of dramatic change remained central to the policies of Nicholas I. Russia's basic system of government, including the organization of conscription and taxation, dated back to the reign of Peter I. State building, supported by cultural achievement and resource mobilization, defined Peter's reforms. During the reign of Nicholas, Peter's policies remained relevant and seemingly effective, at least from the perspective of administrative and military needs. The Petrine system, it can be said, reached its fullest point of development. The Russian empire appeared strong and defensible. Judging from the archival record, Russia possessed a rule-based government that with some consistency held officials and military commanders accountable for failure to uphold the law. Yet even a cursory reading of literary sources from the time provides a radically different picture of society and government. Instead of good order and bureaucratic rationality, corruption, abuse, and stagnation seem to dominate social and political life. The dichotomy between the images found in official documents and those found in the works of authors such as Nikolai V. Gogol (1809–52), Aleksandr I. Herzen (1812–70), and Fedor M. Dostoevskii (1821–81) is telling. In the reign of Nicholas I, society and government came to represent separate spheres of consciousness and action. In the eighteenth century, Russian educated society consisted of service classes eager to acquire a European cultural voice. By the nineteenth century, educated Russians began to use that voice for their own purposes, separate from and increasingly in opposition to the government. Russian absolute monarchy, while more modern and rational in a bureaucratic sense, also appeared more arbitrary and alien from the viewpoint of independent society.

Chapter 9

To Speak for the Russian People

For much of the eighteenth century the process of importing European culture into Russia grew out of government needs such as the education of personnel and the building of institutions. Russian letters, arts, and sciences produced largely derivative works which either applied European learning to Russian conditions or explained Russian experience in European terms. In the first decades of the nineteenth century, the period of intensive cultural borrowing reached a seemingly miraculous end. Although educated Russians continued to look to Europe for cultural inspiration and guidance, the assimilated European models became so thoroughly Russianized that they cohered as something identifiably Russian in content, form, and meaning. If the eighteenth century constituted the crucible of modern Russian culture, the first half of the nineteenth century represented its coming of age – the moment when the educated service classes became an educated public or independent society (*obshchestvo*), when the Russian literary language acquired its modern form, when political opposition and modern political thought burst onto the Russian scene, and when Russia's Europeanized writers, artists, and composers began to present the world, and Russia's place in the world, in specifically Russian terms.

But with cultural maturation also came intellectual pluralism and dissonance. The remarkable unity of outlook previously shared by the Russian monarchy and educated classes crumbled in the face of uncertainty about the progress of enlightenment.[1] What did the spread of civilization mean in a country populated overwhelmingly by uneducated peasants, about half of whom lived in outright bondage? How could educated Russians, the putative carriers of civilization to the people, satisfy their Enlightenment yearning for individual autonomy and moral self-development at the same time that they remained the subjects of an absolute monarch? Regardless, moreover, of whether Russia's (and their own)

Europeanization had been genuine or artificial, a troubling question in itself, after roughly a century of conscious borrowing, what else could be learned from Europe? Perhaps more important, had Russia benefited from the openness to foreign influences, or had the adoption of European models undermined Russian traditions? In the first half of the nineteenth century, as nationalism spread across the European continent, educated Russians came to believe that their country too possessed, and should follow, her own unique path of historical development. But what was the Russian path, and what did it mean to be Russian in a multiethnic, multiconfessional empire where a small Europeanized elite lived in social and cultural isolation from the mass of the "nation(s)"? Within the halls of government, on the Russian stage, from university podiums, and in art, literature, and journalism, a critical mass of independent thought responded to these burning questions. Spurred by the awareness that intellectual and artistic creations represented not services to the monarchy, but contributions to a national culture, educated Russians began to translate ideas into action. Increasingly, they claimed both independence from the government and the right to speak for the Russian people.

Dissonance and Dissent

"Looking at the present condition of my country," wrote Prince Mikhail M. Shcherbatov (1733–90), "I cannot but wonder at the short time in which morals in Russia have everywhere become corrupt." Shcherbatov, scion of an old noble family, wrote *On the Corruption of Morals in Russia* in 1786–7, and he traced Russia's moral decline back to the reforms of Peter I. Peter transformed the sociability of his subjects, making it possible for Russians to take "gigantic steps to correct our outward appearance." At the same time, however, the open sociability unleashed the passions of love and sensuality, which gave rise to luxury, profligacy, and careerism. As a result, Shcherbatov observed, "faith and God's law have been extinguished in our hearts, Divine mysteries have fallen into disrepute, and civil laws have become objects of scorn."[2] Educated, enlightened, and Europeanized, Prince Shcherbatov could not unequivocally condemn Peter I. He praised the great reformer for increasing Russian power and for taking measures to eradicate superstition. But Shcherbatov also decried the careerism and dishonor that resulted from the bureaucratic ennoblement of commoners through the Table of Ranks and from the ability of merchants to buy noble status. Equally disturbing, he concluded that "by taking superstition away from an unenlightened people," Peter had eliminated "love of God and his Holy Law."[3] To Shcherbatov's mind, "voluptuousness" had taken hold, and the very fiber of Russian life had become rotten at the core.

On the Corruption of Morals did not become widely known in Russia until Aleksandr I. Herzen (1812–70), the father of Russian socialism, published the work in London in 1858. By that time, modern forms of political thought had emerged, and Shcherbatov's defense of noble privilege, belief in the natural inequality of human beings, and support for absolute monarchy had become mainstays of Russian conservatism. Yet Shcherbatov could be read in different ways, and in some writings, he seemed to call for aristocratic constitutionalism. His devastating critique of Russian society and government also appeared consistent with Enlightenment reason and even liberal reformism. Like other eighteenth-century intellectuals, Shcherbatov did not so much develop an ideological position as raise unsettling moral questions about Russian reality and the effects of the Europeanization wrought by Peter.[4]

Shcherbatov's younger contemporary, Aleksandr N. Radishchev (1749–1802), represented a different and more overtly dissident intellectual orientation that also echoed among subsequent generations of political thinkers. In 1790 Radishchev published a critique of serfdom and tyranny, *Journey from Petersburg to Moscow*, which led to his arrest and criminal conviction. A radical and uncompromising abolitionist tract, the *Journey* described the most hideous abuses of serfdom and presented peasant rebellion and the murder of landlords as legitimate responses to inescapable cruelty and exploitation. Although Radishchev did not openly advocate revolt, memories of the Pugachev Rebellion (1773–4) and awareness of the unfolding revolution in France made his call for social justice appear dangerous to the Russian monarchy. In 1790 Radishchev received a death sentence, which in 1791 Empress Catherine II commuted to ten years of exile in remote Siberia. There, in the town of Ilimsk, the condemned nobleman remained until 1796, when Emperor Paul allowed him to live on his family estates. Finally, in 1801 Alexander I granted Radishchev a full pardon and recalled him to St Petersburg to serve on a commission appointed to write a new law code. One year later Radishchev committed suicide.[5] Clearly, Alexander did not consider Radishchev a political threat, yet Catherine may not have been off the mark in pronouncing his ideas subversive.[6] Whereas Aleksandr Herzen called Shcherbatov an 'angry old man' nostalgic for the 'tedious and semi-barbarous existence of our forbears,' he admired Radishchev and held him up as a model for his own European-style social radicalism.[7]

Throughout the eighteenth century, the sense of duty to a personal ruler remained strong among noble intellectuals, even disaffected ones, from across the political spectrum. But when an individual's sense of duty clashed with his or her understanding of moral virtue, the results could be emotionally explosive. Dissonance and dissent, whether political or moral, easily assumed the appearance of a personal betrayal directed against the reigning monarch. Both Shcherbatov and Radishchev formulated moral critiques of Russian society and government, and both experienced the conflict between principle and duty (hence the apparent wavering in their political positions). Both also envisioned government constrained by just laws and social relationships grounded in moral virtue. At the same time, Shcherbatov and Radishchev advocated very different principles of social organization. Shcherbatov assumed that privileges represented rewards for the meritorious service of ancestors and thus staunchly defended inequalities based on birth. He considered natural the legal distinctions that ascribed to every Russian subject a social position and occupational function. Radishchev, by contrast, rejected the inequities of social hierarchy and especially serfdom. He assumed that the natural equality of all human beings should be incorporated into social relationships. Ironically, despite their differences on social questions, both men also imagined "constitutionalist" forms of government, for Shcherbatov grounded in the preservation of aristocratic privilege and for Radishchev based on liberal principles and liberties. Ultimately, both accepted the reality of absolute monarchy in Russia, but hoped that political and social life could be reformed according to the dictates of justice, reason, and virtue. Aside from Radishchev's abolitionism, which is well documented, what this might have meant in concrete Russian terms neither man had a chance to say.

Early Political Opposition

Only a handful of dissident voices emerged from eighteenth-century Russia, yet those that did contributed critical themes to the cultural debates of the early nineteenth century. Whether labeled conservative, liberal, radical, monarchist, constitutionalist, or republican, intellectuals such as Shcherbatov and Radishchev handed to the nineteenth century a discourse of moral virtue applied to social and political questions. Transcendent and absolute, like the power of the monarch, this discourse did not provide a language or mode of thought suitable for political negotiation and compromise. Even if it had, moreover, Russia possessed relatively few institutional sites where open political posturing might occur. Policy discussions at court and within the bureaucracy could be called political – factions formed around distinct positions – but these discussions rarely reached into the public arena. Noble assemblies, urban societies, and peasant communes also discussed problems of public concern, though only with reference to the affairs of distinct classes and communities in decidedly local frameworks. The same can be said of cultural and philanthropic organizations, even though eventually they became leading participants in Russian political life. Surely it is no accident that historians interested in the study of civil society or the emergence of political opposition in the first half of the nineteenth century turn to literature and the periodical press for the bulk of their source material. Short of open rebellion, Russian literary culture provided the most significant forum for ideological debate.

In the terminology of modern Europe, Russian political opposition emanated from the "left" and the "right." During the reign of Alexander I, conservative public opinion, grounded in anti-liberal nationalist thought, became a serious political force. Patriotic themes such as love of the fatherland, the moral superiority of Slavs or Russians, and the corruption caused by superficial Europeanization and excessive Francophilia could be found in Russian literature of the later eighteenth century.[8] In the early years of the nineteenth century, as Napoleon's armies spread the principles of the French Revolution across Europe, liberal reformism and Enlightenment universalism began to appear dangerous to growing numbers of policymakers and intellectuals. Gradually, and in a variety of ways, the patriotic themes of the eighteenth century acquired political overtones and became associated with conservative ideologies. Although the ideas that arose in this environment remained diffuse, unsystematic, and changeable, conservative thinkers seemed united in their opposition to the political ways of Britain and France.

Committed to imperial strength and social stability, conservatives insisted that Russian institutions and traditions be preserved, in some instances restored, as fundamental principles of government and cultural life. Romantic nationalists such as Aleksandr S. Shishkov (1754–1841) and Sergei N. Glinka (1776–1847) saw in the culture of the Russian people, especially the peasants, the main line of defense against pernicious influences emanating from Europe. By embracing the authentic, uncorrupted traditions of the peasants, they argued, Russian elites could restore the country to moral strength, bridge the gap that separated the monarchy from its subjects and the educated classes from the common people, and ensure that the nation's development took a proper non-European course. Less enamored with the idea of a superior Russian past, though equally concerned about the problem of moral corruption, cosmopolitan, state-oriented conservatives such as Nikolai M. Karamzin (1766–1826) and Fedor V. Rostopchin (1763–1825) remained comfortable with Russia's Petrine institutions and with the Europeanized lifestyle of the Russian elite. In their view, Russia's greatness and continued progress depended on maintaining the eighteenth-century alliance of absolute monarchy and noble privilege, while also restoring virtue and justice to social and political relationships. Yet another group of conservative thinkers, represented by Aleksandr N. Golitsyn (1773–1844), Roksandra S. Sturdza (1786–1844), and Aleksandr S. Sturdza (1791–1854) feared the potential for discontent in Russia and hoped that Christian spirituality and government-sponsored social work among the poor could bring about both elite and popular reconciliation with the monarchy and established institutions.[9] Clearly, Russia's early conservatives did not oppose change or enlightened reform, but they did tend to understand reform in terms of moral regeneration. They also remained committed to religion, monarchy, and social harmony as necessary principles of Russian historical development.

Russian conservatism in the reign of Alexander I did not add up to a political movement or counter-enlightenment with a coherent ideology and social base. It did, however, represent a body of public opinion capable of influencing official policy. The emperor's flirtation with constitutional reform in 1801–12, legal changes to serfdom in 1801–4, and the Treaty of Tilsit and consequent alliance with Napoleon in 1807–12 caused considerable concern among advocates of social order, noble privilege, absolute monarchy, and the centrality of the church and religion in Russian life. As early as 1806, hostile public opinion forced Adam A. Czartoryski (1770–1861), a personal friend of Alexander, to resign his post as minister of foreign affairs. At a time of French influence in rebellious Poland and of conservative dissatisfaction with the emperor's pro-French policies, Czartoryski's liberalism and Polish origins created suspicions about his loyalty to Russia. Several years later, in 1812, State Secretary Mikhail M. Speranskii (1772–1839), the son of a village priest and hence also an outsider in ruling circles, suffered a similar fate. Speranskii's liberal reformism led powerful critics to see him as pro-French and to accuse him of treasonous designs against Russia. On the eve of Napoleon's invasion, the conservative uproar convinced Alexander to remove Speranskii from office and send him into exile. With this action, the emperor sacrificed his trusted advisor and plans for political reform to the need for unity within the governing elite. Shishkov became state secretary in place of Speranskii, and Rostopchin became Moscow governor-general.[10]

In 1806 and again in 1812, Alexander I appeared to bow to conservative public opinion. Yet neither he nor any subsequent Russian monarch ever came fully under the sway of a particular political grouping. Shishkov's calls to purge Russia, and especially the Russian language, of French influences, which he saw as a source of moral corruption, had no discernible effect on the emperor, who in August 1814, once the military crisis had passed, removed both Shishkov and Rostopchin from office. Less than two years later, in January 1816, Alexander recalled the reform-minded Speranskii to service by appointing him to the governorship of Penza province.[11] In the halls of Russian government, liberal reformers came and went. At no time, moreover, did Alexander or his successors follow the lead of European liberals committed to the development of civil liberties, democratic political institutions, and a capitalist market economy. For the remainder of the imperial period, until the overthrow of the monarchy in February 1917, Russia's rulers wavered uneasily between progressive reform, counter-reform, and maintenance of the status quo. Although conservative nationalists, monarchists, and defenders of noble privilege continued to play an important role in the formulation of foreign and domestic policy, the monarch made all policy decisions and could overrule any majority or minority opinion. At court, in the upper reaches of government, and even in the press, it fell to the ruler to decide between liberal and conservative positions. This is precisely how the liberal reforms of the 1860s came to be. One cannot help but think, therefore, that if Russian conservatives had been less vociferous and less effective in manipulating successive monarchs' sense of duty and commitment to tradition, the empire's political history might have unfolded in a more consistently reformist direction.

But historians cannot tackle "what if" questions, and even though Alexander I sometimes seemed liberal, in the aftermath of the Napoleonic wars, he took nationalist thinking beyond conservative notions of purifying the Russian language, returning Russian culture to authentic popular roots, and restoring social harmony. Alexander imagined nothing less than the creation under Russian leadership of a Christian order in Europe. In proposals for the formation of the Holy Alliance between Russia, Prussia, and Austria, Alexander combined the Enlightenment (and Christian) idea of a single moral law for all peoples and monarchs with a quasi-religious, messianic belief in Russia's world historical mission. Convinced by the victory over Napoleon that Russia had been chosen by God to play a special providential role, Alexander saw in the Holy Alliance the advent of a new age, the coming of the kingdom of Christ, in which Russia and her emperor would bring to the world Christian enlightenment.[12] Fortunately for the world, cooler heads prevailed in the diplomatic reconstruction of Europe. Tamed by Prussian and Austrian opposition, Alexander's plans for a universal Christian republic remained a vision. Nor in everyday life and governance did the emperor's own eschatological expectations and belief in having been chosen by God always hold firm. Although encouraged by contemporaries such as Golitsyn, the Sturdzas, and poet Vasilii A. Zhukovskii (1783–1852), Alexander's messianic nationalism could not easily be applied to concrete policy. Mystical spirituality sent his mind reeling in multiple contradictory directions that are fascinating to behold, though not likely to be understood based on available documentation. For the historian, it can indeed become difficult not to question the emperor's mental stability. That said, the idea of a special world-historical mission for Russia, a highly charged blend of universalism and Russianness, struck deep roots and remains to this day a force in Russian politics and culture.[13]

Under Alexander I's successor, Nicholas I, the conservative thought influential at court became a more reasoned statement of government policy and ideology. Official nationality – the tripartite formula of Orthodoxy, autocracy, and nationality – sought to enshrine the Orthodox religion, Russian absolute monarchy, the Romanov dynasty, and the cultural traditions of the Russian people as unchangeable principles of Russian historical development. Proponents of official nationality defended serfdom, noble privilege, and peasant communal agriculture, but like earlier conservatives, they did not necessarily oppose change, reform, or even European influence. They understood that Russian state power required ongoing cultural advancement, and like the educated servicemen of the eighteenth century, they recognized that Russia needed to learn from Europe in order to compete in the world of international diplomacy and military affairs. But neither did the theorists of official nationality want Russian traditions to get lost in the process, and so they deliberately rejected the intellectual freedom and market transformation that, in their view, had led to revolution in Europe. They firmly believed, erroneously history would prove, that Russia could continue her European education in science, technology, and the arts without succumbing to the social and political upheavals that had led to the collapse of religious and civic institutions further west.[14]

By the second quarter of the nineteenth century, the Russian government and intellectuals from across the political spectrum tended to agree that capitalist economic development had brought social disaster to significant areas of Europe. Almost universally, educated Russians thought it best to avoid the social degradation, exploitation, and conflict caused by the factory system and capitalist market economy.[15] But shared assumptions about the ills of liberal Europe did not produce a common understanding of Russian progress or agreement about solutions to specifically Russian problems. Whereas in the eighteenth century the monarchy and a handful of "projectors" had taken the lead in defining Russia's path to progress and in proposing solutions to problems of public concern, in the nineteenth century Russian society produced a plethora of ideas, circles, organizations, and movements devoted to the development and transformation of the country. As pro-government intellectuals formulated and elaborated the principles of official nationality, the dissonant and ever more oppositionist ideas of radicals, liberals, and romantic nationalists clashed with those of the court and bureaucracy. Increasingly, instead of encouraging educated Russians to develop their intellectual capacities in the service of the common good, the monarchy suspected seditious intent and viewed independent ideas as a threat to social and political order. Of course, officials sometimes had good reason to raise the specter of revolution and impose repressive measures. More often than not, however, the government overreached, treating any form of disturbance and dissent as rebellion, and as a consequence, generating more discontent and actual revolt.

Russia's First Revolution

The "parting of ways" between the government and educated society developed primarily as a struggle to define Russia's future path of development and to speak for the Russian people or nation.[16] In the Decembrist Rebellion of 1825, the struggle produced overt political action which aimed to overthrow or, at a minimum, radically alter the monarchy.[17] Harkening back to the court coups of the eighteenth century, the rebels of 1825 chose to act during a moment of confusion over the succession to the throne. Unbeknownst to the public, in 1822,

Constantine Pavlovich had renounced his right to rule after marrying a Polish noblewoman of non-royal lineage. The crown thus belonged to his younger brother Nicholas. But when on December 14, Guard regiments in St Petersburg assembled to take the oath of allegiance, a mutiny occurred. Led by elite military officers who promised to abolish corporal punishment and shorten the term of service, the rebellious soldiers refused to recognize Nicholas. In addition to obeying their commanders, as soldiers are obligated to do, they no doubt welcomed the opportunity to ease the burdens of military service and also may have been reacting to the unexpected news that Nicholas, not his more popular brother Constantine, had ascended the throne. There is no evidence that the soldiers shared the political and social beliefs of their Decembrist superiors. Regardless of their motives, moreover, the estimated 30 officers and 2,850 soldiers who gathered in Senate Square elicited no concrete action from the greater St Petersburg garrison or from society in general.[18] Only the men of the Chernigov Regiment, part of the Second Army located in Ukraine, marched out to join the uprising, and they were easily rebuffed by troops loyal to Nicholas. By mid-January the Decembrist Rebellion collapsed.

On July 13, 1826, after a judicial investigation, sentencing by the Supreme Criminal Court, and review by the monarch, five Decembrist leaders were executed by hanging. Another 111 leaders faced hard labor or exile in Siberia, and nine were demoted to service as soldiers. In proceedings outside the Supreme Criminal Court, 53 officers, including Vladimir F. Raevskii (1795–1872), under judicial investigation since 1822, suffered punishments of hard labor or exile in Siberia, demotion and service in the lower ranks, imprisonment, and/or surveillance. The authorities sentenced roughly 305 soldiers and noncommissioned officers to corporal punishment, primarily running the gauntlet, followed by service in the Caucasus, and also sent another 4,000 soldiers to serve in the Caucasus. Finally, among the suspected leaders, 120 individuals who had failed to inform on the conspirators received administrative punishments that included demotion to soldier and prison terms of six months to four years.[19] As the number of convicted and punished individuals shows, the influence of the Decembrists reached significant dimensions. Especially after the execution of the punishments, a special aura enveloped those who had suffered so grievously for their beliefs, making them heroes to generations of liberal and opposition-minded Russians Even though the actual rebellion quickly came to naught, it entered historical memory as Russia's "first revolution."

The Decembrists, like later revolutionaries, sought to overturn the Russian social and political order through armed rebellion. Their actions marked the onset of modern political struggle in Imperial Russia. In contrast to the Guard mutineers of the eighteenth century, the Decembrists prepared to act by organizing secret societies and elaborating constitutional programs. As early as 1816, military officers and members of the educated elite in Moscow and St Petersburg organized the Union of Salvation, superseded in 1818 by the Union of Welfare. In an eighteenth-century vein, the Union of Welfare hoped to achieve social and political reforms through the enlightenment and moral development of Russia's governing classes. By 1821, however, the emphasis on moral reformation evolved into political activity. Impatience with the gradualist approach led to the breakup of the Union of Welfare and to the formation of the Northern and Southern Societies, which carried out the rebellion of December 1825.

The Northern Society, based in St Petersburg and representing the more moderate branch of the Decembrist movement, advocated a liberal program in line with the principles of the American and French Revolutions. Spelled out in a draft constitution written by Nikita M. Murav'ev (1795–1843), the program of the Northern Society called for the creation of a federal system composed of fourteen states, each with its own capital and two-chamber governing assembly. The governing assemblies enjoyed significant authority, including the ability to raise taxes and make laws necessary for the administration and public welfare of the states. Above the states, at the head of the federal government, the emperor exercised executive powers similar to those of the president of the United States. Sovereign power belonged to the people, however, the citizens of the empire, and to the elected People's Assembly (*Narodnoe veche*), also a two-chambered body, which possessed full legislative authority. All citizens participated in elections, though men of property enjoyed greater representation, and only they could hold public office. More broadly, all Russians, defined as native inhabitants and children of foreigners born in Russia, were considered "equal before the law." This meant that serfdom, guilds, corporate bodies, and distinctions between nobles and commoners had to be abolished and that every individual benefited from civil liberties such as freedom of religion, freedom of expression, freedom to choose an occupation, and the right to trial by jury. If implemented, Murav'ev's program would have established a constitutional monarchy and given to Russia a government as liberal as any in Europe.[20]

A second group of Decembrists formed the Southern Society, centered in Tul'chin and associated with the more radical ideas of Pavel I. Pestel (1793–1826). Pestel's draft constitution, *The Russian Law*, envisioned a centralized political system which merged all the distinctive nationalities of the empire into a unitary state and culture.[21] Society or the state, the two concepts were not clearly distinguished, consisted of those who commanded (the government) and those who obeyed (the people), an arrangement that served "the welfare of all and each in the state." Although Pestel did not appear to advocate sudden change, which led to turmoil and confusion, he did call for "a complete transformation of the order of government" (no monarch is mentioned) based on the *Russian Law*. He divided the territory of the Russian state into 53 provinces and designated the commercial center of Nizhnii Novgorod as the future capital. Like Murav'ev, he also intended to abolish serfdom, hierarchical estates, and noble privileges; to establish equality before the law, economic and occupational freedom, freedom of the press, and freedom of religion; and finally, to craft a system of political representation based on elected territorial assemblies. After the overthrow of the monarchy, a provisional dictatorship, the Supreme Provisional Administration, would be established to guide the nation – all the peoples of the empire would be merged into a single Russian nation – in the creation of a republic based on popular representation.

Neither Pestel nor Murav'ev fully worked out his political plan, and in their draft constitutions, numerous ambiguities and some outright contradictions are evident. In the end, the Decembrists turned out to be more an ideological orientation than an organized political movement. They shared not a blueprint for action, but a fundamental grievance that in their eyes accounted for "all the evil" in Russian life: "lack of security and respect for the individual, his dignity, his honor, his property, his work, and even his life." The Decembrists assigned responsibility for this state of affairs to the monarchy – to the monarchy as an institution, not merely to a particular monarch – and to "the arbitrariness and whims of its agents."[22] In their ability to link moral grievance to concrete political action and to conceive political action in the abstract terms of a constitutional order, the Decembrists represented, for the Russian case, a newly modern form of political thought and opposition.

—— Cultural Politics and the Consolidation of Radicalism ——

The Decembrist Rebellion of 1825 set the stage for the consolidation of full-blown radicalism in the reign of Nicholas I. The fight between the monarchy and educated classes gathered steam, and although open rebellion did not recur before the 1860s, intellectuals increasingly assumed, or presumed, that they spoke for the Russian people, independent of, and often in opposition to, the government. No longer content to stand at the monarchy's side, educated Russians accepted responsibility for leading the nation to a brighter future. Of course, in practice, their ability to turn the desire for responsibility into concrete action remained exceedingly limited. Although after 1800 the proliferation of independent journals, private philanthropic organizations, charity schools, literary societies, salons, and clubs provided elite men and women with significant opportunities for non-governmental public service, the monarchy continued to deny its subjects basic civil liberties.[23] The educated classes of the early nineteenth century, like the educated service classes of the eighteenth century, generally talked among themselves. In the absence of parliamentary bodies or an institutionalized public opinion capable of passing judgment on specific policies, the cultural activities of the educated classes functioned as a substitute for political contestation. During a period when Russians of exceptional talent began to produce world-renowned artistic classics, lesser cultural figures articulated political concerns of ongoing historical importance. Among the issues that to this day resonate in Russian politics, historians identify: 1) Russia's relationship to Europe or "the West," 2) the role of literature and the arts in Russian society, and 3) the educated elite's relationship to the common people.

The problem of Russia's relationship to Europe – of Russia's cultural and historical identity – resulted directly from the Europeanizing reforms of the eighteenth century. Not until the reign of Nicholas I, however, did Russian national identity become a matter of intense intellectual controversy. The firestorm began in 1836 after the journal *Telescope* published the first of eight "Letters on the Philosophy of History" written by Petr Ia. Chaadaev (ca. 1794–1856)[24]. Public and official reaction to the letter turned so hostile that Chaadaev published nothing more during his lifetime. The Russian government, acting on the monarch's explicit condemnation, quickly shut down *Telescope*, exiled its editor, reprimanded the responsible censor, declared Chaadaev insane, and placed him under house arrest. Nicholas in 1837 lifted the police and medical surveillance on Chaadaev and in 1838 allowed the former editor of *Telescope* to live in St Petersburg, but the public debate instigated by the letter continued to rage. Dated 1829, the first philosophical letter, in the words of Aleksandr I. Herzen, had the "effect of a pistol shot in the dead of night."[25]

The letter set forth a devastating and painfully pessimistic critique of Russian culture and history, which Chaadaev viewed as neither of the East (Asia) nor of the West (Europe). Russia, he claimed, existed in a primeval stage of development, cut off from the great civilizations of humankind. The product of a tragic youth characterized by foreign domination (the Mongol conquest), servitude, and the adoption of Byzantine Christianity, Russia had given nothing of value to the world. In contrast to the historical achievements of European civilization, the offspring of authentic (Catholic) Christianity, Russian culture, imported and imitative, constituted "a blank in the intellectual order."[26] Lacking a past and a future, Russia remained a spiritual wasteland and could become civilized only if she repeated the education of the human race that had brought Europe to a position of cultural superiority. Although Chaadaev did not openly advocate conversion to Catholicism, he strongly implied that Russia had gone astray when her medieval princes adopted the Christianity of the Byzantine Empire.

Chaadaev's first philosophical letter can be read as a cry of despair produced by an isolated and unstable mind. Among contemporaries, however, the letter encouraged creative thinking and debate about Russia's relationship to Europe, place in world history, and path to progress. In what came to be known as the

Slavophile–Westernizer controversy, Chaadaev occupied an idiosyncratic Westernizing position. Chaadaev remained a conservative monarchist, which put him at odds with liberal and radical Westernizers, but like them, he believed that Russia's spiritual and historical progress hinged on becoming European – in his case European in the Catholic tradition and to the exclusion of all that was Russian.[27] Other Westernizers did not go so far as to renounce wholesale their nation's culture, history, and religious traditions, advocating instead the long-established practice of borrowing from Europe whatever could be useful to Russia. Westernizers likewise admired the policies of Peter I, who, in Chaadaev's words, "flung us the mantle of civilization." But Chaadaev also concluded that while "we [Russians] picked up the mantle, . . . we did not touch civilization itself," a position also rejected by most Westernizers.[28] Westernizers may have agreed that Russia remained backward in relation to Europe, but to acknowledge that the empire's western neighbors were more advanced, that Russians should learn from their achievements, or that the path to progress lay in repeating European patterns of development did not necessarily imply abandonment of Russian traditions and customs. Russia shared with Europe the Christian religion and a cultural heritage traceable to ancient Greece and Rome, albeit via the Byzantine Empire, so that to view European civilization as alien or hostile made little sense.

To this day, historians and intellectuals debate whether or not Russian culture belongs to the orbit of European civilization. In the second quarter of the nineteenth century, the influence of romantic nationalism and German idealism gave to the question special poignancy. The idea that each nation or people possesses its own unique history, culture, and destiny appealed to Russians from across the political spectrum. As an extreme Westernizer, Chaadaev went beyond the suggestion that Russia suffered from backwardness or possessed inferior traditions and customs. Chaadaev insisted that Russia completely lacked traditions and customs. Not surprisingly, most Russian intellectuals repudiated this absolutist notion. In response to Chaadaev, thinkers representing a variety of ideological positions set out to define and defend the heritage of the Russian people.

The strongest opposition to Chaadaev and to Westernism in general came from the Slavophiles, who denounced Peter I for forcefully imposing on Russia a European path of development. Thinkers such as Aleksei S. Khomiakov (1804–60), Ivan V. Kireevskii (1806–56), and Konstantin S. Aksakov (1817–60) formulated an intellectual position that combined elements of monarchism, religious faith, romantic nationalism, and populism.[29] According to the Slavophiles, Western civilization, built upon the foundations of ancient Rome and the Catholic Church, produced outer brilliance but inner darkness. The Western emphasis on abstract rationalistic thinking, prescriptive legalism, and formalistic community relationships led to social fragmentation and spiritual torpidity. As a result, European societies suffered from endless conflict and could be unified only by artificial means. Held together through military conquest, legal contracts, and bureaucratic regulation, they lacked true justice and inner wholeness. Traditional Russian society, by contrast, rooted in the patriarchal household, peasant commune, and Eastern Orthodox Christianity, embodied principles of social harmony, spiritual integrity, and organic unity. Legalistic Europe may have shown the world the way to material progress, but organic Russia offered the hope of spiritual progress and development toward true Christian unity, based on freedom and love.

The Slavophiles equated Russian national culture with the customs of the common people, and in so doing, they emerged as critics of the government and educated society (*obshchestvo*). They mistook the limited administrative reach of the Muscovite monarchy for social harmony and cultural integrity, which in their view had been undermined by the imposition of serfdom and by the tyranny and Westernizing reforms of Peter I. Although the Slavophiles accepted the need for absolute monarchy in Russia, they restricted the sphere of legitimate government action to national defense and assumed that officials would not interfere in the internal life of the nonpolitical Russian people. By no means democratic in their political thinking, they nonetheless envisioned a complete separation of society and government. In their critique of Russian society, the Slavophiles blamed the process of Europeanization begun by Peter for creating a cultural cleavage that separated the educated classes from the common people. Spiritual sterility, vulgar materialism, and false enlightenment had engulfed the Europeanized elite, whereas the people, especially the peasants, imbued with organic principles of patriarchy and communalism, had preserved an authentic Russian life to which the educated should return. Only by embracing Russian principles of social organization could the nation escape the spirit of revolt and opposition to the monarchy that long ago had infected the elite and now also threatened to spread throughout society.

The Slavophiles hoped to overcome the social contestation, cultural bifurcation, and bureaucratic politics that permeated Russian life, and they believed that this could be done by uniting the monarchy, educated society, and ordinary Russians in a utopian Christian community. For the Slavophiles, spiritual progress represented the only real form of progress, and the path of spiritual progress required a return to the idealized traditions of a nonexistent historical past. In contrast to policymakers and proponents of official nationality, who thought it possible to pursue the material benefits of European modernity without embracing social and political change, Slavophiles rejected European modernity in all its dimensions, looking instead to spiritual wholeness and Christian community as the source of human happiness.

The Slavophiles faced the question of Russia's relationship to Europe, particularly the painful awareness of Russian backwardness, by positing a spiritual and moral superiority grounded in indigenous traditions, institutions, and religious beliefs. In the process, they brought to the fore the problem of educated society's relationship to the people – a problem for which they, as elite nobles and Europeanized intellectuals, felt a personal responsibility. The Slavophiles shared this sense of responsibility with Westernizing intellectuals, both liberals and radicals, who identified with the European orientation of official policy and Russian historical development, but sparred with the government over issues of individual liberty, freedom of speech, the institution of serfdom, the power of the bureaucracy, and the claim to speak for the nation. In contrast to the Slavophiles, who hoped to remake Russian life in accordance with imagined traditions, Westernizers, not unlike reform-minded officials, hoped to transform Russian reality by continuing to import European ideas. Regardless of the political programs that Westernizers adopted, they generally shared a commitment to the freedom of the individual and the dignity of the human person, found abhorrent the revolutionary upheavals afflicting contemporary Europe, and hoped to transform Russia without compromising cherished principles or unleashing violent class conflict. For a time, in the 1830s and 1840s, the differences between liberal and radical Westernizers could be difficult to distinguish. By the mid-1850s, however, they occupied clearly opposing ideological positions. Liberals advocated a program of gradual change and evolution toward legal equality, civil liberties, and representative constitutional government, while radicals hoped to reorganize social and political relationships based on socialist principles. Some radicals also became proponents of violent revolution.

An early distinction between Westernizing liberals and radicals appeared in attitudes toward the Russian state. Timofei N. Granovskii (1813–55), Konstantin D. Kavelin (1818–85), and Boris N. Chicherin (1828–1904), liberal historians associated with the juridical school of Russian historiography, expected the state, assisted by educated society, to lead the nation to material progress, social justice, and political liberty.[30] Despite their often noble origins, liberals readily embraced enlightened reformism, including the abolition of serfdom and the elimination of hereditary noble privilege, and looked to contemporary Europe as the model of social and political progress. Even though liberals did not consider parliamentary democracy an immediate possibility for Russia, they nonetheless became proponents of individual rights and government based on the rule of law. Their understanding of individual rights encompassed property rights, the freedom to choose an occupation, freedom of conscience (religious toleration), and freedom of speech. At once admirers of Peter I and critics of Russia's privileged hereditary elite, liberals valued national traditions and imagined the Russian people as fellow citizens. At the same time, however, they viewed the state as the embodiment of the nation, assumed that the common people would be brought into the orbit of European civilization (that is, would become like them), and hoped that Russia would follow the modern European path of development.

More than any other ideological grouping in early nineteenth-century Russia, liberals mirrored their counterparts in contemporary Europe. They rejected revolution, but associated historical progress with movement toward political liberty and a capitalist market economy. The intellectual depth of Russian liberals, the clarity of their moral vision, and the moderation of their political tactics have long impressed scholars in Russia, Europe, and the United States. Yet the concrete impact of their ideas proved painfully limited. Vulnerable to the vagaries of government repression and lacking a significant base of social support, liberals had little effect on Russia's long-term historical development. In the annals of Russian history, they invariably take second stage to radicals and especially socialists. The historiographic attention to radicals is of course partly due to later communist successes and to the ideological sympathies of twentieth-century scholars, but it also is a measure of their historical importance. Unlike liberals, who remained politically weak and socially isolated throughout the Imperial period (a pattern that has recurred in the post-communist era), radicals such as Vissarion G. Belinskii (1811–48), Aleksandr I. Herzen (1812–70), and Mikhail A. Bakunin (1814–76) came to be seen as defenders of the people and forefathers of the revolutionary movement.

Vissarion G. Belinskii, the grandson of a priest and the son of an ennobled doctor, achieved renown in the 1840s for his writings on Russian literature. Belinskii shared much with his liberal associates: admiration for Peter I, opposition to the Slavophiles' idealization of the Muscovite past, acceptance of the need to abolish serfdom and establish a government based on the rule of law, and above all, a commitment to human dignity and freedom. Like moderate liberals, Belinskii understood that his larger goal of individual liberty required changes in the social and political conditions of Russia. Where Belinskii diverged from liberals, and ultimately became a hero to revolutionaries, was in his impatience for change, open hostility to the status quo, and passionate social rhetoric. Although Belinskii did not directly denounce the Russian monarchy, he criticized the Orthodox Church for its support of serfdom and tyranny. He also expressed admiration for French Enlightenment thinkers such as Voltaire and for the ideals of liberty, equality, and fraternity proclaimed by French revolutionaries.

In Belinskii's view of the common people, he stood firmly in the Westernizer camp. The people, he believed, needed to be educated and brought up to the cultural level of the Europeanized elite. Belinskii praised the good sense and what he believed to be the innate atheism of the people, but like Westernizers of almost all political stripes, he regarded educated Russians as the representatives of progress and civilization. In contrast to the juridical historians and to officialdom, he did not see in the Russian state the engine of positive change. That role belonged to independent intellectuals and to the arts, particularly to writers, whose works Belinskii judged based on social instead of aesthetic criteria. Only through public engagement and the espousal of politically and socially correct positions could the writer fulfill his or her obligation to defend society "from the black night of Autocracy, Orthodoxy, and Nationalism."[31] Belinskii became an early advocate of a professional journalism that espoused a specific ideological program, and he saw in literature a creator of Russian national consciousness. Although Belinskii went beyond liberals in his criticism of Russian institutions and only late in his life embraced the socialism of many radicals, his ideas, and especially his moral fervor, appealed to a variety of socially conscious intellectuals.

Already in the 1830s socialist ideas began to have a significant impact in Russia, and among Russian radicals, socialism eventually carried the day. By the mid-1840s, the activities of Mikhail V. Butashevich-Petrashevskii (1821–66) and his St Petersburg circle showed that from the monarchy's perspective socialism had become a political problem.[32] A devotee of French utopian socialist Charles Fourier, Petrashevskii began in the early 1840s to invite friends to his home to consult his large library of banned books and to discuss social and political questions. By 1845 attendance at the gatherings grew beyond Petrashevskii's personal friends, and in 1845–6 the *Petrashevtsy*, as members of the circle came to be known, began to publish the *Pocket Dictionary of Foreign Terms*, in which they espoused the principles of scientism, socialism, and atheism. Under the entry for "naturalism," for example, the *Dictionary* declared that 'by thought alone, without the help of tradition, revelation, or divine intervention, man can achieve in real life a state of permanent happiness through the total and independent development of all his natural faculties.' After absorbing pantheism, materialism, and atheism, the entry continued, naturalism 'becomes transformed into anthropotheism,' a science that proclaims 'man himself as a part of nature' to be 'the only supreme being' and that 'considers the universal fact of the recognition of God in positive religion to be a result of man's deification of his own personality and the universal laws of his intellect.'[33] Not surprisingly, government censors intervened at the letter "o" to stop publication of the *Dictionary*.

Although ideologically radical, the *Petrashevtsy* tried to steer a moderate course when it came to political action. They despised absolute monarchy and hoped to see the establishment of a constitutional monarchy or democratic republic in Russia, but also feared peasant revolution and so accepted the need for partial reform through legal struggle. To that end, Petrashevskii in 1847 attempted to create a Fourierist phalanstery on his private estate. Petrashevskii's serfs seemed to endorse the plan, which aimed to organize everyday life and agricultural labor so that the peasants' obligation to work became a source of joy and self-fulfillment. But on the day after some forty families moved from their village huts into the phalanstery, the new building had been burned to the ground. Petrashevskii learned from the experience, and instead of concrete social action, became focused on the spread of enlightenment and the propagation of socialist ideas. The gatherings at his home turned into a regular open house held on Fridays for invited guests. The number and social diversity of the participants increased, and satellite circles also formed. Historians estimate that several hundred individuals eventually took part in the Friday discussions. The great writer Fedor M. Dostoevskii (1821–81) began to attend Petrashevskii's gatherings in the spring of 1847. By the spring of 1848, the Friday meetings became widely known, with about 10 to 20 guests present on any given occasion. The police also took an interest in the circle's activities, especially after revolutions broke out across Europe and after Petrashevskii circulated a petition among the St Petersburg nobility, calling for legal changes that would allow nonnobles to buy landed estates on condition that they convert the status of the purchased peasants from serfs into tenants.

During the winter of 1848–9, at the same time that officials started to investigate Petrashevskii and his activities, some members of the circle became hungry for action. Nikolai A. Speshnev (1821–82), a believer in egalitarian communism and nationalization of the means of production, pushed to transform the Petrashevskii circle into a secret society that would prepare the peasants for armed revolt. Speshnev embraced violent revolution, the use of terrorism, and the development of a conspiratorial organization capable of seizing power at the earliest opportunity. The spread of revolution in Europe had inspired in radicals the hope that change might also be at hand for Russia. But Petrashevskii and most of his associates opposed the extremists in their midst, rejecting communism and the idea that a successful uprising could be carried out at the present time. Instead, Petrashevskii continued to advocate an end to censorship, exposure of official corruption, and reform of the judicial system by legal means. Another member of the circle also suggested that it might be possible to work through the courts to achieve the emancipation of the serfs. Although moderate when compared to the likes of Speshnev, the *Petrashevtsy* did not rule out the possibility of revolution at a future date, and they openly propagated socialist ideas. They saw in the traditional peasant commune "an embryonic socialist community" and believed that Russia would lead the world to socialism.[34]

Clearly, with just a handful of exceptions, the *Petrashevtsy* devoted more attention to ideological struggles within their own circle than to preparing for revolution against the government. But in an absolute monarchy with no independent judiciary or guarantees of civil liberties, radical speech and calls for social justice easily crossed the line into subversion. On April 23–4, 1849, the activities of the Petrashevskii circle came to an end with the arrest of 36 members. Months of judicial investigation and court proceedings ensued, and 21 *Petrashevtsy*, including Fedor Dostoevskii, who had close ties with Speshnev, received death sentences. On December 22, the condemned men were brought to Semenovskii Square and prepared for execution. At the last possible moment, after the first three prisoners had been tied to posts, their heads and bodies covered in shrouds, and after the drums had begun to roll, a military courier arrived carrying an imperial pardon. Instead of death by firing squad, the prisoners faced sentences of prison, exile, or hard labor in Siberia.

The Petrashevskii circle disappeared, but Russian socialism struck deep roots. In 1847, the same year that Fedor Dostoevskii became a regular member of the circle, Aleksandr I. Herzen, accompanied by his family and entire household, left Russia for Paris, never to return.[35] An admirer of French socialist and German idealist philosophers, Herzen became a mouthpiece for Russian progressive thought, especially socialist thought, in Europe and Russia. Born the illegitimate son of a wealthy noble, Herzen received his early education at home, instructed by private tutors, and during the years 1829–33 attended Moscow University, where he heard lectures on literature, philosophy, and natural science. While studying at the university, Herzen and his close friend Nikolai P. Ogarev (1813–77) organized a philosophical circle of freethinkers devoted to socialism and the ideals of the French Revolution. Unabashed in their criticism of social and political conditions in Russia, the members of the circle attracted police attention, and in July 1834 Herzen, Ogarev, and most of their associates were arrested. Herzen spent the next ten months in prison. From 1835 until 1840, he worked in provincial administrative offices in Perm, Viatka, and Vladimir, living under police surveillance. In 1840–1 Herzen briefly returned to Moscow and St Petersburg, but then in June 1841 began a second period of exile in Novgorod, the result of orders from Nicholas I that he be appointed to service outside the capital. Upon retiring from service, Herzen again received permission to live in Moscow, where he took up residence in July 1842. The death of Herzen's father in 1846 made him an independently wealthy man, and he left for Paris the following year.

From 1847 until 1852, Herzen lived in Paris and Nice but also traveled around Switzerland and Italy. His wife died in 1851, and the following year he decided to move to London. There in 1852–3, Herzen established the Free Russian Press, which became a voice for the Russian opposition in Europe and a beacon of free speech for liberals and radicals in Russia. Like other progressive intellectuals, Herzen denounced serfdom, censorship, and absolute monarchy, and he believed that society should be organized so as to ensure the liberty and full development of the individual personality. But his experience of capitalism and revolution in Europe led him also to reject the bourgeois individualism, economic materialism, and mass culture that had accompanied the rise of the European middle classes to a position of social and political prominence. Herzen echoed the Slavophiles in his critique of European modernity and in assigning to Russia a unique historical destiny, distinct from and superior to the European path of development. At the same time, he praised Peter I for bringing dynamic change to Russia and even appreciated the ability of capitalist economies to reduce poverty and raise standards of living. Herzen continued to live the life of Russia's most elite Europeanized nobles;

however, he also became a "noble revolutionary" who embraced socialism as a more advanced form of socioeconomic organization. The leading theoretician of "Russian socialism," Herzen held that the indigenous peasant commune, with its traditions of self-government and communal land ownership, could provide the foundation for the building of a utopian society free of injustice, exploitation, class conflict, and nationalist strife. In Herzen's ideological framework, what had long appeared to be Russian backwardness – whether economic, social, political, or cultural – turned out instead to be the advantage of a youthful society destined to lead the world to a higher form of historical development.

The idea that the Russian peasant commune represented the seed of a future socialist society became a centerpiece of radical thought and agrarian socialism in nineteenth-century Russia. Herzen deservedly has gone down in history as the father of Russian socialism. But at no time did Herzen advocate violent revolution, and after the emancipation of the serfs in 1861, he even accepted that the Russian monarchy might again, as it had in the eighteenth century, become a force for progressive historical change. Toward the end of his life, based on the experience of Britain, Herzen also began to appreciate the role that labor organizations could play in bettering the lot of the common people. Herzen understood that conditions in contemporary Russia would not allow radical intellectuals to lead the Russian peasants into the bright socialist future. The Russian people themselves, assisted of course by intellectuals, needed to achieve internal freedom by evolving into conscious identification with socialist principles. The Russian people, in other words, needed to become reflections of Herzen and his elite associates. Then and only then could Russia assume her rightful place in human history.

By the 1860s, privileged but alienated intellectuals such as Herzen began to identify themselves as members of a distinct sociocultural class, the intelligentsia, and to think seriously about their relationship to the Russian people. Socialists in particular sought to understand how they could forge ties to the people in order to mobilize them for revolutionary action. Moderate socialists accepted that thoroughgoing change could not quickly occur and so focused on preparatory educational work among the people. More radical figures, the anarchist Mikhail A. Bakunin for example, dismissed the need for preparation, believing instead that the time had come to ignite the revolutionary instincts of the oppressed masses. Once the people rebelled, Bakunin imagined, the old order, which depended on institutional coercion, would be destroyed from the bottom up. Freedom would be achieved, and a new society, organized on socialist principles, would spontaneously emerge. From the reign of Nicholas I until the Bolshevik Revolution, and even beyond October 1917 in the emigration, Russian socialists remained divided between those who thought revolutionary action leading to the destruction of the state or to a seizure of political power would bring the socialist utopia into being and those who envisioned an evolutionary process of development toward socialism that built upon traditional communal relationships and the further enlightenment of the people. Both groups regarded Herzen as a forefather and model progressive who had paved the way for their own movements.

Conclusion

Ideological pluralism and dissonance in the first half of the nineteenth century represented the cultural expression of the emergence of independent society in Russia. The educated classes ceased to be primarily educated service classes, employed by and ideologically supportive of the monarchy, becoming instead a plethora of creative individuals and circles devoted to a wide range of social, political, and aesthetic programs. Without belittling the cultural achievements and intellectual depth of eighteenth-century educated Russians, when the products of their minds and imaginations are compared to the artistic and philosophical works produced in even the first decades of the nineteenth century, it is difficult not to conclude that a new age had dawned. In art, literature, theater, and music, the early to mid-nineteenth century represented the moment when a Russian national canon took its rightful place among the great cultures of modern Europe. To describe this process and to pay appropriate homage to its creative geniuses – to the likes of Aleksandr S. Pushkin (1799–1837), Nikolai V. Gogol (1809–52), Ivan S. Turgenev (1818–83), Fedor M. Dostoevskii (1821–81), and Lev N. Tolstoi (1828–1910) – lies beyond the scope of this book. Suffice it say that these and other writers, together with painters and composers, produced artistic works of enduring power that brought to Russian culture world historical status.[36]

In the decades leading up to the Great Reforms, only a handful of Russian creative geniuses rose to positions of public prominence. With the exception of Pushkin's stunning poetry and Gogol's piercing satire, the most important intellectual products of the period lay not in the creations of individual artists and writers – Turgenev, Dostoevskii, and Tolstoi produced their greatest novels after 1860 – but in the collective coming together of a cultural voice that placed the Russian people on an equal footing with other more "advanced" nations in Europe. By the time of the Crimean War, the Russian people had come into their own as Europeans both politically and culturally. The producers and consumers of Russian high culture remained a small and privileged elite, but their social horizon had broadened considerably. No longer dominated by the nobility or focused on transforming themselves into Europeans, they increasingly aimed their activities at educating the Russian people and at bringing social justice and progress to Russia. The moral voice that Russian educated society had developed in the later eighteenth century became a call to action on behalf of the people and in opposition to the government. Of course, educated Russians of the day had only limited contact with the Russian people, and in the decades ahead, radical activists would struggle to bridge the social and cultural gap separating them from "the masses" they sought to represent. Their failure to do so – their inability to develop meaningful and enduring relationships with broad sectors of the population – had momentous consequences for the future of Russia. Due at least in part to the educated classes' continuing isolation from peasants, workers, and minority communities, liberal democracy failed in 1917, and radical conspiratorial socialism succeeded.

Notes

Part I

1 Harold J. Berman, *Law and Revolution: The Formation of the Western Legal Tradition* (Cambridge, MA, 1983); Quentin Skinner, *The Foundations of Modern Political Thought*, 2 vols. (Cambridge, 1978).
2 Fritz Kern, *Kingship and Law in the Middle Ages*, trans. S. B. Chrimes, reprint (Oxford, 1939; New York, 1970); Leonard Krieger, *An Essay on the Theory of Enlightened Despotism* (Chicago, 1975); Marc Raeff, *The Well-Ordered Police State: Social and Institutional Change through Law in the Germanies and Russia, 1600–1800* (New Haven, 1983).
3 James B. Collins, *The State in Early Modern France* (Cambridge, 1995), p. 3.

Chapter 1

1 Gerda Lerner, *The Creation of Feminist Consciousness from the Middle Ages to 1870* (New York, 1993).
2 Nancy Shields Kollmann, "The Seclusion of Elite Muscovite Women," *Russian History* 10 (1983), pp. 170–87; Isolde Thyrêt, *Between God and Tsar: Religious Symbolism and the Royal Women of Muscovite Russia* (DeKalb, IL, 2001).
3 A. G. Man'kov, *Ulozhenie 1649 goda – kodeks feodal'nogo prava Rossii*, 2nd edn (Moscow, 2003).
4 Richard Hellie, *Enserfment and Military Change in Muscovy* (Chicago, 1971), pp. 21–147.
5 N. A. Gorskaia, *Monastyrskie krest'iane Tsentral'noi Rossii v XVII veke* (Moscow, 1977), pp. 239–346; David Moon, *The Russian Peasantry 1600–1930. The World the Peasants Made* (London and New York, 1999), pp. 66–70; Christoph Schmidt, *Leibeigenschaft im Ostseeraum. Versuch einer Typologie* (Cologne, 1997), pp. 63–71; E. N. Shveikovskaia, *Gosudarstvo i krest'iane Rossii. Pomor'e v XVII veke* (Moscow, 1997), pp. 91–7.

6	Ia. E. Vodarskii, *Naselenie Rossii v kontse XVII-nachale XVIII veka* (Moscow, 1977), pp. 91–115, 134.

7	These estimates are based on data that include St Petersburg, the environs of St Petersburg, and the Don Cossack territory, but not Left-Bank (eastern) Ukraine or the Baltic region. Moon, *The Russian Peasantry*, pp. 20–3.

8	Throughout this book I am indebted to David Moon's lucid, sensitive, and highly reliable work on Russian peasants, "the world they made," and the hardships they endured. See Moon, *The Russian Peasantry*.

9	L. V. Danilova et al. *Krest'ianskie chelobitnye XVII v. Iz sobranii Gosudarstvennogo Istoricheskogo muzeia* (Moscow, 1994).

10	Moon, *The Russian Peasantry*, pp. 79–80.

11	Moon, *The Russian Peasantry*, pp. 82–3; John L. H. Keep, *Soldiers of the Tsar: Army and Society in Russia 1462–1874* (New York, 1985), pp. 56–62, 80–92; William C. Fuller, Jr., *Strategy and Power in Russia, 1600–1914* (New York, 1992), p. 7.

12	For discussion of the commune and methods of agricultural production, see Moon, *The Russian Peasantry*, chapters 4 and 6.

13	Moon, *The Russian Peasantry*, pp. 121–3.

14	Moon, *The Russian Peasantry*, pp. 132–3.

15	Moon, *The Russian Peasantry*, pp. 237–54.

16	For discussion of townspeople, see Man'kov, *Ulozhenie*, pp. 185–206; Richard Hellie, "The Stratification of Muscovite Society," *Russian History* 5 (1978), pp. 119–75; and David H. Miller, "State and City in Seventeenth-Century Muscovy," in *The City in Russian History*, ed. Michael F. Hamm (Lexington, KY, 1976), pp. 34–52.

17	Vodarskii, *Naselenie Rossii*, pp. 129–34.

18	Man'kov, *Ulozhenie*, p. 185.

19	For explanation of these terms, see Keep, *Soldiers of the Tsar*, pp. 22–3, 60–79; Hellie, "Stratification of Muscovite Society," pp. 140–4; idem, *Slavery in Russia 1450–1725* (Chicago, 1982), pp. 49–66; A. V. Kazakov, ed. *Terminy i poniatiia voennoi istorii Rusi, Rossii IX-nachala XX veka* (St Petersburg, 1998).

20	Man'kov, *Ulozhenie*, p. 196.

21	Man'kov, *Ulozhenie*, pp. 204–5; Hellie, "Stratification of Muscovite Society," pp. 124–30.

22	Keep, *Soldiers of the Tsar*, pp. 22–3, 60–92; Fuller, *Strategy and Power*, pp. 4–7, 33–4.

23	Keep, *Soldiers of the Tsar*, pp. 80–1.

24	Keep, *Soldiers of the Tsar*, pp. 85–7.

25	On these groups, see Hellie, *Enserfment*, pp. 21–47; Keep, *Soldiers of the Tsar*, pp. 20–55; Valerie A. Kivelson, *Autocracy in the Provinces: The Muscovite Gentry and Political Culture in the Seventeenth Century* (Stanford, CA, 1996), pp. 26–57.

26	Hellie, *Enserfment*, pp. 24–5.

27	Kivelson, *Autocracy in the Provinces*, p. 36.

28	Keep, *Soldiers of the Tsar*, p. 33.

29	Robert O. Crummey, *Aristocrats and Servitors: The Boyar Elite in Russia, 1613–1689* (Princeton, NJ, 1983), pp. 12–64, 175–7.

30 Kivelson, *Autocracy in the Provinces*, pp. 178–80; Crummey, *Aristocrats and Servitors*, pp. 10–11, 35, 136–9; Nancy Shields Kollmann, *By Honor Bound: State and Society in Early Modern Russia* (Ithaca, NY, 1999).

31 Crummey, *Aristocrats and Servitors*, pp. 69–70.

32 Crummey, *Aristocrats and Servitors*, pp. 108–10.

33 Kivelson, *Autocracy in the Provinces*, pp. 101–28; Crummey, *Aristocrats and Servitors*, pp. 107–34.

34 N. F. Demidova, *Sluzhilaia biurokratiia v Rossii XVII v. i ee rol' v formirovanii absoliutizma* (Moscow, 1987), pp. 17–50.

35 The Muscovite Assembly of the Land (*zemskii sobor*), discussed in chapter 2, represented a different sort of body.

36 In 1682 Peter I was crowned ruler and then co-ruler with his half-brother Ivan V, and as co-ruler he remained under the *de facto* regency of his half-sister Sophia until her removal in 1689. Although Ivan did not die until 1696, historians agree that Peter took over the reins of government following his mother's death in 1694.

37 E. V. Anisimov, *Podatnaia reforma Petra I: Vvedenie podushnoi podati v Rossii v 1719–1728* (Leningrad, 1982); V. M. Kabuzan, *Narodonaselenie Rossii v XVIII-pervoi polovine XIX v. (po materialam revizii)* (Moscow, 1963); V. M. Kabuzan and N. M. Shepukova, "Tabel' pervoi revizii narodonaseleniia Rossii (1718–1727 gg.)," *Istoricheskii arkhiv*, no. 3 (1959), pp. 126–65.

38 The history of these categories receives broad treatment in Gregory L. Freeze, "The *Soslovie* (Estate) Paradigm in Russian Social History," *American Historical Review* 91 (1986), pp. 11–36; Elise Kimerling Wirtschafter, *Social Identity in Imperial Russia* (DeKalb, IL, 1997).

39 Elise Kimerling Wirtschafter, *Structures of Society: Imperial Russia's "People of Various Ranks"* (DeKalb, IL, 1994).

40 Anisimov, *Podatnaia reforma*, pp. 107–109.

41 Fuller, *Strategy and Power*, pp. 45–46.

42 Anisimov, *Podatnaia reforma*, pp. 107–109.

43 V. A. Aleksandrov, *Sel'skaia obshchina v Rossii (XVII-nachalo XIX v.)* (Moscow, 1976), pp. 242–93.

44 Elise Kimerling Wirtschafter, *From Serf to Russian Soldier* (Princeton, NJ, 1990), p. 3.

45 Anisimov, *Podatnaia reforma*, pp. 194–5.

46 B. N. Mironov, *Sotsial'naia istoriia Rossii perioda imperii (XVIII-nachalo XX v.). Genezis lichnosti, demokraticheskoi sem'i, grazhdanskogo obshchestva i pravovogo gosudarstva*, 2 vols. (St Petersburg, 1999), vol. 1, pp. 110–11; Wirtschafter, *Social Identity*, pp. 130–2.

47 L. E. Shepelev, *Chinovnyi mir Rossii XVII-nachalo XX v.* (St Petersburg, 1999), pp. 131–57.

48 Marc Raeff, *The Well-Ordered Police State: Social and Institutional Change through Law in the Germanies and Russia, 1600–1800* (New Haven, CT, 1983); Dietrich Geyer, "'Gesellschaft' als staatliche Veranstaltung. Sozialgeschichtliche Aspekte des russischen Behördenstaats im 18. Jahrhundert," in *Wirtschaft und Gesellschaft im vorrevolutionären Russland*, ed. Dietrich Beyrau (Cologne, 1975), pp. 20–52.

——————————————— Chapter 2 ———————————————

1 For a modern statement of the patrimonial thesis, see Richard Pipes, *Russia under the Old Regime* (New York, 1974).
2 Quoted from the Military Statute of 1716 in James Cracraft, *The Petrine Revolution in Russian Culture* (Cambridge, MA, 2004), pp. 74, 126.
3 For an accessible illustration of the anthropological approach to Muscovite political culture, see Nancy Shields Kollmann, "Ritual and Drama at the Muscovite Court," *Slavic Review* 45 (1986), pp. 486–502.
4 Vladimir Val'denberg, *Drevnerusskiia ucheniia o predelakh tsarskoi vlasti: ocherki russkoi politicheskoi literatury ot Vladimira Sviatogo do kontsa XVII veka*, reprint (Petrograd, 1916; The Hague, 1966).
5 Chester S. L. Dunning, *Russia's First Civil War: The Time of Troubles and the Founding of the Romanov Dynasty* (University Park, PA, 2001), pp. 439–60.
6 Dunning, *Russia's First Civil War*, p. 445.
7 Robert O. Crummey, *Aristocrats and Servitors: The Boyar Elite in Russia, 1613–1689* (Princeton, NJ, 1983), pp. 175–7.
8 Peter B. Brown, "Neither Fish nor Fowl: Administrative Legality in Mid- and Late-Seventeenth-Century Russia," *Jahrbücher für Geschichte Osteuropas* 50 (2002), pp. 17–18.
9 L. V. Cherepnin, *Zemskie sobory russkogo gosudarstva v XVI–XVII vv.* (Moscow, 1978), pp. 382–7.
10 Donald Ostrowski lists separate assemblies for 1613, 1614, 1616, 1617, 1619, 1621, 1622, rejecting the notion of a more or less regular assembly meeting from 1613 to 1622. Donald Ostrowski, "The Assembly of the Land (*Zemskii sobor*) as a Representative Institution," in *Modernizing Muscovy: Reform and social change in seventeenth-century Russia*, ed. Jarmo Kotilaine and Marshall Poe (London and New York, 2004), pp. 117–42; Michael Florinsky, *Russia: A History and an Interpretation*, 2 vols. (New York, 1953), vol. 1, pp. 266–9.
11 Dunning, *Russia's First Civil War*, pp. 448–50.
12 Dunning, *Russia's First Civil War*, p. 35.
13 N. F. Demidova, *Sluzhilaia biurokratiia v Rossii XVII v. i ee rol' v formirovanii absoliutizma* (Moscow, 1987), p. 23; Peter B. Brown, "Bureaucratic Administration in Seventeenth-Century Russia," in Kotilaine and Poe, ed. *Modernizing Muscovy*, pp. 64–70; idem, "The Service Land Chancellery Clerks of Seventeenth-Century Russia: Their Regime, Salaries, and Economic Survival," *Jahrbücher für Geschichte Osteuropas* 52 (2004), pp. 33–69; Borivoj Plavsic, "Seventeenth-Century Chanceries and their Staffs," in *Russian Officialdom: The Bureaucratization of Russian Society from the Seventeenth to the Twentieth Century*, ed. Walter McKenzie Pintner and Don Karl Rowney (Chapel Hill, NC, 1980), p. 21, n. 3; N. V. Ustiugov, "Evoliutsiia prikaznogo stroia Russkogo gosudarstva v XVII v.," in *Absoliutizm v Rossii (XVII–XVIII vv.). Sbornik statei k semidesiatiletiiu so dnia rozhdeniia B. B. Kafengauza* (Moscow, 1964), pp. 134–67.
14 Plavsic, "Seventeenth-Century Chanceries," pp. 19–45; Brown, "Neither Fish nor Fowl"; idem, "Bureaucratic Administration." For direct critique of Plavsic's rosy portrait of

Muscovy's chancelleries, see Hans J. Torke, "Crime and Punishment in the Pre-Petrine Civil Service: The Problem of Control," in *Imperial Russia 1700–1917. State, Society, Opposition*, ed. Ezra Mendelsohn and Marshall S. Shatz (DeKalb, IL, 1988), pp. 5–21.

15 For scholarly appraisal, see Demidova, *Sluzhilaia biurokratiia*, pp. 141–46; Hans J. Torke, "Continuity and Change in the Relations between Bureaucracy and Society in Russia, 1613–1861," *Canadian Slavic Studies* 5 (1971), pp. 457–76; Stephen Lovell, Alena Ledeneva, and Andrei Rogachevskii, ed. *Bribery and Blat in Russia: Negotiating Reciprocity from the Middle Ages to the 1990s* (Houndmills and London, 2000).

16 Demidova, *Sluzhilaia biurokratiia*, pp. 21–8, esp. 23.

17 Plavsic, "Seventeenth-Century Chanceries," pp. 25–6.

18 Demidova, *Sluzhilaia biurokratiia*, pp. 28–37, esp. 31, 37.

19 Dunning, *Russia's First Civil War*, pp. 31–2; John Meyendorff, *Byzantium and the Rise of Russia*, reprint (New York, 1981; Crestwood, NY, 1989), pp. 1–23, 268–70; Alexander Schmemann, *The Historical Road of Eastern Orthodoxy* (Crestwood, NY, 2003), pp. 308–13; P. V. Znamenskii, *Istoriia russkoi tserkvi (uchebnoe rukovodstvo)*, reprint (Kazan, 1870; Moscow, 1996), pp. 96–7.

20 Unless otherwise indicated, my discussion of the Russian Orthodox Church in the seventeenth century relies on Znamenskii, *Istoriia russkoi tserkvi*, pp. 223–64; Sviashchennik Aleksei Nikolin, *Tserkov' i gosudarstvo (istoriia pravovykh otnoshenii)* (Moscow, 1997), pp. 66–76; Georg Bernhard Michels, *At War with the Church: Religious Dissent in Seventeenth-Century Russia* (Stanford, CA, 1999); Matthew Spinka, "Patriarch Nikon and the Subjection of the Russian Church to the State," *Church History* 10 (1941), pp. 347–66.

21 Dunning, *Russia's First Civil War*, p. 473; David Moon, *The Russian Peasantry 1600–1930: The World the Peasants Made* (London and New York, 1999), p. 99; E. V. Anisimov, *Podatnaia reforma Petra I: Vvedenie podushnoi podati v Rossii v 1719–1728* (Leningrad, 1982), p. 109.

22 Paul A. Bushkovitch, "The Epiphany Ceremony of the Russian Court in the Sixteenth and Seventeenth Centuries," *Russian Review* 49 (1990), pp. 1–17; Robert O. Crummey, "Court Spectacles in Seventeenth-Century Russia: Illusion and Reality," in *Essays in Honor of A. A. Zimin*, ed. Daniel Waugh (Columbus, OH, 1985), pp. 130–58.

23 On Nikon's reforms, see Paul Meyendorff, *Russia, Ritual, and Reform: The Liturgical Reforms of Nikon in the 17th Century* (Crestwood, NY, 1991).

24 Recent English-language studies of Peter and his reign include: Paul Bushkovitch, *Peter the Great* (Lanham, MD, 2001); idem, *Peter the Great: The Struggle for Power, 1671–1725* (Cambridge, 2001); James Cracraft, *The Petrine Revolution in Russian Culture* (Cambridge, MA, 2004); idem, *The Revolution of Peter the Great* (Cambridge, MA, 2003); idem, *The Petrine Revolution in Russian Imagery* (Chicago, 1997); idem, *The Petrine Revolution in Russian Architecture* (Chicago, 1990); Lindsey Hughes, *Peter the Great: A Biography* (New Haven, CT, 2002); idem, *Russia in the Age of Peter the Great* (New Haven, CT, 1998).

25 Lindsey Hughes gives a figure of 1,182. Hughes, *Peter the Great*, pp. 51–3, 55–7; Hans Joachim Torke, ed. *Russkie tsari 1547–1917* (Rostov on the Don and Moscow, 1997), pp. 189–227.

26 Cracraft, *Revolution of Peter the Great*, pp. 116–18.

27 Hughes, *Peter the Great*, pp. 52–3.

28 Hughes, *Russia in the Age of Peter the Great*, p. 267.

29 For more on the political implications of Petrine entertainments, see Ernest A. Zitser, *The Transfigured Kingdom: Sacred Parody and Charismatic Authority at the Court of Peter the Great* (Ithaca, NY, 2004).

30 Recent accounts of Peter's relationship with Aleksei differ in minor details. See Bushkovitch, *Peter the Great: The Struggle for Power*, pp. 339–425; idem, *Peter the Great*, pp. 126–49; Hughes, *Peter the Great*, pp. 98–100, 122–31; Cracraft, *Revolution of Peter the Great*, pp. 12–16.

31 For a recent account that seems convinced of Aleksei's guilt, see Bushkovitch, *Peter the Great: The Struggle for Power*, pp. 339–425.

32 For the details of Aleksei's return to Russia and his subsequent trial and death, see Hughes, *Peter the Great*, pp. 122–31; Bushkovitch, *Peter the Great*, pp. 143–9; idem, *Peter the Great: The Struggle for Power*, pp. 383–425.

33 A. A. Preobrazhenskii and T. E. Novitskaia, ed. *Zakonodatel'stvo Petra I* (Moscow, 1997), pp. 61–2, 94–6.

34 Evgenii Anisimov, a leading historian of the Petrine era, highlights the human suffering caused by Peter the Great and traces the Soviet police state back to his coercive methods. See Evgenii Anisimov, *Vremia petrovskikh reform* (Leningrad, 1989).

35 A good introduction to these variations can be found in James Cracraft, ed. *Peter the Great Transforms Russia*, 3rd edn (Lexington, MA, 1991).

36 William C. Fuller, Jr., *Strategy and Power in Russia, 1600–1914* (New York, 1992), pp. 1–21; J. T. Kotilaine, "Opening a Window on Europe: Foreign Trade and Military Conquest on Russia's Western Border in the Seventeenth Century," *Jahrbücher für Geschichte Osteuropas* 46 (1998), pp. 494–530.

37 Fuller, *Strategy and Power*, pp. 14–34.

38 Cracraft, *Petrine Revolution in Russian Culture*, pp. 45–51, 57–74, 105–29; Hughes, *Peter the Great*, pp. 22–3.

39 Fuller, *Strategy and Power*, pp. 37–44; Hughes, *Peter the Great*, pp. 92–8, 174–6.

40 Fuller, *Strategy and Power*, p. 34.

41 On the reasons for Russia's eventual victory, see Fuller, *Strategy and Power*, pp. 44–84.

42 For the chronology of the Great Northern War, see Fuller, *Strategy and Power*, pp. 38–44; R. Ernest Dupuy and Trevor N. Dupuy, *The Encyclopedia of Military History from 3500 B.C. to the present*, 2nd rev. edn (New York, 1986), pp. 614–17, 645–51.

43 *Zakonodatel'stvo Petra I*, pp. 60–1.

44 Fuller, *Strategy and Power*, pp. 46, 60; Cracraft, *Petrine Revolution in Russian Culture*, p. 104.

45 Arcadius Kahan, "Continuity in Economic Activity and Policy during the Post-Petrine Period in Russia," *Journal of Economic History* 25 (1965), pp. 61–85; William L. Blackwell, *The Industrialization of Russia: An Historical Perspective*, 2nd edn (Arlington Heights, IL, 1982), pp. 10–12; Elise Kimerling Wirtschafter, *From Serf to Russian Soldier* (Princeton, NJ, 1990), pp. 74–95, 149–51; Hughes, *Russia in the Age of Peter the Great*, pp. 136–44, 150–4; Fuller, *Strategy and Power*, pp. 44–65.

46 Cracraft, *Petrine Revolution in Russian Culture*, pp. 80–7, 131–43, 241–2; Elise Kimerling [Wirtschafter], "Soldiers' Children, 1719–1856: A Study of Social Engineering in Imperial Russia," *Forschungen zur osteuropäischen Geschichte* 30 (1982), pp. 67–8, 99–102; P. N. Miliukov, *Ocherki po istorii russkoi kul'tury*, 3 vols., reprint (Paris, 1937; The Hague, 1964; Moscow, 1993–5), vol. 2, pt. 2, pp. 247–50.

47 The data presented do not include officers above the rank of colonel. M. D. Rabinovich, "Sotsial'noe proiskhozhdenie i imushchestvennoe polozhenie ofitserov reguliarnoi russkoi armii v kontse Severnoi voiny," in *Rossiia v period reform Petra I*, ed. N. I. Pavlenko (Moscow, 1973), pp. 138–40.

48 Marc Raeff, *The Well-Ordered Police State: Social and Institutional Change through Law in the Germanies and Russia 1600–1800* (New Haven, CT, 1983).

49 *Zakonodatel'stvo Petra I*, pp. 63–88, 97–8.

50 James Cracraft, *The Church Reform of Peter the Great* (Palo Alto, CA, 1971), esp. pp. 175–7, 223–5.

51 Cracraft, *Petrine Revolution in Russian Culture*, pp. 172–81.

52 Cracraft, *Church Reform*, pp. 100–7, 184–95, 208, 232, 238–46.

53 Hughes, *Peter the Great*, p. 149; Miliukov, *Ocherki*, vol. 2, pt. 2, pp. 250–3; Gregory L. Freeze, *The Russian Levites: Parish Clergy in the Eighteenth Century* (Cambridge, MA, 1977), pp. 82–96.

54 L. E. Shepelev, *Chinovnyi mir Rossii XVIII-nachalo XX v.* (St Petersburg, 1999), pp. 131–57.

55 Between 1722 and 1917 a total of 33 trusted individuals occupied the post of procurator general. A. G. Zviagintsev and Iu. G. Orlov, *Oko gosudarevo. Rossiiskie prokurory. XVIII vek* (Moscow, 1994); *Zakonodatel'stvo Petra I*, pp. 131–5.

Chapter 3

1 James Cracraft, *The Revolution of Peter the Great* (Cambridge, MA, 2003); idem, *The Petrine Revolution in Russian Culture* (Cambridge, MA, 2004); idem, *The Petrine Revolution in Russian Imagery* (Chicago, 1997); idem, *The Petrine Revolution in Russian Architecture* (Chicago, 1988).

2 On publishing, see Gary Marker, *Publishing, Printing, and the Origins of Intellectual Life in Russia, 1700–1800* (Princeton, NJ, 1985), chap. 1.

3 For overviews, see A. S. Dëmin, *O khudozhestvennosti drevnerusskoi literatury* (Moscow, 1998), pp. 178–98; D. S. Likhachev, ed. *Istoriia russkoi literatury X–XVII vekov* (Moscow, 1980); S. F. Librovicha, *Istoriia knigi v Rossii* (Moscow, 2000); Lindsey Hughes, *Sophia, Regent of Russia 1657–1704* (New Haven, CT, 1990), pp. 165–72.

4 Carolyn J. Pouncy, "Missed Opportunities and the Search for Ivan the Terrible," *Kritika: Explorations in Russian and Eurasian History* 7 (2006), pp. 309–28.

5 Gary Marker, "Russia and the 'Printing Revolution': Notes and Observations," *Slavic Review* 41 (1982), pp. 269–72, 277; Librovicha, *Istoriia knigi*, pp. 35–7; Cracraft, *Petrine Revolution in Russian Imagery*, pp. 149–50.

6 Paul Meyendorff, *Russia, Ritual, and Reform: The Liturgical Reforms of Nikon in the 17th Century* (Crestwood, NY, 1991), pp. 32–4; 95–6; Paul Bushkovitch, *Religion and Society in Russia: The Sixteenth and Seventeenth Centuries* (New York, 1992), pp. 22–6.

7 Meyendorff, *Russia, Ritual, and Reform*, pp. 28–9.

8 Others doubt that the school ever existed, at least in a formal sense. Meyendorff, *Russia, Ritual, and Reform*, p. 120, n. 169; P. N. Miliukov, *Ocherki po istorii russkoi kul'tury* (Moscow, 1994), vol. 2, pt. 2, p. 214.

9 Meyendorff, *Russia, Ritual, and Reform*, pp. 29–34, 101–8.

10 Epifanii also may have operated a Greek-Latin school at the Chudov Monastery.

11 Bushkovitch, *Religion and Society*, pp. 152–60; Meyendorff, *Russia, Ritual, and Reform*, pp. 108–13.

12 Alexander V. Muller, trans. and ed. *The Spiritual Regulation of Peter the Great* (Seattle, WA, 1972), pp. 99–100, n. 137; A. V. Kartashev, *Ocherki po istorii russkoi tserkvi*, 2 vols. (Moscow, 1997), vol. 2, pp. 281–5; Scott M. Kenworthy, "The Struggle for Identity in Russian Orthodoxy since the Seventeenth Century" (unpublished paper presented at Stanford University, February 6, 2006).

13 Until the 1760s, significant numbers of non-Russian clergy became bishops in Russia. Between the death of the last patriarch in 1700 and the death of Peter I in 1725, 61.4 percent of the 44 bishops consecrated were non-Russian: 22 Ukrainian, 16 Russian, 2 Belarusian, and 4 from Serbia, Greece, and the Romanian principalities. See Jan Plamper, "The Russian Orthodox Episcopate, 1721–1917: A Prosopography," *Journal of Social History* 34 (2000), pp. 5–34. http://0-vnweb.hwwilsonweb.com.opac.library. csupomona.edu/hww (accessed March 7, 2006).

14 Ronald Vroon, "Simeon Polotsky," in *Dictionary of Literary Biography. Volume 150: Early Modern Russian Writers, Late Seventeenth and Eighteenth Centuries*, ed. Marcus C. Levitt (Detroit, MI, 1995), pp. 291–307.

15 A. P. Bogdanov questions the notion that Simeon, a graduate of the Kiev-Mogila College, did not master Greek. A. P. Bogdanov, *Moskovskaia publitsistika poslednei chetverti XVII veka* (Moscow, 2001), pp. 286–7.

16 On Simeon, Sil'vestr, continuing religious controversy, and developments in Russian education, see A. P. Bogdanov, "Sil'vestr Medvedev," *Voprosy istorii*, no. 2 (1988), pp. 84–98; idem, *Moskovskaia publitsistika*, pp. 279–428; Hughes, *Sophia*, pp. 126–31, 161–5; Bushkovitch, *Religion and Society*, pp. 163–75; Miliukov, *Ocherki*, vol. 2, pt. 2, pp. 212–22; Kartashev, *Ocherki*, vol. 2, pp. 230–55; P. V. Znamenskii, *Istoriia russkoi tserkvi (uchebnoe rukovodstvo)* (Moscow, 1996), pp. 294–305; Cathy Jean Potter, "The Russian Church and the Politics of Reform in the Second Half of the Seventeenth Century," 2 vols. (Ph.D. diss., Yale University, 1993); Nikolaos A. Chrissidis, "A Jesuit Aristotle in Seventeenth-Century Russia: Cosmology and the Planetary System in the Slavo-Greco-Latin Academy," in *Modernizing Muscovy: Reform and social change in seventeenth-century Russia*, ed. Jarmo Kotilaine and Marshall Poe (London and New York, 2004), pp. 391–416.

17 Chrissidis, "A Jesuit Aristotle," pp. 412–16.

18 Cracraft, *Petrine Revolution in Russian Imagery*, pp. 107–30, 190–3; Hughes, *Sophia*, pp. 10, 134–50; George Heard Hamilton, *The Art and Architecture of Russia* (New York, 1983), pp. 241–57.

19 Hamilton, *Art and Architecture*, pp. 209–40; James Cracraft, "Peter the Great and the Problem of Periodization," in *Architectures of Russian Identity: 1500 to the Present*, ed. James Cracraft and Daniel Rowland (Ithaca, NY, 2003), pp. 7–17; Lindsey Hughes, "Moscow Baroque – A Controversial Style," *Zapiski russkoi akademicheskoi gruppy v S. Sh. A.* 15 (1982), pp. 69–93; idem, *Sophia*, pp. 147–61.

20 At the end of the sixteenth century, troupes of English actors began to tour the European continent, becoming especially popular in the Germanies. A published collection of English plays from their repertoire appeared in 1620, followed by a collection of mainly German titles in 1630. Elise Kimerling Wirtschafter, *The Play of Ideas in Russian Enlightenment Theater* (DeKalb, IL, 2003), pp. 4–7, 204 n.

21 Hughes, *Sophia*, pp. 173–5; Wirtschafter, *Play of Ideas*, pp. 7–8.

22 Viktor Zhivov, *Iz tserkovnoi istorii vremeni Petra Velikogo: Issledovaniia i materialy* (Moscow, 2004), pp. 1–130.

23 Zhivov, *Iz tserkovnoi istorii*, p. 44.

24 The decree on shaving is translated in James Cracraft, ed. *Major Problems in the History of Imperial Russia* (Lexington, MA, 1994), p. 111.

25 Zhivov, *Iz tserkovnoi istorii*.

26 J. B. Schneewind, *The Invention of Autonomy: A History of Modern Moral Philosophy* (New York, 1998); Peter Dear, *Revolutionizing the Sciences: European Knowledge and Its Ambitions, 1500–1700* (Princeton, NJ, 2001).

27 Cracraft, *Petrine Revolution in Russian Culture*, pp. 24–39, 266–7; V. M. Zhivov, *Iazyk i kul'tura v Rossii XVIII veka* (Moscow, 1996), pp. 69–153, 376–96; Sergei Nikolev, "Dimitrii Rostovsky (Daniil Savvich Tuptalo)," in Levitt, ed. *Dictionary of Literary Biography*, pp. 334–8.

28 James Cracraft, "Feofan Prokopovich: a Bibliography of His Works," *Oxford Slavonic Papers*, New Series 8 (1975), pp. 2–3.

29 Cracraft, *Petrine Revolution in Russian Culture*, p. 24.

30 Zhivov, *Iazyk i kul'tura*, pp. 368–509.

31 Cracraft, *Petrine Revolution in Russian Culture*, esp. pp. 260–1, 278, 283; idem, *Revolution of Peter the Great*, pp. 75–113; Marker, *Publishing*, chapter 1.

32 Cracraft, *Petrine Revolution in Russian Culture*, pp. 181–92; idem, *Revolution of Peter the Great*, pp. 181–92; Feofan Prokopovich, "Sermon on Royal Authority and Honor," in *Russian Intellectual History: an Anthology*, ed. Marc Raeff (Amherst, NY, 1966), pp. 13–30.

33 I. T. Pososhkov, *Kniga o skudosti i bogatstve i drugie sochineniia*, ed. B. B. Kafengauz, reprint (Moscow, 1951; St Petersburg, 2004); Marc Raeff, "The Two Facets of the World of Ivan Pososhkov," *Forschungen zur osteuropäischen Geschichte* 50 (1995), pp. 309–28; Ivan Pososhkov, *The Book on Poverty and Wealth*, ed. and trans. A. P. Vlasto and L. R. Lewitter (Stanford, CA, 1987).

34 Lindsey Hughes, *Russia in the Age of Peter the Great* (New Haven, CT, 1998), pp. 280–8.

35 Barbara Alpern Engel, *Women in Russia, 1700–2000* (New York, 2004), p. 11. For the 1701 decree on German clothes, see Cracraft, ed. *Major Problems*, pp. 110–11.

36 Hughes, *Russia*, pp. 186–90, 267–70. For Zubov's etching, see Cracraft, *Revolution of Peter the Great*; idem, *Petrine Revolution in Russian Imagery*, pp. 182–3.

37   Cracraft, *Petrine Revolution in Russian Culture*, pp. 228–35; Elena Lavrent'eva, *Svetskii etiket pushkinskoi pory* (Moscow, 1999), pp. 11–12.

38   James Van Horn Melton, *The Rise of the Public in Enlightenment Europe* (Cambridge, 2001).

39   Wirtschafter, *Play of Ideas*, pp. 7–22.

40   L. P. Gromova, ed. *Istoriia russkoi zhurnalistiki XVIII–XIX vekov. Uchebnik* (St Petersburg, 2003), pp. 16–29; Cracraft, *Petrine Revolution in Russian Culture*, p. 266.

41   Cracraft, *Revolution of Peter the Great*, pp. 106–13; idem, *Petrine Revolution in Russian Culture*, pp. 193–4, 240–55; N. I. Nevskaia, *Letopis' Rossiiskoi Akademii nauk. Vol. 1. 1724–1801* (St Petersburg, 2000).

42   Paul Bushkovitch, *Peter the Great: The Struggle for Power, 1671–1725* (Cambridge, 2001).

Chapter 4

1   Carolyn Johnston Pouncy, ed. and trans. *The Domostroi: Rules for Russian Households in the Time of Ivan the Terrible* (Ithaca, NY, 1994).

2   See Platon's explication of the fifth commandment – "Honor thy father and thy mother, that it may be well with thee, and that thy days may be long upon the earth" – which appears in catechisms published between 1765 and 1800. All are printed in Platon (Levshin), *Pouchitel'nyia slova pri Vysochaishem Dvore Eia Imperatorskago Velichestva . . .* , 20 vols. (Moscow, 1779–1806), vols. 6–9.

3   Platon (Levshin), *Kratkii katikhizis dlia obucheniia malykh detei*, in *Pouchitel'nyia slova*, vol. 6 (Moscow, 1780), p. 184.

4   Elise Kimerling Wirtschafter, *Structures of Society: Imperial Russia's "People of Various Ranks"* (DeKalb, IL, 1994).

5   Wirtschafter, *Structures of Society*, pp. 78–92.

6   David Moon, *The Russian Peasantry 1600–1930: The World the Peasants Made* (London and New York, 1999), pp. 240–54; Andreas Kappeler, *The Russian Empire: A Multiethnic History*, trans. Alfred Clayton (Harlow, Eng., 2001), pp. 153–7, 187.

7   Quoted in Jacob Walkin, *The Rise of Democracy in Pre-Revolutionary Russia: Political and Social Institutions under the Last Three Czars* (New York, 1962), p. 76.

8   Brenda Meehan-Waters, *Autocracy and Aristocracy: The Russian Service Elite of 1730* (New Brunswick, NJ, 1982), pp. 47–8.

9   S. V. Volkov, *Russkii ofitserskii korpus* (Moscow, 1993), pp. 100–2.

10   *Slovar' russkikh pisatelei XVIII veka*, vol. 1 (Leningrad, 1988), pp. 114–17; I. V. Faizova, *"Manifest o vol'nosti" i sluzhba dvorianstva v XVIII stoletii* (Moscow, 1999), pp. 66–7; A. T. Bolotov, *Zhizn' i prikliucheniia Andreia Bolotova, opisannye samim im dlia svoikh potomkov*, 3 vols. 1871–3, reprint (Moscow, 1993), vol. 1, pp. 66–9, 76, 242–7.

11   Paul Dukes, *Catherine the Great and the Russian Nobility* (London, 1967), pp. 159–60; Faizova, *"Manifest o vol'nosti,"* p. 155.

12   Faizova, *"Manifest o vol'nosti,"* pp. 171–2.

13   Faizova, *"Manifest o vol'nosti,"* p. 107.

14   Faizova, *"Manifest o vol'nosti,"* pp. 129–31.

15   David Moon, *The Abolition of Serfdom in Russia* (Harlow and London, 2001), p. 17.

16 Arcadius Kahan, "The Costs of 'Westernization' in Russia: The Gentry and the Economy in the Eighteenth Century," reprinted in *The Structure of Russian History: Interpretive Essays*, ed. Michael Cherniavsky (New York, 1970), pp. 226–8.

17 Robert E. Jones, *The Emancipation of the Russian Nobility, 1761–1785* (Princeton, NJ, 1973).

18 David M. Griffiths and George E. Munro, ed. *Catherine II's Charters of 1785 to the Nobility and the Towns* (Bakersfield, CA, 1990).

19 John P. LeDonne, *Absolutism and Ruling Class: The Formation of the Russian Political Order, 1700–1825* (New York, 1991); idem, *Ruling Russia: Politics and Administration in the Age of Absolutism, 1762–1796* (Princeton, NJ, 1984).

20 Michelle Lamarche Marrese, *A Woman's Kingdom: Noblewomen and the Control of Property in Russia, 1700–1861* (Ithaca, NY, 2002), pp. 218–34.

21 Jones, *Emancipation*, p. 295.

22 Dukes, *Catherine the Great*, pp. 9–15, 141.

23 Elise Kimerling Wirtschafter, "Legal Identity and the Possession of Serfs in Imperial Russia," *Journal of Modern History* 70 (1998), pp. 561–87.

24 The classic works cited in connection with this debate are Marc Raeff, *Origins of the Russian Intelligentsia: The Eighteenth-Century Nobility* (New York, 1966); Michael Confino, *Domaines et seigneurs en Russie vers la fin du XVIIIe siècle* (Paris, 1963); idem, "Histoire et psychologie: À propos de la noblesse russe au XVIIIe siècle," *Annales: Économies-Sociétés-Civilisation* 22 (1967), pp. 1163–205; idem, *Systèmes agraires et progrès agricole: L'assolement triennal en Russie aux XVIIIe–XIXe siècles* (Paris and La Haye, 1969). For a recent treatment, see Valerie A. Kivelson, *Autocracy in the Provinces: The Muscovite Gentry and Political Culture in the Seventeenth Century* (Stanford, CA, 1996).

25 Sergei Aksakov, *A Russian Gentleman*, trans. J. D. Duff (Oxford, 1982).

26 Elise Kimerling Wirtschafter, *The Play of Ideas in Russian Enlightenment Theater* (DeKalb, IL, 2003), pp. 85–9, 138–46.

27 Dominic Lieven, *Russia's Rulers under the Old Regime* (New Haven, CT, 1989), pp. 47–8, 156–67.

28 Bolotov, *Zhizn' i prikliucheniia*; Thomas Newlin, *The Voice in the Garden: Andrei Bolotov and the Anxieties of Russian Pastoral, 1738–1833* (Evanston, IL, 2001).

29 On the lack of change in Russian agriculture, see Confino, *Systèmes agraires*, chapters 4–6.

30 Moon, *The Russian Peasantry*, pp. 18–21, 99. In estimating comparative population figures for "Russia," Moon excludes most territories incorporated into the Russian Empire after the mid-seventeenth century: the Baltic region, Left-Bank Ukraine, Lithuania, Belarus, Poland, Right-Bank Ukraine, Bessarabia, the steppes to the north of the Black Sea (New Russia or southern Ukraine), the Crimea, the Caucasus, Central Asia, and the Pacific Far East. He includes the St Petersburg region and the Don Cossack territory.

31 Steven L. Hoch, "The Serf Economy and the Social Order in Russia," in *Serfdom and Slavery: Studies in Legal Bondage*, ed. M. L. Bush (New York, 1996), pp. 312–14.

32 N. V. Sokolova, "Krest'ianskoe samoupravlenie v tsentral'noi Rossii v 20-e gody XVIII v.," *Istoricheskie zapiski* 7 (125) (Moscow, 2004), pp. 117–74.

33 Edgar Melton, "Household Economies and Communal Conflicts on a Russian Serf Estate, 1800–1817," *Journal of Social History* 26 (1993), pp. 559–85; idem, "Enlightened Seigniorialism and Its Dilemmas in Serf Russia, 1750–1830," *Journal of Modern History* 62 (1990), pp. 675–708; Steven L. Hoch, *Serfdom and Social Control in Russia: Petrovskoe, a Village in Tambov* (Chicago, 1986).

34 See note 31 above.

35 Sokolova, "Krest'ianskoe samoupravlenie." See note 32 above.

36 David Moon, "Peasant Migration and the Settlement of Russia's Frontiers, 1550–1897," *The Historical Journal* 40 (1997), pp. 859–93; idem, *The Russian Peasantry*, pp. 48–65.

37 Melton, "Enlightened Seigniorialism"; E. B. Smilianskaia, *Dvorianskoe gnezdo serediny XVIII veka. Timofei Tekut'ev i ego "Instruktsiia o domashnikh poriadkakh"* (Moscow, 1998).

38 Confino, *Domaines et seigneurs*, pp. 104–76, 255–75; idem, *Systèmes agraires*, pp. 135–269, 279–85, 343–66.

39 Moon, *The Russian Peasantry*, pp. 70–7; Confino, *Domaines et seigneurs*, pp. 186–254.

40 Ian Blanchard, *Russia's 'Age of Silver': Precious-metal production and economic growth in the eighteenth century* (London, 1989), pp. 236–41.

41 Blanchard, *Russia's 'Age of Silver'*, pp. 236–7.

42 Arcadius Kahan, *The Plow, the Hammer, and the Knout: An Economic History of Eighteenth-Century Russia* (Chicago, 1985), pp. 57–9.

43 Edgar Melton, "Proto-Industrialization, Serf Agriculture, and Agrarian Social Structure: Two Estates in Nineteenth-Century Russia," *Past and Present* 115 (1987), pp. 94–6; idem, "Household Economies," pp. 563–8.

44 Melton, "Proto-Industrialization," pp. 81–4.

45 Melton, "Proto-Industrialization," pp. 74–5; Klaus Gestwa, *Proto-Industrialisierung in Russland: Wirtschaft, Herrschaft und Kultur in Ivanovo und Pavlovo, 1741–1932* (Göttingen, 1999), pp. 53–60.

46 Gestwa, *Proto-Industrialisierung*, pp. 75–87; Henry Rosovsky, "The Serf Entrepreneur in Russia," *Explorations in Entrepreneurial History* 6 (1954), pp. 207–33.

47 Kahan, *The Plow*, pp. 267–82.

48 Simon Dixon, *The Modernisation of Russia 1675–1825* (Cambridge, 1999), p. 252.

49 Jan De Vries, "The Industrial Revolution and the Industrious Revolution," *Journal of Economic History* 54 (1994), pp. 249–70, esp. p. 252.

50 Gilbert Rozman, *Urban Networks in Russia, 1750–1800, and Premodern Periodization* (Princeton, NJ, 1976).

51 Moon, *The Russian Peasantry*, pp. 21, 292–3.

52 Kahan, *The Plow*, pp. 120–9, 269–75, 278, 283–318.

53 B. N. Mironov, *Sotsial'naia istoriia Rossii perioda imperii (XVIII-nachalo XX v). Genezis lichnosti, demokraticheskoi sem'i, grazhdanskogo obshchestva i pravovogo gosudarstva*, vol. 1 (St Petersburg, 1999), pp. 129–33.

54 Manfred Hildermeier, "Was war das Meščanstvo? Zur rechtlichen und sozialen Verfassung des unterenstädtischen Standes in Russland," *Forschungen zur osteuropäischen Geschichte* 36 (1985), pp. 15–53; A. A. Kizevetter, *Posadskaia obshchina v Rossii XVIII st.* (Moscow, 1903); Griffiths and Munro, ed. *Catherine's Charters*.

55 P. G. Ryndziunskii, *Gorodskoe grazhdanstvo doreformennoi Rossii* (Moscow, 1958), pp. 40–51, 179–82, 504–53; M. M. Gromyko, "Razvitie Tiumeni kak remeslennogo-torgovogo tsentra v XVIII v.," in *Goroda feodal'noi Rossii: Sbornik statei pamiati I. V. Ustiugova* (Moscow, 1966), pp. 408–9.

56 Judith Pallot and Denis J. B. Shaw, *Landscape and Settlement in Romanov Russia 1613–1917* (New York, 1990), pp. 253–6; B. N. Mironov, "Russkii gorod vo vtoroi polovine XVIII-pervoi polovine XIX veka: Tipologicheskii analiz," *Istoriia SSSR* 5 (1988), pp. 150–68; idem, *Sotsial'naia istoriia*, vol. 1, pp. 284–5.

57 Mironov, *Sotsial'naia istoriia*, vol. 1, p. 296.

58 Wirtschafter, *Structures of Society*, pp. 85–91.

59 Samuel H. Baron, "Entrepreneurs and Entrepreneurship in Sixteenth/Seventeenth-Century Russia," in *Entrepreneurship in Imperial Russia and the Soviet Union*, ed. Gregory Guroff and Fred V. Carstensen (Princeton, NJ, 1985), p. 52; Wallace Daniel, "Entrepreneurship and the Russian Textile Industry: From Peter the Great to Catherine the Great," *Russian Review* 54 (1995), 1–25.

60 A. I. Aksenev, *Genealogiia moskovskogo kupechestva XVIII v.: Iz istorii formirovaniia russkoi burzhuazii* (Moscow, 1988), pp. 61–2; B. N. Mironov, *Russkii gorod v 1740–1860-e gody: Demograficheskoe, sotsial'noe i ekonomicheskoe razvitie* (Leningrad, 1990), pp. 151–69; idem, "Sotsial'naia mobil'nost' rossiiskogo kupechestva v XVIII-nachale XIX veka (opyt izucheniia)," in *Problemy istoricheskoi demografii SSSR*, ed. R. N. Pullat (Tallin, 1977), pp. 207–17.

61 N. P. Durov, "Fedor Vasil'evich Karzhavin," *Russkaia starina* 12 (1875), pp. 272–97.

62 Wirtschafter, *Structures of Society*, pp. 133–8.

63 Elise Kimerling Wirtschafter, *Social Identity in Imperial Russia* (DeKalb, IL, 1997), pp. 80–2; idem, *Play of Ideas*, pp. 12–14.

64 Adrian Jones, "A Russian Bourgeois's Arctic Enlightenment," *The Historical Journal* 48 (2005), pp. 623–40.

65 Muscovite Russians did not imagine themselves as part of a social collective; they lacked "a collective vision, even a collective noun, for their society as an entity." Nancy Shields Kollmann, *By Honor Bound: State and Society in Early Modern Russia* (Ithaca, NY, 1999), p. 59.

66 David L. Ransel, "An Eighteenth-Century Russian Merchant Family in Prosperity and Decline," in *Imperial Russia: New Histories for the Empire*, ed. Jane Burbank and David L. Ransel (Bloomington, 1998), pp. 256–80.

67 Arcadius Kahan, "The Costs of 'Westernization' in Russia: The Gentry and the Economy in the Eighteenth Century," in Cherniavsky, ed. *The Structure of Russian History*, pp. 224–50.

68 B. N. Mironov, "Gramotnost' v Rossii v 1797–1917 godov: Poluchenie novoi istoricheskoi informatsii s pomoshch'iu metodov retrospektivnogo prognozirovaniia," *Istoriia SSSR*, no. 4 (1985), pp. 137–53.

69 James Van Horn Melton, *The Rise of the Public in Enlightenment Europe* (Cambridge, 2001), p. 82.

70 Another estimate of readership calculates that between 1760 and 1800 about 8500 individuals "purchased or subscribed to a least one book or journal." Colum Leckey,

"Patronage and Public Culture in the Russian Free Economic Society, 1765–1796," *Slavic Review* 64 (2005), pp. 355–6, especially n. 1.

71   Margaret C. Jacob, "The Mental Landscape of the Public Sphere: A European Perspective," *Eighteenth-Century Studies* 28 (1994), pp. 95–113.

72   Marc Raeff, "Transfiguration and Modernization: The Paradoxes of Social Disciplining, Paedagogical Leadership, and the Enlightenment in Eighteenth-Century Russia," in *Alteuropa – Ancien Régime – Frühe Neuzeit: Probleme und Methoden der Forschung*, ed. Hans Erich Bödeker and Ernst Hinrichs (Stuttgart and Bad Cannstatt, 1991), p. 109; Anthony G. Netting, "Russian Liberalism: The Years of Promise" (Ph.D. diss., Columbia University, 1967), p. 20.

Chapter 5

1   John P. LeDonne, *The Russian Empire and the World 1700–1917: The Geopolitics of Expansion and Containment* (New York, 1997), pp. 89–104; Alexander Bitis, *Russia and the Eastern Question: Army, Government and Society 1815–1833* (Oxford, 2006), pp. 22–6.

2   On the steppe and Russia's relations with the steppe peoples, see Andreas Kappeler, *The Russian Empire: A Multiethnic History*, trans. Alfred Clayton (Harlow, Eng., 2001); Michael Khodarkovsky, *Russia's Steppe Frontier: The Making of a Colonial Empire, 1500–1800* (Bloomington, IN, 2002); Willard Sunderland, *Taming the Wild Field: Colonization and Empire on the Russian Steppe* (Ithaca, NY, 2004).

3   Khodarkovsky, *Russia's Steppe Frontier*, pp. 227–9.

4   Sunderland, *Taming the Wild Field*, pp. 3–5; John P. LeDonne, *The Grand Strategy of the Russian Empire, 1650–1831* (New York, 2004), pp. 9–11.

5   On the Bashkirs, see Kappeler, *Russian Empire*, pp. 39–42; Khodarkovsky, *Russia's Steppe Frontier*, pp. 156–9; Sunderland, *Taming the Wild Field*, pp. 46–9.

6   Sunderland, *Taming the Wild Field*, p. 60.

7   On the Kalmyks, see Khodarkovsky, *Russia's Steppe Frontier*, pp. 134–46.

8   Kappeler, *Russian Empire*, pp. 44–51.

9   On Ukraine, see Zenon E. Kohut, *Russian Centralism and Ukrainian Autonomy: Imperial Absorption of the Hetmanate, 1760s–1830s* (Cambridge, MA, 1988); Paul Bushkovitch, "The Ukraine in Russian Culture 1790–1860: The Evidence of the Journals," *Jahrbücher für Geschichte Osteuropas* 39 (1991), pp. 339–63; Kappeler, *Russian Empire*, pp. 61–9.

10 Peasants of the Hetmanate retained the right to move, though by 1760 they could depart with nothing but personal property.

11 Zofia Zielińska, "Poland between Prussia and Russia in the Eighteenth Century," in *Constitution and Reform in Eighteenth-Century Poland: The Constitution of 3 May 1791*, ed. Samuel Fiszman (Bloomington, IN, 1997), p. 88.

12 Edward C. Thaden, *Russia's Western Borderlands, 1710–1870* (Princeton, NJ, 1984); Kappeler, *Russian Empire*, pp. 75–94.

13 Uniates were Orthodox Christians who had accepted papal authority at the end of the sixteenth century.

14 John Doyle Klier, *Russia Gathers her Jews: The Origins of the "Jewish Question" in Russia, 1772–1825* (DeKalb, IL, 1986), p. 19.

15 Thaden, *Russia's Western Borderlands*; Kappeler, *Russian Empire*, pp. 71–5.

16 At its inception, the Table of Ranks included the Baltic service hierarchy.

17 Thaden, *Russia's Western Borderlands*, p. 212.

18 Geoffrey Hosking, "The Freudian Frontier," *TLS* (March 10, 1995), p. 27; Hugh Seton-Watson, *The Russian Empire 1801–1917* (Oxford, 1967), pp. 52–5; V. M. Kabuzan, *Narody Rossii v pervoi polovine XIX v. Chislennost' i etnicheskii sostav* (Moscow, 1992), p. 127.

19 Words of V. O. Kliuchevskii. Quoted in Seymour Becker, "The Muslim East in Nineteenth-Century Russian Popular Historiography," *Central Asian Survey* 5 (1986), p. 41.

20 Unless otherwise indicated my account of the eighteenth-century succession struggles is based on I. V. Kurukin, *Epokha "dvorskikh bur'": Ocherki politicheskoi istorii poslepetrovskoi Rossii, 1725–1762 gg.* (Riazan', 2003). Kurukin's book is the most comprehensive, reliable, and astute account of the post-Petrine political struggles published to date. Events that have long been a blur of misinformation and received opinion at last have found a diligent modern scholar. See also E. V. Anisimov, *Rossiia bez Petra: 1725–1740* (St Petersburg, 1994); idem, *Rossiia v seredine XVIII veka: Bor'ba za nasledie Petra* (Moscow, 1986).

21 The Council's other members were P. A. Tolstoi, G. I. Golovkin, F. M. Apraskin, and A. I. Osterman. Kurukin, *Epokha "dvorskikh bur'*," p. 109.

22 Kurukin, *Epokha "dvorskikh bur'*," pp. 109–10, quoting E. V. Anisimov, "Vnutrenniaia politika Verkhovnogo Tainogo soveta (1726–1730 gg.)." Avtoreferat diss. kand. ist. nauk (Leningrad, 1975).

23 Kurukin, *Epokha "dvorskikh bur'*," p. 148.

24 Kurukin, *Epokha "dvorskikh bur'*," pp. 172–3.

25 For details and documentation, see Kurukin, *Epokha "dvorskikh bur'*," pp. 170–91.

26 Kurukin, *Epokha "dvorskikh bur'*," p. 216.

27 Anisimov, *Rossiia bez Petra*, p. 279.

28 Kurukin, *Epokha "dvorskikh bur'*," pp. 288–92.

29 Kurukin, *Epokha "dvorskikh bur'*," pp. 337–8.

30 Kurukin, *Epokha "dvorskikh bur'*," pp. 546–8.

31 Kurukin, *Epokha "dvorskikh bur'*," p. 356.

32 LeDonne, *Grand Strategy*, p. 89.

33 Kurukin, *Epokha "dvorskikh bur'*," pp. 370–2.

34 One of Catherine's most important co-conspirators was the Guard officer Grigorii G. Orlov, the third in a line of lovers she took during her life.

35 Kurukin, *Epokha "dvorskikh bur'*," pp. 415–17.

36 For reliable and accessible accounts of Catherine II, see Isabel de Madariaga, *Catherine the Great: A Short History* (New Haven, CT, 1990); idem, *Russia in the Age of Catherine the Great* (New Haven, CT, 1981); Simon Dixon, *Catherine the Great* (Harlow, Eng., 2001); John T. Alexander, *Catherine the Great: Life and Legend* (Oxford, 1989); A. B. Kamenskii, *"Pod seniiu Ekateriny . . .": Vtoraia polovina XVIII veka* (St Petersburg,

1992); O. A. Omel'chenko, *"Zakonnaia monarkhiia" Ekateriny II: Prosveshchennyi absoliutizm v Rossii* (Moscow, 1993).

37 Elise Kimerling Wirtschafter, *The Play of Ideas in Russian Enlightenment Theater* (DeKalb, IL, 2003), pp. 169–70.

38 E. R. Dashkova, *The Memoirs of Princess Dashkova: Russia in the Age of Catherine the Great*, trans. and ed. Kyril Fitzlyon, reprint (London, 1958; Durham, NC, 1995), p. 181.

39 Dashkova, *Memoirs*, p. 276.

40 Kurukin's data include ranked and unranked officials (*chinovniki* and *prikaznye*). Kurukin, *Epokha "dvorskikh bur'*," pp. 241–2. Data for officials with rank compiled by Boris Mironov indicate a higher concentration of officials – .39 per 1,000 inhabitants in the 1690s and .57 in 1755 and 1796 – but the problem of undergovernment stands. B. N. Mironov, *Sotsial'naia istoriia Rossii perioda imperii (XVIII-nachalo XX v.). Genezis lichnosti, demokraticheskoi sem'i, grazhdanskogo obshchestva i pravovogo gosudarstva*, 2 vols. (St Petersburg, 1999), vol. 2, p. 200. On the fiscal and administrative problems of the post-Petrine era, see also A. B. Kamenskii, *Ot Petra I do Pavla I: Reformy v Rossii XVIII veka. Opyt tselostnogo analiza* (Moscow, 1999), pp. 184–254.

41 Marc Raeff, *The Well-Ordered Police State: Social and Institutional Change through Law in the Germanies and Russia, 1600–1800* (New Haven, CT, 1983).

42 Anisimov, *Rossiia v seredine*, pp. 69–72.

43 My account of the Legislative Commission follows Madariaga, *Catherine the Great*, pp. 24–37.

44 For a sampling of these instructions in English translation, see Gregory L. Freeze, *From Supplication to Revolution: A Documentary Social History of Imperial Russia* (New York, 1988).

45 An English translation of Catherine's Instruction is available in Paul Dukes, ed. *Catherine the Great's Instruction (Nakaz) to the Legislative Commission, 1767* (Newtonville, MA, 1977).

46 Madariaga, *Catherine the Great*, p. 28.

47 Madariaga, *Catherine the Great*, p. 29.

48 According to Madariaga, information gathered through the Legislative Commission influenced the 1775 Statute on Local Administration, the 1781 Salt Code and Code of Commercial Navigation, the 1782 Police Ordinance, the 1785 Charters to the Nobility and the Towns, and the 1786 Statute on National Education. Madariaga, *Catherine the Great*, pp. 33–4.

49 On Catherine's local reforms, see Madariaga, *Catherine the Great*, pp. 66–79; idem, *Russia*, pp. 277–91; John P. LeDonne, *Ruling Russia: Politics and Administration in the Age of Absolutism 1762–1796* (Princeton, NJ, 1984), pp. 67–82, 152–65.

50 For the number of officials with rank, see Mironov, *Sotsial'naia istoriia*, vol. 2, p. 200.

51 N. N. Efremova, *Sudoustroistvo Rossii v XVIII-pervoi polovine XIX vv. (istoriko-pravovoe issledovanie)* (Moscow, 1993), pp. 96–152.

52 There were no special state courts for serfs, whose judge was the noble master. But if serfs became involved in cases with individuals from other social groups, they too might gain access to the local courts.

53 Janet Hartley, "Town Government in St. Petersburg Guberniya after the Charter to the Towns of 1785," *Slavonic and East European Review* 62 (1984), pp. 61–84.

54 David Griffiths, "Introduction: Of Estates, Charters, and Constitutions," in *Catherine II's Charters of 1785 to the Nobility and the Towns*, trans. and ed. David Griffiths and George E. Munro (Bakersfield, CA, 1991), pp. xvii–lxix.

55 On these themes, see Wirtschafter, *Play of Ideas*.

56 Fritz Kern, *Kingship and Law in the Middle Ages*, trans. S. B. Chrimes, reprint (Oxford, 1939; New York, 1970); Vladimir Val'denberg, *Drevnerusskiia ucheniia o predelakh tsarskoi vlasti: Ocherki russkoi politicheskoi literatury ot Vladimira Sviatogo do kontsa XVII veka*, reprint (Petrograd, 1916; The Hague, 1966).

57 Omel'chenko, *"Zakonnaia monarkhiia,"* pp. 45–8, 72; Richard Wortman, *The Development of a Russian Legal Consciousness* (Chicago, 1976), pp. 9–50.

--- Chapter 6 ---

1 Citing the work of Jürgen Habermas, historians of early modern Europe have in recent decades explored the concept of the "bourgeois public sphere" situated between the private sphere of the household and the sphere of public authority represented by the government. From the Habermasian perspective, in the "bourgeois public sphere," so termed because of its roots in the capitalist market economy, the freedom and openness of relationships within the private household spread out into the arena of public authority. Through the development of autonomous civic organizations, the commercialization of print culture, the political assertiveness of corporate bodies, and the formation of communities structured around sites of polite sociability, the "bourgeois public sphere" eventually limited the absolutist power of the monarchy to the point where public authority became the common domain of society and government. Prior to the moment of political actualization, the "bourgeois public sphere" can be thought of as a "prepolitical literary public sphere," which is the appropriate category for eighteenth-century Russia. Jürgen Habermas, *The Structural Transformation of the Public Sphere: An Inquiry into a Category of Bourgeois Society*, trans. Thomas Burger with Frederick Lawrence (Cambridge, MA, 1989).

2 Elise Kimerling Wirtschafter, *The Play of Ideas in Russian Enlightenment Theater* (DeKalb, IL, 2003), p. 72. For the works and ideas of Russia's enlightened prelates, see A. I. Esiukov, *Filosofskie aspekty russkoi bogoslovskoi mysli (vtoraia polovina XVIII-nachalo XIX v.): Monografiia* (Arkhangel'sk, 2003).

3 Wirtschafter, *Play of Ideas*, pp. 8–9.

4 George Heard Hamilton, *The Art and Architecture of Russia* (New York, 1983), pp. 346–7.

5 S. P. Shevyrev, *Istoriia imperatorskogo Moskovskogo universiteta, napisannaia k stoletnemu ego iubileiu*, 1855, reprint (Moscow, 1998), pp. 7–80.

6 Wirtschafter, *Play of Ideas*, pp. 11–15, 25–6; Shevyrev, *Istoriia*, pp. 24–5; L. P. Gromova, ed. *Istoriia russkoi zhurnalistiki XVIII–XIX vekov. Uchebnik* (St Petersburg, 2003), p. 45.

7 Wirtschafter, *Play of Ideas*, pp. 13–21.

8 M. Sh. Fainshtein, *"I slavu Frantsii v Rossii prevzoiti . . ." Rossiiskaia Akademiia (1783–1841) i razvitie kul'tury i gumanitarnykh nauk* (Moscow and St Petersburg, 2002).

9 Wirtschafter, *Play of Ideas*, p. 37.

10   M. Aronson and S. Reiser, *Literaturnye kruzhki i salony*, 1929, reprint (St Petersburg, 2001), pp. 38–49.

11   The discussion of journals relies on Gromova, ed. *Istoriia russkoi zhurnalistiki*, pp. 36–58; Marcus C. Levitt, ed. *Dictionary of Literary Biography. Volume 150: Early Modern Russian Writers, Late Seventeenth and Eighteenth Centuries* (Detroit, MI, 1995); Isabel de Madariaga, *Catherine the Great: A Short History* (New Haven, CT, 1990), pp. 91–103; idem, *Russia in the Age of Catherine the Great* (New Haven, CT, 1981), pp. 327–42; G. A. Gukovskii, *Russkaia literatura XVIII veka*, 1939, reprint (Moscow, 1998), pp. 154–5, 213–51.

12   Gary Marker, "Russian Journals and their Readers in the Late Eighteenth Century," *Oxford Slavonic Papers. New Series* 19 (1986), pp. 88–101; Wirtschafter, *Play of Ideas*, pp. 25–8.

13   On the collaboration between Catherine and Novikov, see W. Gareth Jones, *Nikolay Novikov: Enlightener of Russia* (Cambridge, 1984).

14   Less well-known individuals who published satirical journals in 1769 included Vasilii G. Ruban (*Ni to ni sio*), Ivan F. Rumiantsev and Ignatii A. de Teil's (*Poleznoe s priiatnym*), and V. V. Tuzov (*Podenshchina*).

15   Irina Reyfman, *Vasilii Trediakovsky: The Fool of the "New" Russian Literature* (Stanford, CA, 1990).

16   Roger Bartlett, "The Free Economic Society: The Foundation Years and the Prize Essay Competition of 1766 on Peasant Property," in *Russland zur Zeit Katharinas II. Absolutismus – Aufklärung – Pragmatismus*, ed. Eckhard Hübner, Jan Kusber, and Peter Nitsche (Cologne, 1998), pp. 181–214; Joseph Bradley, "Subjects into Citizens: Societies, Civil Society, and Autocracy in Tsarist Russia," *American Historical Review* 107 (2002), pp. 1094–123; Colum Leckey, "Provincial Readers and Agrarian Reform, 1760s–1770s: The Case of Sloboda Ukraine," *Russian Review* 61 (2002), pp. 535–59; idem, "Patronage and Public Culture in the Russian Free Economic Society, 1765–1796," *Slavic Review* 64 (2005), pp. 355–79.

17   Bartlett, "The Free Economic Society."

18   V. A. Somov, "Dva otveta Vol'tera na Peterburgskom konkurse o krest'ianskoi sobstvennosti," in *Evropeiskoe prosveshchenie i tsivilizatsiia Rossii*, ed. S. Ia. Karp and S. A. Mezin (Moscow, 2004), pp. 149–65.

19   In the early 1790s, an average of 393 Russian-language titles appeared each year, up from the 150 to 160 Russian books published annually in the 1760s. John T. Alexander, "Catherine II, 'The Great,' Empress of Russia," in Levitt, ed. *Dictionary of Literary Biography*, pp. 49–50.

20   Shevyrev, *Istoriia*, pp. 52, 182–4, 201–4, 241–2, 253–4, 259–60, 269–70.

21   Galina Nikolaevna Moiseeva, "Antiokh Dmitrievich Kantemir (1708–1744)," in Levitt, ed. *Dictionary of Literary Biography*, pp. 120–8, quote on p. 120.

22   Kantemir's satires were first published in French (1749 and 1750) and German (1752) prose translations. Although known in Russia in manuscript form, a Russian edition of the satires did not appear until 1762.

23   James Cracraft, *The Petrine Revolution in Russian Culture* (Cambridge, MA, 2004), pp. 212–13.

24   Reyfman, *Vasilii Trediakovsky*, pp. 1–69; idem, "Vasilii Kirillovich Trediakovsky (1703–1769)," in Levitt, ed. *Dictionary of Literary Biography*, pp. 382–93; idem, "Mikhail

Notes 255

Vasil'evich Lomonosov (1711–1765)," in Levitt, ed. *Dictionary of Literary Biography*, pp. 208–21; Marcus Levitt, "Aleksandr Petrovich Sumarokov (1717–1777)," in Levitt, ed. *Dictionary of Literary Biography*, pp. 370–81.

25 Reyfman, "Mikhail Vasil'evich Lomonosov," p. 211.
26 Reyfman, "Mikhail Vasil'evich Lomonosov," p. 218.
27 Reyfman, "Mikhail Vasil'evich Lomonosov," p. 220.
28 Levitt, "Aleksandr Petrovich Sumarokov," p. 372.
29 Levitt, "Aleksandr Petrovich Sumarokov," p. 372.
30 Quoted in Levitt, "Aleksandr Petrovich Sumarokov," pp. 380–1.
31 Andrew Kahn, "Nikolai Karamzin, *Letters of a Russian traveller*," *Studies on Voltaire and the Eighteenth Century*, no. 4 (Oxford, 2003); Gitta Hammarberg, "Nikolai Mikhailovich Karamzin (1 December 1766–2 May 1826)," in Levitt, ed. *Dictionary of Literary Biography*, pp. 135–50.
32 Richard Pipes, ed. and trans. *Karamzin's Memoir on Ancient and Modern Russia. A Translation and Analysis* (New York, 1974).
33 Vera Proskurina, *Mify imperii: Literatura i vlast' v epokhu Ekateriny II* (Moscow, 2006), pp. 285–314; Iurii Vladimirovich Stennik, "Ivan Andreevich Krylov (2 February 1769–9 November 1844)," in Levitt, ed. *Dictionary of Literary Biography*, pp. 197–207.
34 Robert Darnton, *The Forbidden Best-Sellers of Pre-Revolutionary France* (New York, 1996).
35 I. Ia. Shchipanov, ed. *Izbrannye proizvedeniia russkikh myslitelei vtoroi poloviny XVIII veka*, 2 vols. (Moscow, 1952); S. A. Pokrovskii, ed. *Iuridicheskie proizvedeniia progressivnykh russkikh myslitelei. Vtoraia polovina XVIII veka* (Moscow, 1959); T. V. Artem'eva, *Istoriia metafiziki v Rossii XVIII veka* (St Petersburg, 1996); *Slovar' russkikh pisatelei XVIII veka*, 2 vols. (Leningrad, 1988; St Petersburg, 1999); S. S. Ilizarov, *Moskovskaia intelligentsiia XVIII veka* (Moscow, 1999); A. H. Brown, "Adam Smith's First Russian Followers," in *Essays on Adam Smith*, ed. Andrew S. Skinner and Thomas Wilson (Oxford, 1975), pp. 247–73.
36 On architects, painters, and sculptors, see Hamilton, *Art and Architecture*, pp. 258–313, 343–58. On serf painters, see Richard Stites, *Serfdom, Society, and the Arts in Imperial Russia. The Pleasure and the Power* (New Haven, CT, 2005), pp. 332–43.
37 Stites, *Serfdom*; Priscilla Roosevelt, *Life on the Russian Country Estate: A Social and Cultural History* (New Haven, CT, 1995), pp. 102–12, 129–53, 245–67.
38 Stites, *Serfdom*, pp. 71–84, esp. p. 75.
39 A. S. Galitskii, *Nizhegorodskii teatr (1798–1867)* (Nizhnii Novgorod, 1867), pp. 13–19; Wirtschafter, *Play of Ideas*, p. 21.
40 L. Lenskaia, *Repertuar krepostnogo teatra Sheremetevykh. Katalog p'es* (Moscow, 1996).
41 Wirtschafter, *Play of Ideas*, p. 21.
42 Stites, *Serfdom*, p. 293.
43 Gary Marker, "Nikolai Ivanovich Novikov (27 April 1744–31 July 1818)," in Levitt, ed. *Dictionary of Literary Biography*, pp. 249–59; Wirtschafter, *Play of Ideas*, pp. 25–8.
44 Marker, "Nikolai Ivanovich Novikov," p. 255.
45 Emperor Paul ended Radishchev's exile, and he returned to government service under Alexander I. On September 11, 1802, Radishchev committed suicide. Igor Vladimirovich Nemirovsky, "Aleksandr Nikolaevich Radishchev (20 August 1749–11

September 1802)," in Levitt, ed. *Dictionary of Literary Biography*, pp. 323–33; Gary M. Hamburg, "Russian political thought: 1700–1917," in *The Cambridge History of Russia. Volume II: Imperial Russia, 1689–1917*, ed. Dominic Lieven (Cambridge, 2006), p. 121.

46 James Van Horn Melton, *The Rise of the Public in Enlightenment Europe* (Cambridge, 2001), pp. 252–72, quote on p. 254.

47 Douglas Smith, *Working the Rough Stone: Freemasonry and Society in Eighteenth-Century Russia* (DeKalb, IL, 1999), pp. 120–1.

48 Melton, *Rise of the Public*, pp. 254–7.

49 Smith, *Working the Rough Stone*, pp. 18–30.

50 On Voronikhin, see Stites, *Serfdom*, pp. 285–6.

51 The Friendly Learned Society operated informally from 1779. Raffaella Faggionato, *A Rosicrucian Utopia in Eighteenth-Century Russia: The Masonic Circle of N. I. Novikov*, trans. Michael Boyd and Brunello Lotti (Dordrecht, The Netherlands, 2005); W. Gareth Jones, *Nikolay Novikov, Enlightener of Russia* (Cambridge, 1984); Iu. V. Stennik, "Pravoslavie i masonstvo v Rossii XVIII veka (k postanovke problemy)," *Russkaia literatura* 1 (1995), pp. 76–92; Smith, *Working the Rough Stone*; Marker, "Nikolai Ivanovich Novikov."

52 Quoted in Faggionato, *Rosicrucian Utopia*, p. 1.

53 Marker, "Nikolai Ivanovich Novikov," p. 256. Faggionato gives slightly different figures: 397 titles examined, 22 declared suspect, and 6 banned. Faggionato, *Rosicrucian Utopia*, pp. 196–9.

54 Quoted in Faggionato, *Rosicrucian Utopia*, p. 197; Stennik, "Pravoslavie i masonstvo," p. 87.

55 Marker, "Nikolai Ivanovich Novikov," pp. 256–8.

56 Smith, *Working the Rough Stone*, pp. 64–86.

57 V. M. Zhivov, " Gosudarstvennyi mif v epokhu prosveshcheniia i ego razrushenie v Rossii kontsa XVIII veka," in *Iz istorii russkoi kul'tury. Tom 4 (XVIII-nachalo XIX veka)* (Moscow, 1996), p. 670.

58 Daniel Roche, *France in the Enlightenment*, trans. Arthur Goldhammer (Cambridge, MA, 1998), p. 247.

59 Quoted in William B. Edgerton, "Ambivalence as the Key to Kniazhnin's Tragedy *Vadim Novgorodskii*," in *Russia and the World of the Eighteenth Century*, ed. R. P. Bartlett, A. G. Cross, and Karen Rasmussen (Columbus, OH, 1988), pp. 307–8.

60 Wirtschafter, *Play of Ideas*, pp. 166–9.

────────────────────────── Chapter 7 ──────────────────────────

1 Steven M. Beaudoin, ed. *The Industrial Revolution* (Boston, 2003), pp. 47–87 and the works cited herein.

2 Anne Lincoln Fitzpatrick, *The Great Russian Fair: Nizhnii Novgorod, 1840–90* (New York, 1990), p. 3.

3 Arcadius Kahan, *The Plow, the Hammer and the Knout: An Economic History of Eighteenth-Century Russia* (Chicago, 1985), pp. 7–8, 36–7; Peter Gatrell, *The Tsarist*

Economy 1850–1917 (London, 1986), pp. 49–50. Boris Mironov gives similar figures for the population of the empire: 15.6 million in 1719, 37.4 million in 1796, and 74.5 million in 1858. B. N. Mironov, *Sotsial'naia istoriia Rossii perioda imperii (XVIII-nachalo XX v.). Genezis lichnosti, demokraticheskoi sem'i, grazhdanskogo obshchestva i pravovogo gosudarstva*, 2 vols. (St Petersburg, 1999), vol. 1, p. 20.

4 Hugh Seton-Watson, *The Russian Empire 1801–1917* (Oxford, 1967), pp. 246–7; Ian Blanchard, *Russia's 'Age of Silver': Precious metal production and economic growth in the eighteenth century* (London, 1989), p. 274; Judith Pallot and D. J. B. Shaw, *Landscape and Settlement in Romanov Russia 1613–1917* (Oxford, 1990), pp. 197–8; Fitzpatrick, *The Great Russian Fair*, pp. 1–8.

5 Elise Kimerling Wirtschafter, *Social Identity in Imperial Russia* (DeKalb, IL, 1997), pp. 25–6.

6 Specific goods included flax, hemp, wool, silk, linen, hides, soap, potash, paper, glass, sugar, liquor, sunflower oil, grains, fruit, and metals. Pallot and Shaw, *Landscape and Settlement*, p. 197; Priscilla Roosevelt, *Life on the Russian Country Estate: A Social and Cultural History* (New Haven, CT, 1995), pp. 235–8; Arcadius Kahan, "The Costs of 'Westernization' in Russia: The Gentry and the Economy in the Eighteenth Century," reprinted in *The Structure of Russian History: Interpretive Essays*, ed. Michael Cherniavsky (New York, 1970), pp. 236–40; Gatrell, *The Tsarist Economy*, pp. 204–5.

7 Wirtschafter, *Social Identity*, pp. 108–9; Edgar Melton, "Proto-Industrialization, Serf Agriculture, and Agrarian Social Structure: Two Estates in Nineteenth-Century Russia," *Past and Present* 115 (1987), pp. 69–106; idem, "Household Economies and Communal Conflicts on a Russian Serf Estate, 1800–1817," *Journal of Social History* 26 (1993), pp. 559–85.

8 David Moon, *The Russian Peasantry 1600–1930: The World the Peasants Made* (New York and London, 1999), p. 144.

9 Oleg Tarasov, *Icon and Devotion: Sacred Spaces in Imperial Russia*, trans. and ed. Robin Milner-Gulland (London, 2002), pp. 30–2, 50–7; Wirtschafter, *Social Identity*, pp. 110–11; Moon, *The Russian Peasantry*, pp. 144–6.

10 Moon, *The Russian Peasantry*, p. 145; Wirtschafter, *Social Identity*, pp. 109–10.

11 Pallot and Shaw, *Landscape and Settlement*, pp. 221–2; Wirtschafter, *Social Identity*, pp. 109–10.

12 In the period 1721–62, the government allowed merchants to purchase serfs to work in their factories. The serfs remained attached to the factory, not the factory owner, and comprised a special category called possessional serfs.

13 Kahan, *The Knout*, pp. 81–114; Pallot and Shaw, *Landscape and Settlement*, pp. 196–7; Gatrell, *The Tsarist Economy*, pp. 144–5; William L. Blackwell, *The Industrialization of Russia: An Historical Perspective*, 2nd edn (Arlington Heights, IL, 1982), pp. 8–13.

14 Arcadius Kahan, "Continuity in Economic Activity and Policy during the Post-Petrine Period in Russia," *Journal of Economic History* 25 (1965), pp. 66–7; Blackwell, *The Industrialization of Russia*, p. 10.

15 Pallot and Shaw, *Landscape and Settlement*, pp. 196–7; Blackwell, *The Industrialization of Russia*, pp. 10–12.

16   James H. Bater, "The Industrialization of Moscow and St. Petersburg," in *Studies in Russian Historical Geography*, ed. James H. Bater and R. A. French, 2 vols. (London, 1983), vol. 2, pp. 280–2.

17   Blackwell, *The Industrialization of Russia*, p. 14.

18   William L. Blackwell, "The Historical Geography of Industry in Russia during the Nineteenth Century," in Bater and French, ed. *Studies in Russian Historical Geography*, vol. 2, pp. 387–420.

19   Moon, *The Russian Peasantry*, p. 148; O. Platonov, ed. *1000 let russkogo predprinimatel'stva: Iz istorii kupecheskikh rodov* (Moscow, 1995), pp. 94–6.

20   Elise Kimerling Wirtschafter, *Structures of Society: Imperial Russia's "People of Various Ranks"* (DeKalb, IL, 1994), pp. 133–8; idem, *Social Identity*, pp. 72–3.

21   Wirtschafter, *Social Identity*, pp. 78–9.

22   Samuel H. Baron, "Entrepreneurs and Entrepreneurship in Sixteenth/Seventeenth-Century Russia," in *Entrepreneurship in Imperial Russia and the Soviet Union*, ed. Gregory Guroff and Fred V. Carstensen (Princeton, NJ, 1983), p. 46.

23   Fitzpatrick, *The Great Russian Fair*, pp. 92–103, 145–6; Thomas C. Owen, *The Corporation under Russian Law, 1800–1917: A Study in Tsarist Economic Policy* (Cambridge, 1991), pp. 1–59.

24   William Blackwell, "The Russian Entrepreneur in the Tsarist Period: An Overview," in Guroff and Carstensen, ed. *Entrepreneurship*, pp. 18–23.

25   Serf entrepreneurs could also be Old Believers.

26   Platonov, *1000 let russkogo predprinimatel'stva*, pp. 20–1, 126–7; Moon, *The Russian Peasantry*, p. 148; Henry Rosovsky, "The Serf Entrepreneur in Russia," *Explorations in Entrepreneurial History* 4 (1954), pp. 207–33.

27   Gatrell, *The Tsarist Economy*, pp. 208–9.

28   Wirtschafter, *Social Identity*, pp. 81–2.

29   Wirtschafter, *Social Identity*, p. 81; Jo Ann Ruckman, *The Moscow Business Elite: A Social and Cultural Portrait of Two Generations, 1840–1905* (DeKalb, IL, 1984), pp. 1–3, 19, 73–80.

30   Wirtschafter, *Social Identity*, pp. 79–83.

31   A. Iu. Andreev, *Russkie studenty v nemetskikh universitetakh XVIII-pervoi poloviny XIX veka* (Moscow, 2005), pp. 37–58.

32   Wirtschafter, *Structures of Society*, pp. 133–6.

33   Until 1793 soldiers served for life and after that for 25 years. In 1834 the government further reduced the term of service to 20 years with 5 years in the reserve.

34   Elise Kimerling Wirtschafter, *From Serf to Russian Soldier* (Princeton, NJ, 1990), pp. 38–9; idem, "Soldiers' Children, 1719–1856: A Study of Social Engineering in Imperial Russia," *Forschungen zur osteuropäischen Geschichte* 30 (1982), pp. 62–3, 70, 100–20.

35   M. Vladimirskii-Budanov, *Gosudarstvo i narodnoe obrazovanie v Rossii XVIII-go veka*, reprint (Iaroslavl, 1874; Cambridge, 1972), pt. 1, pp. 1–9.

36   Jan Kusber, *Eliten- und Volksbildung im Zarenreich während des 18. und in der ersten Hälfte des 19. Jahrhundert. Studien zu Diskurs, Gesetzgebung und Umsetzung* (Stuttgart, 2004), pp. 165–275.

37   The first two classes in the main schools repeated the two-year course offered in the lower schools.

38 S. V. Rozhdestvenskii, *Istoricheskii obzor deiatel'nosti Ministerstva narodnogo prosveshcheniia 1802–1902* (St Petersburg, 1902), pp. 12–30; idem, "Znachenie komissii ob uchrezhdenii narodnykh uchilishch v istorii politiki narodnogo prosveshcheniia v XVIII–XIX vekakh," in *Opisanie del arkhiva Ministerstva narodnogo prosveshcheniia*, ed. S. F. Platonov and A. S. Nikolaev (Petrograd, 1917), vol. 1, pp. XXXI–LI; P. N. Miliukov, *Ocherki po istorii russkoi kul'tury*, 3 vols., reprint (Paris, 1937; The Hague, 1964; Moscow, 1994), vol. 2, pt. 2, pp. 275–6. Kusber gives slightly different figures for the start of Alexander I's reign: 287 schools with 759 teachers and 22,209 students. Kusber, *Eliten- and Volksbildung*, pp. 271–3.

39 Kusber, *Eliten- und Volksbildung*, pp. 277–436.

40 Warsaw University opened in 1816 but then closed in 1831 following the Polish Rebellion.

41 In the reign of Alexander I, lycées were founded in Tsarskoe Selo, Nezhin in Ukraine, and Odessa. The Demidov School in Iaroslavl became a lycée in 1834. Janet M. Hartley, *Alexander I* (London, 1994), pp. 42–3, 52–5; Michael Florinsky, *Russia: A History and an Interpretation*, 2 vols. (New York, 1970), vol. 2, pp. 725–6; V. R. Leikina-Svirskaia, "Formirovanie raznochinskoi intelligentsii v Rossii v 40-kh godakh XIX v.," *Istoriia SSSR*, no. 1 (1958), p. 85; Miliukov, *Ocherki*, vol. 2, pt. 2, pp. 275–6; Kusber, *Eliten- und Volksbildung*, p. 410.

42 Kusber, *Eliten- und Volksbildung*, pp. 428–30.

43 Miliukov, *Ocherki*, vol. 2, pt. 2, pp. 318–26.

44 Finland became part of the Russian empire in 1809. See chapter 8.

45 L. E. Shepelev, *Otmenennye istoriei chiny, zvaniia i tituly v Rossiiskoi imperii* (Leningrad, 1977), pp. 15–16, 35, 70, 75–6.

46 Hartley, *Alexander I*, pp. 55, 84. For testing requirements in military service, see Wirtschafter, *From Serf to Russian Soldier*, pp. 40–54.

47 Established in the aftermath of the emancipation of the serfs, the *zemstvo* assemblies were all-class bodies of rural self-government elected at the district and provincial levels. Although the assemblies possessed no legislative authority, they enjoyed some powers of taxation and performed important functions of government in education, communications, public health, social welfare, and economic development.

48 Leikina-Svirskaia, "Formirovanie raznochinskoi intelligentsii," pp. 93–4; Wirtschafter, *Social Identity*, pp. 86–96.

49 Elise Kimerling Wirtschafter, *The Play of Ideas in Russian Enlightenment Theater* (DeKalb, IL, 2003), pp. 43–5.

50 Wirtschafter, *Play of Ideas*, p. 84; Marc Raeff, "Transfiguration and Modernization: The Paradoxes of Social Disciplining, Paedagogical Leadership, and the Enlightenment in Eighteenth-Century Russia," in *Alteuropa – Ancien Régime – Frühe Neuzeit: Probleme und Methoden der Forschung*, ed. Hans Erich Bödeker and Ernst Hinrichs (Stuttgart and Bad Cannstatt, 1991), p. 109; Anthony G. Netting, "Russian Liberalism: The Years of Promise" (Ph.D. diss., Columbia University, 1967), p. 20.

51 Wirtschafter, *Structures of Society*, pp. 125–33; Nathaniel Knight, "Was the Intelligentsia Part of the Nation? Visions of Society in Post-Emancipation Russia," *Kritika: Explorations in Russian and Eurasian History* 7 (2006), pp. 733–58.

52 Otto Müller, *Intelligencija. Untersuchungen zur Geschichte eines politischen Schlag-wortes* (Frankfurt, 1971); S. O. Shmidt, "K istorii slova 'intelligentsii'," reprinted in *Obshchestvennoe samosoznanie rossiiskogo blagorodnogo sosloviia, XVII-pervaia tret' XIX veka* (Moscow, 2002), pp. 300–9; S. I. Khasanova, "K voprosu ob izuchenii intel-ligentsii dorevoliutsionnoi Rossii," in *Revoliutsionno-osvoboditel'noe dvizhenie v XIX–XX vv. v Povolzh'e i Priural'e* (Kazan, 1974), pp. 37–54.

53 Michael Confino, "On Intellectuals and Intellectual Traditions in Eighteenth- and Nineteenth-Century Russia," *Daedalus* 101 (1972), pp. 117–49.

54 Wirtschafter, *Play of Ideas.*

55 Nicholas Riasanovsky, *A Parting of Ways: Government and the Educated Public in Russia* (New York, 1976).

56 For recent discussion, see James Van Horn Melton, *The Rise of the Public in Enlightenment Europe* (Cambridge, 2001).

57 A decree of 1822 outlawed Masonic lodges.

58 At the time of the French Revolution in 1789, the provincial *coutumes* numbered over 200. Donald R. Kelley, *The Human Measure: Social Thought in the Western Legal Tradition* (Cambridge, MA, 1990), pp. 202–8.

59 See chapter 9 for more detailed treatment of the Decembrists.

60 Terence Emmons, *The Russian Landed Gentry and the Peasant Emancipation of 1861* (London, 1968).

--- Chapter 8 ---

1 The following account of the French Revolutionary and Napoleonic Wars derives from William C. Fuller, Jr., *Strategy and Power in Russia 1600–1914* (New York, 1992), pp. 177–218; Michael T. Florinsky, *Russia: A History and an Interpretation*, 2 vols. (New York, 1947 and 1953), vol. 1, pp. 617–22; vol. 2, pp. 651–92; Janet M. Hartley, *Alexander I* (New York, 1994); Charles Breunig and Matthew Levinger, *The Revolutionary Era, 1789–1850*, 3rd edn (New York, 2002), pp. 24–32, 82–122; R. Ernest Dupuy and Trevor N. Dupuy, *The Encyclopedia of Military History from 3500 BC to the present*, 2nd rev. edn (New York, 1986); Gunther E. Rothenberg, *The Art of Warfare in the Age of Napoleon* (Bloomington, IN, 1980), pp. 31–60; Paul W. Schroeder, *The Transformation of European Politics 1763–1848* (New York, 1994), pp. 177–582; I. A. Zaichkin and I. N. Pochkaev, *Ekaterininskie orly* (Moscow, 1996), pp. 9–72; A. A. Kersnovskii, *Istoriia russkoi armii*, 4 vols., reprint (Moscow, 1992–4), vol. 1, pp. 171–293.

2 New Style dates are used in discussing the Napoleonic wars. In October 1799, an Anglo-Russian expedition to liberate Holland failed. France took the Ionian Islands in 1797.

3 In March Suvorov also received the rank of Austrian field marshal.

4 In 1802 Napoleon became consul for life and in 1804 emperor.

5 Florinsky, *Russia*, vol. 2, p. 663.

6 The Trianon Tariff of August 1810 imposed heavy duties on colonial products imported on neutral ships.

7 Before receiving Alexander's response, Napoleon became fed up and decided to marry Marie Louise of Austria.

8   Andrei Zorin, *Kormia dvuglavogo orla . . . Literatura i gosudarstvennaia ideologiia v Rossii v poslednei treti XVIII-pervoi treti XIX veka* (Moscow, 2001), chapters 7–9.
9   Fuller, *Strategy and Power*, p. 186.
10 Fuller, *Strategy and Power*, p. 190; Florinsky, *Russia*, vol. 2, p. 676. Janet Hartley gives lower but no less harrowing figures: 50,000 Russian casualties and 40,000 French. Hartley, *Alexander I*, p. 115.
11 Fuller, *Strategy and Power*, pp. 191–2.
12 Fuller, *Strategy and Power*, p. 193.
13 In the summer of 1808, revolt broke out in Spain, and British troops arrived in August. Fighting continued until Napoleon's abdication in April 1814.
14 Schroeder, *Transformation of European Politics*, pp. 523–38.
15 Schroeder, *Transformation of European Politics*, pp. 5–11, 46–52, 575–82.
16 On Russia's conquest of the Caucasus region, see Thomas Sanders, Ernest Tucker, and Gary Hamburg, ed. and trans. *Russian–Muslim Confrontation in the Caucusus. Alternative visions of the conflict between Imam Shamil and the Russians, 1830–1859* (New York, 2004).
17 The discussion of Russia's international position after 1815, including the Crimean War, uses New Style dates and is based on Alexander Bitis, *Russia and the Eastern Question: Army, Government, and Society 1815–1833* (Oxford, 2006); Charles and Barbara Jelavich, *The Establishment of the Balkan National States, 1804–1920* (Seattle, 1977); John Shelton Curtiss, *Russia's Crimean War* (Durham, NC, 1979); Winfried Baumgart, *The Crimean War 1853–1856* (London, 1999); Fuller, *Strategy and Power*, pp. 219–68; Florinsky, *Russia*, vol. 2, pp. 826–78, 947–56; Dupuy and Dupuy, *Encyclopedia of Military History*; Kersnovskii, *Istoriia russkoi armii*, vol. 2, pp. 93–164; Schroeder, *Transformation of European Politics*, pp. 583–804.
18 The Treaty of London (7 May 1832) created the Kingdom of Greece.
19 The Straits connect the Black Sea, Sea of Marmora, and Aegean Sea. They represented the Russian Empire's only outlet to the Mediterranean.
20 Baumgart, *Crimean War*, pp. 3–4.
21 The treaty allowed the Ottoman Empire to maintain a naval fleet in the Straits, but left southern Russia without maritime defenses. Jelavich and Jelavich, *Balkan National States*, pp. 107–8.
22 Fuller, *Strategy and Power*, pp. 259–60.
23 Fuller, *Strategy and Power*, pp. 273–7.
24 Steven L. Hoch, "The Banking Crisis, Peasant Reform, and Economic Development in Russia, 1857–1861," *American Historical Review* 96 (1991), pp. 795–820.
25 E. R. Dashkova, *The Memoirs of Princess Dashkova*, trans. and ed. Kyril Fitzlyon (Durham, NC, 1995), pp. 275–76.
26 Women followed in the line of succession only in the absence of a male heir. On Paul's policies, see E. V. Anisimov and A. B. Kamenskii, *Rossiia v XVIII-pervoi polovine XIX veka: Istoriia. Istorik. Dokument: Eksperimental'noe uchebnoe posobie dlia starshikh klassov* (Moscow, 1994), pp. 217–28; N. N. Efremova, *Sudoustroistvo Rossii v XVIII-pervoi polovine XIX vv. (istoriko-pravovoe issledovanie)* (Moscow, 1993), pp. 148–52; N. P. Eroshkin, *Istoriia gosudarstvennykh uchrezhdenii dorevoliutsionnoi Rossii*, 4th edn. (Moscow, 1997) pp. 109–31; John L. H. Keep, *Soldiers of the Tsar: Army and Society*

in Russia 1462–1874 (New York, 1985), pp. 245–49; Richard S. Wortman, *Scenarios of Power: Myth and Ceremony in Russian Monarchy. Volume I: From Peter the Great to the Death of Nicholas I* (Princeton, NJ, 1995), pp. 171–92; Roderick E. McGrew, *Paul I of Russia* (Oxford, 1992).

27   In the period 1721–62, merchants had been allowed to purchase peasants to work in factories. David Moon, *The Russian Peasantry 1600–1930: The World the Peasants Made* (New York and London, 1999), p. 78.

28   David Moon, *The Abolition of Serfdom in Russia, 1762–1907* (Harlow and London, 2001), pp. 38–41.

29   Paul's military regulations were modeled on those of Frederick the Great.

30   The members of the Unofficial Committee included Prince Adam A. Czartoryski, Count Viktor P. Kochubev, Count Nikolai N. Novosil'tsev, and Count Pavel A. Stroganov.

31   "Project for a Most Graciously Granted Charter to the Russian People (1801)," in *Plans for Political Reform in Imperial Russia, 1730–1905*, ed. Marc Raeff (Englewood Cliffs, NJ, 1966), p. 79.

32   Hartley, *Alexander I*, pp. 30–44; "Project for a Most Graciously Granted Charter," pp. 75–84.

33   "Principles of Government Reform (of the Unofficial Committee, 1802)," in Raeff, ed. *Plans for Political Reform*, pp. 85–91, quote on p. 90.

34   Eroshkin, *Istoriia gosudarstvennykh uchrezhdenii*, pp. 138–41, 148–64. Eroshkin's account covers subsequent changes in the number and distribution of the ministries.

35   The state treasury (*kaznacheistvo*) possessed the rights of a ministry.

36   On Speranskii's reforms and career, see Marc Raeff, *Michael Speransky: Statesman of Imperial Russia 1772–1839* (The Hague, 1957); M. M. Speranskii, *Rukovodstvo k poznaniiu zakonov*, ed. I. D. Osipov (St Petersburg, 2002); I. D. Osipov, *Filosofiia politiki M. M. Speranskogo. K 230-letiiu so dnia rozhdeniia* (St Petersburg, 2002); Hartley, *Alexander I*, pp. 82–101; "Introduction to the Codification of State Laws by M. M. Speransky (1809)," in Raeff, ed. *Plans for Political Reform*, pp. 92–109.

37   Sovereign power referred to the power of the monarch. "Codification of State Laws," pp. 94–5.

38   "Codification of State Laws," pp. 106–7.

39   The king appointed members of the Senate for life.

40   The Polish Rebellion of 1830–1 ended the constitutional period.

41   Hartley, *Alexander I*, p. 132. S. V. Mironenko gives a figure of 100,000 eligible voters. S. V. Mironenko, *Samoderzhavie i reformy: Politicheskaia bor'ba v Rossii v nachale XIX v.* (Moscow, 1989), p. 151.

42   Hartley, *Alexander I*, pp. 132–3; Florinsky, *Russia*, vol. 2, pp. 705–7; Mironenko, *Samoderzhavie*, pp. 150–3.

43   Hartley, *Alexander I*, pp. 166–73; "N. N. Novosil'tsev: Constitutional Charter of the Russian Empire (1818–1820)," in Raeff, ed. *Plans for Political Reform*, pp. 110–20; John P. LeDonne, "Regionalism and Constitutional Reform 1819–1826," *Cahiers du Monde russe* 43 (2003), pp. 5–34; S. V. Mironenko, *Stranitsy tainoi istorii samoderzhaviia: Politicheskaia istoriia Rossii pervoi poloviny XIX stoletiia* (Moscow, 1990), pp. 46–64; idem, *Samoderzhavie*, pp. 147–206.

44   Novosil'tsev used a Russian version of the Polish word *sejm*.

45 "N. N. Novosil'tsev," p. 111.
46 "The law gives equal protection to all citizens without any distinctions." Equal protection from the law should not be confused with equality before the law. "N. N. Novosil'tsev," p. 115.
47 Mironenko, *Stranitsy*, pp. 48–9.
48 Unless otherwise indicated, the discussion of peasant reform is based on Moon, *Abolition of Serfdom*, pp. 38–48.
49 Elise Kimerling Wirtschafter, *Social Identity in Imperial Russia* (DeKalb, IL, 1997), pp. 119, 208n.
50 Moon, *Abolition of Serfdom*, p. 39.
51 Wirtschafter, *Social Identity*, p. 119.
52 Moon, *Abolition of Serfdom*, pp. 45–7.
53 Moon, *Abolition of Serfdom*, p. 47.
54 On the enlightened bureaucracy and preparation for the Great Reforms, including the emancipation settlement of 1861, see W. Bruce Lincoln, *In the Vanguard of Reform: Russia's Enlightened Bureaucrats, 1825–1861* (DeKalb, IL, 1982); I. V. Ruzhitskaia, *Zakonodatel'naia deiatel'nost' v tsarstvovanie Imperatora Nikolaia I* (Moscow, 2005).
55 Quoted in Cynthia H. Whittaker, *The Origins of Modern Russian Education: An Intellectual Biography of Count Sergei Uvarov, 1786–1855* (DeKalb, IL, 1984), p. 4.
56 Raeff, *Michael Speransky*, pp. 320–46, quote on p. 325; W. Bruce Lincoln, *Nicholas I: Emperor and Autocrat of All the Russias* (Bloomington, IN, 1980), p. 100–3; William G. Wagner, *Marriage, Property and Law in Late Imperial Russia* (New York, 1994), pp. 56–7.
57 G. V. Zhirkov, *Istoriia tsenzury v Rossii XIX–XX vv.: Uchebnoe posobie* (Moscow, 2001), pp. 54–71.
58 Elise Kimerling Wirtschafter, *Structures of Society: Imperial Russia's "People of Various Ranks"* (DeKalb, IL, 1994), pp. 139–40.
59 Lincoln, *Nicholas I*, p. 88.
60 Lincoln, *Nicholas I*, pp. 88–9.

Chapter 9

1 Simon Dixon, "*Prosveshchenie*: Enlightenment in Eighteenth-Century Russia," *Studies on Voltaire and the Eighteenth Century* (October 2007); V. M. Zhivov, *Iazyk i kul'tura v Rossii XVIII veka* (Moscow, 1996).
2 M. M. Shcherbatov, *On the Corruption of Morals in Russia*, ed. and trans. A. Lentin (Cambridge, 1969), p. 113.
3 Marc Raeff, "State and Nobility in the Ideology of M. M. Shcherbatov," reprinted in *Political Ideas and Institutions in Imperial Russia* (Boulder, CO, 1994), pp. 268–83; Shcherbatov, *Corruption of Morals*, p. 155.
4 Andrzej Walicki, *A History of Russian Thought from the Enlightenment to Marxism*, trans. Hilda Andrews-Rusiecka (Stanford, CA, 1979), pp. 26–34; Raeff, "State and Nobility"; Lentin, "Introduction," in Shcherbatov, *Corruption of Morals*, pp. 1–102; Richard Pipes, *Russian Conservatism and Its Critics: A Study in Political Culture* (New

Haven, CT, 2005), pp. 76–9; Antony Lentin, "A la Recherche du Prince Méconnu: M. M. Shcherbatov (1733–1790) and his Critical Reception Across Two Centuries," *Canadian-American Slavic Studies* 28 (1994), pp. 361–98.

5 Walicki, *Russian Thought*, pp. 35–52.

6 Recent scholarship downplays the political import of *Journey from Petersburg to Moscow*. Andrew Kahn, "Self and Sensibility in Radishchev's *Journey from St. Petersburg to Moscow*: Dialogism, Relativism, and the Moral Spectator," in *Self and Story in Russian History*, ed. Laura Engelstein and Stephanie Sandler (Ithaca, NY, 2000), pp. 280–304.

7 Quoted in Lentin, "A la Recherche," p. 376.

8 Elise Kimerling Wirtschafter, *The Play of Ideas in Russian Enlightenment Theater* (DeKalb, IL, 2003), pp. 138–46; Hans Rogger, *National Consciousness in Eighteenth-Century Russia* (Cambridge, MA, 1960).

9 Alexander M. Martin, *Romantics, Reformers, Reactionaries: Russian Conservative Thought and Politics in the Reign of Alexander I* (DeKalb, IL, 1997), esp. pp. 4–6.

10 Andrei Zorin, *Kormia dvuglavogo orla . . . Literatura i gosudarstvennaia ideologiia v Rossii v poslednei treti XVIII-pervoi treti XIX veka* (Moscow, 2001), pp. 159–258.

11 Zorin, *Kormia*, pp. 234–54.

12 Zorin, *Kormia*, pp. 269–335.

13 Tim McDaniel, *The Agony of the Russian Idea* (Princeton, NJ, 1996).

14 Cynthia H. Whittaker, *The Origins of Modern Russian Education: An Intellectual Biography of Count Sergei Uvarov, 1786–1855* (DeKalb, IL, 1984).

15 Joachim Zweynert, *Eine Geschichte des ökonomischen Denkens in Russland, 1805–1905* (Marburg, 2002); Esther Kingston-Mann, *In Search of the True West: Culture, Economics, and Problems of Russian Development* (Princeton, NJ, 1999); Walter McKenzie Pintner, *Russian Economic Policy under Nicholas I* (Ithaca, NY, 1967).

16 Nicholas V. Riasanovsky, *A Parting of Ways: Government and the Educated Public in Russia, 1801–1855* (Oxford, 1976).

17 The historical literature on the Decembrists is among the most voluminous in the field of Russian history. I provide only a handful of citations: Anatole G. Mazour, *The First Russian Revolution, 1825* (Stanford, CA, 1961); Marc Raeff, ed. *The Decembrist Movement* (Englewood Cliffs, NJ, 1966); M. V. Nechkina, *Dekabristy*, 2nd edn (Moscow, 1982); V. A. Fedorov, *Dekabristy i ikh vremia* (Moscow, 1992); V. M. Bokova, *Epokha tainykh obshchestv: Russkie obshchestvennye ob"edineniia pervoi treti XIX v.* (Moscow, 2003), pp. 232–556; Patrick O'Meara, *The Decembrist Pavel Pestel: Russia's First Republican* (New York, 2003); David Saunders, *Russia in the Age of Reaction and Reform 1801–1881* (London, 1992), pp. 87–115; John L. H. Keep, *Soldiers of the Tsar: Army and Society in Russia, 1462–1874* (Oxford, 1985), pp. 250–72; Walicki, *Russian Thought*, pp. 57–70.

18 Keep, *Soldiers of the Tsar*, p. 268.

19 Fedorov, *Dekabristy*, pp. 246–58.

20 Raeff, ed. *Decembrist Movement*, pp. 103–18.

21 Raeff, ed. *Decembrist Movement*, pp. 124–56.

22 Raeff, ed. *Decembrist Movement*, p. 15.

23 Bokova, *Epokha tainykh obshchestv*; Wendy Rosslyn, "Benevolent Ladies and their Exertions for the Good of Humankind: V. A. Repnina, S. S. Meshcherskaia, and the

Origins of Female Philanthropy in Early Nineteenth-Century Russia," *Slavonic and East European Review* 84 (2006), pp. 52–82; Adele Lindenmeyr, *Poverty Is Not a Vice: Charity, Society, and the State in Imperial Russia* (Princeton, NJ, 1996).

24 "Petr Iakovlevich Chaadaev, ca. 1794–1856," in *Russian Intellectual History: an Anthology*, ed. Marc Raeff, 1966, reprint (Amherst, NY, 1999), pp. 159–73; Raymond T. Mcnally, *The Major Works of Peter Chaadaev: A Translation and Commentary* (Notre Dame, IN, 1969); Walicki, *Russian Thought*, pp. 81–91.

25 "Petr Iakovlevich Chaadaev," p. 159.

26 "Petr Iakovlevich Chaadaev," p. 167.

27 Pipes, *Russian Conservatism*, pp. 103–9.

28 "Petr Iakovlevich Chaadaev," p. 167.

29 Raeff, ed. *Russian Intellectual History*, pp. 174–251; Walicki, *Russian Thought*, pp. 92–114; Abbott Gleason, *European and Muscovite: Ivan Kireevsky and the Origins of Slavophilism* (Cambridge, MA, 1972).

30 Walicki, *Russian Thought*, pp. 115–51; Raeff, ed. *Russian Intellectual History*, pp. 252–61, 301–21; Derek Offord, *Portraits of Early Russian Liberals: A Study of the Thought of T. N. Granovsky, V. P. Botkin, P. V. Annenkov, A. V. Druzhinin and K. D. Kavelin* (Cambridge, 1985); G. M. Hamburg, *Boris Chicherin and Early Russian Liberalism* (Stanford, CA, 1992); G. M. Hamburg, ed. and trans. *Liberty, Equality, and the Market: Essays by B. N. Chicherin* (New Haven, CT, 1998); Konstantin Shneider, "Was There an 'Early Russian Liberalism'? Perspectives from Russian and Anglo-American Historiography," *Kritika: Explorations in Russian and Eurasian History* 7 (2006), pp. 825–41.

31 Belinskii is referring to the ideology of official nationality. "Vissarion Grigor'evich Belinskii, 1811–1848," in Raeff, ed. *Russian Intellectual History*, p. 258. See also William Mills Todd III, "Periodicals in literary life of the early nineteenth century," in *Literary Journals in Imperial Russia*, ed. Deborah A. Martinsen (Cambridge, 1997), pp. 37–63; Victor Terras, "Belinsky the journalist and Russian literature," in Martinsen, ed. *Literary Journals*, pp. 117–28.

32 B. F. Egorov, *Petrashevtsy* (Leningrad, 1988); Joseph Frank, *Dostoevsky: The Seeds of Revolt, 1821–1849* (Princeton, NJ, 1976), pp. 239–91; Walicki, *Russian Thought*, pp. 152–61.

33 Quoted in Walicki, *Russian Thought*, pp. 157–8.

34 Walicki, *Russian Thought*, p. 156.

35 Franco Venturi, *Roots of Revolution: A History of the Populist and Socialist Movements in Nineteenth-Century Russia*, trans. Francis Haskell (New York, 1966); Martin Malia, *Alexander Herzen and the Birth of Russian Socialism* (New York, 1965); Alexander Herzen, *From the Other Shore and The Russian People and Socialism*, trans. Moura Budberg and Richard Wollheim, 1956, reprint (Oxford, 1979); Walicki, *Russian Thought*, pp. 162–82.

36 For broad coverage, see Richard Stites, *Serfdom, Society, and the Arts in Imperial Russia: The Pleasure and the Power* (New Haven, CT, 2005); W. Bruce Lincoln, *Between Heaven and Hell: The Story of a Thousand Years of Artistic Life in Russia* (New York, 1998); Nicholas Rzhevsky, ed. *An Anthology of Russian Literature from Earliest Writings to Modern Fiction: Introduction to a Culture* (Armonk, NY, 1996).

References

Aleksandrov, V. A. *Sel'skaia obshchina v Rossii (XVII-nachalo XIX v.)*. Moscow, 1976.

Alexander, John T. *Catherine the Great: Life and Legend*. Oxford, 1989.

Aksakov, Sergei. *A Russian Gentleman*. Translated by J. D. Duff. Oxford, 1982.

Aksenev, A. I. *Genealogiia moskovskogo kupechestva XVIII v.: Iz istorii formirovaniia russkoi burzhuazii*. Moscow, 1988.

Andreev, A. Iu. *Russkie studenty v nemetskikh universitetakh XVIII-pervoi poloviny XIX veka*. Moscow, 2005.

Anisimov, E. V. *Podatnaia reforma Petra I: Vvedenie podushnoi podati v Rossii v 1719–1728*. Leningrad, 1982.

Anisimov, E. V. *Rossiia bez Petra: 1725–1740*. St Petersburg, 1994.

Anisimov, E. V. and A. B. Kamenskii. *Rossiia v XVIII-pervoi polovine XIX veka: Istoriia. Istorik. Dokument: Eksperimental'noe uchebnoe posobie dlia starshikh klassov*. Moscow, 1994.

Anisimov, E. V. *Rossiia v seredine XVIII veka: Bor'ba za nasledie Petra*. Moscow, 1986.

Anisimov, Evgenii. *Vremia petrovskikh reform*. Leningrad, 1989.

Aronson, M. and S. Reiser. *Literaturnye kruzhki i salony*. 1929, reprint. St Petersburg, 2001.

Artem'eva, T. V. *Istoriia metafiziki v Rossii XVIII veka*. St Petersburg, 1996.

Baron, Samuel H. "Entrepreneurs and Entrepreneurship in Sixteenth/Seventeenth-Century Russia." In *Entrepreneurship in Imperial Russia and the Soviet Union*. Edited by Gregory Guroff and Fred V. Carstensen. Princeton, 1985.

Bartlett, Roger. "The Free Economic Society: The Foundation Years and the Prize Essay Competition of 1766 on Peasant Property." In *Russland zur Zeit Katharinas II. Absolutismus–Aufklärung–Pragmatismus*. Edited by Eckhard Hübner, Jan Kusber, and Peter Nitsche. Cologne, 1998.

Bater, James H. "The Industrialization of Moscow and St. Petersburg." In *Studies in Russian Historical Geography*. Edited by James H. Bater and R. A. French. 2 vols. London, 1983.

Baumgart, Winfried. *The Crimean War 1853–1856*. London, 1999.

Beaudoin, Steven M., ed. *The Industrial Revoloution*. Boston, 2003.

Becker, Seymour. "The Muslim East in Nineteenth-Century Russian Popular Historiography." *Central Asian Survey* 5 (1986), pp. 25–47.

Berman, Harold J. *Law and Revolution: The Formation of the Western Legal Tradition.* Cambridge, MA, 1983.

Bitis, Alexander. *Russia and the Eastern Question: Army, Government, and Society 1815–1833.* Oxford, 2006.

Blackwell, William L. "The Historical Geography of Industry in Russia during the Nineteenth Century." In *Studies in Russian Historical Geography.* Edited by James H. Bater and R. A. French. 2 vols. London, 1983.

Blackwell, William L. *The Industrialization of Russia: An Historical Perspective.* 2nd edn. Arlington Heights, IL, 1982.

Blackwell, William. "The Russian Entrepreneur in the Tsarist Period: An Overview." In *Entrepreneurship in Imperial Russia and the Soviet Union.* Edited by Gregory Guroff and Fred V. Carstensen. Princeton, 1985.

Blanchard, Ian. *Russia's 'Age of Silver': Precious metal production and economic growth in the eighteenth century.* London, 1989.

Bogdanov, A. P. *Moskovskaia publitsistika poslednei chetverti XVII veka.* Moscow, 2001.

Bogdanov, A. P. "Sil'vestr Medvedev." *Voprosy istorii,* no. 2 (1988), pp. 84–98.

Bokova, V. M. "*Epokha tainykh obshchestv: Russkie obshchestvennye obedineniia pervoi treti XIX v.* Moscow, 2003.

Bolotov, A. T. *Zhizn' i prikliucheniia Andreia Bolotova, opisannye samim im dlia svoikh potomkov.* 3 vols. 1871–3, reprint. Moscow, 1993.

Bradley, Joseph. "Subjects into Citizens: Societies, Civil Society, and Autocracy in Tsarist Russia." *American Historical Review* 107 (2002), pp. 1094–1123.

Breunig, Charles, and Matthew Levinger. *The Revolutionary Era, 1789–1850.* 3rd edn. New York, 2002.

Brown, A. H. "Adam Smith's First Russian Followers." In *Essays on Adam Smith.* Edited by Andrew S. Skinner and Thomas Wilson. Oxford, 1975.

Brown, Peter B. "Bureaucratic Administration in Seventeenth-Century Russia." In *Modernizing Muscovy: Reform and social change in seventeenth-century Russia.* Edited by Jarmo Kotilaine and Marshall Poe. London and New York, 2004.

Brown, Peter B. "Neither Fish nor Fowl: Administrative Legality in Mid- and Late-Seventeenth-Century Russia." *Jahrbücher für Geschichte Osteuropas* 50 (2002), pp. 1–21.

Brown, Peter B. "The Service Land Chancellery Clerks of Seventeenth-Century Russia: Their Regime, Salaries, and Economic Survival." *Jahrbücher für Geschichte Osteuropas* 52 (2004), pp. 33–69.

Bushkovitch, Paul A. "The Epiphany Ceremony of the Russian Court in the Sixteenth and Seventeenth Centuries." *Russian Review* 49 (1990), pp. 1–17.

Bushkovitch, Paul. *Peter the Great.* Lanham, MD, 2001.

Bushkovitch, Paul. *Peter the Great: The Struggle for Power, 1671–1725.* Cambridge, 2001.

Bushkovitch, Paul. *Religion and Society in Russia: The Sixteenth and Seventeenth Centuries.* New York, 1992.

Bushkovitch, Paul. "The Ukraine in Russian Culture 1790–1860: The Evidence of the Journals." *Jahrbücher für Geschichte Osteuropas* 39 (1991), pp. 339–63.

Cherepnin, L. V. *Zemskie sobory russkogo gosudarstva v XVI–XVII vv.* Moscow, 1978.

Chrissidis, Nikolaos A. "A Jesuit Aristotle in Seventeenth-Century Russia: Cosmology and the Planetary System in the Slavo-Greco-Latin Academy." In *Modernizing Muscovy: Reform and social change in seventeenth-century Russia*. Edited by Jarmo Kotilaine and Marshall Poe. London and New York, 2004.

Collins, James B. *The State in Early Modern France*. Cambridge, 1995.

Confino, Michael, *Domaines et seigneurs en Russie vers la fin du XVIIIe siècle*. Paris, 1963.

Confino, Michael, "Histoire et psychologie: À propos de la noblesse russe au XVIIIe siècle." *Annales: Économies-Sociétés-Civilisation* 22 (1967), pp. 1163–1205.

Confino, Michael. "On Intellectuals and Intellectual Traditions in Eighteenth- and Nineteenth-Century Russia." *Daedalus* 101 (1972), pp. 117–49.

Confino, Michael. *Systèmes agraires et progress agricole: L'assolement triennal en Russie aux XVIIIe–XIXe siècles*. Paris and La Haye, 1969.

Cracraft, James. *The Church Reform of Peter the Great*. Palo Alto, CA 1971.

Cracraft, James. "Feofan Prokopovich: a Bibliography of His Works." *Oxford Slavonic Papers*, New Series 8 (1975), pp. 1–36.

Cracraft, James, ed. *Major Problems in the History of Imperial Russia*. Lexington, MA, 1994.

Cracraft, James. "Peter the Great and the Problem of Periodization." In *Architectures of Russian Identity: 1500 to the Present*. Edited by James Cracraft and Daniel Rowland. Ithaca, NY, 2003.

Cracraft, James, ed. *Peter the Great Transforms Russia*. 3rd edn. Lexington, MA, 1991.

Cracraft, James. *The Petrine Revolution in Russian Architecture*. Chicago, 1990.

Cracraft, James. *The Petrine Revolution in Russian Culture*. Cambridge, MA, 2004.

Cracraft, James. *The Petrine Revolution in Russian Imagery*. Chicago, 1997.

Cracraft, James. *The Revolution of Peter the Great*. Cambridge, MA, 2003.

Crummey, Robert O. *Aristocrats and Servitors: The Boyar Elite in Russia, 1613–1689*. Princeton, 1983.

Crummey, Robert O. "Court Spectacles in Seventeenth-Century Russia: Illusion and Reality." In *Essays in Honor of A. A. Zimin*. Edited by Daniel Waugh. Columbus, OH, 1985.

Curtiss, John Shelton. *Russia's Crimean War*. Durham, NC, 1979.

Daniel, Wallace. "Entrepreneurship and the Russian Textile Industry: From Peter the Great to Catherine the Great." *Russian Review* 54 (1995), pp. 1–25.

Danilova, L. V., ed. *Krest'ianskie chelobitnye XVII v. Iz sobranii Gosudarstvennogo Istoricheskogo muzeia*. Moscow, 1994.

Darnton, Robert. *The Forbidden Best-Sellers of Pre-Revolutionary France*. New York, 1996.

Dashkova, E. R. *The Memoirs of Princess Dashkova: Russia in the Age of Catherine the Great*. Translated and edited by Kyril Fitzlyon. Reprint. London, 1958; Durham and London, 1995.

Dear, Peter. *Revolutionizing the Sciences: European Knowledge and Its Ambitions, 1500–1700*. Princeton, 2001.

Demidova, N. F. *Sluzhilaia biurokratiia v Rossii XVII v. i ee rol' v formirovanii absoliutizma*. Moscow, 1987.

Dëmin, A. S. *O khudozhestvennosti drevnerusskoi literatury*. Moscow, 1998.

De Vries, Jan. "The Industrial Revolution and the Industrious Revolution." *Journal of Economic History* 54 (1994), pp. 249–70.

Dixon, Simon. *Catherine the Great*. Harlow, 2001.

Dixon, Simon. *The Modernisation of Russia 1676–1825*. Cambridge, 1999.

Dixon, Simon. "*Prosveshchenie*: Enlightenment in Eighteenth-Century Russia." *Studies on Voltaire and the Eighteenth Century* (October 2007).

Dukes, Paul. *Catherine the Great and the Russian Nobility*. London, 1967.

Dukes, ed. *Catherine the Great's Instruction (Nakaz) to the Legislative Commission, 1767*. Newtonville, MA, 1977.

Dunning, Chester S. L. *Russia's First Civil War: The Time of Troubles and the Founding of the Romanov Dynasty*. University Park, PA, 2001.

Dupuy, R. Ernest, and Trevor N. Dupuy. *The Encyclopedia of Military History from 3500 BC to the Present*. 2nd rev. edn. New York, 1986.

Durov, N. P. "Fedor Vasil'evich Karzhavin." *Russkaia starina* 12 (1875), pp. 272–97.

Edgerton, William B. "Ambivalence as the Key to Kniazhnin's Tragedy *Vadim Novgorodskii*." In *Russia and the World of the Eighteenth Century*. Edited by R. P. Bartlett, A. G. Cross, and Karen Rasmussen. Columbus, OH, 1988.

Efremova, N. N. *Sudoustroistvo Rossii v XVIII-pervoi polovine XIX vv. (istoriko-pravovoe issledovanie)*. Moscow, 1993.

Egorov, B. F. *Petrashevtsy*. Leningrad, 1988.

Emmons, Terence. *The Russian Landed Gentry and the Peasant Emancipation of 1861*. London, 1968.

Engel, Barbara Alpern. *Women in Russia, 1700–2000*. New York, 2004.

Eroshkin, N. P. *Istoriia gosudarstvennykh uchrezhdenii dorevoliutsionnoi Rossii*. 4th edn. Moscow, 1997.

Esiukov, A. I. *Filosofskie aspekty russkoi bogoslovskoi mysli (vtoraia polovina XVIII-nachalo XIX v.): Monografiia*. Arkhangel'sk, 2003.

Faggionato, Raffaella. *A Rosicrucian Utopia in Eighteenth-Century Russia: The Masonic Circle of N. I. Novikov*. Translated by Michael Boyd and Brunello Lotti. Dordrecht, The Netherlands, 2005.

Fainshtein, M. Sh. "*I slavu Frantsii v Rossii prevzoiti . . .*" *Rossiiskaia Akademiia (1783–1841) i razvitie kul'tury i gumanitarnykh nauk*. Moscow and St Petersburg, 2002.

Faizova, I. V. "*Manifest o vol'nosti*" *i sluzhba dvorianstva v XVIII stoletii*. Moscow, 1999.

Fedorov, V. A. *Dekabristy i ikh vremia*. Moscow, 1992.

Fitzpatrick, Anne Lincoln. *The Great Russian Fair: Nizhnii Novgorod, 1840–90*. New York, 1990.

Florinsky, Michael. *Russia: A History and An Interpretation*. 2 vols. New York, 1953.

Frank, Joseph. *Dostoevsky: The Seeds of Revolt, 1821–1849*. Princeton, 1976.

Freeze, Gregory L. *The Russian Levites: Parish Clergy in the Eighteenth Century*. Cambridge, MA, 1977.

Freeze, Gregory L. "The *Soslovie* (Estate) Paradigm in Russian Social History." *American Historical Review* 91 (1986), pp. 11–36.

Freeze, Gregory L. *From Supplication to Revolution: A Documentary Social History of Imperial Russia*. New York, 1988.

Fuller, William C., Jr. *Strategy and Power in Russia, 1600–1914*. New York, 1992.

Galitskii, A. S. *Nizhegorodskii teatr (1798–1867)*. Nizhnii Novgorod, 1867.

Gatrell, Peter. *The Tsarist Economy 1850–1917*. London, 1986.

Gestwa, Klaus. *Proto-Industrialisierung in Russland: Wirtschaft, Herrschaft und Kultur in Ivanovo und Pavlovo, 1741–1932.* Göttingen, 1999.

Geyer, Dietrich. " 'Gesellschaft' als Staatliche Veranstaltung. Sozialgeschichtliche Aspekte des russischen Behördenstaats im 18. Jahrhundert." In *Wirtschaft und Gesellschaft im vorrevolutionären Russland.* Edited by Dietrich Beyrau. Cologne, 1975.

Gleason, Abbott. *European and Muscovite: Ivan Kireevsky and the Origins of Slavophilism.* Cambridge, MA, 1972.

Gorskaia, N. A. *Monastyrskie krest'iane Tsentral'noi Rossii v XVII veke.* Moscow, 1977.

Griffiths, David. "Introduction: of Estates, Charters, and Constitutions." In *Catherine II's Charters of 1785 to the Nobility and the Towns.* Translated and edited by David Griffiths and George E. Munro. Bakersfield, CA, 1991.

Gromova, L. P., ed. *Istoriia russkoi zhurnalistiki XVIII–XIX vekov. Uchebnik.* St Petersburg, 2003.

Gromyko, M. M. "Razvitie Tiumeni kak remeslennogo-torgovogo tsentra v XVIII v." In *Goroda feodal'noi Rossii: Sbornik statei pamiati I. V. Ustiugova.* Moscow, 1966.

Gukovskii, G. A. *Russkaia literatura XVIII veka.* 1939, reprint. Moscow, 1998.

Habermas, Jürgen. *The Structural Transformation of the Public Sphere: An Inquiry into a Category of Bourgeois Society.* Tranlsated by Thomas Burger with Frederick Lawrence. Cambridge, MA, 1989.

Hamburg, G. M. *Boris Chicherin and Early Russian Liberalism.* Stanford, CA, 1992.

Hamburg, G. M. ed. and trans. *Liberty, Equality, and the Market: Essays by B. N. Chicherin.* New Haven, CT, 1998.

Hamburg, Gary M. "Russian political thought: 1700–1917." In *The Cambridge History of Russia. Volume II: Imperial Russia, 1689–1917.* Edited by Dominic Lieven. Cambridge, 2006.

Hamilton, George Heard. *The Art and Architecture of Russia.* New York, 1983.

Hartley, Janet M. *Alexander I.* London, 1994.

Hartley, Janet. "Town Government in St. Petersburg Guberniya after the Charter to the Towns of 1785." *Slavonic and East European Review* 62 (1984), pp. 61–84.

Hellie, Richard. *Enserfment and Military Change in Muscovy.* Chicago, 1971.

Hellie, Richard. *Slavery in Russia 1450–1725.* Chicago, 1982.

Hellie, Richard. "The Stratification of Muscovite Society." *Russian History* 5 (1978), pp. 119–75.

Herzen, Alexander. *From the Other Shore and The Russian People and Socialism.* Translated by Moura Budberg and Richard Wollheim. 1956, reprint. Oxford, 1979.

Hildermeier, Manfred. "Was war das Meščanstvo? Zur rechtlichen und sozialen Verfassung des unterenstädtischen Standes in Russland." *Forschungen zur osteuropäischen Geschichte* 36 (1985), pp. 15–53.

Hoch, Steven L. "The Banking Crisis, Peasant Reform, and Economic Development in Russia, 1857–1861." *American Historical Review* 96 (1991), pp. 795–820.

Hoch, Steven L. *Serfdom and Social Control in Russia: Petrovskoe, a Village in Tambov.* Chicago, 1986.

Hoch, Steven L. "The Serf Economy and the Social Order in Russia." In *Serfdom and Slavery: Studies in Legal Bondage.* Edited by M. L. Bush. New York, 1996.

Hosking, Geoffrey. "The Freudian Frontier." *TLS* (March 10, 1995), p. 27.

Hughes, Lindsey. "Moscow Baroque – A Controversial Style." *Zapiski russkoi akademich-eskoi gruppy v S. Sh. A.* 15 (1982), pp. 147–61.

Hughes, Lindsey. *Peter the Great: A Biography.* New Haven, 2002.

Hughes, Lindsey. *Russia in the Age of Peter the Great.* New Haven, 1998.

Hughes, Lindsey. *Sophia, Regent of Russia 1657–1704.* New Haven and London, 1990.

Ilizarov, S. S. *Moskovskaia intelligentsiia XVIII veka.* Moscow, 1999.

Jacob, Margaret C. "The Mental Landscape of the Public Sphere: A European Perspective." *Eighteenth-Century Studies* 28 (1994), pp. 95–113.

Jelavich, Charles and Barbara. *The Establishment of the Balkan National States, 1804–1920.* Seattle, 1977.

Jones, Adrian. "A Russian Bourgeois's Arctic Enlightenment." *The Historical Journal* 48 (2005), pp. 623–40.

Jones, Robert E. *The Emancipation of the Russian Nobility, 1761–1785.* Princeton, 1973.

Jones, W. Gareth. *Nikolay Novikov, Enlightener of Russia.* Cambridge, 1984.

Kabuzan, V. M. *Narodonaselenie Rossii v XVIII-pervoi polovine XIX v. (po materialam revizii).* Moscow, 1963.

Kabuzan, V. M. *Narody Rossii v pervoi polovine XIX v. Chislennost' i etnicheskii sostav.* Moscow, 1992.

Kabuzan, V. M. and N. M. Shepukova, "Tabel' pervoi revizii narodonaseleniia Rossii (1718–1727 gg.)." *Istoricheskii arkhiv,* no. 3 (1959), pp. 126–65.

Kahan, Arcadius. "Continuity in Economic Activity and Policy during the Post-Petrine Period in Russia." *Journal of Economic History* 25 (1965), pp. 61–85.

Kahan, Arcadius. "The Costs of 'Westernization' in Russia: The Gentry and the Economy in the Eighteenth Century." 1966. Reprinted in *The Structure of Russian History: Interpretive Essays.* Edited by Michael Cherniavsky. New York, 1970.

Kahan, Arcadius. *The Plow, the Hammer, and the Knout: An Economic History of Eighteenth-Century Russia.* Chicago, 1985.

Kahn, Andrew. "Nikolai Karamzin, *Letters of a Russian traveller.*" *Studies on Voltaire and the Eighteenth Century,* no. 4. Oxford, 2003.

Kahn, Andrew. "Self and Sensibility in Radishchev's *Journey from St. Petersburg to Moscow*: Dialogism, Relativism, and the Moral Spectator." In *Self and Story in Russian History.* Edited by Laura Engelstein and Stephanie Sandler. Ithaca, NY, 2000.

Kamenskii, A. B. *Ot Petra I do Pavla I: Reformy v Rossii XVIII veka. Opyt tselostnogo analiza.* Moscow, 1999.

Kamenskii, A. B. *"Pod seniiu Ekateriny . . .": Vtoraia polovina XVIII veka.* St Petersburg, 1992.

Kappeler, Andreas, *The Russian Empire: A Multiethnic History.* Translated by Alfred Clayton. Harlow, Eng., 2001.

Kartashev, A. V. *Ocherki po istorii russkoi tserkvi.* 2 vols. Moscow, 1997.

Kazakov, A. V., ed. *Terminy i poniatiia voennoi istorii Rusi, Rossii IX-nachala XX veka.* St Petersburg, 1998.

Keep, John L. H. *Soldiers of the Tsar: Army and Society in Russia 1462–1874.* New York, 1985.

Kelley, Donald R. *The Human Measure: Social Thought in the Western Legal Tradition.* Cambridge, MA, 1990.

Kenworthy, Scott M. "The Struggle for Identity in Russian Orthodoxy Since the Seventeenth Century." Unpublished paper. February 2006.

Kern, Fritz. *Kingship and Law in the Middle Ages.* Translated by S. B. Chrimes. Reprint. Oxford, 1939; New York, 1970.

Kersnovskii, A. A. *Istoriia russkoi armii.* 4 vols. Reprint. Moscow, 1992–94.

Khasanova, S. I. "K voprosu ob izuchenii intelligentsii dorevoliutsionnoi Rossii." In *Revoliutsionno-osvoboditel'noe dvizhenie v XIX–XX vv. v Povolzh'e i Priural'e.* Kazan, 1974.

Khodarkovsky, Michael. *Russia's Steppe Frontier: The Making of a Colonial Empire, 1500–1800.* Bloomington, IN, 2002.

Kingston-Mann, Esther. *In Search of the True West: Culture, Economics, and Problems of Russian Development.* Princeton, NJ, 1999.

Kivelson, Valerie A. *Autocracy in the Provinces: The Muscovite Gentry and Political Culture in the Seventeenth Century.* Stanford, 1996.

Kizevetter, A. A. *Posadskaia obshchina v Rossii XVIII st.* Moscow, 1903.

Klier, John Doyle. *Russia Gathers her Jews: The Origins of the "Jewish Question" in Russia, 1772–1825.* DeKalb, IL, 1986.

Knight, Nathaniel. "Was the Intelligentsia Part of the Nation? Visions of Society in Post-Emancipation Russia." *Kritika: Explorations in Russian and Eurasian History* 7 (2006), pp. 733–58.

Kohut, Zenon E. *Russian Centralism and Ukrainian Autonomy: Imperial Absorption of the Hetmanate, 1760s–1830s.* Cambridge, MA, 1988.

Kollmann, Nancy Shields. *By Honor Bound: State and Society in Early Modern Russia.* Ithaca, NY, 1999.

Kollmann, Nancy Shields. "Ritual and Drama at the Muscovite Court." *Slavic Review* 45 (1986), pp. 486–502.

Kollmann, Nancy Shields. "The Seclusion of Elite Muscovite Women." *Russian History* 10 (1983), pp. 170–87.

Kotilaine, J. T. "Opening a Window on Europe: Foreign Trade and Military Conquest on Russia's Western Border in the Seventeenth Century." *Jahrbücher für Geschichte Osteuropas* 46 (1998), pp. 494–530.

Krieger, Leonard. *An Essay on the Theory of Enlightened Despotism.* Chicago, 1975.

Kurukin, I. V. *Epokha "dvorskikh bur'": Ocherki politicheskoi istorii poslepetrovskoi Rossii, 1725–1762 gg.* Riazan', 2003.

Kusber, Jan. *Eliten- und Volksbildung im Zarenreich während des 18. und in der ersten Hälfte des 19. Jahrhunderts. Studien zu Diskurs, Gesetzgebung und Umsetzung.* Stuttgart, 2004.

Lavrent'eva, Elena. *Svetskii etiket pushkinskoi pory.* Moscow, 1999.

Leckey, Colum. "Provincial Readers and Agrarian Reform, 1760s–1770s: The Case of Sloboda Ukraine." *Russian Review* 61 (2002), pp. 535–59.

Leckey, Colum. "Patronage and Public Culture in the Russian Free Economic Society, 1765–1796." *Slavic Review* 64 (2005), pp. 355–79.

LeDonne, John P. *Absolutism and Ruling Class: The Formation of the Russian Political Order, 1700–1825.* New York, 1991.

LeDonne, John P. *The Grand Strategy of the Russian Empire, 1650–1831.* New York, 2004.

LeDonne, John P. "Regionalism and Constitutional Reform 1819–1826." *Cahiers du Monde russe* 43 (2003), pp. 5–34.

LeDonne, John P. *The Russian Empire and the World 1700–1917: The Geopolitics of Expansion and Containment.* New York, 1997.

LeDonne, John P. *Ruling Russia: Politics and Administration in the Age of Absolutism, 1762–1796.* Princeton, 1984.

Leikina-Svirskaia, V. R. "Formirovanie raznochinskoi intelligentsii v Rossii v 40-kh godakh XIX v." *Istoriia SSSR,* no. 1 (1958), pp. 83–104.

Lenskaia, L. *Repertuar krepostnogo teatra Sheremetevykh. Katalog p'es.* Moscow, 1996.

Lentin, Antony. "A la Recherche du Prince Méconnu: M. M. Shcherbatov (1733–1790) and his Critical Reception Across Two Centuries." *Canadian-American Slavic Studies* 28 (1994), pp. 361–98.

Lerner, Gerda. *The Creation of Feminist Consciousness from the Middle Ages to 1870.* New York, 1993.

Levitt, Marcus, ed. *Dictionary of Literary Biography. Volume 150: Early Modern Russian Writers, Late Seventeenth and Eighteenth Centuries.* Detroit, MI, 1995.

Levshin, Platon. *Pouchitel'nyia slova pri Vysochaishem Dvore Eia Imperatorskago Velichestva. . . .* 20 vols. Moscow, 1779–1806.

Librovicha, S.F. *Istoriia knigi v Rossii.* Moscow, 2000.

Likhachev, D. S., ed. *Istoriia russkoi literatury X–XVII vekov.* Moscow, 1980.

Lieven, Dominic. *Russia's Rulers Under the Old Regime.* New Haven, 1989.

Lincoln, W. Bruce. *Between Heaven and Hell: The Story of a Thousand Years of Artistic Life in Russia.* New York, 1998.

Lincoln, W. Bruce. *In the Vanguard of Reform: Russia's Enlightened Bureaucrats, 1825–1861.* DeKalb, IL, 1982.

Lincoln, W. Bruce. *Nicholas I: Emperor and Autocrat of All the Russias.* Bloomington, IN, 1980.

Lindenmeyr, Adele. *Poverty Is Not a Vice: Charity, Society, and the State in Imperial Russia.* Princeton, 1996.

Lovell, Stephen, Alena Ledeneva, and Andrei Rogachevskii, ed. *Bribery and Blat in Russia: Negotiating Reciprocity from the Middle Ages to the 1990s.* Houndmills and London, 2000.

Madariaga, Isabel de. *Catherine the Great: A Short History.* New Haven and London, 1990.

Madariaga, Isabel de. *Russia in the Age of Catherine the Great.* New Haven and London, 1981.

Malia, Martin. *Alexander Herzen and the Birth of Russian Socialism.* New York, 1965.

Man'kov, A. G. *Ulozhenie 1649 god – kodeks feodal'nogo prava Rossii.* 2nd edn. Moscow, 2003.

Marker, Gary. *Publishing, Printing, and the Origins of Intellectual Life in Russia, 1700–1800.* Princeton, 1985.

Marker, Gary. "Russia and the 'Printing Revolution': Notes and Observations." *Slavic Review* 41 (1982), pp. 266–83.

Marker, Gary. "Russian Journals and their Readers in the Late Eighteenth Century." *Oxford Slavonic Papers.* New Series 19 (1986), pp. 88–101.

Marrese, Michelle Lamarche. *A Woman's Kingdom: Noblewomen and the Control of Property in Russia, 1700–1861.* Ithaca, NY, 2002.

Martin, Alexander M. *Romantics, Reformers, Reactionaries: Russian Conservative Thought and Politics in the Reign of Alexander I.* DeKalb, IL, 1997.

Martinsen, Deborah A., ed. *Literary Journals in Imperial Russia*. Cambridge, 1997.

Mazour, Anatole G. *The First Russian Revolution, 1825*. Stanford, CA, 1961.

McDaniel, Tim. *The Agony of the Russian Idea*. Princeton, NJ, 1996.

McGrew, Roderick E. *Paul I of Russia*. Oxford, 1992.

McNally, Raymond T., ed. *The Major Works of Peter Chaadaev: A Translation and Commentary*. Notre Dame, IN, 1969.

Meehan-Waters, Brenda. *Autocracy and Aristocracy: The Russian Service Elite of 1730*. New Brunswick, NJ, 1982.

Melton, Edgar. "Enlightened Seigniorialism and Its Dilemmas in Serf Russia, 1750– 1830." *Journal of Modern History* 62 (1990), pp. 675–708.

Melton, Edgar. "Household Economies and Communal Conflicts on a Russian Serf Estate, 1800–1817." *Journal of Social History* 26 (1993), pp. 559–85.

Melton, Edgar. "Proto-Industrialization, Serf Agriculture, and Agrarian Social Structure: Two Estates in Nineteenth-Century Russia." *Past and Present* 115 (1997), pp. 69–106.

Melton, James Van Horn. *The Rise of the Public in Enlightenment Europe*. Cambridge, 2001.

Meyendorff, John. *Byzantium and the Rise of Russia*. Reprint. New York, 1981; Crestwood, NY, 1989.

Meyendorff, Paul. *Russia, Ritual, and Reform: The Liturgical Reforms of Nikon in the 17th Century*. Crestwood, NY, 1991.

Michels, Georg Bernhard. *At War with the Church: Religious Dissent in Seventeenth-Century Russia*. Stanford, 1999.

Miliukov, P. N. *Ocherki po istorii russkoi kul'tury*, 3 vols. Reprint. Paris, 1937; The Hague, 1964; Moscow, 1993–95.

Miller, David H. "State and City in Seventeenth-Century Muscovy." In *The City in Russian History*. Edited by Michael F. Hamm. Lexington, KY, 1976.

Mironenko, S. V. *Samoderzhavie i reformy: Politicheskaia bor'ba v Rossii v nachale XIX v.* Moscow, 1989.

Mironenko, S. V. *Stranitsy tainoi istorii samoderzhaviia: Politicheskaia istoriia Rossii pervoi poloviny XIX stoletiia*. Moscow, 1990.

Mironov, B. N. "Gramotnost' v Rossii v 1797–1917 godov: Poluchenie novoi istoricheskoi informatsii s pomoshch'iu metodov retrospektivnogo prognozirovaniia." *Istoriia SSSR*, no. 4 (1985), pp. 137–53.

Mironov, B. N. *Russkii gorod v 1740–1860-e gody: Demograficheskoe, sotsial'noe i eko-nomicheskoe razvitie*. Leningrad, 1990.

Mironov, B. N. "Russkii gorod vo vtoroi polovine XVIII-pervoi polovine XIX veka: Tipologicheskii analiz." *Istoriia SSSR* 5 (1988), pp. 150–68.

Mironov, B. N. *Sotsial'naia istoriia Rossii perioda imperii (XVIII-nachalo XX v.). Genezis lichnosti, demokraticheskoi sem'i, grazhdanskogo obshchestva i pravovogo gosudarstva*, 2 vols. St Petersburg, 1999.

Mironov, B. N. "Sotsial'naia mobil'nost' rossiiskogo kupechestva v XVIII- nachale XIX veka (opyt izucheniia)." In *Problemy istoricheskoi demografii SSSR*. Edited by R. N. Pullat. Tallin, 1977.

Moon, David. *The Abolition of Serfdom in Russia*. Harlow and London, 2001.

Moon, David. "Peasant Migration and the Settlement of Russia's Frontiers, 1550–1897." *The Historical Journal* 40 (1997), pp. 859–93.

Moon, David. *The Russian Peasantry 1600–1930. The World the Peasants Made*. London and New York, 1999.

Muller, Alexander V., trans. and ed. *The Spiritual Regulation of Peter the Great*. Seattle, WA, 1971.

Müller, Otto. *Intelligencija. Untersuchungen zur Geschichte eines politischen Schlagwortes*. Frankfurt, 1971.

Nechkina, M. V. *Dekabristy*. 2nd edn. Moscow, 1982.

Netting, Anthony G. "Russian Liberalism: The Years of Promise." Ph.D. diss., Columbia University, 1967.

Nevskaia, N. I. *Letopis' Rossiiskoi Akademii nauk. Vol. 1. 1724–1801*. St Petersburg, 2000.

Newlin. Thomas. *The Voice in the Garden: Andrei Bolotov and the Anxieties of Russian Pastoral, 1783–1833*. Evanston, IL, 2001.

Nikolin, Aleksei. *Tserkov' i gosudarstvo (istoriia pravovykh otnoshenii)*. Moscow, 1997.

Offord, Derek. *Portraits of Early Russian Liberals: A Study of the Thought of T. N. Granovsky, V. P. Botkin, P. V. Annenkov, A. V. Druzhinin, and K. D. Kavelin*. Cambridge, 1985.

O'Meara, Patrick. *The Decembrist Pavel Pestel: Russia's First Republican*. New York, 2003.

Omel'chenko, O. A. *"Zakonnaia monarkhiia" Ekateriny II: Prosveshchennyi absoliutizm v Rossii*. Moscow, 1993.

Osipov, I. D. *Filosofiia politiki M. M. Speranskogo. K 230-letiiu so dnia rozhdeniia*. St Petersburg, 2002.

Ostrowski, Donald. "The Assembly of the Land (*Zemskii sobor*) as a Representative Institution." In *Modernizing Muscovy: Reform and social change in seventeenth- century Russia*. Edited by Jarmo Kotilaine and Marshall Poe. London and New York, 2004.

Owen, Thomas C. *The Corporation under Russian Law, 1800–1917: A Study in Tsarist Economic Policy*. Cambridge, 1991.

Pallot, Judith, and Denis J. B. Shaw. *Landscape and Settlement in Romanov Russia 1613–1917*. New York, 1990.

Pintner, Walter McKenzie. *Russian Economic Policy under Nicholas I*. Ithaca, NY, 1967.

Pipes, Richard, ed. and trans. *Karamzin's Memoir on Ancient and Modern Russia. A Translation and Analysis*. New York, 1974.

Pipes, Richard. *Russia under the Old Regime*. New York, 1974.

Pipes, Richard. *Russian Conservatism and Its Critics: A Study in Political Culture*. New Haven, CT, 2005.

Plamper, Jan. "The Russian Orthodox Episcopate, 1721–1917: A Prosopography." *Journal of Social History* 34 (2000), pp. 5–34.

Platonov, O., ed. *1000 let russkogo predprinimatel'stva: Iz istorii kupecheskikh rodov*. Moscow, 1995.

Plavsic, Borivoj. "Seventeenth-Century Chanceries and their Staffs." In *Russian Officialdom: The Bureaucratization of Russian Society from the Seventeenth to the Twentieth Century*. Edited by Walter McKenzie Pintner and Don Karl Rowney. Chapel Hill, NC, 1980.

Pokrovskii, S. A., ed. *Iuridicheskie proizvedeniia progressivnykh russkikh myslitelei. Vtoraia polovina XVIII veka*. Moscow, 1959.

Potter, Cathy Jean. "The Russian Church and the Politics of Reform in the Second Half of the Seventeenth Century." 2 vols. Ph.D. diss., Yale University, 1993.

Pososhkov, I. T. *Kniga o skudosti i bogatstve i drugie sochineniia.* Edited by B. B. Kafengauz. Reprint. Moscow, 1951; St Petersburg, 2004.

Pososhkov, Ivan. *The Book on Poverty and Wealth.* Edited and translated by A. P. Vlasto and L. R. Lewitter. Stanford, 1987.

Pouncy, Carolyn Johnston, ed. and trans. *The Domostroi: Rules for Russian Households in the Time of Ivan the Terrible.* Ithaca, NY, 1994.

Pouncy, Carolyn Johnston. "Missed Opportunities and the Search for Ivan the Terrible." *Kritika: Explorations in Russian and Eurasian History* 7 (2006), pp. 309–28.

Preobrazhenskii, A. A. and T. E. Novitskaia, eds. *Zakonodatel'stvo Petra I.* Moscow, 1997.

Proskurina, Vera. *Mify imperii: Literatura i vlast' v epokhu Ekateriny II.* Moscow, 2006.

Rabinovich, M. D. "Sotsial'noe proiskhozhdenie i imushchestvennoe polozhenie ofitserov reguliarnoi russkoi armii v kontse Severnoi voiny." In *Rossiia v period reform Petra I.* Edited by N. I. Pavlenko. Moscow, 1973.

Raeff, Marc, ed. *The Decembrist Movement.* Englewood Cliffs, NJ, 1966.

Raeff, Marc. *Michael Speransky: Statesman of Imperial Russia 1772–1839.* The Hague, 1957.

Raeff, Marc. *Origins of the Russian Intelligentsia: The Eighteenth-Century Nobility.* New York, 1966.

Raeff, Marc, ed. *Plans for Political Reform in Imperial Russia, 1730–1905.* Englewood Cliffs, NJ, 1966.

Raeff, Marc, ed. *Russian Intellectual History: an Anthology.* 1966, reprint. Amherst, NY, 1999.

Raeff, Marc. "State and Nobility in the Ideology of M. M. Shcherbatov." Reprinted in *Political Ideas and Institutions in Imperial Russia.* Boulder, CO, 1994.

Raeff, Marc. "Transfiguration and Modernization: The Paradoxes of Social Disciplining, Paedagogical Leadership, and the Enlightenment in Eighteenth-Century Russia." In *Alteuropa–Ancien Régime –Frühe Neuzeit: Probleme und Methoden der Forschung.* Edited by Hans Erich Bödeker and Ernst Hinrichs. Stuttgart and Bad Cannstatt, 1991.

Raeff, Marc. "The Two Facets of the World of Ivan Pososhkov." *Forschungen zur osteuropäischen Geschichte* 50 (1995), pp. 309–28.

Raeff, Marc. *The Well-Ordered Police State: Social and Institutional Change through Law in the Germanies and Russia, 1600–1800.* New Haven, 1983.

Ransel, David L. "An Eighteenth-Century Russian Merchant Family in Prosperity and Decline." In *Imperial Russia: New Histories for the Empire.* Edited by Jane Burbank and David L. Ransel. Bloomington, 1998.

Reyfman, Irina. *Vasilii Trediakovsky: The Fool of the "New" Russian Literature.* Stanford, CA, 1990.

Riasanovsky, Nicholas. *A Parting of Ways: Government and the Educated Public in Russia.* New York, 1976.

Roche, Daniel. *France in the Enlightenment.* Translated by Arthur Goldhammer. Cambridge, MA, 1998.

Rogger, Hans. *National Consciousness in Eighteenth-Century Russia.* Cambridge, MA, 1960.

Roosevelt, Priscilla. *Life on the Russian Country Estate: A Social and Cultural History.* New Haven, CT, 1995.

Rosslyn, Wendy. "Benevolent Ladies and their Exertions for the Good of Humankind: V.A. Repnina, S. S. Meshcherskaia, and the Origins of Female Philanthropy in Early Nineteenth-Century Russia." *Slavonic and East European Review* 84 (2006), pp. 52–82.

Rosovsky, Henry. "The Serf Entrepreneur in Russia." *Explorations in Entrepreneurial History* 6 (1954), pp. 207–33.

Rothenberg, Gunther E. *The Art of Warfare in the Age of Napoleon*. Bloomington, IN, 1980.

Rozhdestvenskii, S. V. *Istoricheskii obzor deiatel'nosti Ministerstva narodnogo prosveshcheniia 1802–1902*. St Petersburg, 1902.

Rozhdestvenskii, S. V. "Znachenie komissii ob uchrezhdenii narodnykh uchilishch v istorii politiki narodnogo prosveshcheniia v XVIII–XIX vekakh." In *Opisanie del arkhiva Ministerstva narodnogo prosveshcheniia*. Edited by S. F. Platonov and A. S. Nikolaev. Petrograd, 1917.

Rozman, Gilbert. *Urban Networks in Russia, 1750–1800, and Premodern Periodization*. Princeton, 1976.

Ruckman, Jo Ann. *The Moscow Business Elite: A Social and Cultural Portrait of Two Generations, 1840–1905*. DeKalb, IL, 1984.

Russkie pisateli 1800–1917. Biograficheskii slovar'. 4 vols. to date. Moscow, 1992.

Ruzhitskaia, I. V. *Zakonodatel'naia deiatel'nost' v tsarstvovanie Imperatora Nikolaia I*. Moscow, 2005.

Ryndziunskii, P. G. *Gorodskoe grazhdanstvo doreformennoi Rossii*. Moscow, 1958.

Rzhevsky, Nicholas, ed. *An Anthology of Russian Literature from Earliest Writings to Modern Fiction: Introduction to a Culture*. Armonk, NY, 1996.

Sanders, Thomas, Ernest Tucker, and Gary Hamburg, ed. and trans. *Russian–Muslim Confrontation in the Caucasus. Alternative visions of the conflict between Imam Shamil and the Russians, 1830–1859*. New York, 2004.

Saunders, David. *Russia in the Age of Reaction and Reform 1801–1881*. London, 1992.

Shchipanov, I. Ia., ed. *Izbrannye proizvedeniia russkikh myslitelei vtoroi poloviny XVIII veka*. 2 vols. Moscow, 1952.

Schmemann, Alexander. *The Historical Road of Eastern Orthodoxy*. Crestwood, NY, 2003.

Schmidt, Christoph. *Leibeigenschaft im Ostseeraum. Versuch einer Typologie*. Cologne, 1997.

Shmidt, S. O. "K istorii slova 'intelligentsii'." Reprinted in *Obshchestvennoe samosoznanie rossiiskogo blagorodnogo sosloviia, XVII-pervaia tret' XIX veka*. Moscow, 2002.

Schneewind, J. B. *The Invention of Autonomy: A History of Modern Moral Philosophy*. New York, 1998.

Schroeder, Paul W. *The Transformation of European Politics 1763–1848*. New York, 1994.

Seton-Watson, Hugh. *The Russian Empire 1801–1917*. Oxford, 1967.

Shcherbatov, M. M. *On the Corruption of Morals in Russia*. Edited and translated by A. Lentin. Cambridge, 1969.

Shepelev, L. E. *Chinovnyi mir Rossii XVII-nachalo XX v*. St Petersburg, 1999.

Shepelev, L. E. *Otmenennye istoriei chiny, zvaniia i tituly v Rossiiskoi imperii*. Leningrad, 1977.

Shevyrev, S. P. *Istoriia imperatorskogo Moskovskogo universiteta, napisannaia k stoletnemu ego iubileiu*. 1855, reprint. Moscow, 1998.

Shneider, Konstantin. "Was There an 'Early Russian Liberalism'? Perspectives from Russian and Anglo-American Historiography." *Kritika: Explorations in Russian and Eurasian History* 7 (2006), pp. 825–41.

Shveikovskaia, E. N. *Gosudarstvo i krest'iane Rossii. Pomor'e v XVII veke*. Moscow, 1997.

Skinner, Quentin. *The Foundations of Modern Political Thought.* 2 vols. Cambridge, 1978.

Slovar' russkikh pisatelei XVIII veka. 2 vols. to date. Leningrad, 1988; St Petersburg, 1999.

Smilianskaia, E. B. *Dvorianskoe gnezdo serediny XVIII veka. Timofei Tekut'ev i ego "Instruktsiia o domashnikh poriadkakh."* Moscow, 1998.

Smith, Douglas. *Working the Rough Stone: Freemasonry and Society in Eighteenth-Century Russia.* DeKalb, IL, 1999.

Sokolova, N. V. "Krest'ianskoe samoupravlenie v tsentral'noi Rossii v 20-e gody XVIII v." *Istoricheskie zapiski* 7 (125) (2004), pp. 117–74.

Somov, V. A. "Dva otveta Vol'tera na Peterburgskom konkurse o krest'ianskoi sobstvennosti." In *Evropeiskoe prosveshchenie i tsivilizatsiia Rossii.* Edited by S. Ia. Karp and S. A. Mezin. Moscow, 2004.

Speranskii, M. M. *Rukovodstvo k poznaniiu zakonov.* Edited by I. D. Osipov. St Petersburg, 2002.

Spinka, Matthew. "Patriarch Nikon and the Subjection of the Russian Church to the State." *Church History* 10 (1941), pp. 347–66.

Stennik, Iu. V. "Pravoslavie i masonstvo v Rossii XVIII veka (k postanovke problemy)." *Russkaia literatura* 1 (1995), pp. 76–92.

Stites, Richard. *Serfdom, Society, and the Arts in Imperial Russia: The Pleasure and the Power.* New Haven, CT, 2005.

Sunderland, Willard. *Taming the Wild Field: Colonization and Empire on the Russian Steppe.* Ithaca, NY, 2004.

Tarasov, Oleg. *Icon and Devotion: Sacred Spaces in Imperial Russia.* Translated and edited by Robin Millner-Gulland. London, 2002.

Terras, Victor. "Belinsky the journalist and Russian literature." In *Literary Journals in Imperial Russia.* Edited by Deborah A. Martinsen. Cambridge, 1997.

Thaden, Edward C. *Russia's Western Borderlands, 1710–1870.* Princeton, 1984.

Thyrêt, Isolde. *Between God and Tsar: Religious Symbolism and the Royal Women of Muscovite Russia.* DeKalb, IL, 2001.

Todd, William Mills, III. "Periodicals in literary life of the early nineteenth century." In *Literary Journals in Imperial Russia.* Edited by Deborah A. Martinsen. Cambridge, 1997.

Torke, Hans J. "Continuity and Change in the Relations between Bureaucracy and Society in Russia, 1613–1861." *Canadian Slavic Studies* 5 (1971), pp. 457–76.

Torke, Hans J. "Crime and Punishment in the Pre-Petrine Civil Service: The Problem of Control." In *Imperial Russia 1700–1917. State, Society, Opposition.* Edited by Ezra Mendelsohn and Marshall S. Shatz. DeKalb, IL, 1988.

Torke, Hans Joachim, ed. *Russkie tsari 1547–1917.* Rostov on the Don and Moscow, 1997.

Ustiugov, N. V. "Evoliutsiia prikaznogo stroia Russkogo gosudarstva v XVII v." In *Absoliutizm v Rossii (XVII–XVIII vv.). Sbornik statei k semidesiatiletiiu so dnia rozhdeniia B. B. Kafengauza.* Moscow, 1964.

Val'denberg, Vladimir. *Drevnerusskiia ucheniia o predelakh tsarskoi vlasti: ocherki russkoi politicheskoi literatury ot Vladimira Sviatogo do kontsa XVII veka.* Reprint. Petrograd, 1916; The Hague, 1966.

Venturi, Franco. *Roots of Revolution: A History of the Populist and Socialist Movements in Nineteenth-Century Russia.* Translated by Francis Haskell. New York, 1966.

Vladimirskii-Budanov, M. *Gosudarstvo i narodnoe obrazovanie v Rossii XVIII-go veka.* Reprint. Iaroslavl, 1874; Cambridge, 1972.

Vodarskii, Ia. E. *Naselenie Rossii v kontse XVII-nachale XVIII veka.* Moscow, 1977.

Volkov, S. V. *Russkii ofitserskii korpus.* Moscow, 1993.

Wagner, William G. *Marriage, Property and Law in Late Imperial Russia.* New York, 1994.

Walkin, Jacob. *The Rise of Democracy in Pre-Revolutionary Russia: Political and Social Institutions under the Last Three Czars.* New York, 1962.

Walicki, Andrzej. *A History of Russian Thought from the Enlightenment to Marxism.* Translated by Hilda Andrews-Rusiecka. Stanford, CA, 1979.

Whittaker, Cynthia H. *The Origins of Modern Russian Education: An Intellectual Biography of Count Sergei Uvarov, 1786–1855.* DeKalb, IL, 1984.

Wirtschafter, Elise Kimerling. *From Serf to Russian Soldier.* Princeton, NJ, 1990.

Wirtschafter, Elise Kimerling. "Legal Identity and the Possession of Serfs in Imperial Russia." *Journal of Modern History* 70 (1998), pp. 561–87.

Wirtschafter, Elise Kimerling. *The Play of Ideas in Russian Enlightenment Theater.* DeKalb, IL, 2003.

Wirtschafter, Elise Kimerling. *Social Identity in Imperial Russia.* DeKalb, IL, 1997.

[Wirtschafter], Elise Kimerling. "Soldiers' Children, 1719–1856: A Study of Social Engineering in Imperial Russia." *Forschungen zur osteuropäischen Geschichte* 30 (1982), pp. 61–136.

Wirtschafter, Elise Kimerling. *Structures of Society: Imperial Russia's "People of Various Ranks."* DeKalb, IL, 1994.

Wortman, Richard. *The Development of a Russian Legal Consciousness.* Chicago, 1976.

Wortman, Richard S. *Scenarios of Power: Myth and Ceremony in Russian Monarchy. Volume I: From Peter the Great to the Death of Nicholas I.* Princeton, NJ, 1995.

Zaichkin, I. A. and I. N. Pochkaev. *Ekaterininskie orly.* Moscow, 1996.

Zhirkov, G. V. *Istoriia tsenzury v Rossii XIX–XX vv.: Uchebnoe posobie.* Moscow, 2001.

Zielińska, Zofia. "Poland between Prussia and Russia in the Eighteenth Century." In *Constitution and Reform in Eighteenth-Century Poland: The Constitution of 3 May 1791.* Edited by Samuel Fiszman. Bloomington, IN, 1997.

Zhivov, V. M. "Gosudarstvennyi mif v epokhu prosveshcheniia i ego razrushenie v Rossii kontsa XVIII veka." In *Iz istorii russkoi kul'tury. Tom 4 (XVIII-nachalo XIX veka).* Moscow, 1996.

Zhivov, V. M. *Iazyk i kul'tura v Rossii XVIII veka.* Moscow, 1996.

Zhivov, Victor. *Iz tserkovnoi istorii vremeni Petra Velikogo: Issledovaniia i materialy.* Moscow, 2004.

Zitser, Ernest A. *The Transfigured Kingdom: Sacred Parody and Charismatic Authority at the Court of Peter the Great.* Ithaca, NY, 2004.

Znamenskii, P. V. *Istoriia russkoi tserkvi (uchebnoe rukovodstvo).* Reprint. Kazan, 1870; Moscow, 1996.

Zorin, Andrei. *Kormia dvuglavogo orla . . . Literatura i gosudarstvennaia ideologiia v Rossii v poslednei treti XVIII-pervoi treti XIX veka.* Moscow, 2001.

Zviagintsev, A. G. and Iu. G. Orlov. *Oko gosudarevo. Rossiiskie prokurory. XVIII vek.* Moscow, 1994.

Zweynert, Joachim. *Eine Geschichte des ökonomischen Denkens in Russland, 1805–1905.* Marburg, 2002.

Index

Close relations of rulers and some rulers are referred to by Christian name and patronymic, e.g., "Aleksei Mikhailovich."

schools,
  development 178
  and Enlightenment culture 145
  expansion 180–2
  and soldiers' sons 179–80
Schwarz, Johann Georg 152, 161
science 67–8, 152
Second Coalition, French war 191–2
Secret Chancellery 47
Semenovskii Guard Regiment *see* Guards
  regiments
Senate 119, 124, 127, 130, 205
  and Paul 202, 203
  and Peter I 19, 52, 54
serfs and serfdom 8–14, 92–100, 157–8,
  201–2, 208–9, 221
  emancipation 169, 211
  and industry 174, 176
  institutionalization 81–2
  and nobility 88, 90
service 26–7, 30–58, 167
  recruitment for 16, 17
servicemen, hereditary 17–18
Seven Years War 127, 129–30
Shafirov, Petr P. 74
Shakhovskoi, Nikolai G. 158
Shcherbatov, Mikhail M. 216–18
Sheremetev family 97, 98, 158, 171–3,
  176
shipbuilding 44, 173, 174
Shishkov, Aleksandr S. 219, 220
Shuvalov, Ivan L. 146
Siberia 11, 12, 109
Sil'vestr (Medvedev) 66, 67
Simeon (Polotskii) 65–6, 69, 72, 78
Slavonic, as church language 37–8
Slavophile–Westernizer controversy
  226–9, 233
social order 83–5
social organization 5–28
socialism 233–4
society 169–89
  and civic life 103–6
Society of Lovers of Learnedness 152

Society for the Translation of Foreign
  Books 152
Sokolov, Ivan Ia. 142
Sophia Alekseevna 43, 67
Southern Society 224–5
Speranskii, Mikhail M. 203, 204, 206,
  212–13, 220
Speshnev, Nikolai A. 231
Stalin 13
State Council 206–7
state peasants 10, 93, 210–11
Stefan (Iavorskii) 74
Stoglav Council 40, 62
Stroganov, Aleksandr S. 160
Sturdza family 219, 221
succession 48, 118–33, 135
Sumarokov, Aleksandr P. 72, 76, 146,
  149–50, 151, 183–4
  as man of letters 154, 155
Supreme Privy Council 119, 120, 121,
  122, 123, 124
Suvorov, Aleksandr V. 191
Sweden 108–9, 173, 196
  and French wars 192, 195
  Great Northern War 50–2, 108, 173
  and Peter I 48–9

Table of Ranks 27, 55–6, 182–3, 216
Tatishchev, Vasilii N. 153–4
taxation 10, 15
  see also poll tax
technological change 170
Teplov, Grigorii N. 78, 157
terem 5, 75
textiles 172, 174, 176
theater 78, 103, 145, 158, 164
  expansion 146–8, 185
  and Peter I 69, 76
Third Coalition, French war 192–3
Third Section of His Majesty's Personal
  Chancery 213
Thirteen Years War 10, 114
Time of Troubles 3, 32, 33
Titov, Vasilii 69